**EMBRACING THE OTHER**

# EMBRACING THE OTHER

## PHILOSOPHICAL, PSYCHOLOGICAL, AND HISTORICAL PERSPECTIVES ON ALTRUISM

*Edited by Pearl M. Oliner, Samuel P. Oliner, Lawrence Baron, Lawrence A. Blum, Dennis L. Krebs, and M. Zuzanna Smolenska*

**NEW YORK UNIVERSITY PRESS**
**New York and London**

NEW YORK UNIVERSITY PRESS
New York and London

Copyright © 1992 by New York University

Library of Congress Cataloging-in-Publication Data
Embracing the other : philopophical, psychological, and historical
perspectives on altruism / edited by Pearl M. Oliner ... [et al.].
p.    cm.
Papers preseted at the conference. Theoretical and social implications of rescuing
people in extreme situtations: another look at altruism, held in Radziejowice,
Poland, in June 1989.
Includes bibliographical references and index.
ISBN 0-8147-6175-5 (hard : alk. paper)
1. Righteous Gentiles in the Holocaust—Psychology—Congresses.   2. World
War, 1939-1945—Jews—Rescue—Congresses.   3. Altruism—Congresses.
4. Motivation (Psychology)—Congresses.   I. Oliner, Pearl M.
DB10.J4E477   1992                                              92-19102
940.54'7794'019—dc20                                            CIP

New York University Press books are printed on acid-free paper,
and their binding materials are chosen for strength and durability.

Manufactured in the United States of America

c 10 9 8 7 6 5 4 3 2 1

*We dedicate this book to all those individuals who reflect the Altruistic Spirit in their words as well as in their deeds.*

# CONTENTS

# CONTRIBUTORS

**Lawrence Baron** is Director of the Lipinsky Institute and Nasatir Professor of Modern Jewish History at San Diego State University. He served as an interviewer and consulting historian for the Altruistic Personality Project.

**Lawrence A. Blum** is Professor of Philosophy at the University of Massachusetts, Boston, and is the author of *Friendship, Altruism and Morality* and (with Victor Seidler) *A Truer Liberty: Simone Weil and Marxism*.

**Daniel M. Boland** is a consultant and writer in private practice in Lincoln City, Oregon. His work focuses on organizational leadership, moral responsibility, and mutual accountability in public and private life.

**Ronald Cohen** is Professor of Anthropology and teaches in the Center for African Studies at the University of Florida. He is the author of books on Africa, methodology, and social evolution.

**Wendy M. Heller** is an author and editor and has taught writing at Humboldt State University, Arcata, California.

**Rachel Hertz-Lazarowitz** is Professor at the School of Education, Haifa University, Israel, and works in introducing innovation to school systems in the areas of organizational development, co-operative learning, and active learning.

**Richard G. Hovannisian** holds the Endowed Chair in Armenian and Near Eastern History at the University of California, Los Angeles.

He is the author or editor of nine books including *The Armenian Genocide: History, Politics, Ethics*.

**Maria Jarymowicz** is Professor of Psychology at the University of Warsaw, Poland, and conducts research on self-identity and its role in non-egocentric social functioning.

**Krzysztof Konarzewski** is Associate Professor at the Institute of Psychology of the Polish Academy of Science, Warsaw, and is the author of *Theoretical Foundations of Moral Education* and *If a Child Says No*.

**Dennis L. Krebs** is Professor of Psychology at Simon Fraser University, Burnaby, British Columbia, and Fellow of the Center for Advanced Study in the Behavioral Sciences. He is the author of numerous works on altruism and moral development.

**Ewa Kurek-Lesik** is a historian at the University of Lublin, Poland.

**Hoda Mahmoudi** is Associate Dean for Academic Affairs and Associate Professor of Sociology at California Lutheran University, Thousand Oaks.

**Elizabeth Midlarsky** is Professor of Clinical Psychology at Columbia University, Teachers College. Her research is on altruism and helping in persons of diverse ages and particularly under conditions of extreme stress.

**Leo Montada** is Professor of Psychology at the University of Trier, Germany, and conducts research on social justice, altruism, responsibility, and social emotions.

**Pearl M. Oliner** is Professor of Education and Research Director of the Altruistic Personality and Prosocial Behavior Institute, Humboldt State University, Arcata, California.

**Samuel P. Oliner** is Professor of Sociology at Humboldt State University, Arcata, California, and is the founder and director of the Altruistic Personality and Prosocial Behavior Institute.

**Wiktor Osiatynski** is Program Director at the Center for Study and Education in Human Rights, Warsaw, Poland, and Codirector of the Center for the Study of Constitutionalism in Eastern Europe at the University of Chicago Law School.

**Janusz Reykowski** is Professor of Psychology at the Polish Academy of Science, Warsaw. He is the author of several books on personality, motivation, and emotions and has conducted extensive research on prosocial behavior.

**Victor J. Seidler** is Senior Lecturer in Social Theory and Philosophy at Goldsmiths' College, University of London. His most recent book is *The Moral Limits of Modernity: Love, Inequality, and Oppression.*

**M. Zuzanna Smolenska** is Assistant Professor of Psychology at the Polish Academy of Science, Warsaw. She has conducted research on prosocial behavior and developmental changes in values.

**Ervin Staub** is Professor of Psychology at the University of Massachusetts, Amherst, and author of *The Roots of Evil: The Origins of Genocide and Other Group Violence* and *Positive Social Behavior and Morality*, Vols. 1 and 2.

**Frank Van Hesteren** is Professor of Educational Psychology at the University of Saskatchewan. He has a longstanding interest in the development of altruism as an aspect of personality and in developmental approaches to teaching and counselor education.

**Ian Vine** teaches psychology at the University of Bradford, England, and is a founder-member of the MOSAIC morality research network, studying the sociobiology of moral consciousness.

# PART ONE

# PREFACE AND INTRODUCTION

# PREFACE

*Janusz Reykowski*

This book was initiated at the international conference titled "Theoretical and Social Implications of Rescuing People in Extreme Situations: Another Look at Altruism," held in Radziejowice (Poland) in June 1989. The purpose of the conference was to discuss the implications of studies concerning the capability of human beings to perform brave, enduring altruistic actions. The inspiration for such an approach came from the Altruistic Personality Project—the large-scale study originated and directed by Professor Samuel Oliner. The project focuses on people who were willing, despite grave risk and consequence, to help others—to rescue Jews during the Holocaust—and it was supposed to shed new light on the psychological and concomitant social implications of such actions. It was based on a sample of approximately seven hundred rescuers, nonrescuers (controls), and rescued survivors in various countries under Nazi occupation, and provided a large database concerning the social and family background of the subjects, their childhood experience, their social relations before and after rescuing actions ensued, and many other related factors. The results of the project were presented in the book written by Samuel P. Oliner and Pearl S. Oliner titled *The Altruistic Personality: Rescuers of Jews in Nazi Europe* (Free Press, 1988).

It should be kept in mind that reflection about human nature is heavily influenced by the studies uncovering its various flaws and imperfections. One of the first great sources of disillusionment about human nature was Freud's discovery of the unconscious, with its primitive sexual and aggressive urges. Subsequent studies on the authoritarian personality, prejudice, Machiavellianism,

3

"crimes of obedience," cognitive biases, etc., contributed to the reinforcement of a rather unflattering picture of the human being. There were, though, some attempts to look at human nature in different ways—the proponents of humanistic psychology claimed that an individual, freed from imposed constraints and undue pressures, will manifest a capacity for empathy and creative self-realization. But the foundations of this claim were rather shaky. In fact, it was more an expression of the personal convictions of its authors than a proposition supported by some kind of scientific evidence.

Nevertheless, over the last two decades there has been an increasing number of empirical studies focusing on the "positive" forms of human behavior—on the psychological mechanism of prosocial actions: helping, sharing, and caring for others. Many of these studies were conducted in laboratory settings. But their real significance could not be fully appreciated as long as there was not enough data linking laboratory situations with real life. The studies of real-life altruism provide this missing link. They show the phenomenon that in the laboratory may have a rather elusive and "ghostly" existence, but that under certain conditions can become very robust; prosocial forces can sustain themselves under the most adverse conditions.

The studies of altruism indicate that the idea that empathy and altruism as a natural propensity of a human being must inevitably appear, if the conditions that suppress it are eliminated, is rather simpleminded. The real mechanisms of prosocial action are apparently much more complex. As the understanding of these mechanisms grows, many of our old views about human beings may require major revisions.

This was, in fact, the basic assumption of the organizers of the conference. They believed that through the analysis of these mechanisms we could shed new light on a number of issues: on theories of personality, social attitudes, and culture; on family relationships, education, and public policy; on moral, philosophical, and religious considerations. Of course, one cannot in the framework of one conference exhaust all the possible considerations dealing with this topic. Its major goal was therefore more modest; it was to instigate thought about the implications of the studies on altruism for our approach to different spheres of social life. And this is also the aim of this book, which is the outcome of that conference.

The organizers of the conference would like to express their appreciation to the following institutions, which by offering their generous support made the whole undertaking possible: the Institute of Psychology of the Polish Academy of Science, the Altruistic Personality and Prosocial Behavior Institute, and the Institute of Noetic Sciences.

# INTRODUCTION

## Pearl M. Oliner

In the summer of 1989, we met with a group of international scholars in Poland to exchange views on a particular type of altruism: the kind that some have called "heroic" altruism and that the conference organizers described as altruistic activity undertaken in extreme situations.

The topic of the conference emerged largely from recent studies of rescue activities undertaken by non-Jews on behalf of Jews during the Nazi occupation of Europe during World War II. Rescuers, as they are popularly called, risked their lives and frequently those of their families as well to help Jews survive the Nazi Holocaust. In a very real sense, rescue was an embrace: an act of enclosure and protective care in the midst of an ocean of unrelieved brutality. Moreover, the "other" whom rescuers embraced were neither family members nor coreligionists; in some cases, they were not even conationals. In many cases, rescuers helped Jews despite their "outsider" status, the consequence of national and ethnic definitions that excluded them. While their numbers were very small— even by the most generous estimates, no more than one half of 1 percent of the total population under Nazi occupation—the very existence of rescuers suggests something important about the human spirit and its potential. In light of it, it seems less naive to envision a future without genocides and war, and even possible to imagine a global society marked by care.

Just as the topic evoked images of extreme evil and hope, so did the site of our meeting and its timing. Poland suffered one of the most cruel Nazi occupations and was the center of most of their exterminating centers, yet it also mounted an impressive resistance. Testimonies about that period were everywhere: in the monuments on every few streets to those who had died, in the Warsaw ghetto remnants in the heart of the city, in Auschwitz where we visited, and in conversations with Poles. The scarcity of goods on store shelves, the long lines of people waiting patiently to enter the shops, and the unrepaired facades on buildings attested to the economic hardships Poles endured in the years following. But during that very summer of our conference, Communist and Solidarity representatives were meeting at the round table to see if they could forge unprecedented cooperative means to bring the country to a new political structure without violence. The symbolic significance of these multiple events—simultaneously grim and hopeful—was keenly felt by all of us.

The conference participants were a highly diverse group. Composed of scholars from multiple disciplines (historians, psychologists, social psychologists, sociologists, philosophers, educators, and social welfare representatives) and nations, their approaches to the topic ranged from highly theoretical to strongly pragmatic. Inherent in such diversity is both a threat and a promise: the threat of increasing fragmentation, polarization, and disconnectedness, and the promise of bringing mutual enrichment and cohesion out of isolating specializations and cultural specificities. The threat was quickly dissipated, for what eventually marked the lively exchanges and the resultant papers included herein was the sense of commonality of issues and shared problems, albeit expressed in the conceptual language particular to their respective disciplines.

The common underlying motif of the conference, expressed implicitly or explicitly, was the inadequacy of dominant theories to explain altruism—particularly heroic altruism, such as rescue. Such inadequacies focused on central issues.

One issue revolved around prevailing definitions of altruism and its relationship to moral theory. Behaviorist definitions try to avoid motivational issues, while concentrating on objective, measurable criteria. Other definitions have included motivational aspects, some insisting for example on specific internal states, such as empathy, lack of concern with restitution, specific values (such as love or compassion), personal norms, or principles of justice. Conference participants almost unanimously rejected behaviorist definitions as adequate. And while they also did not accept the

motivations identified by others as quite sufficient to explain rescue, they largely agreed that the issue of motivation was essential
to any adequate definition of altruism.

Another issue revolved around the relationship of altruism generally and rescue specifically to morality and moral theory. While
none disputed the idea that altruism resonates with moral implications, rescue itself appeared to imply moral themes that extended beyond Western conceptions of morality and prevailing
moral theories. Neither the Kantian notions of justice nor insist-
ence on pure selflessness appeared satisfactory to address altruism
generally or the particular moral virtues of rescue.

The continuing debate over the paradox of altruism in the context of evolutionary theory surfaced as yet another issue. While
notions of kinship and reciprocity might help explain some cases
of altruism, they appeared inadequate to explain rescue behavior
that was directed toward outsiders who were often strangers, and
who constituted poor prospects for future reciprocity claims. Yet
to rely on cultural explanations alone appeared equally unacceptable in view of real human biological constraints. Could evolutionary theory be reconciled or modified to account for behaviors
such as rescue?

Just as evolutionary theory appeared inadequate to explain rescue, so did social psychological theory. If altruism is a trait that
some people have and others do not, as implied in the notion of
"an altruistic personality," then the world can presumably be divided into altruists and nonaltruists. But people often behave altruistically in one context and selfishly in another, and the quality
of their altruistic responses also varies in the sense of their effectiveness and comprehensiveness. Given that many aspects of cognition and affect are subject to development, might it not be the
case that altruism itself is an incremental developmental stage
process, the potential for which all people have but not all develop
fully?

Nor could social psychological theory adequately account for
the influence of culture and the demands of specific situations.
While apparently altruistic acts might share behavioral similarities, the meaning of such acts often differs depending on the culture
in which they occurred. Thus, for example, rescue in the case of
Denmark appeared to be largely an affirmation of national political
traditions, whereas among Christian Reformed groups in Holland,

it appeared to be largely an affirmation of religious culture in which Jews were perceived as God's chosen people.

Finally, conferees unanimously agreed that the pragmatic implications of their work were of the utmost importance. The hope they shared in common was that their work would illuminate practice designed to create a better world society.

These issues, initially expressed at the conference, were subsequently refined in the written articles that followed thereafter. They serve as the organizational framework for this volume.

## PART 2: PHILOSOPHICAL, DEFINITIONAL, AND CONCEPTUAL ISSUES

The authors of part 2 address three central questions: What is an adequate definition of "altruism"? How is altruism related to rescue particularly and morality generally? And how well do our traditions of moral thought illuminate the phenomenon of altruism?

Rejecting ordinary forms of prosocial behavior as manifestations of altruism, Krzysztof Konarzewski (chapter 1) begins by arguing that the rescue of Jews during the Holocaust was a prototypical form of moral altruism. Heroic altruism of this type, says Konarzewski, requires both empathy and protest, two quite different motivational orientations. Whereas the former depends on some degree of social dependency or conformism, the latter requires a principled independence based on recognition of and commitment to the axiological foundations of community life. Since these are rooted in quite different and apparently irreconcilable psychological orientations, Konarzewski asks how both can be cultivated simultaneously in the same individual.

While Lawrence Blum (chapter 2) agrees emphatically that rescue was a qualitatively different activity from that implied in more routine kindly acts, he finds the term "altruism" itself insufficient to capture the moral resonances of rescue. Although agreeing with Konarzewski that rescue was unquestionably an altruistic act and an act of protest, Blum nonetheless argues that rescue involved moral principles beyond altruism. While acknowledging that morality requires universality—that is, extending one's concern to all human beings—he adds a distinctly innovative component by introducing the moral value of "affirming cultures." Whereas universality denies differences and obscures them, preserving people as a distinct people affirms their valued specificity.

Victor Seidler (chapter 3) takes Blum's argument further. Rather than liberating people and embracing them, the universalistic rational tradition, rooted in Enlightenment thought, is predicated on an abstract humanity from which cultural identity is to be trajected. In this tradition, feelings and self are regarded as manifestations of egoism; thus, the price of freedom and equality is self-denial. Seidler argues that Western moral theorists have embraced this notion with pernicious consequences. Inasmuch as the language of altruism is tied to Christian/Kantian thought, neither the concept of altruism nor conventional Western notions of morality or moral theory suffice to explain rescue. By way of contrast with this tradition, which emphasizes "ethical purity," he offers the tradition of Judaism, which, he says, accepts emotions, self, and individuality as well as social context as part of the human condition and integral to moral behavior rather than in conflict with it.

**PART 3: SOCIOBIOLOGY AND MORAL ALTRUISM**

Given that altruism is maladaptive at the individual level, in the sense of being incompatible with reproductive success, how can altruism generally and rescue behavior particularly be explained in terms of evolutionary theory? Rejecting both exclusively biologically based and exclusively culturally based explanations for this paradox, Ian Vine (chapter 4) and Ronald Cohen (chapter 5) attribute altruism to an interaction between biologically based altruistic dispositions and cultural inputs. While kin selection, reciprocity, and manipulation help explain altruism in part, says Vine, they are inadequate to explain the self-sacrificial behavior toward "outsiders" as evidenced in rescue behavior. He proposes instead that an evolved subjective self-system enables humans to transcend biological constraints and develop sympathy and a sense of identity with a broad range of others. What genes do is provide a range of possible behaviors, but it is culture and learning that shape the selection of the range. Hence, he concludes, "our biology encourages us to be saints in some contexts and allows us to in others. . . . But it remains a matter of choice which human options we cultivate."

Although he conceptualizes it somewhat differently, Cohen also proposes an interactionist model between biology and culture, in which choice features. Altruism, including rescue, says Cohen, is based on both genetic and sociocultural evolution. Its genetic basis lies in an innate capacity for restraint that modifies dominance striving and provides a basis for morality. Congruent with the "dual inheritance model" advanced by Boyd and Richerson, he argues that while biological and cultural evolution are logically and empirically separate domains, "they are nonetheless united phenomenologically into a single process of descent with modification." Hence, while not divorced from reproductive inheritance, both biology and culture are modifiable, the latter most particularly through role recruitment, population migrations, and diffusion of traits. Current societal trends (e.g., a rising concern with public versus private concerns, the end of Cold War tensions, and an increase in the nuclearization of family life), coupled with the phenomenon of rescue itself, lead Cohen to a very optimistic view regarding the possibilities for the evolution of what he calls "civil society," in which norms and behaviors toward other persons and groups will take their welfare into account.

## PART 4: THE DEVELOPMENT AND ENACTMENT OF ALTRUISM

The chapters in this section address the growth of altruism over the life span and the internal and external factors that mediate altruistic behavior. Dennis Krebs and Frank Van Hesteren (chapter 6) begin by asking whether there really are altruists and egoists or whether we are all a little bit of both. Rather than a trait that some people have and others do not, altruism, they argue, is shared to a greater or lesser degree by all people, and the capacity for it grows with social and cognitive development. Claiming that past approaches have failed to adequately address the stages of altruistic development and its interactional aspect, Krebs and Van Hesteren propose a "developmental-interactional" model consisting of seven cognitively based stage structures, the apex of which is "integrated altruism." What distinguishes individuals possessing advanced stages is their more direct focus on enhancing the welfare of others as an end in itself, and their capacity to perform a broader array of more altruistic acts, as well as their capacity to respond more adequately. Van Hesteren (chapter 7) expands on the developmental aspect of the model, particularly as it relates to the most highly developed, ideal type. Drawing on theory and empirical research, he elaborates on the characteristics of this type, describing the coordination of characteristics within the personality, the forces that drive it, and the internal dynamics that mediate between structures and altruistic behavior. At the most advanced stage of "ideal" altruism, says Van Hesteren, individuals achieve a powerful and highly integrated sense of self-identity. Acutely self-aware, they are thus ever mindful of their internal standards and consistently "on the watch" for situations involving altruism.

The importance of self-awareness in altruism is also highlighted by Maria Jarymowicz (chapter 8). Whereas "endocentric" altruism—which stems from a focus on one's own norms and standards—may result in an appropriate altruistic response when directed toward similar others, "exocentric" altruism—which stems from centering on the other—is more likely to result in an appropriate response when directed toward those who are dissimilar as well. Exocentric altruism, says Jarymowicz, is more likely to occur among those who have a strong sense of self-other distinctiveness. On the basis of results from several empirical studies, she suggests that people with low self-distinctiveness experience identity problems; thus they have a greater need to differentiate themselves from in-group members, and are more likely to discriminate against dissimilar "out-group" others.

Like Krebs and Van Hesteren, as well as Jarymowicz, Zuzanna Smolenska and Janusz Reykowski (chapter 9) also distinguish among types of altruism and altruistic motivation, and apply their conceptual framework to an analysis of rescuers' motivations. The motives of rescuers, they claim, were basically of three types: allocentric, normocentric, and axiological. Whereas allocentric motivations are induced by direct contact with a person in need and attention on his/her cognitive and affective state, normocentric motivations (similar to stages 3 and 4 in Krebs and Van Hesteren's model) are induced by the norms of significant reference groups, which, however, may be internalized in varying degrees. Axiological altruism (similar to stages 5 and 6 in the Krebs and Van Hesteren model) is motivated by indignation at the violation of moral principles relating to care and justice.

Leo Montada (chapter 10) also finds evidence to support the concept that people display different kinds of altruism in different situations. The motivation for prosocial activities, says Montada, varies with the social structure and the relationships between the potential helper and the needy. On the basis of two empirical studies, Montada reports that moral outrage coupled with existential guilt were the best predictors of prosocial commitment with respect to disadvantaged people who are not personally known. However, in personal relationships between middle-aged daughters and elderly mothers, the best predictor was love realized as part of individual role behavior, such as the daughter's customary behavior, personal normative consideration, and the opportunity to help.

If developmental theorists are correct, the capacity for higher-stage altruism should increase with age. Elizabeth Midlarsky's studies (chapter 11) suggest that this implication may be correct. Individuals aged sixty-five to seventy-five were more likely to volunteer for a first-aid course than younger candidates (as long as the fee was not too high) and were more likely to give more altruistic reasons for doing so than younger volunteers. In general, the elderly reported a high involvement in helping behavior, and most attributed it to intrinsic factors.

Is heroic altruism, such as rescue, then a manifestation of advanced altruism? While none of the above authors tackle this question directly, they imply that without an understanding of its underlying motives and cognitive structures, the behavior itself cannot be properly assessed.

**PART 5: EMBRACING THE "OUTSIDER"**

Whereas the chapters described above concentrate on conceptual issues, the authors of this section discuss altruism in the context of concrete historical events. In highlighting the acts of Turks who saved the lives of Armenians during the Genocide of 1915, Richard Hovannisian (chapter 12) not only contributes a pioneering study of this phenomenon but also raises the issue of its cultural meaning. Although he attributes much of this activity to humanitarian motives, he is not certain they were altruistic. "How," he asks, "should one view the childless couple, or the family with no male children, who rescued, converted, and adopted Armenian infants and youngsters and loved and provided for them while forcing them to forget their ethnic and religious origins?" Hovannisian implies that by failing to affirm their cultures, these interveners failed to do what the highest level of morality requires—a point with which Blum and Seidler would probably agree. Yet Hovannisian acknowledges that conversion and Turkification occurred in an historical and cultural context where they implied both the physical and spiritual well-being of their wards. Moreover, he asks, "If altruism means that there is no profit motive or gain for the intervener," then how does one categorize those who profited from their labor? The difficulty arises because in rural societies, "even the most humanitarian families required labor of all family members."

Whereas Hovannisian only alludes to the cultural context, Lawrence Baron (chapter 13) and Ewa Kurek-Lesik (chapter 14) emphasize it. Dutch involvement in rescue, says Baron, was facilitated by an historical tradition of religious tolerance and the high rate of Jewish assimilation into the mainstream. Despite these culturally supportive elements, however, the percentage of Dutch Jews who perished was among the highest in all of Nazi-dominated Europe, largely the consequence of an unfortunate convergence of specific situational characteristics and events that inhibited rescue. However, the Polish nuns who saved Jewish children did so despite pervasive Polish values and Catholic thought, which were permeated with anti-Semitism. Yet, as Kurek-Lesik observes, this same Catholic tradition also motivated them to help, for embedded within it was the ideal of responding to the suffering of all humanity. Unlike Hovannisian, she has no difficulty in categorizing their behavior as altruistic, even when they baptized and converted them. Given their commitment to save lives as the highest goal, and their belief that this was the best way to ensure their physical and spiritual salvation, as well as the absence of cultural norms regarding alternatively appropriate behaviors toward their charges, the sisters acted according to the best interests of their charges as they saw them.

As implied by the above authors, situations and culture can facilitate altruism, but only as they intersect with personal attributes and personal meaning. In the case of Dov Yirmiya, personal and political culture merged to produce what Rachel Hertz-Lazarowitz (chapter 15) describes as a "political altruist." A passionately committed Israeli who fought in the War of Independence and the Lebanon War, Yirmiya is currently devoting all his time to helping Palestinians. Hertz-Lazarowitz calls his motivation empathic and political altruism, but his efforts to reconcile his particularist attachments—strong loyalty to his country and people—with the universalistic values implied by socialist/Zionist ideology has put him at the margins of Israeli society. In describing him as an individual committed "to people" as well as "to abstract principles of justice, the national legitimacy of groups, equality, moral conduct and humanism," Hertz-Lazarowitz highlights the tension that frequently accompanies such dualities, as well as the mode of their integration as suggested by the interactionist model proposed by Krebs and Van Hesteren.

## PART 6: PROMOTING ALTRUISTIC BONDS

If society were to self-consciously decide to support the promotion of altruism, how might it do so? Noting that rescuers were marked by what they call "extensivity"—that is, a dual orientation toward attachments in interpersonal relationships as well as an inclusive sense of obligation toward multiple groups—Pearl and Samuel Oliner (chapter 16) launch this section by proposing eight social processes that can encourage an extensive orientation. Four of the processes they identify relate primarily to forming attachments to known others; they include bonding, empathizing, learning caring norms, and participating in caring behaviors. The remaining four deal primarily with developing a sense of obligation toward the broader society; they include diversifying, networking, reasoning, and forming global connections. This framework, they propose, can serve as a conceptual lens for analyzing current social institutions with the view of reinforcing, modifying, or adding components as necessary.

"What kind of socialization is required to raise caring, cooperative, helpful persons?" asks Ervin Staub (chapter 17). Pointing to the role of a society's ideals and the actual experiences of children, and drawing on empirical research, he makes specific recommendations regarding the nature of such experiences in families and schools. Socialization experiences to promote caring help children develop what Staub calls "connected identities." Rather than merely autonomous or independent on the one hand, or embedded on the other hand, people with connected identities have a sense of themselves in relation. Thus, they feel both connected to others as well as apart, and at times can stand in opposition to others.

Whereas Staub addresses the institutions of family and schools generally, Daniel Boland (chapter 18) cites the case of Alcoholics Anonymous as a concrete example of altruism. What alcoholics offer each other in this context is nonintrusive listening, personal knowledge of the experience and its accompanying despair, nonthreatening intimacy, honest supportive reassurances, as well as tireless concern, time, attention, and empathy with no expectations of personal reward. While recovering alcoholics practice altruism through their supportive interchanges, adherents of the Bahá'í faith, according to Wendy Heller and Hoda Mahmoudi (chapter 19), learn extensive altruistic norms primarily through its central teachings. Rather than being focused on personal enlightenment or salvation, its sacred texts are intended to transform civilization by personal action that transforms individuals and their social institutions. Spirituality, belief, and practice are inseparable in the Bahá'í conception, say Heller and Mahmoudi, and they are integrally joined to promote equality, equitable distribution of resources, elimination of prejudice, and world peace.

Whereas autonomy, voluntarism, and choice are noted among many contributors to this volume, for Wiktor Osiatynski (chapter 20), they are cardinal preconditions for altruism. On the basis of an analysis of the collectivist model developed in the USSR, as well as the collectivist rural village and the Russian Orthodox religion of pre-Communist times, Osiatynski develops the idea that philanthropy and charity may be possible in a paternalistic or autocratic collectivist society, but that altruism cannot exist in it.

# PART TWO

# PHILOSOPHICAL, DEFINITIONAL, AND CONCEPTUAL ISSUES

*Edited by Lawrence A. Blum*

# INTRODUCTION

## *Lawrence A. Blum*

In Plato's *Republic*, Thrasymachus argues that self-interest motivates all our behavior, even behavior that appears to show consideration for the interests of others. Plato rejects Thrasymachus's view, but the controversy is still with us. The papers in this section address three questions within this controversy: (1) What is an adequate and workable definition for "altruism"? (2) What are the basic types of and motives for altruism? (3) How is altruism related to morality more generally? How well do our inherited traditions of moral thought illuminate the phenomenon of altruism?

Krzysztof Konarzewski, a Polish psychologist, dismisses most ordinary forms of prosocial behavior as not real altruism. Konarzewski suggests two quite distinct motives for rescue: (1) "Empathy" is a direct concern for the rescuee as a vicarious self. It involves an inclusiveness that breaks through the boundaries of social categories (such as "Jew"). (2) "Protest" involves aiding the rescuee as a way of attacking or protesting against the regime or social order (or one's position in it).

Konarzewski emphasizes the sense of individual independence necessary for protest-inspired rescue—an independence from the values of the social order and its leaders, nurtured by encouragement to reflect critically on the validity of what one has been taught. Konarzewski suggests that empathy and protest are difficult to combine in one individual, for empathic people are more dependent on and sensitive to the situations and opinions of others, thus tending to lack the independence necessary for protest motivation.

Lawrence Blum, an American philosopher, explores distinct aspects of the moral accomplishment of rescuers. He distinguishes between altruism as the concern for another person's welfare as such, and resistance to evil (including resistance to persecution, racism, and genocide). This distinction is very much like Konarzewski's but with two important differences. Blum thinks it unlikely that a rescuer would engage in rescue *purely* from the motive of protest or resistance to evil, since he/she would not be likely to see the regime as evil unless he/she also had some altruistic concern for its victims.

Second, Blum does not see protest or resistance to evil strictly as a form of *altruism* at all, but rather as a distinct moral principle involved in rescue activity. Saving a Jewish life was not just like saving a victim of an accident or natural disaster (an act prompted solely by altruism), but implicitly involved resistance to the evil of Nazism. Thus, according to Blum rescue cannot serve as a paradigm for theories of altruistic personality per se, for rescue (of the persecuted) requires an appreciation of other distinct values as well.

Victor Seidler, an English philosopher and social theorist, offers a wide-ranging discussion of the traditions of thought that he sees as making it difficult to acknowledge the human possibilities of altruism. Seidler especially criticizes Kantianism—as an expression of Enlightenment thought—for its overvaluing of reason and duty and its neglect or denigration of emotion-based motivation like compassion, without which altruism is impossible (the emotion-grounded nature of altruism is presupposed in Konarzewski's notion of empathy and Blum's of altruism). Seidler sees both reason and duty as having the potentiality for diverting the individual from his/her deepest impulses—including impulses to care for others—toward an abstract, rigid, and rule-bound morality.

Seidler also questions the customary posing of the issue of altruism as a choice or opposition between altruism and egoism. Seidler argues that the true altruist is not a self-sacrificer. While Seidler is not denying that rescue activities involve risk, he follows the Oliners' findings that the source of specific acts of rescue lie in a structure of personality; and Seidler wants to emphasize that in choosing to engage in this, as in other, altruistic activities, "altruistic personalities" are acting from their own deepest sense of value and identity.

Seidler's rejection of the dichotomies of egoism/altruism and duty/inclination dovetail with his rejection of the idea that rescuers have superior moral merit. He cites the Oliners' book as well as Philip Hallie's account of the villagers of Le Chambon (in *Lest Innocent Blood Be Shed*), where rescuers almost uniformly rejected a view of themselves as especially meritorious. They regarded themselves as doing what simply needed to be done. In this sense Seidler questions the sharp distinction drawn by Konarzewski between everyday prosocial behavior (not counted as truly altruistic by Konarzewski) and altruism in extreme circumstances. For Seidler, this behavior should all be seen as founded in human concern and care. Conferring special merit on rescuers lets bystanders off the hook morally, allowing them not to take responsibility for the human concern that the situation calls for.

Finally, Seidler criticizes the ignoring of cultural identity in Kantian and Enlightenment thought, where only what is common or universal to all humanity is emphasized as the basis of morality. Seidler points out that such an outlook encouraged Jews (especially in Germany) to downplay their cultural heritage and distinctness, and thus in a sense to betray themselves. Blum relates this issue of cultural identity to morality in another way. He claims that the preservation of any distinct people, such as the Jews, is a separate value over and above altruistic concern for individual members of that group; but that most rescuers were not in touch with this value, and expressed their motivation to rescue in purely universal terms. As Konarzewski says, the rescuers saw past all the social categorizations dividing persons from one another. But Seidler and Blum point out that as high an ideal as this may be, it does neglect what ought also to be taken as a value in its own right, namely, respect for specific cultural identity, in oneself and in others.

# 1

# EMPATHY AND PROTEST: TWO ROOTS OF HEROIC ALTRUISM

## Krzysztof Konarzewski

As the world moves away from the impersonal ideologies inherited from the nineteenth century, altruism becomes one of the least questioned educational goals and one of the most popular objects of psychological inquiry. About altruism almost everything seems to be known, and if we do not experience it in our everyday life, this is attributed only to the insufficient effort we put into preaching and striving for it. What contribution could then be made by a new book about altruism by Samuel and Pearl Oliner (1988) to the theory of character education? The answer looks straightforward. It is the authors' attempt at discovering the psychological roots of true altruism that makes the book important for educational studies, and educators. The remainder of this paper is an elaboration of that answer.

### EMPATHY AND PROTEST: CONCEPTUAL DISTINCTIONS

From the Oliners' interpretations two hypotheses may, I believe, be extracted. The first explains altruism by empathy, the second, by protest. Conceptually they are quite distinct from one another: the first considers altruism as an act *on behalf of* somebody, while the second as an act *against* somebody or something.

The hypothesis of empathy says that an individual shows an inclination to help another person if that person has been "incorporated into himself" in the sense that the fear and pain of another becomes his own fear and pain. He rescues others as he would rescue himself if he were in a similar situation. The other becomes the vicarious self. Rescuing of the other is rescuing the self-in-the-other.

The hypothesis of protest says that the tendency to help another person stems from disagreement with the existing state of affairs or the social order. An individual may disagree either with the world itself or his position in it. The world in which lawlessness is rampant, brute force is the last resort, and innocent people are condemned to torture and death—that world may elicit the protest in various forms, among them, altruistic protest. An individual may endeavor to sabotage the regime by means of helping people whom the regime considers enemies and persecutes the most. The protest may also stem from the recognition of one's own position as unjustly disadvantageous relative to others. By helping the oppressed an individual may try to undermine the social order that put him on such unequal terms with them. Leo Montada (in this volume) has aptly called these two forms of protest "moral outrage" and "existential guilt."

At the core of altruistic motivation, according to the first hypothesis, lies the unfortunate other who may have to be physically or symbolically present. According to the second, this position is occupied by the world that has been pulled out of its proper form by the hostile forces. Hence the altruistic acts may not be dependent on the presence of the persecuted other. In fact, such persons may be actively sought. There is another, equally obvious difference between the two hypotheses. While the first requires the victim to be personally attractive to the potential rescuer, and considers love as the surest way to altruism, the second makes no claim of that sort. One may come to the victim's aid even if he personally dislikes him and would have quit the relationship had the victim been in a more favorable situation.

### PSYCHOLOGICAL PREREQUISITES: INCLUSIVENESS OR INDEPENDENCE

The two hypotheses assume different psychological prerequisites of altruistic behavior. According to the first, it is *inclusiveness*— that is, perceiving of other people as essentially similar to the self, regardless of the ways they are socially categorized. As the Oliners (1988) put it, we would expect a person involved in the act of altruism to be one whose "ego boundaries were sufficiently broadened so that other people were experienced as part of the self" (183). The main obstacle to altruism is everything that splits people into separate categories, makes them different from others—in short, blocks the process of the "stimulus generalization."

The second hypothesis assumes *independence* as the basic prerequisite of altruism. It is independence of a special kind, however: independence from the "factual" on behalf of the "actual." By the latter I mean not the habitual forms of community life but rather their axiological foundation. The opposition of the independence, and hence the main enemy of altruism, is conformity to current leaders and movements. Dependent people easily admit all elements forced out by the present to be relics of the past, and eagerly accept the changes as historical necessity, an outcrop of collective justice, and so on. Many mental adaptations of this kind have in fact an opportunistic basis. That can be seen from the fact that people are usually more ready to accept some new order if it is introduced by the powerful, prestigious, or conquering agents that could hardly be resisted.

Since the condition just described has two sides—independence from the new changes and loyalty to the old foundation—it may be called conservatism as well. But this is not ordinary, inert conservatism that pushes an individual aside from the social life. It is rather an active rejection of the new order if it does not keep within the bounds of decency.

### EDUCATION FOR INCLUSIVENESS AND INDEPENDENCE

The two psychological prerequisites of altruism are acquired in different educational settings. Inclusiveness requires an education that creates the climate of universal solidarity of men on the, so to speak, biological basis. It can be achieved by the rejection of all social categories in introducing people to the child. Such an education consists of making the child interact with others—regardless of their gender, ethnicity, social class, religious affiliation, and the like—by means of setting tasks, modeling, suasion, etc.

It is obvious that education of that kind is almost impossible. Social differentiation of people reflects the social structure. To introduce the child into that structure is an important task of any socialization, which by definition aims at the reproduction of some social order. An education aiming at the formless community of the whole mankind would have to take place, as in the pedagogy of J. J. Rousseau, outside the society and against it. There is, however, some way to soften this limitation. I would say that what is conducive to inclusiveness is to instruct a child about a social category *after*, and not *before* his experience with concrete representatives of the category. The information "This is a Jew" in relation to somebody whom I know very well contributes little to my representation of that person. If I, however, do not know any Jews personally, this word labels all my uncertainty relating to the whole group of people. "Jew" as an attribute of otherwise known persons makes me intensify my interaction with them in order to explore this new difference. "Jew" as an attribute of strangers prevents me from getting in touch with them while it opens my ears to everything "people say about" them.

We could then set two educational strategies against each other. In the first, differences between people are *discovered*, while in the second they are *assumed* at the point of departure. From that point of view it is very interesting that in the Oliners' sample only 4 percent of rescuers, in contrast to 13 percent of nonrescuers, reported that they hadn't known if there were any Jews in their vicinity before the war (114). I suspect that among that 13 percent of the respondents' confessions of the sort "I hate the word *Jew*, it sounds so rotten" could be easily found. As the assumed difference seemingly fills informational gaps, it reduces the need for unbiased inquiry, and strengthens the primitive impulse of in-group solidarity (Tajfel et al. 1971). The discovered difference, by contrast, motivates the processes of both cognitive repeal of the strangeness it implies, and preservation of its descriptive sense. That is my interpretation of the slightly ambiguous passage from the Oliners' book that says that rescuers "feel more comfortable dealing with people different from themselves and are readier to emphasize the likeness that binds them to others than the distinctions that separate them" (250).

What can be said about independence? It grows, I believe, in educational contexts that require the child to reflect on the validity of various claims set up for him by other people, and teach him to resist the claims regarded as unjustifiable. Basic means of such education are examples of moral examination of the mutual claims in the family and the practice of appropriate reasoning in the course of everyday life. At the opposite pole is an education that puts the main emphasis on obedience.

Two kinds of obedience may be distinguished: "positional" and mercenary. The first implies uncritical acceptance of claims advanced by persons of higher social rank. In families that B. Bernstein (1971) has called positional, questioning of the validity of claims is seen as unnecessary or is even prohibited. It is known in advance that the father, as head of the family, is always right, that the mother is right unless the father opposes her, and so on. The world of the child splits into two circles: one contains all the persons whom he has to obey, another those whom he does not. It has been keenly observed the satisfaction with which the obedient child ignores the claims of adults belonging to the latter group. Mercenary obedience also makes the control of the validity of claims unnecessary, since it is based on profit and loss accounting. Many parents introduce their offspring into dull pragmatism by explicating moral duties in terms of profitability, and by disdaining reasons that may bring, if observed, unpleasant consequences.

Many a fact from the vast pool of facts collected by the Oliners confirms this description. It should be noted that members of the middle and upper-middle classes—where, according to Bernstein (1971), positional families are rare—were clearly overrepresented in the sample of rescuers. That can mean that many rescuers had the opportunity in their childhood to learn to examine the validity of claims or at least had avoided severe obedience training. Indeed, the rescuers reported more often than nonrescuers that their parents rejected both blind obedience and pragmatic attitudes toward conflict situations. Even more interesting are the differences in disciplinary measures used by the parents. Both rescuers and nonrescuers reported that their parents used punishment of various sorts, but the former more often mentioned that the parental disapproval was accompanied by the verbal explication of their reasons. The authors interpret that effect in a rather complex way as a modeling of the correct relation of the strong to the weak: when parents—the stronger part in the interaction—explain why they are dissatisfied with the child instead of just scolding or spanking him, they demonstrate to him how to resign the domination over the weaker part. I think it can be seen in a simpler way. Giving the reasons for parental disapproval instructs the child to take a reflective, critical attitude toward every claim before he accepts it. Unwarranted disapproval, on the other hand, shifts his attention from the claim itself to the position of its source. Little wonder that many nonrescuers perceived punishments inflicted upon them as a mere unloading of parents' emotions rather than a deliberate response to the intrinsic evil of their deeds (183).

Special attention should be paid in this context to the role of religion. Despite the saliency of religious motives of the rescuers in the eyes of the Jews themselves, the rescuers did not differ from the nonrescuers in religiousness just before the war. It appeared, however, that the rescuers were significantly more religious in childhood and had more religious fathers (156). A possible interpretation of this result assumes that early religious experience weakens in the child the feeling of dependence on others. I have found some support for this in my research on the attributions of school successes and failure made by adolescents. Boys and girls who attributed their successes and failures to God clearly rejected the idea that the help of their classmates and the moods of their teachers may have been responsible for the respective outcomes. It looks as if the feeling of dependence on the supernatural helps the young person to deny his or her dependence on mundane powers.

### HEROIC ALTRUISM AS EMPATHY AND PROTEST

The Oliners insist that any single hypothesis fails to explain the altruistic acts, and I shall agree with them. The hypothesis of protest, if taken alone, seems to them particularly inadequate. Protest is a response that is primarily destructive: it aims at eliminating the malefactor, not saving his victims. Indeed, only 17 percent of rescuers mentioned their hatred of the invaders as a motive for their activity, in contrast to 37 percent of the members of the underground. Patriotism and hatred facilitate armed resistance rather than the acts of altruism, as table 6.2 from *The Altruistic Personality* clearly shows. These facts stimulate the authors to question the relationship between independence and moral courage. They even suggest that great ideas or abstract principles may harden people to the sufferings of real individuals.

That criticism should not, however, imply the acceptance of the hypothesis of empathy. Compassion fails to explain those acts of help that put the rescuer himself in the situation to be pitied. Incorporation of the other into the self makes understandable that the person, in order to ease the other's distress, makes attempts similar to those he would make, should he suffer himself. But there is a limit to those attempts: the sufferings he exposes himself to. If someone denied it, he would have to admit that the cues of others' distress could screen out the cues of one's own distress. However, it is inconceivable on the grounds that empathic altruism is in fact rescuing oneself—in-the-other. Perhaps one should be reminded here that when the Bible lays down the empathy-based law for interpersonal relations, it commands the believer to love his neighbor as he loves himself—but no more.

We should conclude that altruism studied by the Oliners must be determined by both empathy and protest. Both roots of heroic altruism are indispensable as they limit and complement each other. The readiness to the empathic response focuses the protest on the victims and prevents entering into the vicious circle of violence. The ability to protest gives the readiness to help a quality of heroic self-sacrifice.

Without taking into account these two abilities, true altruism is deeply mysterious. But with them it becomes by no means clear. The point is that between the two abilities there is some incompatibility, both psychological and educational.

Psychologically, empathy implies some dependence on others. In my research (Konarzewski and Zychlinska 1978) on prosocial behavior I have found that female university students who worked hard on behalf of an anonymous partner perceived the partner as more similar to them, and—what is of prime interest here—were more field dependent than students who worked poorly. According to Witkin et al. (1962), who introduced the notion of field dependency to personality theory, people high on that measure experience themselves in a way influenced by others, while people low on that measure (i.e., field independent) can better realize their needs, feelings, and traits as well as perceive them as distinct from those of other persons. Hence if a person is able to respond empathically to another's needs, he or she is likely also to be socially dependent, which may prevent the acts of protest.

Educationally, the projects that promote interpersonal contacts in the climate of universal tolerance seem to distract students' attention from the axiological basis of the social order. The students' interpretations of social phenomena take on a psychological color as they rely on the notion of social competencies of interacting individuals. Hence, possible collective constraints of their behavior may escape notice.

The combination of the training of empathy with the training of protest, while not logically impossible, is by no means easy to achieve. That may explain why the acts of heroic altruism only rarely brightened up the darkness of the Holocaust.

## REFERENCES

Bernstein, B. (1971) *Class, Code, and Control: Theoretical Studies towards a Sociology of Language.* Vol. 1. London: Routledge and Kegan Paul.

Konarzewski, K., and G. Zychlinska (1978) The effect of psychological differentiation and perceived similarity on allocentric behavior. *Psychologia Wychowawcza:* 1, 21–36 (in Polish).

Oliner, S. P., and P. M. Oliner (1988) *The Altruistic Personality: Rescuers of Jews in Nazi Europe.* New York: Free Press.

Tajfel, H., M. B. Billig, R. P. Bundy, and C. Flamet (1971) Social categorization and intergroup behavior. *European Journal of Social Psychology:* 1, 149–75.

Witkin, H. A., R. B. Dyk, H. F. Faterson, D. R. Goodenough, and S. A. Karp (1962) *Psychological Differentiation: Studies of Development.* New York: Wiley.

# 2

# ALTRUISM AND THE MORAL VALUE OF RESCUE: RESISTING PERSECUTION, RACISM, AND GENOCIDE

*Lawrence A. Blum*

Samuel and Pearl Oliner's book *The Altruistic Personality* elicits our great admiration and gratitude for the few who risked so much to shelter Jews in Nazi Europe. The Oliners suggest that these individuals had "altruistic personalities" and that by studying their histories we can learn how to promote altruism in others. I will suggest that the concept of "altruism" by itself is insufficient to express the moral accomplishment of these rescuers. I will argue that there are other moral values implicated in such rescue activities that supplement and enrich—but are distinct from—the value of altruism per se. First is the moral value of resistance to evil. Acts of rescue constituted resistance to Nazism, specifically resistance to both persecution and racism, in addition to being acts of altruism per se. Second is the value of resistance to genocide, which implies a positive value being placed on the existence of the Jewish people as a people (over and above the value embodied in altruism per se, of saving individual Jews). I will also discuss the issue of risk and sacrifice as a dimension of altruistic action distinct from altruism per se. My argument will attempt to place altruism within the scheme of these other related though distinct values.

## ALTRUISM AS AN AGENT-CENTERED VALUE

"Altruism" as a positive value is necessarily an "agent-centered" value, rather than a "consequence-centered" value. To call an act

altruistic is to say more than that it produces beneficial consequences for someone; it is to confer praise on the agent of that
action. That is, altruism refers necessarily to an agent's motivation.

Social scientists have understandably found this element of the
notion of altruism troublesome. For it is notoriously difficult to be
certain of people's motivations—hence difficult to study it in the
way social scientists wish to do. For this reason social scientific
writers on altruism sometimes try to deny, or at least to mute, the
agent-centered nature of altruism by defining it without its full
motivational reality. Thus, in *The Altruistic Personality* Pearl and
Samuel Oliner say, "For the purpose of our study, we prefer a
definition [of 'altruism'] which relies on objective measurable criteria" (6), and the Oliners take their definition to avoid reference
to "internal psychological states."

However, the subsequent discussion in the Oliners' book belies
this aspiration. In fact the rescuers cited in the book all appear to
(and are taken by the Oliners to) have acted from concern for the
rescuee or from moral principle. That is, a condition referring to
motivation is in fact adopted in the Oliners' working definition of
"altruism," and this is in accordance with their implicit recognition that altruism is necessarily an agent-centered concept.

In fact rescue presents a less problematic case of genuine moral
motivation than other beneficent acts. Rescuers who received
monetary reward were not counted (by the Oliners). Most rescuers
could not have acted for the egoistic goal of social approval, first
because it was too risky to let others know that one was engaged
in rescue, and second because in most cases the norms prevailing
in one's society or community did not approve of such rescue anyway. Furthermore, even if a rescuer were concerned about approval
(of the rescuees, or of a few confidants who knew of the rescue),
the personal gain in such approval was so obviously outweighed
by the risk to life and freedom in engaging in the rescue that a
desire for such approval could not intelligibly be regarded as the
motive for rescue.

**ALTRUISM AND RISK**

Some psychologists and philosophers oversimplify the nature of
altruism and its value by defining it as involving sacrifice, or at
least the risk of it. The element of risk is of course central to the
case of rescue and surely does constitute an important part of why

rescue activities are admirable. Nevertheless, building self-sacrifice into the very definition of altruism generally (heroic rescue being only one type of altruism) is misleading. For it masks the fact that it can be morally good or admirable to be genuinely concerned about the welfare of others even when there is no risk or loss to the self. The epithets "compassionate," "thoughtful," and "kind" all refer to admirable traits that involve altruism (in the sense of genuine concern for others), yet none of them actually requires loss or sacrifice to the agent.

What altruism does require for the specific value that it has is an absence of concern for the self—a direct concern only for the other. But absence of concern for the self is not the same thing as sacrifice or risk to the self. In many ordinary circumstances it is possible to be helpful to someone out of compassion or sympathy, and yet to lose absolutely nothing (though gain nothing either). Sacrifice and risk are indeed an important part of what gives rescue its value. But the concern for others shown in that rescue is a separately valuable element, which can exist without the risk.

## ALTRUISTIC SPECIALIZATION

While concern for others may be ceteris paribus a good thing (independent of the sacrifice involved), we do not actually *admire* persons or confer positive agent-centered worth on their concerned actions in all contexts. For example, normally we do not admire someone for her concern for family members or friends. Rather, this is simply expected.

Yet if an average degree of concern or altruism does not constitute something positively valuable, how wide in scope does altruism have to be before we count it praiseworthy?

Let us take an example here, which will help to illustrate both the value of altruism and the value of rescue: Jacek is deeply devoted to the welfare of his community. He lives in a relatively poor neighborhood and is always helping his neighbors individually, attempting to secure better services for them, organizing them to articulate their own needs politically, and the like. Jacek is genuinely compassionate and caring toward his neighbors. He is tireless and selfless, energetic and imaginative in his efforts to help.

Let us note, however, that Jacek's altruism involves a degree of what we might call "moral specialization" (or "altruistic specialization"). His altruism is targeted to a specific group of persons—

defined residentially or by a shared condition. To explore the significance of this fact, let us imagine that a political refugee who is of a different race or ethnic group moves into Jacek's community and either by herself or through an intermediary asks Jacek—as a knowledgeable and helpful person in the community—for help and refuge. Let us further imagine the refugee as a Salvadoran, who is in danger of being killed if she returns to El Salvador. The U.S. government will not grant her political refugee status and she is thus threatened with deportation.

Suppose that Jacek refuses to be concerned about the Salvadoran refugee. He feels he has enough to do taking care of the people already in his community; they have urgent needs too, and he spends all his time helping them.

What do we think of Jacek in light of his response to the refugee? Do we reconsider or withdraw our previous judgment that he is an altruistic person deserving of admiration? Let us be clear that his unwillingness to help the refugee does not call into question the authenticity and sincerity of his altruistic efforts on behalf of his community. It is not like discovering that all along Jacek has been secretly employed by a wealthy benefactor who is paying him to help the community.

It is true that Jacek has all along been altruistically specialized. But we knew this about him from the beginning and it did not affect our initial judgment of his worthiness. In any case most people are in some ways morally specialized. Their moral efforts are targeted primarily to members of specific groups, whether defined in terms of proximity to the agent or as sharing some characteristic. Are we entirely to reevaluate our moral judgments about the admirability of morally specialized altruism?

At the same time, Jacek's response to the Salvadoran refugee does reflect on Jacek's moral character, and casts a new light on his previous altruism on behalf of his community. The moral specialization becomes a kind of moral parochialism, for the appearance of the refugee creates a new situation. While in usual circumstances Jacek's moral specialization is not inappropriate and does not render his altruism less than admirable, in this new situation his failure to go beyond that specialization does mark a deficiency in his altruism. This is partly because the refugee's life is in danger; she is in a situation of greater and more urgent need than the members of Jacek's neighborhood. But this is not the only reason. Even if her need were at the same level as his neighbors, it would still be a deficiency were he to fail to have some concern for her and willingness to help.

It would, I think, be too harsh to say that Jacek's altruism towards his community is entirely deprived of moral worth in light of his failure to help the refugee. Yet it seems importantly diminished in moral worth.

It seems, then, that in some situations mere altruism—understood as concern for others besides oneself (and, let us stipulate, beyond the bounds of family and friends)—is not enough. The altruism has to have a particular degree of scope or inclusiveness to warrant full worth and admiration. It must at least go beyond a narrower or customary ethnocentrism or other group centeredness to include groups "different" from oneself.

This analysis is implicit in judgments many of us make about rescue and other altruistic efforts in the context of Nazi occupation. We regard it as a failure of some kind if a Christian was not able to extend her willingness to help, or at least her concern, to Jews, refugees from other countries, and other groups perceived as different from herself. For example, no matter how heroic a Polish Christian was in sheltering members of the Polish underground from the Nazis, if such an individual refused to be concerned about the plight of Jews as well, then something was lacking.

This is not to make a blanket judgment of condemnation of, say, Polish Christians who did not help Jews. The penalty for helping was death to the helpers (visited upon at least two thousand Polish rescuers), and no one is in a position to condenm those who failed to take such risk—especially not those who have never faced anything like such risks themselves. What can be said with more justification, however, is that a person whose refusal to help a Jew stemmed not from fear of the consequences but rather from an inability to extend her altruistic concern beyond national and religious boundaries evidenced a less-than-admirable trait of character. Professor Maria Einhorn-Susulowska (in discussion at the altruism conference) put this point by saying that no one can condemn a Polish non-Jew for failing to help Jews; but one can condemn the many for their indifference to the Jews' plight.

## UNIVERSALISTIC ALTRUISM AS AN IDEAL

In light of reflection on the Nazi context, and on other situations in which the normal moral specializations prove insufficient or inadequate, it might be tempting to define altruism not as concern for others but as concern for others *simply as human beings*—thus building inclusiveness or universality into the concept of altruism itself. For if one is concerned about someone simply as a human being, then one does not exclude from one's concern any human being, no matter what her relation to oneself. If it were true of Jacek that he is concerned about members of his community simply as human beings, then he could not fail to be concerned about the Salvadoran refugee. Such a definition of altruism requires that differences of race, religion, ethnicity, national origin, class, and the like not affect one's caring for others—or else this caring is not to count as "altruism." Jacek's failure to care for the Salvadoran refugee shows that he cares for his neighbors not simply as human beings but rather as persons standing in a certain relation to himself.

The temptation to so define altruism should be resisted. My suggestion would be to retain this universalistic or fully inclusive concept of altruism as an *ideal*, but to reject it as a *definition*. Otherwise one has deprived all altruistic specializations of any of the moral value attaching to "altruism," and I have argued that this goes too far and is untrue to our reflective moral understanding.

My proposal acknowledges the value perspective informing the Oliners' book—that universalistic altruism is a "higher" form of altruism than specialized altruism. (To put it another way: The more inclusive the altruism, the more worth it has.) Beyond this, I have argued also that in some circumstances universalistic altruism is not only an ideal, but constitutes a standard against which specialized altruism becomes parochial and loses much (though not all) of its worth.

## ALTRUISM AND RESISTANCE TO EVIL

While universality or inclusiveness must supplement and qualify altruism in order for it to provide an adequate conceptual framework to express the moral accomplishment of rescuers of Jews under Nazi occupation, I want to argue that a full understanding of this accomplishment and its distinct worth requires an appreciation of several other values distinct from—and not merely qualifying—altruism itself. The first of these is the extraordinary riskiness and danger of rescue activities.

I will discuss two further dimensions of rescue of Jews in Nazi Europe—resistance to evil, and preservation of the Jewish people. It is a morally significant feature of rescue in the Nazi context that to save a Jew was to resist evil—the evil of Nazism. This evil in turn has at least two distinguishable aspects—persecution and racism. The Jews were a persecuted group, and were persecuted because of their ethnicity or religion (their [alleged] "race").

Resistance to evil is a morally distinct feature from altruism itself. The perspective of altruism sees the persecuted Jew as a person in need, whose life is under threat of death. The motive of altruism is activated in the altruist insofar as she sees the other as a person in need (or, more generally, as a person whom she can benefit).

But to help, or to save the life of, someone who is persecuted is to do more than just to save life, as in a flood or accident. It is to recognize a further evil—the evil of persecution (by which I refer here to state-sponsored persecution)—and to resist that evil by saying that one will not let persecution be successful in the case of this particular individual. This is why the Salvadoran political refugee implicitly presents to Jacek a moral issue over and above the urgency of her individual need. She presents an issue (persecution) that is not present in the neighbors who are the usual subjects of Jacek's helping activities.

If a rescuer who acts with the recognition that in helping the persecuted person one does more than save a life but also resists persecution, the notion of altruism alone is insufficient to express her moral accomplishment. Many of the rescuers in *The Altruistic Personality* articulated this dimension of rescue in the Nazi context, by speaking for example of the wrongness of punishing the innocent (see Oliner and Oliner 1988, 166–67). Beyond those who explicitly voice this dimension, many others can be presumed to have seen their rescue activities at least partly in this light. For the fact that Jews were being persecuted was known to virtually everyone in the Nazi-occupied countries, and certainly to all rescuers. Thus rescuers were aware that in saving a Jewish life they were also saving the life of a persecuted person, and so were resisting or in a sense protesting against persecution. They can be presumed to have understood that saving a Jew from the Nazis was in this regard not simply like helping the victims of natural or technological disasters.

The failure to mention the aspect of persecution could stem

partly from the fact that the rescuers took its significance for granted. But there may be another reason as well. While the existence of persecution was evident, it is also a more abstract consideration than the more immediate one of the danger to the particular, individual Jew or Jews who are potential rescuees. It is not surprising that 76 percent of the rescuers focus on the needy condition of the potential rescuee (Oliner and Oliner 1988, 168); this is the most immediate consideration. Yet it is not the only one, and no doubt a smaller number of persons would, upon reflection on their experience, regard assertion of various moral principles that express the wrongness of persecution as a salient consideration in their motivation, or in their understanding of their actions.

In fact the language of "motivation to engage in rescue" may serve us ill in trying to comprehend the full meaning and moral significance of acts of rescue in the Nazi context. For what directly "moves" a person to act does not exhaust the meaning that the action has for the person. It does not exhaust the agent's self-understanding of her action. This point is illustrated in the film *Angry Harvest* (German: *Bittere Ernte*, directed by Agnieszka Holland, 1986), which deals with the rescue phenomenon in its Polish setting. A well-to-do but lonely and sexually frustrated Polish farmer comes upon a hungry and terrified Jewish woman in his woods; he takes her to his home and shelters her. His "motive" in initially helping her would naturally be described as compassion. At the same time the farmer might well not have had such a compassionate reaction to a Jewish male. What young females represent (e.g., wife, helpless dependent, sexual partner) to this farmer's complex and unhealthy consciousness may have been not a direct motive itself but nevertheless a condition of the actual motive of compassion operating.

To say that rescue of the persecuted involves a further moral dimension beyond that of altruism alone is not to say that a persecuted individual's life is worth more than the life of a nonpersecuted person (e.g., of a drowning person, or a victim of natural disaster). It is not to say that the refugee's life has greater worth than the community residents' life (in the example of Jacek), nor that a Jew's life was more valuable than a German soldier's. The point has nothing to do with the worth of persons, but with the moral character of rescue activities.

I say that resistance to the evil of persecution is an element over and above altruism in the rescue of Jews, and it is an element that need not (though it may) function as a direct motive. But can it also be an actual motivation all its own, operating in some cases in the absence of altruism altogether? The Oliners say that some rescuers were motivated primarily by their hostility toward Nazis. They quote one rescued survivor describing his rescuer's motivation: "He explained it to me in very simple words: 'I decided to fight the Germans by saving those persecuted by them. Who were the most persecuted? The Jews.'" (Oliner and Oliner 1988, 144).

One must here distinguish the motive of resistance from that of revenge or hatred. Revenge or hatred does not have a moral character at all, even if one's reason for hating or for wanting revenge stems from the immorality of the object of hatred or intended revenge. By contrast, resistance to evil is a moral motive whose goal is to prevent evil, or at least to take a stand against it—and not merely to vent hatred or revenge.

Keeping this distinction in mind, it seems to me difficult to believe that a person who rescued Jews as a form of resistance to the Nazis was not at least in some small degree motivated by altruism as well. For in recognizing what is evil about Nazism one recognizes the harm it does to human beings, to those whom it persecutes. Care for human beings must be part of the recognition of the evilness of Nazism in the first place. Hence some of the overall motive (of, for example, the Nazi-resisting individual quoted above) in rescuing must surely involve altruistic concern for the potential rescuee.

Yet this is not to deny that resistance to evil can function as a distinct motive, nor that some persons are more dominantly motivated by resistance and others by altruism. Certainly once some underground resistance movements officially adopted the position that rescuing Jews was to be taken on as a resistance activity, some persons whose altruistic motivation by itself was insufficient to get them to engage in rescue began to engage in rescue activities.

## ALTRUISM AND RESISTANCE TO RACISM

So far, I have discussed persecution as one part of the evil that rescue activities resist. But a further distinguishable part of this evil is the racism involved in the Nazis' persecution of Jews. (By "racism" I mean here the victimization of persons because of their [imagined or actual] race, ethnicity, religious affiliation, national heritage, and the like.) Racism is a particularly virulent scourge, beyond that of persecution itself, which can be visited upon someone for nonracist reasons. One can see this in the case of Jacek and the refugee. If Jacek's refusal to help the refugee stems (in part) from racist sentiments, his inaction is more blameworthy than if he fails to help because his moral energies and imagination are too limited in being bounded by his neighborhood community. (One can envision the latter situation if one imagines the refugee to be of the same race as Jacek himself.)

That racism adds a dimension of moral turpitude to an action that is also wrong on other grounds is sometimes recognized in the law as well. A racial attack on an individual is treated more harshly than an attack grounded in jealousy or economic gain, even if the harmed individuals are harmed equally in both situations. In the former case the attack can be a civil rights violation in addition to being an assault.

Thus resistance to racism constitutes a further good element of an action that is morally good on other grounds as well, for example, as an act of rescue. A white sheltering a black on the Underground Railroad during slavery (in the U.S.), a Turk saving an Armenian driven from his home at the time of the Armenian Holocaust (as discussed by Richard Hovannisian in his paper in this volume), and a Christian sheltering a Jew—all these actions by their very nature resist the evil of racism being perpetrated against the groups in question. They all do more than save an individual, or even a persecuted individual; they assert the fundamental principle of human equality across racial, religious, and national differences. They help to keep the evil of racism from being triumphant.

Again, many of the rescuers interviewed in *The Altruistic Personality* recognized this antiracist dimension of their actions. Yet, as in the case of persecution more generally, the fact that some rescuers did not articulate this dimension of their actions does not mean that they were unaware of it, or that it failed to play a role in their action. In fact all rescuers were certainly aware that the Jews were being persecuted for their religion/ethnicity (and alleged race), and most (though not necessarily all) of those engaged in rescue can be presumed to have thought such racial persecution wrong.

In looking back at the activities of these rescuers, and in honoring them for their moral accomplishment, I think we implicitly place these acts in a wider framework than that of altruism alone. We see the actions as resisting the evil of Nazism—as asserting the wrongness of persecution and of racism. This is part, I think, of what accounts for our generally unqualified admiration for these actions. If the actions were solely ones in which one person risked her life and often those of her loved ones and other members of her household to save the life of another endangered person, it is not clear that many such acts—for example, ones in which several lives were risked to save one Jew—would not be regarded as foolhardy rather than courageous and morally honorable. If I am in a burning building with two of my children and I endanger their lives and mine to attempt to rescue another person in the building, there would at least be disagreement as to how morally admirable such an action is.

And yet we do admire rescuers who endangered their own and their loved ones' lives to rescue Jews. I have often been troubled by the easy and seemingly unambivalent admiration that those involved in the study of rescuers (including myself) feel for these rescuers, and assume that others will feel as well. I think the reason that such an attitude is ultimately justified is that the situation of non-Jewish rescuers of Jews (and Turkish and Arab rescuers of Armenians) is only partly analogous to the burning house situation. The analogy is in the motivation to preserve life and in the risk to one's own life and (sometimes) those of loved ones and other members of one's household. (The Oliners report that 84 percent of rescuers lived with other persons, 27 percent with children ten years or younger, all of whom were endangered by rescue activities.) But the disanalogy is that in the rescue context something larger than saving lives per se is at stake—namely resistance to a great evil. This is why it is not merely a matter of one life against another, but rather of fundamental human principles and values at stake on top of (though not apart from) the saving of life. The actions of rescue have an historical importance in their role as countering the hegemony of Nazi power and Nazi values.

Perhaps this point deserves some qualification. I think some moral perspectives would admire actions of rescue involving nothing more than the risking of one's own life to save that of another. In this volume, Ewa Kurek-Lesik cites a moving example of a nun from the Order of the Immaculate Conception describing a meeting called by one of the sisters, Wanda Garczynska, to decide whether to continue sheltering several (possibly many) children and adult Jews. The nun remembers,

She explained that she did not wish to jeopardize the house, the sisters, the community. She knew what could be awaiting us. There was no thought of self. She knew: you should love one another as I have loved you. How? So that He gave His life.

The example suggests a Christian, Christlike moral outlook in which risking one's own life to save another—independent of whether the threat to that life arises through persecution and/ or racism—is itself a high, or even the highest, form of moral endeavor.

In any case, I suspect that most admirers of rescuers do not share the moral standard involved in the literal interpretation of sister Wanda Garczynska's remarks. If this is so, I suggest that their reaction of unqualified admiration of most instances of rescue depends partly on taking account of the context of resistance to racial persecution as an important element of the action.

Our moral reaction to rescuers is one necessarily made from the historical vantage point of hindsight. We see, in retrospect, that acts of rescue were part of a resistance to Nazism. We see their significance as the historical one of asserting a different way of living and different values than those of the Nazis—an assertion not made by bystanders (those who did nothing to help), whatever their actual disagreements with the Nazi regime and philosophy. We see individual acts of rescue, whatever their detailed self-understanding, as imbued with this historical significance—a significance that not everyone needed to have been explicitly aware of at the time (though some certainly were).

To summarize, then: Rescuers are altruistic, and this is certainly part of what we admire in their actions. But it is not only altruism—understood as a concern for the need of the other—that confers on rescuers their exceptional place in our moral evaluation. Aside from the obvious point of risk and sacrifice is the dimension of resistance to evil that their actions involve. In this way the title of the Oliners' book—*The Altruistic Personality*—is in some ways misleading in implying that the notion of altruism itself is sufficient to conceptualize the moral significance of rescue. Rescuers were also resisters of persecution and racism, and these are distinct elements in our understanding of their moral accomplishment.

## ALTRUISM AND AFFIRMING CULTURES

Finally, there is one further element of moral significance, beyond altruism pure and simple, involved (at least potentially) in the rescue situation—and that is preservation of the Jewish people as a people. In contrast to resistance to evil, this aspect was (or could be inferred to be) *seldom* present in the self-understanding (explicit or implicit) of rescuers.

"Preservation of the Jewish people as a people" is one example of a general value, which I will refer to as "affirming cultures." That value is embodied in valuing the existence of any distinct people (though the boundaries of a "people" may be hard to define), with their distinctive culture, values, traditions, and ways of life (such as the Iroquois, Poles, Afro-Americans, Gypsies, Lithuanians, Armenians, Turks, Germans). Octavio Paz states this value well, in the context of an attack on a certain notion of "progress":

By suppressing differences and peculiarities, by eliminating different civilizations and cultures, progress weakens life and favors death.... Every view of the world that becomes extinct, every culture that disappears, diminishes a possibility of life.

Thus for a Turk to help an Armenian, with an understanding that in doing so he was helping to preserve the Armenians as a people, would be to instantiate the same value I am referring to in the case of the Jews.

The Jewish form of this value as applicable in the Nazi context is this: Under the Nazis the Jews as a distinct cultural, ethnic, religious group were threatened with extermination; this was the goal of Nazi policy. In rescuing an individual Jew or Jews, a rescuer did more than save an individual life; she contributed to preserving the Jews as a people. By helping to keep alive a bearer of the Jewish tradition, she helped to preserve that culture and tradition, with its particular values and ways of life.

In asserting the distinct value of this preservation of a people, I am not asserting that the Jews have a special worth that other peoples do not have. Because of the Jewish notion of the "chosen people," and the way that this has been used against Jews even in the present day (for example by Cardinal Glemp, Poland's Catholic primate, in 1989), it is particularly important to distinguish *distinct worth* from *special worth*. "Special worth" implies a greater worthiness than other groups. But "distinct worth" simply implies a kind of worth that is different from but neither more nor less than that of other peoples. The value of preserving Jews is thus one example of a general value. The salience of this general value in the case of Jews stems, of course, from the fact that the Nazis were declaring Jews as a people unworthy of existence, and were attempting to realize their view in genocidal action.

The value of affirming cultures or peoples is recognized in the category of "genocide" as a particularly heinous crime, expressed for example in the 1946 United Nations Convention on the Prevention and Punishment of the Crime of Genocide. The implication is that in wiping out a people one does something more evil, in a sense, than killing the same number of individuals. A people is more than a collection of individual or human beings, and there is value in preserving a people that is over and above the value of saving individual lives. (Genocide can also be practiced without directly taking lives, for example by preventing a people from reproducing, such as by sterilization or forcible conversion.)

Preservation of the Jewish people as a people is of course related to the value and goal discussed earlier of resisting racism against the Jews. But it is by no means the same thing. The resister of racism declares a human equality and human kinship in the face of its denial. Thus the resister of racism rescues the Jew as a fellow human being (and some rescuers explicitly articulate this dimension: "Jewish people are the same; all people are the same" [Oliner and Oliner 1988, 166].) But she does not necessarily rescue him as a Jew—that is, as the bearer of the specific cultural and religious traditions of Jews. It is those traditions that are affirmed by the rescuer who sees the Jew as a Jew. The antiracist rescuer, by contrast, does not necessarily assert the worth of Judaism or Jewishness as a specific culture or religion. What she does is to resist its denial as that denial is used to denigrate the Jew. What she does positively assert is simply the worth of the Jew *as a human being*.

The difference between the antiracist perspective and the perspective of asserting the specific value of Jewishness or of the Jewish people is evident in the fact that very few rescuers seemed to embody the latter value, but many (at least implicitly) adhered to the former and saw their rescue activities in light of it. Rescuers interviewed for *The Altruistic Personality* who mentioned the Jewishness of Jews generally did so only to assert the wrongness of victimizing Jews, and to say that they, in contrast to the Germans, saw the Jew as a human being. Several expressed this by saying, in essence, "I did not see him as a Jew, but as a human being." (see Oliner and Oliner 1988, 154: "I did not help them because they were Jewish," attributed to several rescuers.)

Polish rescuers, for example, almost never saw the value in Jewishness per se. Anti-Semitism ran so deep in Polish culture that the moral accomplishment of the Polish rescuer was to be able to rise above that anti-Semitism to see the Jew as a fellow human being. (Nechama Tec emphasizes this point in her study, *When Light Pierced the Darkness: Christian Rescue of Jews in Nazi-Occupied Poland.*) Iwona Irwin-Zarecka points out in her book, *Neutralizing Memory: The Jew in Contemporary Poland,* that Poles have almost always regarded the Jew as "other," as a problem, defined from the point of view of (non-Jewish) Polish society. They almost never saw Jews from the point of view of the Jews themselves; hence they were not able to appreciate the value of Jewishness in its own right. This has been true even of Poles who are not actually anti-Semitic in the sense of having negative, racist attitudes toward Jews. Given this history, the rarity of the Polish rescuer who was able to see the distinct value of preserving Jews as a people is hardly surprising—though given the particularly rich form of Jewish life in Poland for so many centuries, it is a deeply painful fact.

The value of preserving a people is not only a value over and above saving the life of individuals, though it is that too. It is also a value connected with the sense of identity of the rescued individual. Even when the converting of Jews was done for pure security reasons and with no sense of "spiritual advantage" to the Jew to become a Christian, it must be recognized that this conversion constituted a violation of the Jew's identity (unless of course she herself chose to be converted for heartfelt religious reasons). As she describes in this volume, Ewa Kurek-Lesik found that some of the nuns rescuing Jewish children appreciated this fact, and did not convert them, while others had no compunctions about converting them. Still others presumably had positions in between, recognizing that it might constitute a kind of violation of a Jewish child to baptize and convert her, but feeling that considerations of security (to both the rescuers and rescuees) weighed more strongly in favor of doing so.

One group that did have a sense of the value of Jews as a distinct people were members of the Dutch Calvinists discussed in Lawrence Baron's chapter in this book, "The Dutchness of Dutch Rescuers: The National Dimension of Altruism." It was part of the theological outlook of these Calvinists to take seriously the sacredness of the Old Testament, the Jewish origins of Christianity, and the fact that Jews were regarded as God's chosen people. In saving an individual Jew, a member of this faith saw herself as doing more than saving life—she was also helping to preserve a religious group that she saw as valuable.

Yet these Dutch Calvinists embody only one form of the recognition of the value of preserving the Jews as a people—and in a way it is a less-than-ideal one. For it depends on the idea that Jews possess a special value—as the "chosen people"—the form of which value, therefore, could not be applicable to other peoples. Hence the way the Dutch Calvinists value Jews would not be transferable to other peoples, and would give no grounds for their valuing, for example, a Muslim or Buddhist people. It is thus not an example of the general value of affirming cultures or peoples.

**ALTRUISM AND EXTENSIVITY**

The value of affirming particular cultures and peoples does not involve a retreat from the universalism involved in the notion of "extensivity." The Oliners articulate two paths to universal extensivity, which I will call "care" and "principle." (This usage departs somewhat from the Oliners' own use of these terms.) I will show that affirming culture is actually a path to, or an expression of, extensivity itself, distinct from but complementary to these two other paths.

A (universal) extensivity based on "principle" involves possessing explicitly universalistic principles affirming the worth of all persons, the obligation to help persons in need, the principle of benevolence or love toward all human beings, and the like. By contrast, (universal) extensivity based on "care" involves caring about each individual who presents herself to one—responding directly (without appeal to principle) to each individual's need—just because that individual is a human being and independent of her racial, ethnic, religious (and the like) differences from oneself. This distinction between a caring and a principled universalist is well-illustrated by Magda and André Trocmé, two now well-known rescuers of Jews, described in Philip Hallie's *Lest Innocent Blood Be Shed*.

Affirming the value of distinct peoples is, or anyway can be, a third extensive value as well, embracing almost all persons. For almost every person has some cultural identity and is part of some cultural, ethnic, religious, national, etc., group. Theoretically at least, affirming the plethora of distinct cultures can encompass all the cultures giving identity to specific individuals.

Yet this value should not be seen as an *alternative* to care and principle. That is, affirming the value of peoples—and of an individual's cultural identity—is not a different way of reaching the exact same place (helping someone because she is a human being); it is not analogous to the way that care and principle are different ways of reaching that place. Rather, affirming cultures is a complement to both care and principle. Recognizing a person's distinct cultural identity does not detract from caring for her as a human being; but it is not simply a *way* of caring for her as a human being either. One might say that it is a way of caring for her as a specific individual (with her specific cultural identity); this is a kind of enriching of a care for her as a human being. One takes her specific individual identity into account in a way that the notion of "caring for someone as a human being" does not quite express.

Thus, while affirming the value of Jews as Jews (Armenians as Armenians, etc.) is in one way more particularistic—in encompassing and valuing a particular cultural/religious/ethnic identity—than a principled obligation to all humankind, it is nevertheless barely less extensive or universalist.

**CONCLUSION**

I have argued in this paper that attention to the moral significance of non-Jewish rescuers of Jews can help to place the concept of "altruism" in its proper value perspective. Altruism is of value in its own right. But in addition several other dimensions—some of which are present in all cases of this rescue, and all of which can be present—are distinct sources of value. These other sources are sacrifice or risk; extensivity or universality (extending one's concern to all human beings); resistance to evil in the form of persecution; resistance to evil in the form of racism; and valuing and preserving a people (specifically the Jewish people) as a people. The moral accomplishment—and historical moral significance— of these rescuers can only be understood if these factors are taken into account. "Altruism" alone cannot express that accomplishment and that significance.

## BIBLIOGRAPHY

Blum, L. (1988) "Moral Exemplars: Reflections on Schindler, the Trocmés, and Others." *Midwest Studies in Philosophy 12: Character and Virtue*. Notre Dame: University of Notre Dame Press.

Gilligan, C. (1982) *In a Different Voice*. Cambridge: Harvard University Press.

Irwin-Zarecka, I. (1989) *Neutralizing Memory: The Jew in Contemporary Poland*. Oxford: Transaction.

Noddings, N. (1984) *Caring: A Feminine Approach to Ethics and Education*. Berkeley: University of California Press.

Oliner, S., and P. Oliner. (1988) *The Altruistic Personality: Rescuers of Jews in Nazi Europe*. New York: Free Press.

Slote, M. (1987) *Commonsense Morality and Consequentialism*. London: Routledge and Kegan Paul.

———. (1989) *Beyond Optimizing: A Study of Rational Choice*. Cambridge: Harvard University Press.

Sorokin. P. (1967 [1954]) *The Ways and Power of Love*. Chicago: Henry Regnery.

Tec, N. (1986) *When Light Pierced the Darkness: Christian Rescue of Jews in Nazi-Occupied Poland*. New York: Oxford University Press.

# 3

# RESCUE, RIGHTEOUSNESS, AND MORALITY

*Victor J. Seidler*

## 1. MORALITY AND MODERNITY

Can our moral theory help us illuminate the darkness of the holo-caust? This remains a disturbing and haunting question for those of us who have been educated in philosophy, psychology, and so-ciology departments in the 1950s and 1960s. This central event in the history and experience of Western culture has largely been passed over in silence. Our prevailing moral theories, still largely shaped within a Kantian or utilitarian tradition, have continued to present themselves as viable, even if they seem powerless to illuminate what seems most important to us. The period of Nazi rule and the extermination of European Jewry has in large part been treated as an aberration—as a sustained moment of mad-ness—that could not be grasped in the prevailing language of rea-son. It was a period of irrationality that has to be explained in historical terms. In this deeper and more pervasive sense there has been a denial of the holocaust at the heart of our postwar intel-lectual culture. It has failed, as Saul Friedlander has pointed out, to shift the terms of intellectual, moral, and political discussion, as did the slaughter of the first world war for generations to follow. To repeat, in large part it has been passed over in silence.

This has not always been an easy silence. Auschwitz has found its place in the deeper unspoken recesses of European conscious-ness. It remains a challenge to the visions of humanity and progress that are part of an Enlightenment tradition. It questions the very terms of modernity and of the philosophical tradition that has in large part sustained this tradition. At the close of the 1980s, when the dream of science and progress begins to fade and as we become more aware of the injuries that we have done to the planet in their name, there is more talk about the "crisis of modernity." There is even a lot of vague talk about "postmodernity" and a radical shift in cultural and intellectual sensibility. But it is the holocaust that provides the crisis for a modernity that has been organized according to the principles of Enlightenment rationalism. It is a crisis in our prevailing moral and political traditions that we face when we meditate upon those who rescued Jews during the painful days of the holocaust.

In large part our moral theory remains tied to assumptions that were set by the Enlightenment. We tend to accept in the moral theory of Kant and in the social theory of Durkheim a "dualistic" vision of human nature. We inherit Protestant assumptions that are presented to us in secular and universal terms. The fundamental notion is that "human nature" is radically evil and that left to ourselves individuals would be selfish and egoistic. This Hobbesian vision is at the source of our Enlightenment rationalism. It means that individuals have to be saved from themselves, for we cannot find redemption from within our "natures." For Kant it is crucial to separate our "reason" from our "natures," for it is only as rational beings that we can rely upon an independent and autonomous faculty of reason to discern the duties and principles that are available to us within an "intelligible realm." This is the source of both our freedom and morality. It is only if we act against our "inclinations"—our emotions and desires that would seek to determine our behavior from the outside, externally—that we can find freedom through following the inner voice of reason. Kant's vision has been crucial in defining an inherited sense of morality and freedom.

Put crudely, this means that we cannot find freedom and morality by listening to our "natures." We have to deny these parts of ourselves that would interfere with our capacity to follow the path of reason and morality. What is crucial is the way that "reason" is set against "nature" in such a complete and radical manner. This helps form a particular sense of rationality and a notion of the self as a "rational agent" that has become central to liberal moral and political theory. It tends to identify the moment of freedom with the moment of choice. It tends to see emotions and feelings as essentially "selfish" and "irrational" and so tends to present moral education as a denial of our emotional lives. Our inner lives can only be occupied by reason alone, for our emotions and feelings are presented as essentially external—as determining our behavior from the outside and so being forms of unfreedom. It is crucial to recognize that Kant identifies the inner life with the realm of reason so that freedom, as an inner quality, can be guaranteed by reason alone. So it is that our relationship to our emotional lives is essentially an externalized relationship that plays no part in our dignity or transcendence as individuals. It is only as "rational selves" that we can know ourselves as individuals. So it is that the realm of emotional life is separated from the sphere of morality. It is only as rational/moral beings that our lives have dignity. It is only by separating ourselves from our "animal natures" that we can find dignity and self-respect as moral beings. These assumptions have set the terms for the pervasive framework that sets "egoism" in opposition to "altruism" and that takes the central task of moral theory to provide "reasons" for why people should act altruistically towards others. It is assumed that left to our natures we will act selfishly and egoistically.

## 2. RESCUE AND SILENCE

We have come to know those people who helped to save Jews from the Nazi plans for extermination as "righteous gentiles." These were people who helped to save Jews at considerable risk to themselves, often of torture and death. They took these grave risks at no benefit to themselves. It is important that their actions be honored by the Jewish community at large, as at Yad Vashem. At the conference "Remembering for the Future" at Oxford in 1988, Dr. Mordecai Paldiel spoke in a moving way about his work at Yad Vashem. In meeting many of the rescuers he was struck by just how "ordinary" they often were and how far removed from our image of "righteousness." They did not want to be thought of as anything special and often felt that they simply did what "had to be done" in the situation.

This connects to the fact that it was not education that characterized those who took the risks of rescue. This is supported by the work the Oliners did on "the altruistic personality." It was often the professionals who turned a blind eye to what was going on and who sometimes colluded in Nazi rule, especially in Germany. How many doctors and lawyers protested loudly at the treatment of their fellow Jews? This question touches on the effectiveness of a Kantian morality of duty and principle for which such a morality could sustain individual voices of conscience, and we have to be struck by how few they were. If this was not part of Kant's intention, it has to be recognized as a consequence within the broader moral culture. In Germany this had to do with the notion of "citizenship" and the ways that it connected to the authority of the state. As reason was to be the faculty with authority over our "natures," so the state as the impartial voice of reason could be seen as having authority in relation to citizens. In both cases it legislates principles and laws that we supposedly give to ourselves. Crucial questions about the relationship of "citizenship" to "morality" emerge when people learn to be "good citizens" by learning to "obey the law" and often to do this without questions.

Within the liberal-democratic state citizenship can serve as a guarantee of morality. People learn that they "can do no wrong" as long as they do not break the law or as long as they do not infringe upon the rights of others. So it is that law is identified with justice. People do not have to feel care and concern for the sufferings of others, for they can feel free to pursue their own interests, knowing that the welfare state will look after the well-being of those less fortunate than themselves. With Hitler's rule in Germany, the suffering of the Jews was thought by many to be a small price to pay for returning Germany to its former glory among the nations. It was assumed that Hitler knew what he was doing. The Jews were dispensable. It was crucial that when the Jews were deprived of their rights as citizens they were deprived of their humanity within a moral culture that identified respect for the person with respecting the rights of others. It is only our rights that stand as a guarantee of our dignity as human beings. Our natures are bereft of any dignity within a Kantian tradition.

It could be argued that the Jews in Germany had disempowered themselves by learning to separate themselves from any specific Jewish history and culture. This is the sacrifice they had made for emancipation, unclear that it might mean presenting themselves as "other" than they are. It is as if they could only *be accepted* as equal citizens to the extent that they learned to minimize and marginalize anything that would draw attention to their specificity as Jews. But this was part of an Enlightenment trap, for it made Jews susceptible as a community to the charge of "hiding" who they were. It was as if the liberal notion of citizenship was flawed within European cultures that insisted upon assimilation into the dominant culture as the price of acceptance. It is only as "citizens" that we can be "free and equal." This made the Jews particularly vulnerable, for it was as if they could not be accepted *as* Jews, but only to the extent that they would betray themselves.

A similar tension is highlighted in the relationship between Catholics and Jews in Poland. In his article "Poland and the Jews" Abraham Brumberg quotes Jan Blonski's article, "A Poor Pole Looks at the Ghetto":

"We accepted Jews into our house, but told them to live in the basement. When they wanted to enter the rooms, we promised them admission if they ceased to be Jews, if they became civilized, as they used to say in the nineteenth century, and not only in Poland.... There were some Jews who were ready to accept this condition. Then talk began about the invasion of Jews, the dangers posed by their entrance into Polish society! We began ... to post conditions, such as stipulating that only Jews who would co-operate in limiting Jewish influences would be accepted as Poles. That is—to put it plainly—only those who would turn against their own kind, or against their parents! Eventually we lost our house and the new oc-cupants began to kill Jews. Did we show any solidarity by offering help? How many of us asserted that it wasn't our business? ... We didn't even manage to respect and welcome the survivors, however embittered, lost, or even irritating they might have been." (19)

In a liberal moral culture our dignity as human beings is in-vested in a vision of rights. But as Simone Weil (1952) argues, this notion is inadequate to the tasks that have been placed on it. Nazi Germany showed that if Jews could be deprived of their rights, it could turn them into "nonpersons"—they could be talked of as "vermin." If people no longer had rights then they were removed beyond the realm of reason and humanity. It was difficult to with-draw from the dominant culture and begin to find meaning, dig-nity, and self-respect in a Judaism that an Enlightenment culture had so long derided as a throwback to an earlier time. That culture shared with orthodox Marxism the idea that religion—if not spir-ituality—would wither away with the state. It had served its his-torical purpose so now it was doomed. This was a version of an older Christian myth that said Judaism was superseded by Chris-tianity, so having outlived its purpose. I am thankful that we are beginning to identify such functionalist arguments and question the vision of progress that they embody.

The impersonality of reason gives it a confidence in its own decisions. So it is also that a language of rights teaches us that we respect others by leaving them alone. We learn not to infringe on their legal and political rights. In some way we learn to leave others to their fate unless they call for our help. We become wary of showing care and concern for others lest this be misinterpreted as interference. It is significant that it has been feminist writers who have talked of an ethic of relationships that has to do with care and concern. Within an Enlightenment tradition that has identified masculinity with reason it was easy to silence the different voice of women, as Carol Gilligan (1982) has called it. This care and concern for others grows out of the involvement and relationships of women. It is a sensitivity to hurt and injury in relationships that men are often less sensitive to (see Seidler 1989). Traditionally, we show our care and concern for others within a liberal moral culture by respecting their rights. So when Jews are denied legal and political rights, this removes them beyond the pale of care and concern. We have lost any other sense of their dignity as human beings. We need a different basis for an ethic of care and concern.

Why did so few stand up against the persecution of the Jews in Nazi Germany? This question still haunts our moral and political theory. It brings into question the Christian rhetoric of "love thy neighbor," which has been rationalized within a Kantian tradition that wanted love to be a rational and universal feeling separated from our relationships and feelings for concrete others. It is difficult to develop a more embodied notion of love within a philosophical tradition that had insisted, as did that of Descartes, on separating mind from body. It is only as rational beings that we have identities. Our emotions and feelings locked into our bodies can be no part of our identities. As Kierkegaard recognizes, unless we can love another person in the right way our love for others is empty. He was suspicious of an empty universalism that was an integral part of an Enlightenment tradition that would teach us to love humanity in the abstract, without helping us with the difficulties of loving those we know (see my *Moral Limits of Modernity: Love, Inequality, and Oppression*). He is critical of an abstract altruism that talks about others as "rational selves" because it is unable to illuminate the hurt that people do to each other. It is a great strength of Freud to bring into focus the hurt and pain that individuals can do to each other in their personal relationships. He helps us to question the pervasive notion, as does feminism, that because it is "personal" it does not matter. It is an insight our moral theory has yet to learn, trapped as it is within a moral psychology, as Iris Murdoch indicates in *The Sovereignty of Good,* that is yet to come to terms with Freud and Marx.

## 3. ALTRUISM AND MORALITY

How should we account for the behavior of those "righteous gentiles" who saved Jews at considerable risk to themselves? Seeing it in terms of an altruism as selfless behavior encourages us to envision moral behavior as a matter of fulfilling our duties regardless of the emotional costs to ourselves, for to act against our "inclinations" is somehow to *prove* the moral worth of our actions. It fails to illuminate the difficulties that the rational self has in understanding the importance of individuality and integrity. It is difficult to reinstate the importance of individuals being true to themselves, which involves trusting their deeper feelings. To put our feelings aside to pursue goals that have been set by reason alone can involve a form of betrayal of the self. But this involves breaking with the Kantian vision of the self as the rational self and allowing a space for our emotions as well as our thoughts, our feelings as well as our beliefs. Sometimes it has been religion that has been able to sustain a connection between truth and politics, as we can learn from Simone Weil or from Josef Tischner's *The Spirit of Solidarity.* But this has to leave us wondering about the place of a language of altruism within a renewed moral theory.

Mordecai Paldiel's article "The Altruism of Righteous Gentiles" (1988) argues that "altruism in its variant forms is an innate human predisposition." He thinks that the situation of the righteous gentiles shows that altruism "can be aroused to dominance over our behavior for short spells of time." It is as if this "altruistic disposition" takes over in quite "normal people" to allow them to act courageously in relation to others for "short periods." This helps Paldiel explain why these people can seem so "normal" when you meet them years later. Yet for Kant it is difficult to make sense of altruism as "an innate human predisposition" since he sees our natural dispositions as essentially selfish and egoistic. It is only through the *external* intervention of reason that we can develop a moral sense at all. Deprived of a rational faculty, we are deprived of our capacity for morality.

The Oliners' study *The Altruistic Personality* (1988) senses the weakness of a moral tradition that would educate us into morality in terms of impartial and universal principles. They look towards an ethic of care and concern, recognizing that some of the rescuers who were interviewed had friends drawn from groups other than their own. It could be that their experience of relationships with others from different backgrounds gave their caring a more sub-stantial reality. It was not simply an abstract caring for others in conformity with universal principles. Tied to this is a recognition that rescuers were less susceptible to stereotypical forms of be-havior, and tended to have worked out for themselves an individual ethic. Crucially, this has to do with individuality and the tension with a Kantian notion of a rational self. If people are keen to be accepted by others to assuage feelings of inadequacy that are deeply structured into a Protestant ethic that regards our natural feelings as selfish, they are often keen to conform to prevailing social obligations. It is a structured anxiety to prove ourselves adequate or worthy in the eyes of others that is continually sub-verting a language of individuality. It is difficult to define our individuality if we are brought up feeling that some of our emotions are unacceptable so that they have to be hidden from others, even ourselves, if we are to sustain the ideal of self that we have set for ourselves.

Much of our inherited moral theory is structured by the idea that those who rescued Jews at great risk to themselves went be-yond what we could rightly expect from people. But this is to separate "righteous gentiles" into a sphere of "saintliness" that is denied by many of those involved, who felt that they were only doing what had to be done in the circumstances. Sometimes they did not like the people they saved but said, "What else could I do?" "Would you not have done the same?" "These people were in grave danger and it was only natural to save them." It is sentiments like this that help Paldiel to think that "altruism" is a natural human response in people. It is not something that has to be "rationally justified" and "argued for" as it must be within moral traditions that assume that individuals are self-seeking and so require "rea-sons" so as to be able to overcome their selfish natures. But as Paldiel recognizes, we can care for others without having to engage in a struggle against our inner natures. This is the weakness of the language of altruism tied as it is to a Christian/Kantian mode of thought. It tends to blind us to the very different responses people can have to the suffering of others.

In *Lest Innocent Blood Be Shed*, Philip Hallie reflects upon the story of the village of Le Chambon and how the Protestant community organized itself to rescue so many Jews. He follows the experience of André and Magda Trocmé, who in the presbytery in Le Chambon helped to organize resistance against German orders and Vichy laws. Though they worked closely together, there were significant differences in their approach to what they were doing. This is how Magda Trocmé summarized to Hallie what the work meant to her at the time:

"I have a kind of principle. I am not a good Christian at all, but I have things that I really believe in. . . . I try not to hunt around to find things to do. I do not hunt around to find people to help. But I never close my door, never refuse to help somebody who comes to me and asks for something. This I think is my kind of religion. You see, it is a way of handling myself." (153)

As Hallie describes it, "her 'principle' did not involve abstract theories, but only a feeling of responsibility to particular people—first of all to her husband, and next to anybody who happened to come to the door of the presbytery" (153). As he says, "this feeling is not one of overflowing affection; it is practical and abrupt, like Magda herself" (153).

Hallie reminds us that in Deuteronomy, a city of refuge takes responsibility for the lives of refugees who come to its gates. Its members do not leave those gates to look for the oppressed; rather, they stand at the gates ready to accept the responsibility people place upon them by coming to the city. Deuteronomy 19:10 reads, "I command you this day to [protect the refugee] lest innocent blood be shed in your land . . . and so the guilt of bloodshed be upon you." Magda Trocmé thinks in terms of people in trouble but she is reluctant to use the word *love* when talking about her work with the refugees, as she is reluctant to use words like *good* and *saintly*. She distrusts a language of theology that would separate deeds of high ethical value. She does not believe that there is such a thing as moral nobility that separates off some people—the saints—from others—the common, decent people.

It is important to give space to set out how Philip Hallie contrasts the ethic of Magda Trocmé with that of her husband. There is something unsettling about the way that the contrast is set out that demands to be thought about further. It throws into relief not simply different personalities, but different ethical sensibilities that are still very much with us.

Magda Trocmé believes that something is evil *because* it hurts people. Hers is an ethic of benevolence: she needed only to look into the eyes of a refugee in order to find her duty.

But her husband had a more complex ethic. He believed that something is evil both because it hurts somebody *and* because it violates an imperative, a commandment given us by God in the Bible and in our particular hearts. He had to look up to some authority beyond the eyes of the refugee to find that commandment, but having found it, his duty, like hers, lay in diminishing the hurt in those eyes.

Magda's ethic can be called a horizontal one: she recognized no imperative from above; she saw only another's need, and felt only a need to satisfy the need as best she could. . . . He did what he did because he wanted to be *with* Jesus. . . . He wanted to be close to Jesus, a loving disciple who put his feet in Jesus's footprints with stubborn devotion.

There was verticality in his ethic, an allegiance to a supernatural being, but there was also in him powerful affections, "almost erotic" feelings for the people around him. . . . He worked and cared for the well-being of the "oppressed and the weak," as he described the refugees, as much as did Magda Trocmé, but he never stopped striving to be close to Jesus and, in Jesus, to God. For him, ethical demands had a vertical axis and a horizontal one, like the cross. (*Lest Innocent Blood Be Shed*, 101–2)

The Trocmés shared a commitment to worldly decency and to human dignity that brought them together in the caring for others. This was the crucial dimension that brought harmony to their relationship. Magda felt a simple responsibility to help a person whom "God or chance" had brought to her door. André had a religious conviction that gave shape and direction to his actions as much as did his own warm temperament. The people of Le Chambon came to agree with Trocmé's response to Prefect Bach, who had just reprimanded him for not seeing that the Jews were corrupting the West and must be gotten rid of: "We do not know what a Jew is. We know only men" (160). They saw, in Hallie's words, "only human beings who were valuable enough to be saved from humiliation, torture and death" (161).

Under the moral leadership of André Trocmé and Édouard Theis, as Hallie describes it, "the people of Le Chambon would not give up life for any price—for their own comfort, for their own safety, for patriotism, or for legality. For them, human life had no price; it had only dignity" (274). This formulation echoes Kant but it is crucial that for Kant human dignity is set against our "animal natures." This undermines, I would argue, the sense of the preciousness or dignity of human life for it means that our emotions, feelings, and desires cannot serve as sources of human dignity. It also means, as we can hear, that there is some tension between being able to save others as human beings and being able to honor and treasure their dignity as Jews. It is a tribute to the rescuers in Le Chambon that they did not try to get Jewish children to convert but respected their Judaism, encouraging Jewish children to observe their own holidays. They recognized that help must only be given for the benefit of the people being helped, not for the benefit of some church. As Hallie describes it, "the life and the integrity of the person helped were more precious than any organization" (55).

André Trocmé had grown up in a family in which, in the end, there was only one prayer: "Teach us to do our duty." Theirs was a religion of duty towards a distant God. The words were clear but the feeling was not there. As Hallie has it, "'Teach us to do our duty' became a formula that kept the individuals in the household from communicating their own feelings to each other, or seemed to make it unnecessary to do so" (55). It was as a member of the Union of Saint-Quentin, a Protestant organization of young people, that he learned about the intimacy of friendship as they prayed aloud, often in tears, to be saved from lying or from sexual impurity. He learned that only in intimacy could people save each other. Le Chambon would provide another intimate community of people praying together to make the Protestant idea of a "priesthood of all believers" work.

Aside from the distinction between good and evil, what was crucial to the ethic of rescue in Le Chambon was the distinction between giving things and giving oneself. As Hallie describes it,

When you give somebody a thing without giving yourself, you degrade both parties by making the receiver utterly passive and by making yourself a benefactor standing there to receive thanks—and even sometimes obedience—as repayment. But when you give yourself, nobody is degraded— in fact, both parties are elevated by a shared joy. When you give yourself, the things you are giving become, to use Trocmé's word, *féconde* (fertile, fruitful). What you give creates new, vigorous life, instead of arrogance on the one hand and passivity on the other. (72)

This giving of oneself is an utterly personal action, because each self is a unique person. This can be in tension with a language of altruism that sees the necessity of putting the self aside in order to help others. It is the impersonality and detachment that is so often part of a Kantian tradition that can make it hard to recognize that caring for others is in its depths personal.

In the intimacy of a household, people want to understand each other in ways that their public lives can never reveal. Magda Trocmé, who worked no less hard for the refugees than did her husband, was more lenient with her children. Hallie says insightfully that "she looked into their eyes and saw needs her husband could not see, needs that she allowed them to satisfy even though doing so sometimes caused pain to her husband" (146). She was far more aware of their feelings so that they never saw her as "hard to take." At the same time her powerful indignation against laziness or ineptitude struck fear into her husband and children whenever it was aroused. There was the constant strain of too much work. But her sensitivity to the feelings of others was also part of her caring. It is part of her care and concern. A sensitivity to feelings and emotions can be part of a recognition of the preciousness of human life. It can help with what Hallie called "an imaginative perception of the connection between the preciousness of my life and the preciousness of other lives" (277).

"Universality" in moral theory can stand in the way of recognizing the different moral qualities that people have and the different relationships we have towards moral duties and responsibilities. We become blind to the plurality of moral traditions as a language of rational moral agency has presented itself as universal and available to all. Often this means that *moral thinking* involves *abstracting* ourselves from the concrete realities and contradictions of the situations we find ourselves in. It is a vision of moral purity and moral action that is *untainted* by the everyday relationships of life. We have all—Christians, Jews, or Moslems—learned to see ourselves through these Christian eyes, so failing to recognize the integrity of different moral traditions. The Enlightenment affirmation of "spirituality," "humanity," and "universalism" meant in André Lacocque's (1972) terms that "the language of speculation replaced the language of events" as Christians sought timeless truths and high spirituality, wishing to divorce themselves from the paradoxes and concreteness ("materialism") of the Old Testament—the Hebrew Bible:

Within such a perspective, it was not without frowning that pious and moral Christians read the records of men too "human" for their taste.

Jacob the liar, Moses the murderer, David the adulterer, Solomon the idolatrous.... The concept of God's intervention in human history is so desperately materialistic and the people's feeling of being elected and chosen so particularistic, that it is really hard to "spiritualize" this Jewish book in order to match it with a truly Christian religiosity. (62)

This fear of people "too human" is structured into a Kantian moral tradition that could distance ourselves from our emotional lives. This is part of the "spiritualization" of our moral language that makes us less sensitive to the injuries that we do to ourselves as well as to the miseries and sufferings of others. As we learn to *separate* from our own emotions and feelings we learn to displace and project onto others emotions and feelings that we cannot accept in ourselves. Freud made this central to psychoanalytic understanding, going some way to grasp it as an inheritance within a Western culture that denied the existence of sexuality, the body, and emotional life. We inherit a tradition in which we are more concerned with our moral salvation than with the sufferings of others. We learn to seek principles and we become self-critical for failing to live up to them. It is in this context that a language of altruism is so easily identified with selflessness. We are trapped into resentments for we seem to be constantly comparing ourselves with others and failing in our own eyes to live up to idealized standards we set for ourselves.

## 4. RIGHTEOUSNESS AND MORALITY

The idea that "the righteous are not exempt from evil" can be understood differently within a Jewish tradition that does not conceive of "moral purity" as the suppression or denial of impulses, feelings, and desires. These are not aspects of an animal nature that have to be denied if we are to respond to the clear light of reason but are part of our condition as human beings and so integral to our moral experience. It is a matter of acknowledging our feelings so that we can come to terms with them. Similarly, it is not a matter of putting our interests and desires aside so that we can act selflessly in the interests of others. It is in this sense that the language of altruism is tied to a Kantian/Christian tradition of selflessness. The words of first-century Rabbi Hillel have echoed through the generations, calling for a different relationship between self and other, between individual and community:

"If I am not for myself, who is for me?
"If I care only for myself, what am I?
"If not now, when?"

If I cannot accept and respect myself, including my feelings and desires, how can I expect the love and respect of others? And yet it is a difficult task to know one's feelings in any situation so that we can be more open and honest with ourselves. Often we have grown up within a moral culture that teaches us that goodness has to do with conforming to the expectations of others—our parents and teachers—rather than being true to ourselves. This language of integrity so often seems dangerously empty within a culture in which we learn that if truth is not an objective standard that exists beyond history, then it has to be relative. We lose the connection between goodness and truth.

The children of Le Chambon did not seem to share Magda Trocmé's anguish that they would have "to unlearn lying after the war, and . . . could, perhaps, never again be able to understand the importance of simply telling the truth" (126). This is to see morality as a matter of principles that have to be obeyed. Truthfulness has a different source in our lives and it connects to the heart and the importance of learning to speak from the heart. This cannot be learned as an issue of will and determination alone for I cannot "decide" to be truthful with myself, though the intention can be important in putting me on the right path. People in Le Chambon were doing what they felt to be right in the situation. They were being true to their beliefs. Magda's daughter, Nelly, pointed out to Philip Hallie that as far as she knew the children never had the problem of unlearning lying. As Hallie describes it, "what the children saw was what the rest of the Chambonnais saw: the *necessity* to help the shivering Jew standing there in your door, and the necessity not to betray him or her to harmdoers. In this way of life the children were raised, and—at least according to Nelly—they did not feel their parents to be guilty of any wrongdoing" (127). For children it is crucial for parents to live out what they believe, rather than to say "do what I say, not what I do." This is a precious gift the value of which is not appreciated within a culture that sees morality in terms of abstract principles. We learn from *who* our parents are, rather than simply from what they had to say.

Hallie records how difficult it was, for instance, for Madame Eyraud to understand what he was getting at in his insistent questioning about why she put herself in such danger to bring refugees

into her house. He was looking for reasons because within a Kantian tradition we assume that to act egoistically requires no reasons,
as it is taken to be "natural"—though as Albert Hirschman (1977)
shows in *The Passions and the Interests*, this vision of a foundation
for ethics that is laid within reason has had a pervasive hold on
our moral theory. But Madame Eyraud was having none of it, as
Hallie learned while under her spell, as he says, "her big, round
eyes stopped sparkling in that happy face, and she said, 'Look.
Look. Who else would have taken care of them if we didn't? They
needed our help, and they needed it *then.*' For her, and for me
under the joyous spell she casts over anybody she smiles upon, the
spade was turned by hitting against a deep rock: there are no
deeper issues than the issues of *people needing help then*" (127).

Most people looked away and European Jewry was largely abandoned to its fate. This is part of a painful history that we cannot
put aside unless we are prepared to come to terms with it. This is
a powerful insight in Claude Lanzmann's (1985) *Shoah*—that anti-
Semitism will be sustained as a way of dealing with the unresolved
guilt at what was not done to help the Jews. This will allow people
to feel justified in doing so little. A rationalist moral psychology
fails to illuminate the weight of our histories and of the compro-
mises that we have made to our integrity. We tend to believe in a
liberal moral culture that says that only if we are caught will we
be made to suffer. We are blind to the power of the inner suffering
for our misdeeds. In this sense every action has a consequence,
though we are blind to it. The perpetration of atrocities—be it in
the Nazis who were responsible for "the final solution" or the
American soldiers who were responsible for the massacre at My
Lai in Vietnam—has consequences that must be lived with. It is
not as easy to put the past behind us as we are often led to think.
It has the power to return to haunt us.

At some level truthfulness is connected to individuality. A striking feature of Nechama Tec's (1986) interviews with people who
rescued Jews in Poland is the individuality of the people concerned—they were very much their own persons. People were acting out of their own beliefs and feeling for what is right, regardless
of what the official church was preaching in Poland. They had to
be ready to stand against the insistent authority of the church to
rely upon their own meaning of Christian love and charity. This
could be difficult to sustain because it was not a matter of individual moral actions but of sustained, often dangerous, difficult,

and frustrating relationships over a considerable period of time. This took considerable moral resources. How can such a sense of moral individuality be sustained? To what extent does it involve separating individualism from egoism and a tradition of possessive individuality? For me, this involves learning to take responsibility for our feelings as much as our thought as we learn to define ourselves more clearly.

We have learned to be suspicious of the truth and to doubt any language of authenticity. Too often it has become an empty jargon, and authorities have claimed to have the monopoly of truth. Orthodox Marxism has suffered from the connection between truth, history, and power. It seems better to give up claims to truth completely. This tendency is given intellectual form within a postmodernist tradition that would separate itself from any linear conception of reason, science, and progress. But this would also deny truth to ourselves, for we are simply left with different constructions of our experience and so with no way of deepening our connection with ourselves.

Those who failed to respond as their neighbors were being dragged off to the concentration camps have to live with the darkness that entered their souls. It is not that they failed to act altruistically and so to accrue moral worth that could have been available to them. This presents the situation too neutrally, for people have to live with both what they do and what they fail to do. People and communities who failed to respond became less than they could be as they compromised their humanity and themselves. This is an issue that is bound to resonate loudly in Poland, and it can be no surprise that a film such as *Shoah* called forth such strong reactions. It is an inescapable historical process, for the holocaust has left a profound mark on both Jewish and Christian cultures. It brings into question some of the deepest claims and aspirations of Western culture.

History is not arbitrary, nor is it simply a construction reflecting the interests of the present, as poststructuralist theories tend to have it. For in coming to terms with our histories we are coming to terms with ourselves. An Enlightenment tradition has largely failed to grasp this connection, thinking that freedom and self-determination involve putting our histories behind us so that we can learn to act independently of them. But this has been a dangerous dream that has disempowered those like blacks, Jews, and women, whose integrity and dignity lies partly in honoring and remembering their separate histories and the pain and suffering of slavery, the witch burnings, and now the holocaust. If this is part of our ancestral history, it is part of ourselves. We have come to terms with it in whatever way we can and with the pain it carries as part of regaining our lost dignity and integrity. It is more importantly not something that others can do for us, but something that both individually and collectively we have to do for ourselves.

We all have to accept our histories if they are not to return to haunt us. At the same time it is crucial to make moral distinctions, as Primo Levi (1988) insists in *The Drowned and the Saved*. It is crucial not to end up blaming the victims for what befell them or to perpetuate myths that somehow it was Jewish passivity that brought Jews to their fate. Jerzy Turowicz's "Polish Reasons and Jewish Questions" (1990), disavowing some of his earlier views, rejects the equation of "the fate of the Jews with those of the Poles" on the grounds that "we, too, were being murdered." As Brumberg (1987) reports it, he demolishes one myth after another—about Jewish "passivity"; about Polish wartime attitudes; about the prewar church and the doctrine of Jewish "deicide," rejected rather belatedly, he suggests, by Vatican II. As Brumberg has it, "he is unambivalent; the discussion of Polish-Jewish relations is not an indulgence or masochism: it is a challenge to which Poles must respond without hesitation, if only for the sake of their collective conscience" (87).

We all have to take responsibility for our lives. The rescuers provide a challenge to their "ordinariness" in their refusal to be treated as anything special. They are clear that what they did others could have done. They do not want to be placed on some kind of pedestal as "righteous gentiles." That is to miss the point. To treat them as moral heroes is to deprive the rest of us of the responsibility for what we do and fail to do in our everyday lives. To remove those who rescued into a separate moral sphere is to avoid crucial issues of individual guilt and responsibility. It is the other side of the same coin that would see the Nazis as monsters or as akin to the devil. This is part of a polarized vision that is deeply embedded within a Western Christian tradition given a secular form within Enlightenment rationalism. It insists on dividing the world into autonomous and independent spheres of "good" and "evil." In contrast, the strength of a Judaic tradition is its refusal to polarize. This can help us recognize both "rescuer" and "Nazi" as being part of "our" moral universe in the West. We cannot reject Nazism as an aberration, but it is crucial to come to terms with it, as Simone Weil (1952) grasps in *The Need for Roots*, within the terms of power and greatness that we inherit within Western culture. This is a task that has barely begun.

## REFERENCES

Blum, L., and V. J. Seidler (1989) *Truer Liberty: Simone Weil and Marxism.* New York: Routledge.

Brumberg, A. (1987) Poland and the Jews. *Tikkun* 2:3 (July/August).

Gilligan, C. (1982) *In a Different Voice.* Cambridge: Harvard University Press.

Griffin, S. (1982) *Pornography and Silence.* London: Women's Press.

Hallie, P. (1979) *Lest Innocent Blood Be Shed.* New York: Harper and Row.

Hirschman, A. (1977) *The Passions and the Interests.* Princeton, N.J.: Princeton University Press.

Lacocque, A. (1972) Encounter with the Old Testament. *Chicago Theological Seminary Register* 2:1, p. 62.

Lanzmann, C. (1985) *Shoah: An Oral History of the Holocaust.* New York: Pantheon.

Levi, P. (1988) *The Drowned and the Saved.* London: Michael Joseph.

Mendelssohn, E. (1986) Inter-war Poland: Good for the Jews or Bad for the Jews? In *The Jews in Poland.* C. Abramsky, M. Jachimczyk, and A. Polonsky (Eds.). Oxford: Oxford University Press.

Murdoch, I. (1971) *The Sovereignty of Good.* New York: Schocken.

——— (1977) *The Fire and the Sun.* Oxford: Oxford University Press.

Oliner, S., and P. Oliner (1988) *The Altruistic Personality.* New York: Free Press.

Paldiel, M. (1988) The Altruism of the Righteous Gentiles. *Holocaust and Genocide Studies.* Pergammon Press: 3:2, pp. 187–96.

Sartre, J. P. (1964) *Anti-Semite and Jew.* New York: Schocken.

Seidler, V. J. (1986) *Kant, Respect and Injustice: The Limits of Liberal Moral Theory.* London: Routledge.

——— (1989) *Rediscovering Masculinity: Reason, Language and Sexuality.* London: Routledge.

——— (1990) *The Moral Limits of Modernity: Love, Inequality, and Oppression.* London: Macmillan.

Tec, N. (1986) *When Light Pierced the Darkness: Christian Rescue of Jews in Nazi-Occupied Poland.* New York: Oxford University Press.

Tischner, J. (1984) *The Spirit of Solidarity.* New York: Harper and Row.

Turowicz, J. (1990) Polish Reasons and Jewish Questions. In *My Brother's Keeper?: Recent Polish Debates on the Holocaust.* A. Polonsky (Ed.), pp. 134–43. London: Routledge.

Weil, S. (1952) *The Need for Roots.* London: Routledge.

# PART THREE

# SOCIOBIOLOGY AND MORAL ALTRUISM

*Edited by Dennis L. Krebs*

# INTRODUCTION

## Dennis L. Krebs

Evidence of altruism, defined as behavior that enhances the biological fitness of another at the expense of the biological fitness of a helper, is paradoxical in the theory of evolution because it seems inconsistent with the principle of natural selection. In the "struggle for existence," altruists (and their altruistic genes) should, by definition, fare poorly in competition with individuals possessing genes that favor more selfish behavior, and thus they should become extinct. In the past, theorists have tended to resolve this paradox either by assuming that all animals are fundamentally selfish by nature, but that some species, such as humans, may be induced to behave altruistically by nurture or culture, or by identifying mechanisms equipped to select altruistic behaviors at levels of selection different from that assumed by Darwin.

The authors of the two chapters in this section, Ian Vine and Ronald Cohen, offer resolutions to the paradox of altruism that reject both exclusively biologically based and exclusively culturally based models. Indeed, the writers of both chapters explicitly reject "either-or" nature versus nurture and biology versus culture dichotomies and the "excesses" of "first-generation" sociobiologists. Cohen partially recants the position he advanced in 1978 advocating the cultural overriding of biologically based hedonism. Both writers advocate models that attribute human altruism to an interaction between biologically based dispositions to acquire characteristics that prepare individuals to learn to behave altruistically and environmental or cultural inputs. Vine traces the origin of altruism ontogenetically to interactions between mothers and children during the first year of life, and Cohen attributes it to more broadly based aspects of culture.

In chapter 4, Vine supplies a succinct and lucid review of sociobiological solutions to the paradox of altruism. Rejecting Darwin's appeal to group selection, he partially accepts the more modern resolutions based on kin selection, reciprocity, and manipulation. Vine concludes that such mechanisms go a considerable distance in the explanation of altruism, but they fall short of explaining the type of self-sacrificial behavior toward strangers and members of outgroups documented by theorists such as Oliner and Oliner in their accounts of the rescue of Jews during World War II. Reviewing three contemporary models of evolution, Vine argues that the only model equipped to explain altruism toward out-group members is one attentive to the functional interaction between biological and social-environmental factors.

Vine allows that individuals may maximize their inclusive fitness by behaving altruistically toward kith and kin, but suggests that unconscious brain structures bias individuals toward egocentric and ethnocentric behavior. However, he suggests, the development in humans of a subjective self-system that extends beyond the bodily self to include identities with others permits mental causation of altruistic behavior toward a broad range of others. He explains how consciousness and self-awareness may have evolved in humans, and suggests that these acquisitions have helped free us from biological constraints on altruism through the inculcation of sympathy.

The difficult task Vine sets for himself is to explain how infants acquire an inclusive identity, which entails integration between self and other while at the same time achieving sufficient differentiation to insure that the prosocial behaviors they direct toward others are not directed toward themselves-in-others, depleting them of altruism. In large part, this entails distinguishing between empathy (responding to others as though they were the self) and sympathy (responding to others on their own terms—as Jarymowicz puts it in chapter 8, "exocentrically"). Vine traces the origin of sympathy, and therefore the origin of altruism, to the affectively charged reciprocal exchanges characteristic of interactions between infants and their mothers during the first year. In contrast to theorists who attribute prosocial responses in infants to empathy based on a lack of differentiation, and thus confusion, between self and other, Vine suggests that infants acquire both a "self-with-

other" schema—a "we" identity—*and* a sense of self-other differentiation during early reciprocal exchanges with their mothers.
Infants develop a differentiated sense of themselves as agents when
they respond to the give and take of exchanges with their mothers,
but this sense of self is a connected one—tied to the reciprocal
reaction of the mother. Thus, argues Vine, infants may feel sympathetic to the objects of their reciprocity as distinct from themselves, while at the same time incorporating these objects into their
identities, as, in a sense, the other half of themselves.

Ronald Cohen opens chapter 5 by partially disavowing a position
he advanced in his earlier work attributing human altruism to
cultural constraints on biological hedonism, and goes on to suggest
that a more tenable position is that the "dynamic duo" of biological
and cultural evolution—working with one another, against one
another, and independently—have mediated the evolution of altruism in the human species. Appealing to Boyd and Richerson's
"dual inheritance" model of biological and cultural evolution,
Cohen points out that both processes are governed by the same
basic principles: descent with modification and selective retention
of variations. While biological evolution has worked slowly, selecting gene frequencies over generations, cultural evolution may
operate at a much more rapid pace.

The dynamics of biological evolution are relatively well understood. Cohen singles out four biologically selected traits as especially important in the interaction with culture in the determination of human altruism: the capacity to restrain dominance
strivings, the proclivity to learn from authority, the acquisition of
a sense of morality, defined broadly as the tendency to label some
phenomena right and others wrong, and the capacity for abstraction mediating critical assessment. Also mentioned are organic
brain mechanisms, guilt, and echo responses to distress signaling.

The dynamics of cultural selection are less well understood.
Cohen suggests that cultural variations evolve primarily through
the process of group selection. Culturally based variations occur
through recruitment of different individuals into the same roles,
migration, and the diffusion of traits from one region to another.
Some selective mechanisms, such as conformity, mediate the
spread of popular variations. Other selective mechanisms, such as
gossip, exert a conservative influence on the status quo. Still other
mechanisms, such as reactions to injustice and the imagined effects
of social change, may exert a more directional influence. Cohen

suggests there may be an optimal range of accepted variation, with resistance to radical change.

In the second half of his chapter, Cohen advances the argument that a civil society is evolving through the dual inheritance process, in which altruism is being incorporated into cultural beliefs, values, and regulations. The evolution of such a society is dependent on the promulgation, selection, and retention of cultural ideas supporting it. Defining features of a civil society are (a) the freedom to assess rules and regulations critically and to make changes on the basis of such assessments, (b) an expansion of the boundaries of the moral universe to include those hitherto considered outgroup members, and (c) an increase in the value of altruism and tendencies toward empathy and sympathy.

What evidence is there for the evolution of civil societies? Cohen mentions three features: the expanding recognition that private fates are affected by public policies; the rejection of conflict and acceptance of more peaceful means of resolving differences on an international level; and nuclearization of family life, which, Cohen argues, encourages the socialization of moral and altruistic emotions. Finally, with many other writers in this volume, Cohen identifies inclusiveness of identity as a key factor in the expansion of altruism. Primary among the factors that enable civil society is the expansion of the moral universe to include all people. Cohen believes that at least some of the individuals who rescued Jews during World War II possessed inclusive identities and high moral principles. He suggests that the Holocaust constituted a cultural event that had a profound impact on the evolution of altruism, making clear on an international level the tremendous costs of constricting the moral universe. The time has come, suggests Cohen, both for the belief that all people have equal moral rights and for the willingness to act on this belief, and he believes these cultural variants are being selected on an increasingly wide scale. Cohen is optimistic. He has faith in the fecundity of cultural variations favoring altruism. When he looks at the international community, he sees evidence that civil societies are beginning to evolve. Others, more steeped in the constraints of evolved dispositions perhaps, will appraise the world scene and come to a less hopeful conclusion.

# 4

# ALTRUISM AND HUMAN NATURE: RESOLVING THE EVOLUTIONARY PARADOX

*Ian Vine*

Almost every society values altruism in some shape or form, and seeks to induce children to acquire relevant dispositions. Yet Western concepts of its moral value hinge upon the assumption that we freely choose to help others for their own sake. Moralists are accordingly uneasy about the role of our biology in either facilitating altruism or hindering it. In fact, the vast majority of psychological attempts to account for prosocial conduct are determinist, and are reductionist in seeing it as ultimately selfish (Batson 1987; Wallach and Wallach 1983). But most students of human nature prefer to gloss over the moral ambiguities of such theories, rather than face them squarely.

Wilson (1975) announced that "sociobiology" had first exposed and then solved a paradox about how traits permitting material self-sacrifice for another individual might ever evolve at all, and then dissolved it. Yet his analysis seemed unashamedly to recast human as well as animal altruism as genetically constrained to serve our strictly reproductive interests. Contemptuous ideological attacks from critics who reject all biogenetic approaches to human social behavior have by no means subsided (Lewontin, Rose, and Kamin 1984). More rigorous but unsympathetic scientific critiques of sociobiology, like that of Kitcher (1985), may finally seem to have undermined all Darwinian attempts to explain altruism. Yet puzzles about its organismic sources remain.

We are born as human animals, and only slowly acquire the full personhood that constitutes us as responsible and accountable moral agents. The excesses of "first-generation" sociobiology must not blind us to its human relevance. A more modest formulation of what its principles really imply can help to make sense of altruism and selfishness by reference to the nature, development, and functioning of our consciously accessible subjective self-systems. The self-system and introspective awareness permit distinctive kinds of mental causation. They transform the social potential of our own species by giving unique flexibility to our motives, sympathies, commitments, and intentions.

We must still expect evolved genetic constraints to have left their mark upon brain subsystems that function mainly beneath the threshold of our awareness. These remain likely to bias our social judgments towards egocentric interests or ethnocentric group loyalties, and against any truly indiscriminate readiness for costly altruism (Vine 1987). Yet that need not make us unable to overcome such temptations and resistances, once we understand the sources of distorted perceptions of people's deservingness. It is evident that people do develop dispositions for being moved to sympathy and for striving to respond generously—sometimes even when those in need are remote strangers or enemies rather than close kith and kin. I shall argue that this is humanly possible because evolutionary pressures fashioned us such that we can extend the self's interests well beyond our own bodies. The extent of our truly altruistic motives reflects how far we learn to embrace others within the awarenesses of the mental self's identities.

### THE DARWINIAN PROBLEM AND ITS LEGACY

For the theory of natural selection to displace religious creationism from the Victorian public mind, it required systematic distortion. If our biological continuity with "lower" species could no longer be denied, then our animal inheritance had to become a scientific substitute for "original sin." The "beast within" could take the blame for human weakness and wickedness, and romantics could still be appeased. When the Russian scientist and anarcho-communist, Prince Peter Kropotkin, advanced the thesis that "mutual aid" (1939 [1902]) was a major factor in evolution, his analysis fell upon deaf ears. Further development of biological insights concerning the adaptive advantages of prosocial activity was long in coming.

Darwin himself had acknowledged prosocial instincts in animals, involving feelings of "sympathy." He saw an inherited readiness for such an affective motivation as the organic root of our human "moral sense." Once elaborated upon by reason and by culture, this might lead anyone "without a moment's hesitation to risk his life for that of a fellow-creature" (Darwin 1957 [1871], 285)—and perhaps a total stranger. Yet this observation sat awkwardly with principles of natural selection that specified that evolution occurs because "the best adapted individuals . . . tend to propagate their kind in larger numbers than the less well adapted" (152). Giving aid to others may well benefit collective survival. But it appears to be individually maladaptive to help reproductive "competitors" at the cost of threatening one's personal capacity to survive and propagate one's own genes.

So how could initially rare mutations favoring altruism ever have been spread and sustained through natural selection? Surely, selfish individuals who merely accepted the altruism of others would thrive and be more reproductively successful? This may be called the biological paradox of altruism. Darwin had no clear, consistent, comprehensive answer to it, and the issue was fudged for a century. Pseudosolutions relied upon the assumption that selection favors the survival of whole breeding groups, or the "good of the species." But once the conceptual and empirical inadequacies of "group selection" began to be exposed (e.g., Maynard Smith 1964), a revised explanatory framework for the evolution of social life was necessary. Wilson's (1975) overenthusiasm for new biological concepts that could explain self-sacrificial behaviors was understandable. But like Dawkins (*The Selfish Gene*, 1976), he was essentially an interpreter of sociobiology's basic theories. One central problem in applying these to humans was that biologists untrained in psychology readily confounded costly consequences of altruism with questions about its motivating causes, including intentional concern for others' needs and interests. Thus a realistic assessment of human altruism must start with what the core theories do strictly imply about our species.

The general evolutionary puzzle is real enough. Adaptively critical traits like readily risking one's life on another's behalf are too widespread in nature to be trivial anomalies. It seems that they should be strongly opposed by natural selection—especially in any species whose behavior is rigidly shaped by genetically specified "instinct" mechanisms. Yet Darwin saw that some evolutionary lines had specialized in parental care to enhance the survival of a few offspring, rather than producing myriads of fertilized eggs, of which only a tiny proportion reach maturity (now known as "K" versus "r" strategies). What counts in evolution is not the individual's survival and longevity as such, but the capacity to reproduce effectively—and thus to replicate segments of what we now identify as one's distinctive set of genes.

So he saw the necessity of parents incurring biological costs to themselves in seeking to rear their young to reproductive maturity. And given the uncertainties of survival, we might expect such efforts sometimes to risk even lethal consequences in the protection of vulnerable offspring. This was only a partical answer; but the insight provided the first key for unlocking the paradox, once population genetics had reached an appropriate degree of sophistication. That and other standard solutions have been effectively presented for nonbiologists before (e.g., Krebs 1987; Ridley and Dawkins 1981). They are presented here only briefly, as the necessary starting point for distinguishing between rival paradigms of human sociobiology.

## SOCIOBIOLOGY'S PRINCIPAL ANSWERS

The crucial advance was Hamilton's (1964) concept of inclusive fitness. Ordinary Darwinian personal fitness can be approximately understood as a measure of parental fecundity, or success in producing and nurturing offspring to maturity. Selection will tend to favor traits according to how well these enhance the replication of one's own genotype. Hamilton simply developed an earlier insight that this can be achieved indirectly as well as directly. His mathematical models showed, in essence, that the fitness benefits of parental care can be extended through helping other family members and their offspring.

The closer a biological relative is to oneself, the more this relatedness ensures above-average genetic commonality. To just that degree, promoting relatives' survival and successful reproduction serves one's own "genetic interests." The inclusive fitness measure therefore adds in such active effects, as indirect increments to one's reproductive success. Inclusive fitness is the most fundamental criterion of adaptiveness; and roughly speaking, new genes will be positively selected, and become incorporated in the characteristic genotype of a species, to the extent that their presence makes some positive behavioral difference to any individual's inclusive fitness.

(But we must remember that such processes are inherently probabilistic, and relative to the fitnesses of individuals with other traits.)

Hamilton's (1964) model proposed what is now usually known as "kin selection" (Maynard Smith 1964) as a basis for how "altruism" could evolve. For the moment it will suffice to note that biologists understand "altruism" and "selfishness" nonteleologically—without any reference to conscious motives, and simply in terms of actual consequences of behavior for fitness. I shall use the terms "bio-altruism" and "bio-selfishness" where such effects are meant, to avoid any possibility of confusion. Social acts are counted as bio-selfish or bio-altruistic simply according to whether they transfer net biological gains or losses to or from the agent, from or to the other individual. The currency has to be some predictor of ultimate reproductive potential. Where predictably fixed net costs of an act of unilateral aid are bio-energetically appreciable, or the probability of incurring further very heavy costs is substantial, we can talk of a high cost/risk penalty, and hence of highly "altruistic" behavior. The question is whether and when selection can favor gene-based traits prompting various degrees of bio-altruism towards various categories of recipients. And it has three main answers, as follows.

### 1. Kinship Selection

Since heritable traits detrimental to personal fitness can evolve just so long as they do enhance inclusive fitness, a nepotistic readiness for bio-altruism towards genetic kin can be favored under certain constraints. If a specified cost/risk penalty from providing a given benefit to my own child is only just compatible with maintaining personal fitness, then the same act directed towards my sibling's child would not be so. This is because half my child's genes are "identical by descent" to my own, but only one quarter of the latter's will be. (These are "coefficients of relatedness," $r$.) Only if helping a nephew or niece was half as costly to me, or gave double the benefit to the child, would my loss of personal fitness be compensated for at the inclusive fitness level. A rare mutated gene arising within one genealogical line, and favoring some indiscriminately bio-altruistic trait, would not normally spread through future generations of a breeding population. For it would tend to reduce the bearer's own reproductive success while enhancing that of beneficiaries unlikely to share the facilitating gene.

As Hamilton shows, what therefore counts is that help with a given cost/risk penalty has to be restricted according to how likely recipients are to have inherited such a trait themselves—as measured by *r*. In effect then, dispositions for even highly sacrificial nepotistically restricted bio-altruism can evolve and stabilize, so long as helpers are sufficiently choosy about the targets for aid. And although Hamilton's model proceeds from rather artificial genetic and other assumptions, the basic results appear relatively robust empirically. In general, it is indeed closest kin who are the main beneficiaries of the most costly and dangerous helping attempts.

The main complications arise when we consider how context-sensitive perfectly efficient fitness maximization would be. If I still have my own dependent child, lethal self-sacrifice to save any life—except perhaps its own—would very rarely make adaptive sense. But naturally selected genes are only likely to be able to construct fairly simple mechanisms for detecting external signs of "deservingness" for bio-altruism—and for using the strength of these, plus relevant internal information, in selecting and triggering one of some limited range of helping responses. At best we can expect an organism to have to rely upon fairly simple optimizing heuristics, or rules of thumb such that how it responds in a given situation is more likely to maximize probable overall fitness consequences than are other realistic options.

The highest cost/risk acts usually occur in emergency situations demanding immediate responses allowing no time for fine and complex discriminations. So matching decisions to the actual levels of likely benefit, and differentiating worthy from unworthy targets, may need to be done crudely—meaning that bio-altruistic reactions may sometimes be "erroneously" directed at remote kin or even nonkin. But in other situations, giving aid may entail little inconvenience or risk of serious costs, yet be very helpful to recipients. So within a relatively inbred group-living species it may well optimize fitness to dispense low cost/risk help quite indiscriminately when eliciting cues are detected.

## 2. Reciprocity Selection

Kin selection can only view bio-altruism towards nonrelatives as occurring by default. If its cost/risk factor is appreciable, it should in principle be selected against. Yet some relatively intelligent higher mammals frequently appear to incur significant risks to fitness on behalf of effectively unrelated individuals. Trivers (1971) invoked active selection for what he called "reciprocal altruism," instead of just attributing all such cases to error.

There is no real biological paradox anyway for prosocial behaviors that can be described as strict cooperation—in which two partners simultaneously help each other to attain a shared goal that neither can reach alone. So long as the division of spoils tends to be mutually equitable and profitable in cost/benefit terms, nothing beyond standard selection for traits enhancing personal fitness is required. But because fitnesses must be measured across whole life spans, what appears bio-altruistic in the short term need not ultimately be so biologically. Thus strict reciprocity is just the temporal extension of self-serving cooperation. Readiness to cooperate or to reciprocate can advantage each partner relative to noncollaborating individuals. As with bio-altruism towards kin, this is particularly so where the cost of either's act of helping is small, yet the benefit to the other is large. Also, repayment of a debt need not necessarily be in kind, since the relevant units of exchange are again those of reproductive potential.

Yet Trivers' reference to "altruism" here was not entirely inappropriate, since there is always some risk that today's unilateral favor or sacrifice will not in fact be repaid tomorrow by a corresponding transfer of fitness potential. Successfully defecting from a supposed deal could be advantageous to the first beneficiary. So selection will also favor exploitative "cheating"—again not necessarily at all conscious—so long as this can escape punishment. But conversely, selection for resisting being cheated would also be strong; and liability to costly punishment could mean that resisting temptations to cheat is equally favored. Trivers thereby sought to explain our evolution of moral emotions like indignation and guilt. His analysis particularly implied that attachment bonds of friendship between nonrelatives would be a firm basis for the trust that is necessary—over and above prosocial feelings as such—to keep reciprocity in its mutually aiding mode (rather than cheating followed by cycles of revenge). Regular interaction facilitates intimate knowledge, as well as frequent chances to exchange small favors, and to develop liking and related dispositions. Thus when the other needs or requests a more major act of assistance, unlikely to be reciprocated for a long time ahead, a confident judgment can be formed of how fully and reliably the "investment" of fitness resources will be repaid.

Interpersonal reciprocity relationships between nonrelatives of the most intelligent species can be strong, and demonstrably beneficial for fitness (Trivers 1985; cf. Axelrod 1984). They are crucial where offspring need extended care from both parents. But a further extension of selection for reciprocity is given prominence by Alexander (1987)—one that has apparently only arisen in our own case. He reidentifies what Trivers (1971) called "generalized" reciprocity—seeing it as a socially indirect reciprocity. Its simplest form involves three persons: A may help B, while B then helps C, and ultimately C helps A. All can thus benefit. One important feature of Alexander's approach is the role given to observational social learning, and to concern for one's public social reputation as a prosocial individual. Indirect reciprocity offers more scope for cheating via deceptive public impressions, which exaggerate one's needs or one's readiness to be generous and to reciprocate reliably and fairly. Thus more social vigilance is needed.

Capacities for indirect reciprocity have evidently encouraged the moral systems whereby human groups promote norms encouraging generalized social responsibility. The synergistic benefits of complex divisions of labor will only benefit most or all members, and sustain social cohesion, if shared norms do successfully regulate resolutions of conflicts of interest. But a readiness to internalize the group's expectations—for altruism, the control of selfishness, and "pulling one's weight"—is what sustains indirect reciprocity most effectively. Within a moral system, everyone's inclusive fitness may theoretically be optimized, even where nonrelatives' conduct begins to approximate to truly indiscriminate bio-altruism. But on Alexander's account, hominid evolution would still have restricted this to within-group prosocial helping— often in the service of hostile intergroup competition.

### 3. Manipulation Selection

Not all acts that help others are bio-altruistic. One animal may accidentally benefit another in the ordinary pursuit of its own "genetic self-interest." For instance, it may unavoidably lead others to a food source that it discovers. No biological altruism necessarily results, so long as the finder gains more personal benefit from the supply than do the later arrivals. But if finding the food took a lot of effort, or if attempting to defend the source from nonkin results in injury, then a net transfer of inclusive fitness to them could easily result. We can refer to incidental bio-altruism whenever an organism accidentally advantages others relative to itself.

But one major category of this is still physically voluntary. That occurs where, either literally or at the adaptive-functional level, the helper "mistakes" the identity of the beneficiary. Likewise in cooperation and reciprocity, a prosocial act may be disguised as less self-serving, or higher in cost/risk properties, than it really is—leading to systematic inequity in an exchange of favors. Such tactics involve the exploitation of voluntary helping through unconscious functional deception, or even from deliberate cheating in intelligent species like ourselves. Yet a far cruder mechanism is a more widespread source of behavior that is formally bio-altruistic. Simple coercion is the limiting case of exploitative social manipulation—and in a loose sense, becoming a predator's meal is the ultimate in cross-species manipulated bio-altruism. Humans are certainly archmanipulators, shrewd opportunists, and frequent coercers. But it must be remembered that manipulative skills can be used equally for prosocial and for selfish ends. Humphrey (1986) vividly illustrates how parents paternalistically induce children into fearful and other aversive social situations, in order to prepare them for facing real-world challenges alone.

## HUMAN ALTRUISM AND SOCIOBIOLOGY'S PARADIGMS

These analyses dissolve most of the bio-altruism paradox. But we have as yet no strong explanation of why humans may make high-risk or predictably costly sacrifices to help nonkin and even outgroup members, unless accidental error or active manipulation by others is involved. Incurring serious bio-energetic penalties deliberately and knowingly is usually uncommon where reciprocal repayments or payoffs to kin are negligibly likely. But they do occur—as revealed by kidney-donor studies (Fellner and Marshall 1981) and rescues of Jews during World War II (Oliner and Oliner 1988). And during modern wars, large numbers of males predictably risk sacrificing their lives for the "national interest"—with some doing so quite intentionally on "kamikaze" missions.

So are these cases triumphs of our human neocortex's relative autonomy to override those lower brain mechanisms that are more tightly programmed for optimizing inclusive fitness? If so, just how does it do this? Or is it that we are peculiarly prone to incidental bio-altruism, because natural controls on prosocial responding have been rendered out of date by the rapid socioecological changes of modern civilization? Perhaps we are simply less self-sacrificing of inclusive fitness than we seem—because we are so expert at masking self-interest? Are we masters of manipulatively inducing strangers to be highly altruistic towards us, while their expertise in self-deception helps to disable their inhibitions? Or is our reliance upon the neocortex simply maladaptive, because we constantly misjudge risks to our fitness? Subsequent discussion of self-system processes below will suggest partial answers. But first, competing paradigms for how to apply sociobiological theories to specific predictions about human conduct need to be outlined.

Since evolutionary biology is primarily a functional approach to understanding organisms' attributes, general models of how natural selection favors fitness-enhancing traits do not need to specify the proximate causal mechanisms that achieve such effects. Successful replication of DNA is the "bottom line" of biological evolution; but genes are only partial and often very indirect causes of their own reproduction. All that sociobiological theorizing is bound to assume is that selection tends to ensure that most genes of a successful species typically make some positive contribution to traits that tend to aid the inclusive reproductive success of each organism who carries them. Thus as Crook (1980) insists, sociobiologists do not need to get bogged down in the details of endless nature/nurture disputes. If learning processes have predictable enough phenotypic results for selection to build upon these, our genes need only specify "open programs," whose details are filled in through developmental experience.

Dawkins (1976) emphasized that genes—whose "goal" is to "manipulate" their bearers "selfishly" into acting as copying machines—took a great "evolutionary gamble" in higher animals. By "investing" in building intelligent brains, they risked such species' members acting systematically against their genetic interests. But the advantage of the relative autonomy of the brain as a mediator of behavior is of course the flexibility to cope rapidly with changing environments and new adaptive niches. The success of *Homo sapiens* shows that so far the gamble has paid off overall. But if DNA instructions only canalize the ontogenetic growth of the brain, then we may in, and perhaps even on, principle learn traits that oppose our inclusive fitness. It is simply that doing so will be appreciably more difficult than acquiring dispositions that our genes have prepared us to learn easily.

Early efforts in human sociobiology tended to neglect these and other subtleties, and hence made misleading claims about human altruism and selfishness. The errors will become clearer if three somewhat idealized paradigms are distinguished—to be referred to as the "instinct extrapolation," "functional extrapolation," and "functional interaction" approaches. It must be stressed that they all acknowledge the same processes of kinship, reciprocity, and manipulation selection. Where they differ is in assumptions about how these affected species with the rapidly growing intelligence of our own hominid ancestors.

## 1. Instinct Extrapolation (IE)

Even in its most simplistic forms, sociobiologizing about human behavior makes few claims for genetically programmed stimulus/response automatisms. But it does see us as directed by the same broad motivational systems ("drives," or "open instincts") as other mammals. Any such system—like that for sexual activity, or for parental care—is assumed to have its several fundamental motivational directions, or preset goals, rather rigidly programmed. Which basic cue stimuli and sensations relevant to any goal or its subgoals are inherently arousing and rewarding or punishing is also given innately.

Associative conditioning and other passively mechanistic learning can modify our cue responsiveness; and intelligence can alter our means/ends strategies and subgoals. Yet we cannot really escape from the genetically specified priority ordering of our central motivations. Consciously, we may see our actions in quite different terms—but our ego-centered bodily and reproductive interests will unconsciously reign supreme. It is clear that the IE approach does deserve the accusation that it takes both biological reductionism and appreciable genetic determinism as axiomatic for human nature.

## 2. Functional Extrapolation (FE)

This approach retains an indirect, functional variant of biological reductionism, but moves away from strong genetic determinist assumptions. It takes appreciably more seriously the emergent properties resulting from our high intelligence and conscious awareness. Thus the role given to cognitively mediated learning, complex inference processes, and creative imagination is far greater. Associated capacities for long-range foresight and hind-sight help us to defer many goal satisfactions and to pursue multiple and often distant goals in parallel. All this means that we are far less tightly constrained by immediate emotional impulses than IE theorists imply.

In particular, the FE approach gives far more acknowledgment to how linguistic communication and mental coding of our experience permit the collective definition of shared symbolic meanings for human actions. To this extent, we can erect culturally valued goals that appear quite remote from fitness interests—such as moral and religious ideals. And cultural transmission processes that trade upon our need for social approval can induce us to internalize these and pursue them quite deliberately. In fact, most of the adaptive wisdom of the human species can be carried in the realm of cultural ideas. But it is assumed that our genes hold us "on a leash" because the "epigenetic rules" canalizing development are tight. So cultural traits predominantly optimize fitness, for most individuals at least (Lumsden and Wilson 1983).

In principle this assumption is plausible. Unlimited flexibility of behavior opens up options for grossly maladaptive culturally transmitted traits. This would then generate counterselection against flexibility itself (Barkow 1989). So we may indeed be biologically resistant, in a host of psychologically subtle ways, to acting upon particular categories of social injunctions likely to undermine inclusive fitness. What is difficult to predict is the specificity and strength of such genetically rooted biases; but they would have to be fairly crude, and based upon immediate external and internal cues. The more temporally remote and unforeseeable any damage to fitness is, the less probably will our biology help to protect us from avoiding it.

The FE viewpoint certainly gestures towards the complexities of our intentional choices, and the impact of cultural systems upon our natures. It is usually admitted that cultures often manipulate at least a minority of individuals into sacrificing their fitness interests. And FE theorists like Alexander (1987) are careful to insist that we are not strictly obliged by our genetic makeup to behave selfishly and nepotistically—even though it so predisposes us. Yet he explicitly equates normative conduct with "social investment" in our own extended and ultimate reproductive success. And he lays great stress upon deception and self-deception within the moral rhetoric that he implicitly sees as largely a mask for our self-interest.

In the final analysis, the thrust of the FE theorist's assumptions is still that everyone's "ultimate" interests are "reproductive, whether or not and to whatever extent (a) such knowledge is conscious and (b) evolutionary novelties in the environment thwart realization" of them (Alexander 1987, 139). So we still remain largely bound by the supreme evolutionary imperative. The mental freedoms of the intelligent human brain can never add up to much more than greater sophistication in just how we seek our fitness, coupled with elaborate webs of myth and self-deception that protect us when we jeopardize it.

## 3. Functional Interaction (FI)

The FE approach offers many insights, but fails to shake off a Panglossian optimism about the invincibility of natural selection. A more modest view of the impact of genetic evolution on the fitness-optimizing properties of brains must admit that we simply do not have decisive reasons for supposing that genes can fine tune our goals to serve fitness functions reliably. Intelligent purposiveness means that we direct actions teleologically, towards states of affairs that can be consciously anticipated. The extent of our power to give priority to biologically maladaptive goals is an empirically open issue. It is foolhardy to write off all traits at variance with fitness a priori, as errors and products of manipulation and self-deception. The interactionist approach is adopted here, and takes the principle of novel "emergent properties" of complex brains entirely seriously. Given the almost unlimited range of goal states that our symbolic language permits us to define for ourselves, it stretches credibility to suppose that our preprogramming is as efficient as IE and FE accounts suppose.

The mysterious brain processes permitting reflective partial awareness of our states and processes of mind are likely to play a crucial role. Crook (1980, 242) argues that "the most crucial evolutionary emergent in the phylogeny of human powers is the ability whereby the person conceives of himself as an active agent distinguishable as an entity from others and about which propositions can be entertained." As he also says, it seems likely that the dispositions to feel autonomously in control of one's actions, and to feel self-esteem when these achieve desired consequences, were originally selected for because they enhanced effective striving towards consciously envisaged goals that did serve inclusive fitness (cf. Barkow 1989). But our sense of active agency can equally well contribute to deliberate self-sacrifice on behalf of socially remote others. A "second-generation" human sociobiology is beginning to take the self-system's powers seriously, and so can at last bring evolutionary theory into rich areas of psychological research.

Hinde (1987) perhaps best exemplifies the caution that the FI approach demands when dealing with social phenomena progressively more removed from features of individuals shared with pre-symbolic species. He highlights the multilevel shaping of our mental realities, through dialectical causal influences within and between once-only social encounters, enduring intimate relationships, group dynamics, and the structures of societal cultural organization. Many higher-level and holistic features of our sociality are neither appropriately reducible to, nor predictable from, the properties of materially separate individuals. And such emergent attributes will have autonomous functional properties quite remote from biological processes and functions. Yet to insist that nothing in sociobiology's core theories can preclude human creativity and freedom is not to prove that we can in fact adhere to philosophical ideals of true altruism. At the very least, it remains necessary to outline a biologically coherent account of the means by which we may have become able to enter new realms of social purposiveness, motivated by authentic concern for another's well-being.

## HUMAN MOTIVATIONAL ALTRUISM

Before addressing this most difficult residue of the altruism paradox, it is necessary to turn briefly to remaining definitional problems. Undoubtedly much of our helping behavior is adaptively self-serving in the long run, or only marginally more bio-altruistic in its material consequences than optimizing inclusive fitness would dictate. Modestly expensive prosocial acts invite cynical interpretations if the prepotency of egocentrism is always assumed. And where prosocial traits occasionally lead to acts that do incur serious cost/risk penalties, such effects will often not have been fully anticipated (as with much self-sacrificial impulsive emergency helping or heroism in warfare). Yet such acts are sometimes both deliberate and supererogatory—going beyond moral duties laid down by normative cultural expectations. These cases will often not be readily intelligible in terms of cultural pressures manipulating us into sacrificing fitness. And to invoke self-deceptions or conscious psychologically hedonistic motives as the norm for such examples must require very good evidence.

Definitions themselves will not settle whether we can ever fully transcend facades and distortions in our consciously prosocial conduct. But the problem of what to count as "altruism" is difficult for psychology as well as for sociobiology—since most theorists are reluctant to define it such that it can violate reinforcement principles by yielding neither material nor subjective payoffs to the altruist (Krebs 1987). In broad accord with ordinary language, I shall take an authentically altruistic act to be any intentionally prosocial behavior likely to benefit its recipient, where the agent has primarily altruistic motivation. An altruistic motive refers only to intended goals, and embodies an active commitment to the needs and interests of the recipient—typically motivated by feelings of sympathy. Such efforts do not have to be successful in every case. And as in similar formulations, like "regard for the good of another person for his own sake" (Blum 1980, 9; cf. chapter 2; part 2 of this volume), significant sacrifice of one's own overall interests is not necessarily entailed. So true altruism need not exclude consequential personal benefits like praise, enhanced self-esteem, avoiding guilt—or even material payoffs contributing directly to inclusive fitness (Vine 1983). But on my account, nor is some anticipation of personal payoffs precluded entirely.

The advantage of these definitions is to allow a motivational continuum between "pure" altruism and egoism, with mixed motives in between. Acts qualify as more or less altruistic so long as concern for another's interests is a sufficient goal to cause them—making any awareness of benefits to the agent strictly superfluous. Predominantly egoistic goals make helping into self-interested pseudoaltruism. Yet ego-centered self-interest can still yield prosocially helpful conduct, and so differs from selfishness. I shall take the latter to be present when someone fails to show authentic altruism or reciprocity where it is normatively appropriate. Giving total priority to one's own psychological or biological interests in social contexts is virtually always selfish. But these distinctions avoid giving pejorative connotations to "private self-interest"— the pursuit of one's own satisfactions where there is no social reason not to do so.

Moral cynics may claim that all apparent altruism is nothing but disguised self-interest, because we simply repress our real dominant motivations from consciousness by means of self-deception. This assertion appears to be empirical. Yet like many categorical "psychodynamic" claims, it offers us no means of falsification. Without proof, it inherently denies the validity of those criteria and tests whereby we normally do identify some—but not all— apparent altruists as innocent of such masquerades. Otherwise it is a point of logic that we are bound to do what we expect to yield most subjective satisfaction; and this variant of hedonism only makes sense as an empty tautology (e.g., Midgley 1978;). To accept it only obfuscates the important difference between altruistic and egocentric acts at the level of who is meant to benefit most from them.

Whereas sociobiologists are typically only concerned about actual fitness-related costs and benefits of helping, these do not directly determine whether it should qualify as truly altruistic—even if it is the most personally costly acts that accrue most moral merit. Batson (1987) has made admirable efforts to clarify the possible range of real motives for helping others, and to distinguish these empirically between authentic altruism and pseudoaltruism given that we can only infer another's subjective motivations from verbal and other behaviors. His theory attributes true altruism only where other-directed sympathetic/empathic feelings, aimed at relieving a victim's distress, are sufficient to motivate helping. His experiments show that this is distinguishable from acting to avoid personal distress at their suffering, and that in some persons and contexts sympathy does dominate the latter as a source of giving aid. But he has not as yet been able to rule out anticipated guilt if personal norms of helping were not followed, nor the anticipated satisfactions from being efficacious.

More seriously for the approach that I shall pursue below, Batson dismisses all accounts that invoke tension-reduction goals— including ones that become other directed through mental assimilation of those in need to the subjective self (e.g., Hornstein 1978). Yet he does this on the basis of experiments in which subjects feeling less concern for a victim proved less ready to help if they could more readily "escape" and avoid encountering the person again. However, his studies fell far short of encompassing the complexities of when, how, and with what personal effects one may feel a sense of shared identity with another person as a "we" (in the rich and enduring sense that Hornstein and others mean). It is therefore premature to suppose that he has ruled out motives in which the self/other distinction is partly dissolved.

It may be precisely the mental capacity to assimilate other persons to the subjective self that makes voluntary altruism possible, even when personal costs are psychologically salient, and attention is not exclusively other directed. Comparisons with other species do hint that human bio-altruistic dispositions can only extend beyond fitness constraints just because we are self-aware goal seekers. If so, a capacity to feel shared identities with other persons may be our most basic source of prosocial motivation. Until we attain a much deeper insight into relevant mental mechanisms, it is unwise to interpret the other-directed-concern criterion for authentic altruism too restrictively. Even the liberal, FI paradigm of sociobiology should lead us to look for a way in which nonegoistic motives can be seen to grow out of the egoism that we appear to be born with. It is now appropriate, therefore, to examine first the evolution and then the ontogenetic development of the self-system—including how social experience shapes how readily and extensively we can embrace others within it.

## THE EVOLUTION OF SELF-AWARENESS

Our subjective selves, as defined and individually accessible in awareness, are by no means isomorphic with our material organism, or bodily ego. It is also necessary to think of any immediate content of self-awareness as one of a number of introspectible selves, or one part or facet of a broader self-system of connected, but not always consistent processes. Conscious self-system goals can evidently go beyond or against the ego's needs. Therefore, the claim that we are programmed to promote our "self-interest" above all else will mean quite different things when understood subjectively rather than materially—especially if the experienced self sometimes embraces other persons (including ones beyond our circles of close kith and kin).

Capacities for self-awareness appear to develop universally, even if self-system contents are culturally variable. We may assume that our species genotype provides basic "open program" instructions to create a self-system, consciously monitors parts of our inner as well as outer worlds, and attempts to direct social and other behaviors towards self-related ends that we envisage through our minds' eyes. Yet the forms and dynamics of our introspectible selves are shaped within a powerful social nexus. As perhaps the most schematically and flexibly preprogrammed feature of our brains, we must expect much of the self-system's content to result from the manipulative efforts of those near and dear to us—particularly in our early years. Complex casual interactions, between what socializing agents expect and our own inborn ego-centered desires, appear to set broad limits upon how far our self-mediated social motives are likely to expand beyond ego concerns. But the key issue concerns the basic means by which any self can come to identify with others at all. It is when we do this, and accept their interests as our own, that our self-governed intentions somehow direct the bodily ego to act on behalf of what others want for and from us—or even what we think they want for themselves.

The self-system's fundamental "design features" will be adapted for coping with the hunting-and-gathering lifestyle and socioecology of our hominid ancestors. If we can extrapolate from what we know from palaeontology and from remaining hunter-gatherer societies, they lived a semi-nomadic life in predominantly cooperative, fairly egalitarian, quite stable, and somewhat inbred bands of typically a few dozen persons. In this adaptive context, ties of kinship and friendship would have overlapped; the need to share activities and the lack of privacy made for high social intimacy and susceptibility to group pressure; and conditions were ideal for the spread of genes facilitating reciprocity dispositions (e.g., Trivers 1971). I have hypothesized that a socially molded self-system evolved as a valuable means for regulating the complex requirements of direct and eventually indirect reciprocity in advantageously flexible ways (Vine 1987). And as Hallowell (1959) first argued, subjective self-objectification allowed social systems to become normative moral orders, such that a new, rapid, symbolic-cultural mode of adaptation and evolution could transform our history.

For such claims to be appreciated, the source, nature, and essential functional uses of self-awareness need to be identified. We remain very far from anything but the most elementary and tentative understanding of the relations between our self-systems and our organic structures, or from a definitive account of how awareness and related behavioral functions did evolve. Even so, there is already far more theorizing and suggestive evidence than I can do justice to here (Alexander 1987; Barkow 1989; Byrne and Whiten 1988; Crook 1980, 1988; Humphrey 1983, 1986). It is apparent that self-system properties do play important roles in our own intentionally goal-directed social acts—including substantially bio-altruistic ones directed well beyond the boundaries of our primary groups. But we must first ask how "knowing their own minds" would have enhanced fitness for our more distant hominid ancestors.

My interpretation draws particularly upon Humphrey's insights, although with some conceptual refinements and extensions. We are virtually obliged to credit the higher primates with quite rich cognitive capacities—allowing that they use mental models, maps, plans, and expectancies in at least a rudimentary way (Walker 1983). Most of these powers may well not be exercised consciously. But it is plausible to assume that their subjective experience extends at least to conscious sentience—understood here as awareness of sensations like pains and bodily pleasures, and of affective and volitional states of immediate desire or aversion. Humphrey's thesis argues that the everyday demands of coping with their physical environments only require other primates to deploy relatively routinized, mechanistic forms of problem solving—well below the levels of reasoning some show on laboratory tasks. Their creative intelligence is normally only used to improve social prediction skills; and its extent sets limits on the richness of their social life.

The central claim is that self-awareness was a vital evolutionary innovation for enhancing social anticipation and manipulation of others' social moves. Thereby, our rather puny earliest ancestors were able to flourish in demanding and dangerous savannah environments. Being self-aware was initially useful for doing "natural psychology"—using self-knowledge of how one would react personally to some situation as a basis for predicting others' actions from their assumed private feelings and dispositions. The adaptive advantage accrues because in a complex, dynamic social nexus of manipulative individuals, every second can count in many types of encounters. Success in exploitative deception, resisting manipulation, or avoiding incidentally disruptive social interference with one's own goal seeking can all be enhanced through superior predictive skills. But so can the formation of flexible and productive social alliances. The complex possibilities for "plot and counterplot" in multiway interactions within groups are vast. In familiar situations with familiar individuals, past behavioral experience may permit mechanistic forms of prediction. But with somewhat fluid group membership, and novel environmental demands and affordances, self-aware individuals could do better than this. In fact as well as theory, "Machiavellian apes" (Byrne and Whiten 1988) can act as if they are deploying empathic role-taking skills to imagine a social scene from another's perspective, then attribute to others what they would themselves perceive, feel, and intend in such situations.

The most primitive form of self-consciousness can be called an ego awareness. It involves some kind of mental access to a crossmodal sensory, and affective, model of one's bodily ego. But this may include unseen features—implying that one can envisage one's ego from an outside observer's standpoint. And there is experimental evidence for such "self-recognition" in how chimpanzees react to their own mirror images—providing that they have not been reared in social isolation (Gallup 1977). Human infants' capacities in such tests begin to develop steadily from late in their first year (Bertenthal and Fischer 1978), although awareness of enduring mental self-attributes starts appreciably later and develops slowly (Damon and Hart 1982). And making correct mental attributions to others requires both coordinating ego's own sensory outlook with theirs, and then linking personal introspections with inferences about the internal states of other egos. In effect this implies that both ego and self must be discerned as social entities by comparison and contrast with other egos and selves (Mead 1913).

Given the relative privacy of others' subjective experiences (especially in the absence of language), an individual must make an assumptive leap of faith that similar stimulus conditions yield similar kinds of awareness in other minds as well. Idiosyncratic variability not withstanding, this is a sound first approximation precisely because even "unrelated" members of a species will have essentially similar genomes and developmental histories—ensuring that members' brains do indeed function on very similar principles. Role-taking skills imply a capacity to locate others on a mental map of one's immediate socioecological environment. But that map must be naturally centered upon one's own bodily ego and include this—which requires awareness of self. Anticipating another's social moves before they are made requires the mental skill to reorient the map at will, imagining how another individual could occupy its center and look out towards oneself.

If the same genes favoring acquisition of relevant introspective/projective capacities could simultaneously predispose one to assume a "theory of mind" whereby differing subjective experiences depend simply upon viewpoints, then a basis for primitive intersubjective understanding would be developmentally secured. Yet as Crook (1988, 399) points out, to be effective in this sphere, "empathic sensitivity to another must...be distinguishable from experiences of self." Role taking must feel different from direct experience—in a way that avoids intersubjective confusions of self and other—if it is to serve rather than impede inclusive fitness. The mechanism remains obscure—but in the human case at least, one's own perceptions, affective reactions, and volitions do normally have a special feeling quality (as well as being more vivid).

This quality is very difficult to specify or measure, but may reveal why adaptive "mind reading" has to involve subjective personal awareness. Self-consciousness has a peculiar property, captured in James's (1962 [1892]) distinction between "I" and "me"— the self as agent and knower, versus the self as patient or known object of experience. One's "I-self" aspect cannot become a focus of attention without becoming objectified as a "me-self," yet is normally present in peripheral awareness when we are almost fully engrossed in outer-directed activities. In envisaging others' mental states while making plans with reference to how those egos are represented on one's social map, such empathically vicarious experiences need to be tagged with their actual owners' identities rather than one's own. The phenomenology of experience seems to suggest that this is possible because only one's own ego-bound mental states can be felt directly or recreated with any I-self aspect present. The experiences of others can only be imagined in an objectified form, corresponding to the me-self aspect of reflecting upon personal experiences.

The private sense of self as an enduring, distinct subject and intentional agent cannot be studied directly with objective empirical methods. Indirect evidence suggests that awareness of ego's physical powers emerges clearly in the second year (Kagan 1981)—while knowledge that different egos can experience the same event differently is said to emerge somewhat later (Hoffman 1981). And the full capacity to relate together awareness of self as agent and of self as object may not be reached until after puberty. While many questions remain, it does seem clear that doing natural psychology reliably is demanding, and relies upon slowly acquired skills of social cognition. Children lack sensitivity to the nuances of awareness that ensure that social planning involving mind reading is never undermined by confusions between their own viewpoints and feelings and those vicarious experiences that they must attribute to others' egos. This is why they will often be very susceptible to social manipulation by adults, at the fundamental level of how one comes to define various self-attributes, self-goals, and sources of self-esteem feelings. And I shall shortly argue that the elasticity of early self-conceptions, and their vulnerability to self/other "confusions," is the key to socializing individuals into a variety of social loyalties that can generate personally "maladaptive" voluntary bio-altruism.

A sense of one's autonomous personhood—with abilities to strive for alternative goals according to which accords best with internalized standards for anticipated self-satisfaction, or with the progressive actualization of some ideal "possible self"—is certainly not sufficient to guarantee that helping others qualifies as strictly altruistic. Yet it is one prerequisite for any self-reflective moral awareness of how feelings and social expectations of other persons deserve consideration alongside one's narrowly ego-centered interests, and should sometimes override these. And I have proposed that it was the pliability of children's self-systems that made possible the internalizing of normative expectations, and acquisition of socially inclusive self-definitions, that were able to offer our ancestors the socially synergistic benefits of indirect reciprocity and divisions of labor within groups (Vine 1987).

**THE SELF'S IDENTITIES AND INTERESTS**

Perceiving another person as sharing a social category with oneself can be understood as assimilating them, their interests, and their goals to one's own self and its aims. If such a social self-identity has total mental priority at a given time, these elements will be experienced as inseparable. If the conscious self both embraces the other and yet retains its ego-centered perspective and volitional capacity, we have a basis for freely choosing self-governed actions for another's benefit (to the extent that their need is perceived as greater). If we do take such conduct to qualify as "authentically altruistic," then the scope of our altruism is predominantly limited just by how fully we allow others to share our subjective identities.

I hypothesize that this, rather than simply the empathic role taking that enables us to know precisely how they feel, generates sympathetic or more impersonal affect, and so motivates helping those in need. Krebs is among the few theorists who do not confound empathy and sympathy, and do acknowledge the latter as a more reliable source for helping others (Krebs 1987; Krebs and Russell 1981). Hoffman (e.g., 1981) has sought to chart how empathic awareness of another's distress can develop out of those more primitive emotional contagions of early infancy that do involve self/other confusions. But while he accepts an empathy/sympathy distinction, he has no explanation of just how compassion can arise as a reaction to initial empathic responses.

No full account of the structure and dynamics of a self-system capable of generating sacrifice of the ego's interests can be attempted here. But the processes of experiencing temporary identifications of the subjectively defined self with whole groups—when relevant internal and external cues are present to make an inclusive group identity salient—have been thoroughly explored in research on the "social categorization" identity theory of intergroup relations due to Tajfel (e.g., 1981). Merely acknowledging that ego and others share the same significant social category can lead to treating them preferentially in comparison with an ego-exclusive group's members. Also, various cognitive polarization effects ensue while any group identity is salient—exaggerating similarities and affiliations within groups, and differences and distrust between them. Of most relevance here is what Turner's (1987) extension of the theory identifies as self-stereotyping—which induces attempts to conform to a normative image of the ideal responsible and loyal member. The pursuit of self-esteem is translated into such terms, and so becomes an important factor promoting cooperation and altruism towards an in-group's members.

In considering the evolutionary pressures on ancestral hominids' readiness to acquire such group-oriented self-processes, I have argued that we should in fact expect to find that the individual shows inbuilt systematic ego biases—which somewhat undermine the idealized picture (Vine 1987). Greenwald's (1980) concept of the "totalitarian ego" suggests that their primary function is always to preserve the psychological integrity of the self-system itself (as clearly required by any organism that relies upon such mediating processes for its adaptive behavior). Even a functional interactionist sociobiology can predict biases in self-processes; and these cognitive failings and self-deceptions mean that one's own ego's interests are likely to be given somewhat exaggerated, often stronger weightings than those of other egos—even when an inclusive identity of the self does embrace others.

This is not to predict that we can never learn to live by authentic principles of universal moral equality—only that such ideally impartial commitments and altruistic traits of character are fragile and rather rare (Vine 1986; cf. Krebs and Van Hesteren chapter 6 in this volume). In identity theory terms, an all-encompassing human identity of the self can be subjectively formulated on the basis of everyone's shared humanity. But it will be rarely salient in most persons, because ego biases can be supposed to exert stronger effects according to how far the grouping encompassed within a social identity departs from the evolutionary prototype of the small and intimate band.

Many of Tajfel's and Turner's insights should apply in the area of interpersonal relations, where they envisage one's idiosyncratic and more ego-bound "personal identity" of the self as determining social conduct. I shall refer to social identities (rather than group identities) in cases where the existence of one-to-one attachment relationships can be taken to mean that enduring liking or love for an individual has generated a special self-identity—which ties them closely to one's ego by "we" bonds of intimate attraction. When such a person's presence becomes mentally salient, we can envisage this as evoking a dyadic self-identity that subjectively includes them.

Symbolic interactionists claim that the raw materials for our earliest self-ascriptions and standards are provided by "significant others" like parents, and later by inferring and adopting the impersonal standpoint of the "generalized other" in any group to which we belong (Hewitt 1984). If such experiences provide at least much of our self-system's contents for our primary social identities, then our readiness to acquire the self-control of ego impulses that altruistic sacrifices demand can begin to be explained. In particular, if bands of our hominid ancestors were able to encourage children to develop loyalty to all their group's members by highlighting the ego-inclusive identity and norms that defined any band as a whole, then the basis for shared and socially inclusive self-processes supportive of indirect reciprocity could be firmly laid.

### CONCLUSION: THE BOND OF SELF-WITH-OTHER

Although some features of self-identity have been outlined, no explanation has yet been given for how socially inclusive identities can become accessible parts of the active self-system. The principal uncertainties can be addressed through an hypothesized account of how our very first conscious self-identity arises during infancy. Most of the large body of developmental research on early social relations and attachments makes no attempt to infer what the infant experiences, or to confront acquisition of the I/me dialectic of subjective intentional agency. Yet some recent studies of mother-infant interaction offer clues to a major source for initial acquisition of I-self awareness of autonomous personal capacities—how she engages him in communication games. Almost from birth, infants are sometimes highly attentive and motorically responsive to mothers and their actions. And well before self-awareness can be clearly identified, they appear to have learned to engage intentionally with the most familiar and predictable segments of their social worlds—on the basis of the shared anticipations and meanings that develop within the reciprocity of turn-taking exchanges (e.g., Butterworth and Light 1982; Kaye 1982; Stern 1977).

Through presymbolic interaction sequences, the infant gains experience in roles that must be coordinated with the mother's, and for which certain social expectations come to apply on both sides. Trevarthen (1982) claims to detect innate preadaptations and motives for entering into early cooperation and reciprocity—although Sylvester-Bradley (1985) failed to find supposedly very early intentional communicative rapport with persons as such. It appears safer to infer that young infants can rapidly learn to detect causal contingencies between their own movements and interesting feedback—thus acquiring sensory-motor "expectancies" that motivate active and affectively satisfying efforts to exert efficacious control over their own experiences (e.g., Lewis, Sullivan, and Brooks-Gunn 1985). A sensitive mother, whose expressive responsiveness provides the child with repeated contingency experiences, is initially just perceived as an exceptionally potent and familiar source of rewarding stimulation. This is the likely basis for initial attachment bonds (Vine 1973).

From the middle of the first year there is great enthusiasm for teasing games like "peekaboo"—where a simple turn-taking rule structure that suits the infant's desires and powers can be assimilated, and the alternation between active and passive phases of involvement in a rewarding social exchange can be learned (Bruner and Sherwood 1976). Soon a richer "intersubjectivity" of sharing meanings than that of merely fitting into behavioral routines begins to appear. Trevarthen (1982, 100) may then be right that "exclamatory or request utterances of infant proto-language clearly conceive of others having interests, purposes, and helpful powers." Also by the end of the first year, the child may sometimes obey instructions, offer objects to the mother, and so on—clearly appreciating that he or she figures in her purposes, as well as knowing how to recruit her help in the exercise of the child's internal power to control response-contingent stimulation.

It appears that the infant's incipient, nonintrospectible I/me differentiation, and I-self grasp of intentionality, may be particularly encouraged by purely communicative, and then object-oriented, reciprocal social interchanges that provide vital prereflective experience for later self-acquisition. (It is no surprise if our human genotype does at least indirectly prime us for all this, given the importance of communicative skills and attachment bonds in our highly social mode of adaptation.) But it should not be assumed that the self-system's sources are exclusively social. Kagan (1981, 144) interprets his studies of nonsocial strivings during the second year to mean that perhaps "all that is required for the capacities called 'self-awareness' to appear is any information resulting from the child's actions and feelings"—that is, contingent feedback as such, involving a grasp of self/object rather than self/other differentiation.

Infants are visibly active partners in maternally "scaffolded" interactive games. But a difficulty in inferring innate preadaptations for altruistic helping and socially inclusive definitions of self stems from the impact of the Western ideology of individualism upon our theories. We oppose sharp awareness of personal uniqueness against infantile social confusions involving overassimilation or overaccommodation. In thus implicitly derogating members of small-scale societies where the self is predominantly experienced in a more collectivist or group-oriented way, we also radically obscure the basic form in which the human self-system first evolved within hunter-gatherer bands. Stern (1988) argues—somewhat speculatively but plausibly—that the complex two-way dynamics of early mother/infant interaction suggest a preprogrammed readiness to attain early schemas of "self-with-other," rather than of ego differentiated from other egos. The intersubjective sharing of awareness that develops is at the heart of our human capacity for intimacy or "connectedness." This is a more dialectically balanced, equilibrated intermental relationship between persons than normal individualistic concepts of autonomous selves readily support.

On this account, our early interpersonal attachments and processes of identification with others are poorly represented by psychological theories that focus rather exclusively upon one or both partners' ego-centered need satisfactions. A "we-self" identity need not involve self/other confusion regarding intentionality and causality. A strong sense of interdependency with the other, capable of permitting altruistic sympathy, requires that ego's and other's viewpoints can be distinguished clearly but coordinated through mental operations of reciprocity. Effective social mothering should produce precisely this. Mutual feelings of competence and enjoyment derive from alternating processes of give-and-take, geared to their interest in shared projects and involving each respecting and responding to the agency of the other. The earliest roots for compassionate feeling should thus be predominantly in the joyous efficacy an infant feels when successful in meeting maternal requests, which is contingently associated with reciprocal experience of having the infant's also met by her. But when she does happen to show signs of distress, and disrupts attention to their reciprocal exchanges, it is not just a primary ego satisfaction that is threatened, but their connectedness itself. Her inability to participate is likely to be perceived as mutually frustrating to them both. Although the child's concern, and any comforting attempts, could be seen as means to the child's own ends, the child's conscious goal is their mutual satisfaction. Surely the child wants her relief from distress equally with his or her relief from frustration?

Such hypothesized perceptions and feeling reactions still stop short of describing how an infant can begin to appropriate conscious understanding of meanings from interactions—and thus

acknowledge his or her own capacity to act upon subjective formulations of the end that his or her attempts to restore their
harmonious mutualism are actually for. In this respect the gradual discovery of his or her actions as intentional and self-governed
remains shrouded in theoretical mystery. However, Shotter and
Gregory (1976) are surely right to insist on the importance of the
mother's role as a "double agent" for the infant—initially taking
responsibility for supplying the meaning of the infant's actions
as well as of her own. Their vital insight is that she erroneously
attributes intentions to communicate, well before the infant's
preverbal gestures can have symbolic meaning for the infant. In
reacting as if specific situationally appropriate meanings were
intended, she seeks to draw the infant's attention to what his or
her acts could be socially expected to signify. Her effort on behalf
of the infant's incipient agency does all that could be done to
facilitate the infant's spontaneous grasp of the power of actions
that are directed by attending to fleeting internal images, and
by striving to fit actual perceptions to these.

Mothers deploy considerable natural pedagogic skill—mostly
without realizing what they are doing either—to teach their infants
how to intend self-initiated actions, and above all to understand
that many desires can only be met cooperatively (since even the
mother's competence is limited in situations requiring social alternation). In eventually grasping this, the infant learns that human relations are social partnerships of mutual effort and mutual
aid on each other's behalf. I suggest that the infant's first significant
realizations of conscious agency occur in these contexts of social
familiarity, cooperation, and supportive interdependencies. If so,
the first active, conscious self-identities appropriated from public
and concrete engagement with the world will involve we/us intentions inclusive of attachment figures (with full I/you/me intentionality coming later).

If initial awarenesses of self are "we-cognitions" of self-with-
other, and "we-volitions" of self-for-other, the possibility of altruism becomes real. And once the biological gulf between ego
desires and other-concern has been crossed in prototypic form in
this first social identity, there is no mystery in principle regarding
our human power to escape from the enclosed worlds of evolutionary imperatives. These tied us rigidly to the pursuit of fitness
only until humans jointly created and discovered their subjective,
but still functionally real, social selves.

## BIBLIOGRAPHY

Alexander, R. D. (1987) *The biology of moral systems.* New York: Aldine De Gruyter.

Axelrod, R. (1984) *The evolution of co-operation.* New York: Basic.

Barkow, J. H. (1989) *Darwin, sex, and status: Biological approaches to mind and culture.* Toronto: University of Toronto Press.

Batson, C. D. (1987) Prosocial motivation: Is it ever truly altruistic? In L. Berkowitz (Ed.), *Advances in experimental social psychology.* Vol. 20, pp. 65–122. San Diego, CA: Academic.

Bertenthal, B. I., and Fischer, K. W. (1978) Development of self-recognition in the infant. *Developmental Psychology.* 14:44–50.

Blum, L. A. (1980) *Friendship, altruism, and morality.* London: Routledge and Kegan Paul.

Bruner, J. S., and Sherwood, V. (1976) Early rule structure: The case of "peekaboo." In R. Harré (Ed.), *Life sentences: Aspects of the social role of language.* Pp. 55–62. London: Wiley.

Butterworth, G., and Light, P. (Eds) (1982) *Social cognition: Studies of the development of understanding.* Brighton, Sussex: Harvester.

Byrne, R., and Whiten, A. (Eds.) (1988) *Machiavellian intelligence: Social expertise and the evolution of intellect in monkeys, apes, and humans.* Oxford: Clarendon.

Crook, J. H. (1980) *The evolution of human consciousness.* Oxford: Clarendon.

——— (1988) The nature of conscious awareness. In C. Blakemore and S. Greenfield (Eds.), *Mindwaves.* Pp. 383–402. Oxford: Blackwell.

Damon, W., and Hart, D. (1982) The development of self-understanding from infancy through adolescence. *Child Development.* 53:841–64.

Darwin, C. (1957) Extracts from "The descent of man in relation to sex." In M. Bates and P. S. Humphrey (Eds.). *The Darwin reader.* London: Macmillan. (Originally published by John Murray, London, 1871.)

Dawkins, R. (1976) *The selfish gene.* Oxford: Oxford University Press.

Dennett, D. C. (and commentators) (1983) Intentional systems in cognitive ethology: The "Panglossian paradigm" defended. *Behavioral and Brain Sciences.* 6:343–90.

Fellner, C. H., and Marshall, J. R. (1981) Kidney donors revisited. In J. P. Rushton and R. M. Sorrentino (Eds.), *Altruism and helping behavior: Social, personality, and developmental perspectives.* Pp. 351–66. Hillsdale, NJ: Erlbaum.

Gallup, G. G., Jr. (1977) Self-recognition in primates: A comparative approach to the bidirectional properties of consciousness. *American Psychologist.* 32:329–38.

Greenwald, A. G. (1980) The totalitarian ego: Fabrication and revision of personal history. *American Psychologist.* 35:603–18.

Hallowell, A. I. (1959) Behavioral evolution and the emergence of the self. In B. J. Meggers (Ed.), *Evolution and anthropology: A centennial appraisal.* Pp. 36–60. Washington, DC: Anthropological Society of Washington.

Hamilton, W. D. (1964) The genetical evolution of social behaviour. Parts I and II. *Journal of Theoretical Biology.* 7:1–16 and 17–52.

Hewitt, J. P. (1984) *Self and society: A symbolic interactionist social psychology,* 3d ed. Boston, MA: Allyn and Bacon.

Hinde, R. A. (1987) *Individuals, relationships, and culture: Links between ethology and the social sciences.* Cambridge: Cambridge University Press.

Hoffman, M. L. (1981) The development of empathy. In J. P. Rushton and R. M. Sorrentino (Eds.), *Altruism and helping behavior: Social, personality, and developmental perspectives.* Pp. 41–63. Hillsdale, NJ: Erlbaum.

Hornstein, H. A. (1978) Promotive tension and prosocial behavior: A Lewinian analysis. In L. Wispé (Ed.), *Altruism, sympathy, and helping: Psychological and sociological principles.* Pp. 177–207. New York: Academic.

Humphrey, N. K. (1983) *Consciousness regained: Chapters in the development of mind.* Oxford: Oxford University Press.

―――― (1986) *The inner eye.* London: Faber and Faber/Channel Four Books.

James, W. (1962) *Psychology: Briefer course.* New York: Collier. (Originally published, Henry Holt, New York, 1892.)

Kagan, J. (1981) *The second year: The emergence of self-awareness.* Cambridge, MA: Harvard University Press.

Kaye, K. (1982) *The mental and social life of babies: How parents create persons.* Brighton, Sussex: Harvester.

Kitcher, P. (1985) *Vaulting ambition: Sociobiology and the quest for human nature.* Cambridge, MA: M.I.T. Press.

Krebs, D. (1987) The challenge of altruism in biology and psychology. In C. B. Crawford, M. S. Smith, and D. Krebs (Eds.), *Sociobiology and psychology: Ideas, issues, and applications.* Pp. 81–118. Hillsdale, NJ: Erlbaum.

Krebs, D., and Russell, C. (1981) Role-taking and altruism: When you put yourself in the shoes of another, will they take you to their owner's aid? In J. P. Rushton and R. M. Sorrentino (Eds.), *Altruism and helping behavior: Social, personality, and developmental perspectives.* Pp. 137–65. Hillsdale, NJ: Erlbaum.

Kropotkin, P. (1939) *Mutual aid: A factor of evolution.* Harmondsworth, Middlesex: Penguin. (Originally published, Heinemann, London, 1902.)

Lewis, M., Sullivan, M. W., and Brooks-Gunn, J. (1985) Emotional behavior during the learning of a contingency in early infancy. *British Journal of Developmental Psychology.* 3:307–16.

Lewontin, R. C., Rose, S., and Kamin, L. J. (1984) *Not in our genes: Biology, ideology, and human nature.* Harmondsworth, Middlesex: Penguin.

Lumsden, C. J., and Wilson, E. O. (1983) *Promethean fire: Reflections on the origins of mind.* Cambridge, MA: Harvard University Press.

Markova, I. (1987) *Human awareness: Its social development.* London: Hutchinson.

Maynard Smith, J. (1964) Group selection and kin selection. *Nature.* 201:1145–47.

Mead, G. H. (1913) The social self. *Journal of Philosophy, Psychology, and Scientific Methods.* 10:374–80.

Midgley, M. (1978) *Beast and man: Roots of human nature.* Hassocks, Sussex: Harvester.

Oliner, S. P., and Oliner, P. M. (1988) *The altruistic personality: Rescuers of Jews in Nazi Europe.* New York: Free Press.

Ridley, M., and Dawkins, R. (1981) The natural selection of altruism. In J. P. Rushton and R. M. Sorrentino (Eds.), *Altruism and helping behavior: Social, personality, and developmental perspectives.* Pp. 19–39. Hillsdale, NJ: Erlbaum.

Shotter, J., and Gregory, S. (1976) On first gaining the idea of oneself as a person. In R. Harré (Ed.), *Life sentences: Aspects of the social role of language.* Pp. 3–9. London: Wiley.

Sodian, B. (1991) The development of deception in young children. *British Journal of Developmental Psychology.* 9:173–88.

Stern, D. N. (1977) *The first relationship: Infant and mother.* Cambridge, MA: Harvard University Press.

——— (1988) The early development of schemas of self, other, and "self with other." In J. D. Lichtenberg and S. Kaplan (Eds.), *Reflections on self psychology.* Pp. 49–84. Hillsdale, NJ: Erlbaum/Analytic Press.

Sylvester-Bradley, B. (1985) Failure to distinguish between people and things in early infancy. *British Journal of Developmental Psychology.* 3:281–92.

Tajfel, H. (1981) *Human groups and social categories: Studies in social psychology.* Cambridge: Cambridge University Press.

Trevarthen, C. (1982) The primary motives for cooperative understanding. In G. Butterworth and P. Light (Eds), *Social cognition: Studies of the development of understanding.* Pp. 77–109. Brighton, Sussex: Harvester.

Trivers, R. L. (1971) The evolution of reciprocal altruism. *Quarterly Review of Biology.* 46 (4): 35–57.

——— (1985) *Social evolution.* Menlo Park, CA: Benjamin/Cummings.

Turner, J. C. (1987) *Rediscovering the social group: A self-categorization theory.* Oxford: Blackwell.

Vine, I. (1973) The role of facial-visual signalling in early social development. In M. von Cranach and I. Vine (Eds.), *Social communication and movement: Studies of interaction and expression in man and chimpanzee.* Pp. 195–208. London: Academic.

——— (1983) Sociobiology and social psychology: Rivalry or symbiosis? The explanation of altruism. *British Journal of Social Psychology.* 22:1–11.

——— (1986) Moral maturity in socio-cultural perspective: Are Kohlberg's stages universal? In S. Modgil and C. Modgil (Eds.), *Lawrence Kohlberg: Consensus and commentary.* Pp. 431–53. Brighton, Sussex: Falmer.

——— (1987) Inclusive fitness and the self-system: The roles of human nature and sociocultural processes in intergroup discrimination. In V. Reynolds, V. S. E. Falger, and I. Vine (Eds.), *The sociobiology of ethnocentrism: Evolutionary bases of xenophobia, discrimination, racism, and nationalism.* Pp. 60–80. London: Croom Helm.

——— (1990) From "having in mind" to motivated consciousness. Paper presented at the annual meeting of the British Psychological Society, History and Philosophy of Psychology Section, Lincoln, 2–4 April.

Walker, S. (1983) *Animal thought.* London: Routledge and Kegan Paul.

Wallach, M. A., and Wallach, L. (1983) *Psychology's sanction for selfishness: The error of egoism in theory and therapy.* San Francisco: Freeman.

Wilson, E. O. (1975) *Sociobiology: The new synthesis.* Cambridge, MA: Belknap.

# 5

# ALTRUISM AND THE EVOLUTION
# OF CIVIL SOCIETY

*Ronald Cohen*

## INTRODUCTION

The question of what people did in the Holocaust to protect Jews and why—how individuals reacted altruistically to that horror— contains vital information for our survival as a species. What I wish to do in this chapter is to ask whether, as so many argue, this feature is an inbuilt quality of our genetic heritage. If it is, we have little to worry about. The "selfish genes" can be depended upon for behavioral instructions that predetermine our ennobling and sacrificial choices in order that the gene pool be provided with the most efficient stochastic search for biochemical durability through natural selection.

Fortunately, or unfortunately, things are not so simple. What I will argue is that altruism is based on both genetic and sociocultural evolution. These intertwined forces work together to produce a more humane and civil sociocultural life for the species as a whole. In this view the genetic basis of altruism is not simply a capacity for sacrifice that somehow increases fitness, but includes as well restraint, which in turn fosters morality, understanding, and criticism that constrains egoistic behavior. And these qualities create the opportunity for a more civil, more universalistic morality in both belief and practice—if we choose, individually and collectively, to make it so.

## Culture and Altruism

Some years ago I argued (Cohen 1978) that the standard wisdom of the sociobiologists on altruism was oversimplified. Human altruism is learned, not innate. Simply put, I viewed it as part of sociocultural evolution, its primary features being the way individuals and groups are coached to empathize, sympathize with, even sacrifice for others, thereby counteracting the dominantly hedonic nature provided by genetic inheritance. Culture constrains this force, asking us instead to interfere with these genetic instructions for the adaptive rewards of group life. To illustrate the point, I first showed how altruistic cultural rules can, and very often are, translated into self-serving ends when actually performed by individuals and institutions. Thus among hunters and gatherers cultural norms require that individuals sacrifice the proceeds of their own hunting for the welfare of the group through customs that prescribe obligatory food sharing. The practice is reciprocal, but better hunters give away much more food than they receive. This enables hunters to use altruistic regulations to enhance individual prestige, heighten interpersonal competition, and enable power seeking (Cohen 1978). Individuals seek rewards, social life demands cooperation, and culture provides symbols and values that allow people to internalize altruism. Once internalized (variously in the population), norms provide for genuinely experienced optimization by individuals through conformity to the learned goals (cf. Margolis 1984). I also argued that cultures vary the degree of altruism they demand from members, as well as the degree to which altruistic regulations are highly valued aspects of custom and character development.

The argument is based firmly on the Darwinian assumption that individual actors are predominantly hedonistic. Given scarcity and variation, organisms with greater capacity for capturing scarce requirements possess greater "fitness"—that is, they have a greater potentiality to succeed reproductively. Those who strive harder and more skillfully do better. Logically, then, genetically endorsed dominance striving is the inevitable outcome of competition amidst scarcity. This provides a motor or energizing force for action but no necessary basis in genetic inheritance for the evolution of altruism. As we know it in our culture, altruism (empathy, sympathy, and gratuitous generosity) is the cultural evolution of compensatory rules of behaviors, which offset the effects of individuated reward seeking and dominance striving when the latter drive decreases the competitive position of a group in relation to other groups seeking to exploit the same resources.

Campbell (1978) added an elegant feature by showing that the original theorizing on altruism is based upon life among social insects. These genera *first* evolve sterile castes. Only when this development is accomplished does it become possible to evolve fully sacrificial genetic instructions. More precisely, only when reproductive competition between individual members of an insect community has been first set aside because of the prior evolution of an entire caste of steriles (Campbell 1978, 45–46), then and only then can a species move through a "narrow window" (E. O. Wilson's term) of evolutionary potential to a genetically induced and fully sacrificial (i.e., altruistic) set of behaviors. Even though many animals have some of this, it is universally accepted that the "higher social insects greatly exceed (in [biological] 'altruism') that of any nonhuman vertebrate" (ibid, 49–50). On their part, humans are extremely interdependent as a species, while the individual is an optimizer whose collective life requires more cooperation than almost any other organism except insects (ibid., 51 ff.). Unlike with impersonally intimate insects, the competition among humans remains; but there are no sterile castes whose reproductive sacrifice provides increased survival potential for the group as a whole. In order therefore to achieve the necessary level of cooperation, humanity has a highly evolved set of social systems that "scold... selfishness and cowardice" even though human individual action "is often destructive of the collective good" (ibid., 51, 53).

To his credit, and characteristically, Campbell asked a new question. Namely, in how many species and among which ones can we find how various is the genetic basis for self-sacrifice and cooperativeness, and what triggers its evolutionary intensification? The sociobiologists assumed that once modeled in general terms and applied successfully to any species or genus, their theory could be used to explain any and all cooperative or sacrificially interpreted behavior almost always attributed heretofore to culture and learning. Contrarily, but actually in agreement, I assumed that if I took the opposite tack, starting with an hedonic actor, and then showed how individuals and groups behave selfishly even under conditions of regulated altruism, I would then demonstrate the lack of genetic etiology for altruistic norms and behaviors. If I then demonstrated variation in altruistic behaviors across cultures—associated with an assumedly constant genetic feature—I would weaken or dismiss altruism's biological basis. Campbell went to the interstices between the two paradigms and found the sociobiological argument wanting. This brought his argument and my own to the same point—the defense of sociocultural as opposed to genetic evolution to explain human altruism. And that's where it stands.

But intellectual styles change. Those of us who had an initial "knee-jerk" reaction to sociobiological reasoning have become less uncomfortable with the notion of biologically and socioculturally intertwined causal models. On the other hand, much of my earlier argument about the sociocultural basis for altruism remains valid. Nothing written since leads me to reject the sociocultural determination of altruism observable in human behavior. Nevertheless, in the interim a number of interrelations among biological and behavioral features at the species level have shown the way to a more integrated logic. Clearly, human altruism does have some biological bases. And, even more importantly, in the interim social scientists have begun to accept the need for normative or critical theorizing, not only about the causes of evolution but also about how to influence its direction—in a world worth the effort if we *choose* to make it so.

### The Dual Inheritance Model

The most important fusion of biological and sociocultural reasoning in the past few decades is that of the "dual inheritance model" (Boyd and Richerson 1985). Many have worked on this same set of issues from a similar perspective (see for example, Waddington 1960; Campbell 1965; Cohen 1981). The importance of the Boyd and Richerson (1985) approach is its intricate working out of a theory that simultaneously includes both genetic and cultural evolutionary processes. Each, they argue, evolves in response to logically similar mechanisms but reacts to different selectors operating at differing rates, in differing enabling environments, all the while interacting and affecting each other. Conceptually, biological and cultural evolution are logically and empirically separate domains, but phenomenologically they are united into a single process of "descent with modification". The theory is not only intellectually satisfying and aesthetically pleasing, but it also provides a counterargument to the sociobiological strategy of searching for explanations that rely solely on fitness logics through

biological reproduction. Boyd and Richerson (1985) go beyond this
by adding cultural transmissions that can be selectively retained
and extinguished behaviorally.

Under the classic sociobiological argument (e.g., Trivers 1971;
Wilson 1975), cultural practices evolve to foster and express genetic
fitness; culture is the ultimate product of, and is utilized by, the
"selfish gene" to enhance reproductive success. That's what culture
is; that's why it's here. In contrast, dual inheritance theory makes
the case for a more multicausal set of processes. In effect dual
inheritance posits that changes in adaptation that are selected and
retained originate from and are transmitted by reproductive activity in both the behavioral and the genetic domains.

For example, in some instances cultural regulations may demand self-sacrificial behavior that ensures the survival of the culture and its bearers and in so doing acts to increase the frequency
of genetically *deleterious* variants (Boyd and Richerson 1985, 202)—
the exact reverse of biologically caused behavior. In sociobiology
natural selection among gene frequencies is the predicated source
of self-sacrifice, or altruism, by individuals towards their genetic
relatives. On the other hand, using dual inheritance theory it is
just as logical to have culture evolve sacrificial prescriptions making these demands part of the inheritable transmissions (or learning) required for acceptable membership in the society or a
particular segment of it that shares the same rules.

As a dramatic example of this point the authors (ibid., 202–3)
show how a priest opts for celibacy to become the servant of his
"flock." In doing so he sacrifices his reproductive capacity to devote
more time and energy to propagating the faith. His success is measured by his capacity to reproduce culturally, not biologically, even
though his genes may deliver quite the opposite message to his
everyday interactions. Unlike the insect analogues used in sociobiological arguments, he is not sterile. And that creates problems
of biological versus cultural determination of priestly behavior
evidenced by the fact that a small proportion of priests find it
impossible to refrain from sexual relations. Nevertheless, the sift-
ing and winnowing of variants through time have shown that the
demands of celibacy enhance an individual's total dedication to
the Church, and contribute to the institution's survival in a cultural
sense.

For the most part, sociobiologists have concluded that group
selection is improbable (Barash 1982). Possibly then the priest's

celibacy is a form of inclusive fitness—that is, he sacrifices his own reproductive capacity so his genes will have a better chance of being reproduced through advantages derived from his actions by his kin. Since priests are obligated to help everyone, to minister to the faithful no matter what their relationship, and to work tirelessly for the survival and expansion of the Church, it is not evident why their kinsfolk's fitness would be especially advantaged by their celibacy and obligatory altruism. Alternatively, dual inheritance theory highlights conflicts between culturally derived behavior on the one hand, and genetically determined egoistic motivations on the other. In the dual inheritance model, the survival of the Church is best served if the cultural variant of celibacy is selected for by human actors choosing among alternatives. The mechanisms that produce such selection involve all of the factors that determine directions of social and cultural change and their relations to both individual *and* group behavior and beliefs (cf. Cohen 1981).

Boyd and Richerson (1985, 204–40) put it this way: the empirical facts of cooperation and altruistic behavior cannot easily overcome the egoistic nature of individual actors. To do so, theory must first "account for the evolution of humans who cooperate on a large scale with genetically unrelated individuals. Second, given that individuals belong to many different groups, it must specify with which group (or groups) an individual will identify" (ibid., 236). Alternatively, a more plausible way of explaining such behavior is that of "cultural group selection" (ibid.), which assumes that humans inherit at least some portion of their values and beliefs as part of cultural transmissions.

Membership in groups always requires some sacrifice of personal interests. Humans must live in interacting groups to survive, with role differentiation more and less developed. Each generation must recruit new occupants, each of whom varies in her or his capacity to fill the roles successfully, their conformity to learning pressures to conform to older norms, their capacity to cooperate with or even sacrifice for others, and their assessments about the contemporary merits of older norms that are to be applied to new or changing conditions. But there are always regulations, inheritable through learning, which prescribe individual sacrifice in terms of group interests rather than their own or even those of their close kin.

Even among the simplest societies observers have recorded concepts of the public good for which egoistic motives must be sacrificed or else everyone in the group will suffer. Thus Freuchen (1961) observed an Eskimo encampment in which an individual was killed by common consent after continually breaking rules about the proper etiquette in his treatment of scarce animal kills. The danger that the surviving animal spirits would not cooperate anymore with humans, thus starving the group as a whole, was the rationale, and the man chosen as executioner was a close relative so that no intergroup feuding would result from the death of the miscreant. Proper treatment of animals was a public good. The executioner (a kinsman) was performing a public service—sacrificing his close kinsman for the public welfare and group survival. The beliefs and laws of this group are adaptations to a food-scarce environment. A complex theology has evolved linking animals and humans into a single morally interdependent network of actors. And this results in culturally transmissable conservation practices that help maintain the food supply. These local beliefs about the cause-effect relations that determine optimal animal population numbers have been selected and transmitted down the generations along with the altruistic behavior of kinsmen as executioners. The example illustrates how humans act in terms of an evolved rationality for group survival rather than the simple arithmetic of individual or even inclusive fitness.

In effect, many of the most important intergenerational transmissions among humans have evolved from selection and retention of sociocultural factors that contribute to group rather than individual survival. This acts through a set of selective relations such as role-model pressures from the older generations, from learning and assessments by individuals about the merits of traits that bias his/her adoption of transmitted instructions, or even from frequencies that suggest which transmissions are the most popular and most important to conform to (ibid., 206–8). Elsewhere I have suggested that a number of factors in normal human group life tend to bias our transmittable inheritance regulations and performances away from random or simple genetic determination of trait distribution (see Cohen 1981). First and foremost among these is role recruitment. The constant changeover among social roles required by aging means that each new person occupying the role can and does vary the way roles are performed. This provides a pool of potentially new and adaptive shifts in role behavior performance, transmissability, and normative regulations governing the role. Secondly, migrations provide for variants in transmissable behavioral terms similar to those observed in biased sampling effects or genetic drift. European migrants to Australia were not a representative sample of the English homeland, and this significantly affected their development. Thirdly, variations in behavior and beliefs are affected by "flow" or diffusion of traits from one region to another. Adoption of new plant varieties as well as more complex and subtle beliefs, move across populations through contacts among them.

Selection occurs in many ways. Boyd and Richerson (1985) suggest a number of these, including frequency effects—choosing to be altruistic because so many others seem to be doing it—and merit effects. Actors, they note, can choose to be altruistic because they can calculate and imagine the social benefits of their own sacrifices. I have suggested (Cohen 1981) normalizing effects such as gossip, accusations of wrongdoing, and other regulations that disfavor new variants. I also posit balanced selective mechanisms that allow for some acceptance of new behavioral and belief features, but within limits. Like the selection of sickling in biological reproduction, above and below such limits the new trait is disfavored. At the sociocultural level, there is always some room in a society's role set for dissent, and even acceptance of roles that contradict the dominant values. Finally, there are clear-cut forms of directional selection at the sociocultural level. The welfare state reforms of Scandinavia are a collective reaction to the inequalities and injustices of early capitalism. Over a number of years each new reform carried these societies a step further to a political culture that has turned the state into the manager of altruistic regulations. Each individual recognizes the obligation to give up income for utilitarian goals. The vast majority of the population supports the sacrifices that each individual and each family must make for societal welfare. There are also unintended costs. The resultant culture has shifted the locus of morality away from the person to the state, and is now fostering a syndrome of serious social and personal problems in these societies (Wolfe 1989). But the overall point is clear. There are at the sociocultural level selective factors that can be used to explain a counteregoistic altruism based on the fitness of the behaviors in terms of group selection and survival.

Such transmissions may resonate with and strengthen genetic codings, act independently of them, or stand in direct opposition. They evolve at enormously accelerated rates because they are based on brain-processed, rather than gene-processed information transfers. Where genes must await biological reproduction effects on population genetics, sociocultural and behavioral selection can change many times faster, based as they are on behavior and its diffusion rather than on biology. This means that hedonic reward-seeking human actors can evolve altruistic behavioral traits and themes in their cultures that may counteract self-seeking dominance striving—the natural genetic outcome of scarcity and individual needs. The novel idea here, seen most clearly by Boyd and Richerson (1985), is that even though group selection is an improbable explanation in terms of genetic fitness, it makes perfectly good and plausible sense in explaining why humans opt for and transmit patterns of behavior and belief in the realm of cultural adaptation.

### The Genetic Basis of Altruism Reinterpreted

Does this mean that as organisms we have evolved beyond the selfish gene because culture has taken over to ensure a better, more adaptive species through social learning and individual adaptation of the learning? In older nature/nurture terms one could say that I wish to score for nurture and do battle with the nonrandom inheritance of traits through genetic selection. Nothing could be further from my intention. That old battle, like so many in science, is dead—or it should be—because it set up spurious polarities between two theories, each with reliable and sensible claims on validity.

No, what I wish to look for is a set of genetically evolved features whose evolutionary potential makes probable the emergence of the "dynamic duo," both cultural and biological inheritance trajectories and the increase in fitness provided for by their interactions and independence. Here I would vote for a set of features adapted recently (Cohen 1981) from earlier work (Waddington 1960). These are restraint, learning from authority—therefore the capacity to take instruction—and a sense of right and wrong, or morality, which I see as evolving from the brain's capacity for abstraction (which has many other deep and important potentialities). To these suggestive beginnings I would add echo responses to distress signaling from recent work in psychology. Let me summarize these genetic codings briefly before going on to a new perspective on sociocultural syndromes, including altruism, that I now imagine to have evolved as a biological and sociocultural set of traits—and that are still evolving to enhance our fitness as a species.

### Restraint as Fitness

Dominance seeking without a complementary or dialectical counterforce is injurious to reproductive success. As noted above, dominance is an inevitable outcome of competition and scarcity. However, it must be reconciled with group life. Although we have evolved from a primate background shot through with dominance striving, it is at the same time tempered with restraint capabilities that are just as necessary to survival. Kaplan's (1976) work on rhesus macaque hostile encounters, and Kummer's (1971) provocative work on baboon courting behavior both support the conclusion that normal behavioral arenas of dominance striving (fighting and courting) have associated restraint features in the behavioral repertoires of competing males. These balancing features run counter to dominance hierarchy but enable group structure and constituent relations to survive. In a significant number of dominance fights Kaplan (1976) observed subdominants unite to protect one of their members, stimulating restraint by the dominant but no overall change in group structure. Kummer (1971) found that regardless of dominance, once a courtship relation had been established it stimulated restraint behavior by the noncourting male. Certainly it has been noticed for many years that peripherals in primate groups who restrain sexual drives, learning when, and when not, to advance behind the back of the dominant male toward the oestrus females, do better than the "hotheads." Restraint capacity controls dominance and reward seeking, allowing the animal to assess perceptual signals, process the information, and make a more advantageous response. Given the drive feature of dominance and gratification striving, restraint capacities—holding back on reward seeking to plan a strategy, learning how to avoid an enemy, or to outwit a rival—is a modifier that is associated with increased fitness. Dominance striving is best served, then, by a balanced selection for restraint, which in turn selects for more capable and efficient information processing, and patterned reactions to this information that allow for more adaptive responses—that is, for learning.

### Learning—from Authority

Having to constrain to achieve rewards within a group enables other forms of advances to be made in the direction of greater neural capacities. The greater the rewards and the fitness accorded to individual and group behavior, the greater the need for restraint and the greater the capacity for learning by information transfers, signals, and the passage of adaptive capacities in nongenetic forms of acquired—that is, learned—traits. To carry this down generations we must bond to authority figures, generally parents, and have a genetically evolved capacity to copy, or learn from them (Waddington 1960). In this sense, authority, and heeding authority models, aids fitness, if the information being learned contributes to increased reproductive success.

### Morality: The Transmission of Tradition

Learning capacity and tradition imply another biologically based trait system—morality or oughtness. The passing of information and instructions through learning and authority subsumes the inherent ability to label some variants right, others wrong. More broadly, and logically, long-term and stable tool traditions such as presapiens Mousterian, and the later and more various paleolithic industries associated with the rise of our own species, employed reinforcements to learning over several millenia of fairly stabilized transmissions of behavioral features through nongenetic means. That is to say, for cultural tradition to appear and obtain its dominant position in our adaptation as a species, there had to be ways to restrict behavioral variances in order to sustain the identifiable cultural patterns down the generations. The most efficient form of heritable transmission is through normalizing selection in which variants are disfavored and previously evolved patterns are favored in the learning process. Other explanations would logically involve copying, which produces more frequent variations, or each generation learning the tradition anew, which would produce even more variants. Logically then it is plausible that heritable transmission of tradition by learning requires acquiring a sense of "right" and "wrong" through instructions, followed by "right" and "wrong" behavioral responses for doing things "culturally." It follows that a capacity to evaluate one's own behavior and that of others *in moral terms* is a basic prerequisite for the working of the dual inheritance model—meaning our capacity to use both genes and culture as adaptive modes. I am postulating, therefore, that *morality should be seen as a cause, not a result, of culture.* Humankind the tool maker was above all an animal with a genetic capacity to label and teach and enforce a "sense" of right and wrong. The material remains survive and so we mistakenly give them causal priority. But somehow our ancestors made the jump to cultural life, tool making, burials, and the prohibition of incest behavior, among a myriad of transmissable regulations, by assessing some activities correct, right, acceptable, and some beyond a tolerated variance. Some things done, produced, or acted out were incorrect, wrong, and unacceptable. Consensus among group members about patterned behaviors increased the fitness of individuals who were able to attach normative significance to patterned transmissable behaviors. Incest behavior predates incest prohibitions in evolution. The prohibition turns the adaptive pattern into a cultural rule that reinforces and adds adaptive capacities to any genetic instructions that determine the behavior, without the prohibition. In effect, and of central importance to cultural evolution, moral assessments building on the enabling capacity of genetically determined dominance striving, restraint, and learning have combined to become the governing features of nongenetically transmitted information. Cultural transmission of information down the generations requires some kind of restriction or censor on variance away from selected adaptations. In this sense morality—the capacity to sense oughtness—is a prerequisite of cultural tradition.

### Criticism: The Fundamental Adaptation

And underlying this set of biological instructions is an even more generic one: that of *abstraction*, the capacity to perceive and remember similarities among differences, and differences across similarities, and then to recall these for comparison with other abstractions. This allows us to *assess*. Other animals do this as well. We do it in a quantum leap of expanded capacity that is the basis for our most exorbitantly human quality: that of creating brain images for comparisons of quantities, qualities, relations, and modalities—that is, of significance and explanation. Beyond this most general level, which also explains generalization, the perception of causality, and of metaphor—the bases of human understanding—is the notion of critical assessment. What we learn, and learn to expect, can be compared with what we experience, and the degree of similarity or difference can be assessed. We are thus programmed for appraisal of our culture as well as for learning, transmission, and conformity. When our learned patterns, moralized into rightness and wrongness, don't fit, we can compare expectations and imagine a better "fit" between behavior and goals. In this sense critical analysis, and examining our hedonic reward-seeking goals in relation to the constraints of sociocultural traditions (intergenerational transmission of learned behavior) is a major means for natural selection at the nongenetic level. We not only transmit adaptation behaviorally, but we can also select new or low-frequency variants and increase their frequency when they prove adaptive.

### Psychobiological Factors

The above features summarize some of the biologically based capacities not discussed in my original assumption of an hedonic actor constrained into adaptive behavior through the evolution of altruistic rules and moral teachings. There are, no doubt, many others. For example, research on prosocial behavior in psychology has produced promising results in the search for brain mechanisms that foster specifiable behavioral outcomes. This has led to theories and research on the opiad hypothesis (Panskepp 1986, 22–49) of social affect. This work correlates brain opiad systems with separation distress, echo response to distress signals, and the strengthening of social bonds. Proponents believe that this particular research strategy has already uncovered an important basis in genetically programmed brain organization and its development among maturing individuals for gregariousness, maternal behavior, dominance, sexual behavior, social displays, affective vocalizations, and social bonding. Ultimately, although still hypothetical, it is suggested that this thrust may lead researchers to posit organically influenced brain features that stimulate altruistic activity in the biological sense (ibid., 44). And there is more. Humans are unique in the amount of guilt they can bring to bear on their own reactions. Dogs have been observed to produce some of it, and chimpanzees show an ability to make reparations for wrongdoing. Nevertheless, humans show by far the greatest (biologically based?) capacity both for experiencing guilt and for bringing shame and blame on others (Zahn-Waxler 1986, 312). Clearly, this feature enables and supports the development of behaviorally transmittable moral teachings. There are, in other words, a number of biologically evolved features that together provide humans with a bundle of capacities for the selection and retention of the more complex form of altruism embodied in our cultural traditions.

The field is complex. Still, it is clear that genetic coding for brain-organized reactions is a necessary foundation for the varied architecture of altruism manifest in human sociocultural systems. Simply assuming an hedonic actor constrained by the adaptive features of evolved traditions of altruism overlooks the enabling role of genetic evolution. Although I would still opt for the primary or at least necessary causal status of cultural factors whose evolution has produced altruism as we know it, there is no doubt they interact with and build on biologically based features.

## THE EVOLUTION OF CIVIL SOCIETY

Having established the dual origins of our altruistic capacities as a species, let me now discuss how this feature helps produce what I call civil society. This is an emergent quality that selects for the rapid expansion of commonly held moral constraints. Kant's notion of universal moral imperatives was wrong for his times, right for a future that has now arrived. In effect an increasing number of societies are beginning to accept universally agreed-upon moral rulings applicable to all persons. Between 1928 and 1980 there have been well over one hundred declarations by international and regional organizations and unions of states concerning the rights of persons and collectivities. No other period in world history has witnessed such a flood of universally applicable and widely endorsed moral principles. Although this admittedly optimistic view can always be defeated by events, one of the major selective factors in this historic pulse of proclamations was the Holocaust of World War II, an event so powerful in its impact that it promulgated a shift in the way we as a species see our responsibilities to one another. In the rest of this essay I wish to expand on these ideas sufficiently to explain this rather turgid summary.

### Civil Society

The idea of civil society has been with us for a long time. Early Enlightenment writers used it to refer to humanity's gain under a social contract in which unrestrained egoism is restricted in accordance with the legitimate rights of others, guaranteed by an authoritative state (Locke 1946, 343). Others (e.g., Burke 1987, 237) suggested that religious teaching indicated civility to be part of God's will, although sacerdotal origins were just as often disputed (Rousseau 1946, 121–22; Hooker 1946, 333–37). For these early thinkers civil society meant the rules of a tranquil and ordered social life, government, and the functions performed by moral obligations in a society whose members respect, obey, and enforce virtue.

Later, civil society expanded to include society's nongovernmental realm. This view argues that without "political society" the private sector or civil society was one of unrestrained Hobbesian egoism pitting individuals against one another outside the restraining capacity of the state (Giddens 1971, 5) This approach (put forward most forcefully by Hegel) sees civil society as chaos requiring order, justice, and authority by the state to represent and enforce the moral consciousness of society as a whole (Kolakowski 1978, 1:94–96). Marx (1977) decried the separation of civil and political realms, calling for a "revolutionary" integration of state and society. Civil and political activity will eventually be unified within a new Socialist/postcapitalist human personality, making the restraining power of the state unnecessary. Evolution will then stop because of the triumph of true civility—the natural outcome of a just and classless social order (brought into being by the absolute power of revolutionary leaders).

In more recent times civic culture is more often associated with democratization. Using economic theory, Hayek (1973) argues that optimizing individuals are a constant selective pressure for increased democratization because this organizational context maximizes their personal degrees of freedom. Almond (1988) theorizes that human evolution involves an inevitable increase in liberal democracy, or what he calls the *civic culture*. Operationally, this means the selection and retention of more enlightened political forms—universal suffrage, representative government, political decisions made through rational and deliberative processes, and the protection of human rights. Theoretically, these optimistic outcomes will supplant more authoritarian forms. And worldwide trends in this direction, plus the failure of many overcentralized governments (Wunsch and Olowu 1990), have now revived interest in these earlier ideas.

Elsewhere (Cohen 1992), I have theorized that the capacity for assessment, for the evolution of increased force and scope of altruistic cultural demands, and a capacity for critical reaction to social and political life are embodied in a redefinition of civil society. This is a normative concept of individual and collective reactions and rule making that isolates processes by which populations come to demand greater democracy and rights protection. It includes within it both civil (i.e., nongovernmental social) life, and civility, or rules and behaviors toward other persons and groups that take their welfare into account as well as one's own. So far I have isolated three levels of interaction in which such rules and performances occur; these are (1) reactions by individuals and groups to rules and performances that create just and unjust outcomes, (2) reactions propagated by the culture to the public or even humanity's interest rather than one's own individual or parochial group membership(s), and (3) the degree of civility that can be and should be expected in everyday life. In this latter dimension the civil society concept refers to a culturally defined obligation to positively value and practice norms of sympathy and empathy for others, and to exhibit active or measurable concern for their welfare beyond the boundaries of ethnicity and kinship.

The first quality refers to humanity's capacity to critically assess fairness outcomes of both governmental and private performances. This provides a constant selective pressure from aggregated grievances for changes in the rules and their performances. It is a quality I have called "endless tears," which embodies the notion that governed populations ultimately select (morally significant) reforms through pressure and choice. The entire process is dependent upon the degree to which "rights talk" (Ackerman 1980) is allowed in a society. Critical assessment from pulpits, the arts, the press, social science, and autonomous organizations constantly attempt to aggregate individual unfairness reactions to initiate reform. The degrees of freedom (or democratization) allowed in the society then predicts to its capacity to marshal the critical capacity of individuals for adaptive purposes (Cohen 1992). The second aspect refers to the evolution of increased scale in the inclusiveness of the moral universe (see below), which extends moral injunctions to groups and individuals previously excluded. The third component refers to the cultural evolution of more, not less, altruistic beliefs, customs, and performances—that is, empathic, sympathetic, and gratuitous generosity or sacrifice. Together these features make up what I am calling the civil society, one in which altruistic actions can become incorporated into cultural regulations.

All of this is just a start. It is apparent in the above that I see civil society as a kind of "ideal type"—a teleological causality, in evolutionary terms, or a goal towards which humanity is learning to set its course, is struggling towards, selecting variants that further its force (intensity within individual character) and scope (degree to which it pervades numbers and kinds of institutions) in our cultures. It is being selected for, at the very least, because of its obvious merits and the frequency of its acceptance among more developed societies. Although the concept of civility needs more work, it is clear that similar ideas underlie many of humanity's most revered religious and political teachings (Aron 1980). In effect, it is a systematic attempt to find the best form of social life and the means to its achievement (Wolfe 1989). In evolutionary terms, because I prefer that paradigm, it is a target we can aim at intentionally, and in so doing obtain increased fitness for an uncertain future.

### Selective Factors

There is a vast array of factors that theoretically select for civil society. Generally, such selection involves some contribution or sacrifice of personal rewards for the benefits of a larger group. Unfortunately, this sociobiological criterion is somewhat specious at the sociocultural level since it is easy to rationalize personal benefits resulting from individual sacrifice for the larger group. This being so, let me point to a number of candidates for selective pressures, ending with the one most apposite to the focus of this volume.

First and foremost there is the rising concern around the world with public over private concerns. However it comes about, whatever are the local and the more general causes, the principle remains the same. As people become more convinced that their private fates are deeply and directly affected by publicly based activity, concern with public affairs increases. Sacrificing time and resources for more public, more collective good, always considered to be morally desirable, is becoming more customary. Even large business corporations are devoting resources to "community relations," corporate responsibilities, and business ethics. Reasons for such actions may be prudential rather than altruistic but the end result is a more civil society, one whose actors perform more altruistically. In the West an enormous increase in home ownership since World War II (30 percent in 1940, 66 percent in 1980) has turned people's attention to problems of property and investment and to the local governments whose policies and actions affect this enormous stake in personal wealth. Added to this are problems of education, crime, and, most recently, the environment—a problem that links local to national and global affairs, thereby imposing public concerns onto private welfare. In the rest of the world, access to scarce resources, massive public sector corruption, human rights, personal security and liberties known to be enjoyed elsewhere, the importance of cultural traditions challenged by modernism and the state, and a host of other factors have led to increased concern for, attempts to participate in, and efforts to obtain greater control over, the public life of the state. Because of its critical and moral basis this effort has in some instances led to religious fundamentalism, or radical political movements, ethnic conflict, civil wars, and so on. But it is also leading to a worldwide democracy movement that is pressing for wider participation in, and sacrifice for, social groups beyond kin and ethnicity in the economy and the polity. A very probable outcome is the strengthening of civility—cultural demands and regulations that call for increased fairness, less egoistic, less parochial, and more civic-minded performances.

Secondly, the end of Cold War tensions has eroded the backdrop of conflict influencing an inordinate amount of postwar public affairs. If the major powers are seeking a more civil way of solving differences, if time and effort spent on conflict is decreasing in the major arenas of national and international life, and if the means to increased development and human welfare do not in fact lie so clearly in conflict, then possibly we are on the verge of rejecting conflict as a viable or even fruitful way to solve problems. There are indications from all round the world that conflict-laden issues and relations are calming down, and that peaceful, more just, more civil solutions are not impossible. A cultural theme that has worldwide appeal, one of peaceful and hopefully increasingly fair resolutions of conflict, is quite measurably blanketing the world. Possibly it is just a momentary pause resulting from a lack of successful outcomes in the last few decades. Viet Nam and Afghanistan come to mind, but interethnic conflicts in the Third World, and both leftist and rightist extremism almost everywhere, illustrate the point just as well. The Near East may be an exception or a means by which the world community unites to try to suppress older-style conflicts. The Hegelian-Marxian notion that progress can result only from struggle may be giving way to a more Kropotkinlike vision. That human advance is dependent on peaceful cooperation, a sense of common problems and shared destiny, along with a sense that local problems should be handled locally. Whatever it is, or why, there is very little doubt in my mind that it is upon us—a new and infectious spirit of peace, strengthening the hands of those who seek more civil ways of handling conflict, both within and between societies. Perchance it is ephemeral. On the other hand, it is a trait or syndrome whose time of selection for world and local conflict resolution has arrived—possibly because older, more conflict-laden solutions have failed. Whether of long or short duration, it seems clear that while it is upon us, this new mood of *Pax humana* will help us to overcome some terrifying or just irritating conflicts and to go forward in our capacity to invent lasting techniques for doing so. Hopefully, this means developing cultural traditions and political techniques for greater degrees of conflict resolution and therefore for enhanced civility. In evolution nothing is certain. Actual, rather than hoped-for, directions are apparent only after the fact—and as with all life forms, extinction is always an option.

Thirdly, and hearkening back to my previous work (Cohen 1978), there are worldwide indications for an increase in nuclearization of family life. As I pointed out in that paper, sociocultural "scolding," as Campbell (1978) described it, has a much greater chance of becoming an actual feature of people's internalized dispositions and behavior when families are nuclear and role models both impart and reward the development of affect in human relationships. In effect this means that the change from shame to guilt, to having civility and its altruistic components as part of individual character structure rather than cultural regulation, is a function of the nuclearization process. And within that process the internalization occurs, I suggest, most fulsomely under conditions of long-term stable parent-child relations. Affectivity is a major component determining our capacity for empathy and sympathy as an important part of the maturation process. In many societies mothers reject their children as part of the weaning process. In large extended families with high turnover of personnel, emotional investment in persons is destructive for the smooth operations of households

(Cohen 1971). In more general terms, the affective aspects of adult personality can be inhibited by cultural regulations that call for early childhood rejection, by high divorce rates (over 50 percent of all marriages end in breakups), and by large extended family settings where children are taught to respond unemotionally to rules governing roles rather than developing the capacity to invest emotionally in interpersonal relations (Cohen 1978). Altruism in cultural traditions without affective depth in individuals produces an incapacity to genuinely internalize such teachings (ibid.). This in turn produces a tension in which altruistic acts are more likely to be used for self-gratification, competition, and increased personal status. However, the increase in family nuclearization, if it is paired with low divorce rates (under 50 percent of unions end in divorce) and family stability during children's younger years, is theoretically associated with increased development of affectivity, and an increased capacity to internalize altruistic demands and behave more civilly (ibid.). This argument requires more space than I am able to devote to it here, and it should now be integrated into a dual inheritance model that incorporates biologically stimulated behaviors such as echo responses. In any event, this line of theorizing leads plausibly to the conclusion that evolutionary trends among sociocultural patterns spreading across many societies are moving in the direction of greater psychosocial expressions and performances of civility and its altruistic components.

## FROM TRIBALISM TO UNIVERSALISM: ALTRUISM AS THE END OF MORAL BOUNDARY

The most powerful selective factor in bringing about a civil society is that of increased scale in the scope of the moral universe. The development and ideological emergence of civil society is constrained by cultural definitions of membership. Most often these are in ethnic terms—that is, a process of we/they dichotomizations triggered by multiple markers that define common memberships (Cohen 1978a). These markers—religion, physical appearance, language, citizenship, region of birth, common customs, and so on— define ethnic boundaries. They also vary enormously in scale. For example, as an empirically valid cultural identity "Christendom" cross-cuts nationalities, languages, and other localized markers of common descent. Thus triggering variables are not always in exact congruence. One's religion may incorporate a number of group memberships, one's region of birth another set, and one's citizenship still another. This lack of necessary congruence among identities makes ethnicity into a process as much as an entity. Different determinants, especially situations, conflicts, ambitious leaders looking for followers, and other factors constantly trigger our loyalties to separate groupings defined by a distinguishing identity marker. I may be loyal or concerned as a citizen in one situation, and react against other citizens as a member of a region or town in other situations. Thus identities are multiple and varying in their scope of inclusion. The we of me is an accordianlike set of features.

Secondly, ethnic boundaries often define the applicable loci of moral injunction. Outside an ethnically defined moral universe the individual finds himself and herself in the realm of potential enemies. But the moral universe refers to two levels of inclusiveness. First there is the level of belief and of moral teaching, second the level of actual practice—the group one feels closest to in terms of a shared moral tradition. In many cultures there are often fellow creatures outside the group to whom moral rules apply either in belief terms or practice, or both. For most of human social evolution these moral boundaries are delimited primarily by ethnicity. But there are always penumbral arenas at the edges of the moral universe where interacting persons and groups are partly in, partly outside the boundaries. Thus, among the Orakaiva of New Guinea (Williams 1936) intervillage warfare was endemic. The people also practiced strict village exogamy. Visiting one's in-laws, or even arranging a marriage, or a wedding, could easily end or even begin with violence. Under such circumstances women became ambassadors back to their home territories, and marriage ceremonies often involved mock battles in which the bride was ritually captured. On the other side of the world among the Bura of Nigeria, where I have done field work, and where intervillage hostility is still remembered, intervillage marriages were often planned as a kind of fake kidnapping (some were real). The bride was ritually captured amid a show of violence to sever her forcibly from her kin while arranging to compensate her group for the loss in order to restore peace. In both places the boundary of the moral universe is the village community itself. But the surrounding villages may be dealt with and some mutual agreements reached to alleviate their status as outsiders, enemies, people beyond the sphere of mutual trust to whom moral rules do not apply. The same thing occurs for institutions of blood brotherhood, in which a stranger, for reasons of trade or some other form of alliance, is turned into kin in order to travel safely across the boundaries of the moral universe.

One more point is important. In a few instances, the traditions of moral injunctions have universalistic qualities so that the moral universe, the "we" to whom moral rules apply, is all of humanity, or all living things, or even all entities since spiritual existence may be extended to include beings and objects identified by traditions and personal experience. But as already noted, this is not always congruent with other we/they dichotomizations. Thus Israelis and Palestinians each practice universalistic religions that grant moral rights to all humans, but many in each ethnic group see the other as outsider, beyond the practical and realistic boundaries of each other's moral universe. (See the chapter by Ian Vine in this volume.)

In Europe, as Marx (1977) pointed out, the Jew has always been the stranger in our midst, inside economy and society, outside religion—that is to say outside the most profound symbolic expression of European morality. The same thesis was put forward more recently by the anthropologist Sir Edmund Leach (1984) in his attempt to explain the work of Jewish anthropologists in Britain. He notes how these men tried desperately, and pathetically he claims, to become part of the non-Jewish intellectual establishment. And this he feels, with Marx (ibid.), is part of the timeless Jewish dilemma, to ask for full membership in the sociocultural and political community of Christendom, and yet also to demand the right to remain outside its buttressing beliefs, and therefore its version of, and regulatory teachings about, morality and legitimacy. What both these authors miss is the fundamental claim of catholicity in Christendom's vision of the moral universe and the enormous overlap in the content of both religions' moral regulations. More importantly for the present discussion, both Christianity and Judaism profess species-wide applicability and membership in their conception of the God-given bounds of the moral universe. The Judeo-Christian tradition is clearly one in which morality ordained by a universal God applies to humanity as a whole, not only to coreligionists. In practice of course each religious community has a more limited scale of inclusiveness, involving primarily those others with whom, historically, the force of the moral life is more intensely shared. Those outside these groups are less deserving, less likely to be included in the moral universe. In this sense each community challenges the universality of the other's moral principles. In the rest of the world similar problems abound. The place of the Afro-American in U.S. culture, the struggle for human rights in multiethnic societies of Africa—indeed wherever pluralism exists, or should exist, the moral universe as idealized versus its practice is in conflict and tension. Marx (ibid.) suggested that such differentiation—he used the Jew as an appropriate example—could never succeed in producing a "species-being," one concerned with, and morally involved in, all humanity. Only a common ideology, communism, and the overthrow of older class differences could in his view produce an appropriate support for a species-wide moral universe that was practicable as well as ideal.

But in fact we are, all of us, aware of the universality intrinsically woven into our moral teachings. A few, because of factors of rearing, of communal life, and of role models in school, in church, and in peer groups, are fortunate or unfortunate enough to have internalized these ideal scoldings as a determinant characterological trait. This quality of personality, of integrity (i.e., integration of ideal and real), makes such individuals difficult to live with, moral irritants in a world of compromise. But by the same token, activating the ideal keeps it alive. When a culture possesses a universally applicable concept of the moral universe that *ought* to be applied universally, but that is limited in practice, then the very existence of such teaching guarantees variance in practice. No matter how few, there are bound to be those who have internalized the larger-scaled, more inclusive bonds of the moral universe into fully incorporated personal norms. This was the meaning and the function of the rescuing behavior of Jews during the Holocaust. Caught in a conflict between the abrogation of moral rules for the sake of safety and conformity and compliance with the ideals internalized into their characters, a few non-Jews could not act against their own character and understanding. For them rescue behavior was the only possible response to a society acting contrary to its own most hallowed virtues.

There is clearly more to it than that. In terms of my own theoretical argument, and those of other chapters in this volume, these people were the products of upbringings that produced the altruistic or civil response, one that made them sympathetic and empathic with the sufferers. Their generosity and possible sacrifice of personal safety for Jewish victims was, however, in my view, the activation of critical assessments (or "extensivity") that defined a moral universe in which Jews were included, even though the theme of the day was to ratify and legitimize Leach's position, that Jews are self-selected for exclusion by the heritable transmission of their own outsider culture. Once the definition of universal moral universe is made, cognitively, then affect responses that determine sympathy and empathy intensify the civility/altruism, making the saving behavior logical, albeit in no way less heroic.

## CONCLUSION

As we move forward in a direction (among many possible out-comes) toward a world in which the moral universe is no longer defined by our particular subspecies memberships, we also move towards the achievement of what I call the "civil society" (Cohen 1992). In this essay I have tried to show how our human altruism is involved in that possible outcome, how we are evolving a cultural conception of a civil society, and how a number of factors are operating to select for such an outcome. The rescuing behavior of non-Jews towards Jews was a milestone, as in even more intense ways was the Holocaust itself, in the evolution of universally applicable moral rules. Kant's categorical imperatives have come of age. Now to survive we must expand our moral universe to include humanity as a whole. And the process seems to be underway.

The meaning and the importance of the Holocaust is both singular and selective for our evolutionary next steps. It is singular in that its use of a partial and ethnicized moral universe led to the abrogation of all claims of moral legitimacy. Using insider/outsider distinctions leaves a social space for victimization that in the modern world can mean horror on a massive and unjust scale. On a more general evolutionary level it means we have been challenged to make sure that all claims to moral legitimacy are, and must be, based on the species-wide relevance and practice of our moral rules. There is no room left for parochialism in the moral universes of our many cultures. And this is now a rising pressure selecting among possibilities for our future. As with almost everything else, something good came out of something awesomely evil.

## REFERENCES

Ackerman, B. 1980. *Social Justice in the Liberal State.* New Haven: Yale University Press.

Almond, G. A. 1988. The Intellectual History of the Civic Culture Concept. In L. J. Cantori and A. H. Zeigler, Jr. (eds.), *Politics in the Post-Behavioral Era.* Boulder, Co.: Reiner.

Aron, R. 1980. *War and the Industrial Society.* Westport, Conn.: Greenwood.

Barash, D. P. 1982. *Sociobiology and Behavior.* New York: Elsevier.

Boyd, R., and P. J. Richerson, 1985. *Culture and the Evolutionary Process.* Chicago: University of Chicago Press.

Burke, E. 1987. Reflections on the Revolution in France. In J. Waldron (ed.), *"Nonsense upon Stilts": Bentham, Burke, and Marx on the Rights of Man.* London: Methuen.

Campbell, D. T. 1965. Variation and Selective Retention in Sociocultural Evolution. In H. R. Barringer, G. I. Blanksten, and R. W. Mack (eds.), *Social Changes in Developing Areas.* Cambridge: Schenkman.

―――― 1978. On the Genetics of Altruism and Counterhedonic Components in Human Culture. In L. Wispé (ed.), *Altruism, Helping, and Sympathy.* Pp.39–57. New York: Academic.

Cohen. R. 1971. *Dominance and Defiance.* Washington, D.C.: American Anthropological Association.

―――― 1978. Altruism: Human, Culture or What? In L. Wispé (ed.), *Altruism, Helping, and Sympathy.* Pp. 79–98. New York: Academic.

―――― 1978a. Ethnicity. *Annual Review of Anthropology* 7: 379–404. Palo Alto, Cal.: Annual Reviews.

―――― 1981. Evolutionary Epistemology and Human Values. *Current Anthropology* 22 (3): 201–18.

―――― 1992. Endless Tears: An Introduction. In R. Cohen, G. Hyden, and W. Nagan (eds.), *Human Rights and Governance in Africa.* Gainesville: University of Florida Press.

Freuchen, D. 1961. *The Book of the Eskimo.* New York: World Publishing.

Geertz, C. 1968. *Islam Observed.* New Haven: Yale University Press.

Giddens, A. 1971. *Capitalism and Modern Social Theory.* Cambridge: Cambridge University Press.

Hayek, F. A. 1973. *Law, Legislation, and Liberty.* Vol. 1, *Rules and Order.* Chicago: University of Chicago Press.

Hooker, R. 1946. Laws of Ecclesiastical Polity. In M. Curtis (ed.), *The Great Political Theories.* Pp 331–37. New York: Avon.

Kaplan, J. 1976. Patterns of Interference and the Control of Aggression in a Group of Free-Ranging Rhesus Monkeys. Ph.D Dissertation (Anthropology), Northwestern University.

Kolakowski, L. 1978. *Main Currents of Marxism.* Vol. 1, *The Founders.* Oxford: Oxford University Press.

Kummer, H. 1971. *Primate Societies.* Chicago: Aldine Atherton.

Leach, E. R. 1984. Glimpses of the Unmentionable in the History of British Social Anthropology. *Annual Review of Anthropology* 13:1–23.

Locke, J. 1946. The Second Treatise of Civil Government. In M. Curtis (ed.), *The Great Political Theories*. Pp. 337–54. New York: Avon.

Margolis, H. 1984. *Selfishness, Altruism, and Rationality*. Chicago: University of Chicago Press.

Marx, K. 1977. On the Jewish Question. In D. McLellan (ed.), *Karl Marx: Selected Writings*. Oxford: Oxford University Press.

Panskepp, J. 1986. The Psychobiology of Prosocial Behavior. In C. Zahn-Waxler, E. M. Cummings, and R. Iannotti (eds.), *Altruism and Aggression: Biological and Social Origins*. Pp. 19–49. Cambridge: Cambridge University Press.

Rousseau, J. J. 1946. Excerpts. In M. Laski (ed.), *Political Thought From Bentham to Locke*. Oxford: Clarendon.

Trivers, R. 1971. The Evolution of Reciprocal Altruism. *Quarterly Review of Biology* 46:35–57.

Waddington, C. H. 1960. *The Ethical Animal*. London: Allen and Unwin.

Waldron, J. 1987. *"Nonsense upon Stilts": Bentham, Burke, and Marx on the Rights of Man*. London: Methuen.

Williams, F. E. 1936. *Papuans of the Trans-Fly*. Oxford: Clarendon.

Wilson, E. O. 1975. *Sociobiology: The New Synthesis*. Cambridge: Harvard University Press.

Wolfe, A. 1989. *Whose Keeper?* Berkeley: University of California Press.

Wunsch, J. S., and D. Olowu. 1990. *The Failure of the Centralized State: Institutions and Self-Government in Africa*. Boulder, Co.: Westview.

Zahn-Waxler, C. 1986. Conclusions. In C. Zahn-Waxler, E. M. Cummings, and R. Iannotti (eds.), *Altruism and Aggression: Biological and Social Origins*. Pp. 303–24. Cambridge: Cambridge University Press.

# PART FOUR

# THE DEVELOPMENT AND ENACTMENT OF ALTRUISM

*Edited by Dennis L. Krebs and M. Zuzanna Smolenska*

# INTRODUCTION

*Dennis L. Krebs and M. Zuzanna Smolenska*

As the title suggests, the chapters in this section concern the growth of altruism over the life span and the internal and external factors that mediate altruistic behavior. In chapter 6, Krebs and Van Hesteren advance a "developmental-interactional" approach to altruistic personality that, they claim, counteracts the problems of past approaches. Krebs and Van Hesteren maintain that the patterns of altruistic behavior people display stem from and are shaped by the stages of development they have achieved, and that the forms of prosocial behavior that stem from higher stage structures are more altruistic than the forms that stem from lower stage structures. They suggest that the stages of development described by theorists such as Maslow, Piaget, Loevinger, Kegan, Selman, Hoffman, Haan, Kohlberg, Gilligan, and Eisenberg correspond to one another along basic structural dimensions, and that each set of corresponding stage structures exerts a press toward a different type of altruism. The writers outline eight ideal types of altruism derived from the defining characteristics of corresponding stages of development, which they call *undifferentiated responsiveness* (Stage 0), *egocentric accommodation* (Stage 1), *instrumental cooperation* (Stage 2), *mutual* (Stage 3), *conscientious* (Stage 4), *autonomous* (Stage 5), *integrated* (Stage 6), and *universal love* ("stage 7").

The developmental-interactional approach to altruism advanced by Krebs and Van Hesteren raises several challenging questions. First, how do different cognitively based stage structures give rise to different types of altruistic behavior; what internal processes mediate the link between thought and action? Second, in what sense—on what basis—can the forms of prosocial behavior that stem from relatively high stages be said to be more altruistic than the forms that stem from lower stages? Third, to what extent do the stages of development people are "in" correspond to one another, and, thus, to what extent do individuals display one form of altruism?

In answer to the first question, Krebs and Van Hesteren identify the process of perspective taking, the motivational state of empathy, and the need to behave in ways consistent with one's self-concept and ideal self as central in the link between structures of knowing and forms of altruistic behavior. In response to the second question, Krebs and Van Hesteren advance six main reasons why the forms of prosocial behavior that stem from relatively high stages are more altruistic than the forms that stem from lower stages, namely, because they give rise to an increasingly sensitive understanding of others' needs, because they mediate increasingly precise distinctions between the needs of others and one's own needs, because they encompass an increasingly broad range of recipients (the Oliners' "extensivity"), because they are increasingly effective at enhancing the welfare of others, because they are increasingly precisely directed toward deserving recipients, and because they mediate an increasingly focused acceptance of responsibility.

Finally—and this represents the interactional aspect of the model—Krebs and Van Hesteren depart from highly constructivistic stage theories and assume (a) that individuals retain old stage structures after they acquire new ones, (b) that individuals may acquire different modal stages in different domains of development, and (c) that the forms of altruism individuals display are a product of the interaction between the stage structures they have acquired and the demands of the situations they face. Although stages may tend to converge structurally, and although individuals may tend to display patterns of altruism that stem from their modal stages, the model advanced by Krebs and Van Hesteren allows for considerable inconsistency across situations.

Building on the developmental (but not the interactional) model advanced by Krebs and Van Hesteren, Van Hesteren advances a bold assertion in chapter 7, namely that "it is not unreasonable to assume that some individuals reach the final stages of development across all domains," and that the defining feature of the personalities of such people is their advanced capacity for altruism. According to Van Hesteren, individuals who have achieved the apogee of altruism have reached the post–formal operational stage of cognitive development and the final stages in the development of perspective taking, empathy, care, justice, and, in general, self, or ego. Van Hesteren identifies Albert Schweitzer and Mother Teresa as individuals who have achieved this developmental acquisition. Van Hesteren invokes Maslow's portrait of the self-actualizing personality as the best sketch of his ideally altruistic type.

There are four main reasons why Van Hesteren's assertion is bold. First, it implies that domains of development may be highly integrated in some individuals at the highest levels. Second, related to the first point, it implies that the tension between care and justice noted by theorists such as Gilligan and Blum may be resolved at the highest stages. Third, in contrast with the interactional assumption of the model advanced by Krebs and Van Hesteren, it implies that altruistic behavior is highly consistent within individuals who have reached the final stages of development. And finally, it implies that *the* defining characteristic of advanced development is altruism.

In support of the first assumption, Van Hesteren argues that one of the basic functions of ego development is to integrate personality; indeed, Loevinger refers to her last stage of ego development as the stage of integration. Thus, almost by definition, individuals who have reached advanced stages of ego development also will have achieved advanced stages of development in other domains.

In support of the idea that considerations of care and justice are integrated at the highest stages, Van Hesteren appeals to evidence that post–formal operational thinking is equipped to coordinate the "left hemisphere" type of propositional logic involved in justice reasoning and the "right hemisphere" type of contextualized feelings involved in considerations of care. He cites Kohlberg and Power in support of the notion that care and justice are integrated at the "Stage 7" "ethic of responsible universal love, service, or sacrifice," or *agape*. However, as indicated by other theorists cited by Van Hesteren, the relationship between care and justice is far from resolved.

The assumption that altruistic behavior is consistent across situations at the highest stages stems from the model advanced by Van Hesteren of the internal dynamics mediating between forms of development and altruistic behavior. This model is based on the assumption that the driving force behind both "vertical" development and "horizontal" consistency in behavior is the need to uphold the values in one's ideal self and to be true to one's self (to behave in accordance with one's self-schema). Van Hesteren argues that altruism is an integral aspect of the identities of self-actualizing people, and thus that such people strive to behave altruistically. It is not entirely clear how the value of altruism achieves such regnancy in the self-actualized, but it seems to stem from ego development, advanced perspective-taking abilities, and the moral ideals of care and justice.

The heart of Van Hesteren's chapter is devoted to an explication of the dynamics mediating between internal cognitive and affective processes and altruistic behaviors in the altruistic personality. To this end, Van Hesteren draws from cognitive-developmental theory, humanistic writings, personality theory, information-processing models, social cognition, and research on the relationship between attitudes and behavior. On the affective side, Van Hesteren suggests that those who have reached the apogee of altruism are acutely and broadly empathic. Their advanced perspective-taking abilities enable them to understand clearly and exactly the needs of others and to adopt a broadly based social perspective. Drawing from Hoffman, Van Hesteren suggests that empathic affective charges may become associated with high-level principles of caring and justice, and such charges may be released in empathy-evoking situations, increasing the probability that individuals will behave in accordance with their moral principles.

More cognitive-developmentally, Van Hesteren cites Kohlberg in support of the idea that there is a monotonic increase in sense of responsibility with stage of moral development, and he quotes Blasi to the effect that this sense of responsibility stems from the need to be consistent with one's self, and that it mediates moral behavior. Hoffman also identifies a broadly based sense of responsibility for the "general plight" of the disadvantaged and an accompanying sense of existential guilt as inducements to altruism. (Montada supplies empirical support for the relationship between existential guilt and prosocial commitment in chapter 10.)

Finally, from a social cognitive perspective, Van Hesteren argues that exemplars of altruism possess an acute sense of self-awareness that reminds them of their internal standards and motivates them to behave in accord with them. In such people, altruistic constructs are readily accessible, and such people, in effect, maintain a "watching brief" for situations involving altruism. It is for reasons

such as these that such people tend to behave consistently altruistically across situations.

One of the main themes of this volume, woven through this section
and others, is that individuals with an extensive identification with
and sense of connectedness to others tend to behave more altruistically than individuals with more limited identities. In chapter
8, Maria Jarymowicz establishes that there is more to altruism
than integration between self and other; inasmuch as altruism
involves attending to the unique or distinct needs and qualities of
others, it may be confounded by an absence of differentiation between self and other. Jarymowicz argues that self-other distinctiveness is necessary for "exocentric" altruism—altruism centered
on the other, rather than on oneself—as opposed to "endocentric"
altruism stemming from a focus on one's own norms and standards.
Although individuals who have not adequately differentiated themselves from others might end up behaving altruistically to those
who are similar to them, their altruistic overtures are apt to be
inappropriate when directed toward those who are dissimilar.
Lack of self-distinctiveness induces projection of one's own perspective and needs on others, rather than a sense of respect for
others on their own terms.

Maria Jarymowicz summarizes the results of several empirical
studies that explore the effects of self-distinctiveness. She suggests
that people who have not adequately differentiated themselves
from others experience identity problems, and shows that identity
problems create a self-focus and "egocentricizing tension" inconsistent with exocentric altruism. People with identity problems
display a need to differentiate themselves from in-group members, suggesting that me-we differentiation is more important for
identity formation than me-they differentiation. And low self-
distinctiveness is associated with imbalances in interpersonal
control.

Jarymowicz also explores the implications of an absence of me-
we distinctiveness, showing that individuals with low me-we distinctiveness feel more negative than individuals with high me-we
self-distinctiveness toward individuals who are dissimilar to them,
and that they are more prone to discriminate against members of
out-groups. Apparently, a sense of distinctiveness between oneself
and one's reference group is necessary to take the perspective of

people outside one's reference group, and the absence of this differentiation leads to an exclusionary tendency to treat out-group members with prejudice and hostility.

In chapter 9, Smolenska and Reykowski outline a model of altruistic motivation and the connection between cognitive processes and altruistic behavior. The first step toward altruism involves the recognition that another person is in need. Different people respond to such information in different ways. For some it is simply factual. For others it is upsetting, but it does not impel them to action. For others, it leads them to form a mental representation of a solution to the problem. But even this, argue Smolenska and Reykowski, is not enough to guarantee helping. In order for a "goal image" to evoke action, it must be charged with affect, and such affective charges define the motives of those who behave altruistically.

With this model in mind, Smolenska and Reykowski analyze the motives of individuals who rescued Jews during the Nazi occupation of Europe. Smolenska and Reykowski classify the motives of rescuers in three main categories: allocentric, normocentric, and axiological. Allocentric motives tend to be evoked by direct contact with a person in need. The focus of the helper's attention is on the cognitive and affective state of the victim. Normocentric motives stem from the activation of norms relevant to helping. Normocentric helping often occurs in groups and is facilitated by support from others. Norms may differ in the degree of internalization, ranging from those that are tied closely to the rules and roles of reference groups, through those that stem from a commitment to socializing institutions, to those that stem from the helper's self-concept and sense of identity. Axiological motives are instigated by violations of moral principles relating to care and justice. Axiological helping tends to be impersonal; it is often directed toward groups.

In common with Jarymowicz and Krebs and Van Hesteren, Smolenska and Reykowski distinguish among types of altruism. It is interesting to note the similarities and differences among the types of altruism derived by the different writers on the basis of their own data and theoretical orientations. Smolenska and Reykowski's allocentric motives correspond quite closely to Jarymowicz's exocentric type of altruism; and Smolenska and Reykowski's normocentric (and perhaps axiological) motives correspond to Jarymowicz's endocentric altruism. Krebs and Van Hesteren's "Stage 3" mutual and "Stage 4" conscientious altruism correspond to Smolenska and Reykowski's normocentric types, and Krebs and Van Hesteren's "Stage 5" autonomous and "Stage 6" integrated altruism correspond to the axiological type.

These similarities notwithstanding, there are significant differences among the schemes. First, the Polish psychologists view each type of motive as developmentally equivalent and equal in altruism, whereas Krebs and Van Hesteren assert that the higher-stage forms are more altruistic than the lower-stage forms on several criteria. Second, in defining types of altruism on the basis of transformations in cognitive structure, Krebs and Van Hesteren make distinctions within types not made by the Polish theorists. For example, Krebs and Van Hesteren distinguish among types of empathy-based allocentric and exocentric motives on the basis of the stages of perspective taking that structure them, and they distinguish between types of normocentric and axiological motives in terms of the degree of internalization and universality of norms and principles.

A final difference lies in the extent to which each theorist defines types of people in terms of type of motive. Smolenska and Reykowski assume that all motives may coexist in the same person. Jarymowicz seems to assume more that different individuals are differentially prone to exocentric and endocentric forms of altruism on the basis of their degree of self-distinctiveness. Krebs and Van Hesteren adopt an additive-inclusive model that implies that individuals who have reached high stages of development may display all forms of altruism, but individuals fixated at lower stages will not have the higher forms available to them. Van Hesteren implies that individuals who have reached the highest stages of development will consistently display the highest forms of altruism.

In chapter 10, Leo Montada reports the results of two empirical studies designed to predict prosocial commitment, in the first case to three groups of disadvantaged people and in the second to mothers from their daughters. Montada finds that affective variables such as sympathy, moral outrage, and existential guilt were the best predictors of intentions to help the disadvantaged. Although sympathy predicted prosocial commitment quite well in itself, its effect was moderated significantly when combined with moral outrage and existential guilt. One may feel sorry for the unfortunate, but unless one feels that they do not deserve their fate and that they are unable to help themselves, one may not feel inclined to help them. Unlike sympathy, moral outrage and existential guilt are associated with moral cognitions—giving rise to normocentric or axiological motives, in Smolenska and Reykowski's terminology. These moral emotions are associated with and housed in cognitions such as the perception of injustice to the disadvantaged, a sense of discrepancy between one's own privileged position and the position of the disadvantaged, and endorsement of the principle of need rather than the principle of equity. Individuals who feel moral outrage do not feel they are personally responsible for improving the plight of the disadvantaged, whereas those who feel existential guilt do.

When you change the social context and role relationships between individuals, the dynamics of prosocial behavior undergo a dramatic change. In the second study, Montada reports the results of a study on the prosocial commitment of middle-age daughters for their elderly mothers. Montada found that the factors that predicted prosocial commitment to the disadvantaged did not predict prosocial commitment to mothers. Although justice-related considerations such as the legitimacy of the mothers' needs and the daughters' sense of obligation affected the daughters' *intentions* to help, these factors failed to predict actual helping behavior. The best predictors of actual helping were role-related, normative factors such as the daughter's customary behavior toward her mother, the opportunity to help, the daughters' general attitudes toward supporting mothers, and the daughters' general willingness to accept responsibility. On the more affective side, as we would expect, daughters who were involved in mutually caring relationships with their mothers were more supportive than those who were not.

Montada's findings are consistent with the interactional aspect of the model advanced by Krebs and Van Hesteren and the motivational distinctions made by Smolenska and Reykowski—people display different kinds of altruism in different situations. When recipients of altruism are connected to their benefactors in role relationships, "normocentric" motives come into play, but when the needy are impersonal members of socially disadvantaged categories, "axiological" motives become more relevant.

Appropriately, the final chapter in this section, chapter 11, deals with altruism in the elderly. There is a pervasive tendency to view the elderly as dependent and in need of help; however, as implied by both developmental and evolutionary models of altruism, there is good reason to expect the capacity for altruism to advance with age. Elizabeth Midlarsky reports the results of four studies that demonstrate that the elderly are more prone to altruism than most people assume. In the first study, Midlarsky reports an increase with age in the number of people who stopped in a shopping mall to donate to a fund for infants with birth defects. In the second study, Midlarsky reports that individuals aged sixty-five to seventy-five were more likely to volunteer for a first-aid course than younger adults, as long as the fee was not too high. When asked why they volunteered, the elderly gave more altruistic reasons than the younger volunteers, such as those based on the desire to be an effective helper. In an interesting offshoot of this study, Midlarsky exposed groups of trained and untrained subjects to a staged emergency. Although the younger subjects were more prone than the older subjects to intervene, the older subjects who had first-aid training were more likely to help than those who did not, and of all helpers, they were the most effective.

In the third study, Midlarsky asked a sample of elderly people, aged sixty-two to one hundred years, to report on their attitudes toward altruism and their history of altruistic behavior. Two-thirds of the sample reported providing considerable help to others, and although 39 percent said their level of helping had declined with age, 43 percent said they had maintained it at a relatively constant level, and 18 percent said their level of helping had increased over the years. The elderly reported a rich array of helping behaviors directed toward a variety of recipients. When asked why they helped, some cited external rewards, but most attributed their helping to intrinsic factors.

In the final study reported in the chapter, Midlarsky describes sending a sample of elderly people a personalized brochure outlining opportunities for volunteer work appropriate for them. She found that this intervention increased the level of self-esteem in the recipients. Midlarsky concludes that the elderly are well equipped to provide many kinds of effective help in our social system; they are a fertile but relatively untapped resource. Promoting opportunities for helping in the elderly is a worthy enterprise: the elderly have a lot to offer, and helping others makes them feel good about themselves.

# 6

# THE DEVELOPMENT OF ALTRUISTIC PERSONALITY

*Dennis L. Krebs and Frank Van Hesteren*

Social scientists from several theoretical orientations have adduced evidence that some individuals possess an "altruistic personality"—a pervasive disposition to help others ("alters"), more or less as an end in itself. We will open this chapter with a critique of these approaches, then outline a model we feel counteracts their limitations. We will propose that individuals normally acquire the capacity to perform increasingly adequate types of altruism as they develop, and that individual differences in altruism stem from the interaction between the stage structures individuals have acquired and the opportunities and demands of the social contexts they create and encounter. In contrast to approaches that assume that the amount of altruism in an individual is a function of the frequency of helping behaviors he or she displays, we will argue that there are different types of altruistic personality. Everybody possesses the capacity to engage in some forms of altruism, but individuals who have acquired the competencies intrinsic to advanced stages of development possess the potential to perform a broader array of more altruistic acts than individuals who have not acquired these competencies.

## THE BEHAVIORAL CONSISTENCY APPROACH

The most prevalent psychological approach to altruistic personality is based on the assumption that individuals who consistently display a relatively high incidence of prosocial behavior across different situations possess an internal personality trait of altruism. A major proponent of this approach, Rushton (1982), argues that because many studies have found significant positive correlations between two or more "behavioral indicies of altruism," such as donating to charity and picking up "accidentally" spilled index cards, we should conclude that "some people are more consistently altruistic than others" (432), and therefore that they possess an "altruistic personality."

As pointed out by Krebs (1982) and Krebs and Miller (1985), however, evidence of cross-situational consistency in prosocial behavior does not constitute sufficient evidence of altruism. There are four basic problems with the behavioral consistency approach, two conceptual and two methodological. The conceptual problems stem from the tendency of behaviorally oriented researchers to define altruism phenotypically, in terms of its external form or consequences (benefit to another), rather than in terms of its underlying motives, goals, and purposes. The assumption that behaviors that have the consequence of helping others stem from altruistic motives is gratuitous. Even if, with behaviorally oriented theorists, one is willing to assume that a *behavior* may be characterized as altruistic by its consequences, surely the only basis on which to characterize a *person* as altruistic—to say he or she has an altruistic personality—is in terms of an internal, intrinsically altruistic, person-defining source of behavior.

The behavioral approach also defines consistency from the outside, in terms of the external form and consequences of a behavior. For example, a child who helps an experimenter pick up spilled index cards in one situation and donates to charity in another is assumed to have behaved consistently because he or she performed two acts of helping. Imagine, however, that the reason why a young girl picked up spilled index cards was because she wanted to please the experimenter, and the reason why she donated to charity was because she felt sorry for poor children. Though consistent phenotypically—the subject helped others in both cases—the behaviors are inconsistent genotypically—they stem from different motives (ingratiation and sympathy), and are guided by different purposes (see Krebs 1982).

Turning to the methodological problems with the behavioral approach, experimental research on altruistic personality rarely assesses ecologically valid samples of altruistic behavior (see Krebs and Miller 1985). Experimenters select measures of altruism prifpmarily for their convenience in measurement, not for their ability to represent the forms of altruism subjects display naturally. Of what relevance is the amount of money children donate to charity or the number of "accidentally spilled" index cards they pick up to the type of helping behavior they display in their everyday lives?

Finally, most evidence for altruistic personality stems from research on children. Can children possess an altruistic personality, or is altruism a quality restricted to mature adults? With Poplawski (1986, 204), we will argue that the types of helping behavior typically displayed by children are significantly less altruistic than the types of helping behavior typically displayed by mature adults.

## THE PSYCHOMETRIC APPROACH

Another popular approach to altruistic personality is based on the assumption that if altruism is a personality trait, psychometricians should be able to develop a test to assess it. Investigators such as Rushton, Chrisjohn, and Fekken (1981) and Romer, Gruder, and Lizzadro (1986) have developed pencil-and-paper tests that purport to assess the personality trait of altruism. The Rushton, Chrisjohn, and Fekken test invites respondents to endorse or reject statements such as "I have helped push a stranger's car out of the snow," and the Romer, Gruder, and Lizzadro test asks respondents to complete hypothetical statements such as "A child riding his or her tricycle past your house appears to be lost. You ... "

The psychometric approach is equipped to assess a much larger sample of ecologically valid prosocial behaviors than the behavioral consistency approach; however, it too is limited conceptually and methodologically. Altruism is defined phenotypically and quantitatively in self-report tests as the *number* of *different* incidents of helping *selected by the test maker* that respondents *say* they have emitted or would emit. Though the range of behaviors assessed in self-report tests tends to be broader than the range of behaviors assessed in lab-based research (it is easier to ask people what they would do or what they have done in various situations than to expose them to the situations and see what they actually do), they nonetheless fail to constitute a representative sample of the types of helping behavior engaged in by the different types of people (e.g., males and females, young people and old people ) who take the test. Each incident of helping is given the same weight—that is, all are considered equally altruistic. Self-report measures fail to assess the motives guiding the helping behaviors subjects report, and they fail to distinguish between the quality of altruism intrinsic to different acts. Was the stranger in need an unattractive member of the same sex or an attractive member of the opposite sex? Whose needs were fulfilled by the prosocial overture?

Methodologically, the psychometric approach suffers from the well-known limitations of self-report measures. Unfortunately, people are not very dependable sources of information about themselves (see Gelfand and Hartmann 1982; Krebs et al. 1989). Thus, it is not really surprising that pencil-and-paper tests of altruism fare poorly on accepted criteria of validity. For example, the Rushton, Chrisjohn and Fekker test correlated only .21 with peer ratings (.33 when corrected for attenuation), and there is no evidence that individuals to whom altruistic personalities are attributed on the basis of behavioral consistency also are defined as altruistic on the basis of scores on personality tests.

In a variation of the psychometric approach, Staub (1974) gave subjects a set of conventional (validated) personality tests, and extracted a factor consisting of high scores on prosocial personality traits and values such as "responsibility," "helpful," and "equality," and low scores on personality traits and values such as "Machiavellianism," "comfortable life," and "ambition." Scores on this factor correlated between .40 and .50 with behavioral measures of helping across four situations.

Staub's approach goes further than those based on self-report tests in assessing an underlying personality structure that relates to actual samples of helping behavior. The results of Staub's research, however, do not support the notion that some individuals possess personality traits that induce them to behave "consistently" altruistically across different situations. In Staub's (1974) words, "the relationships [between personality traits and altruistic behaviors] were affected by the surrounding conditions (treatments), the exact nature of the personality characteristics, and the nature of the help needed" (329).

In order to establish that a test assesses a personality trait of altruism, investigators must demonstrate that the trait in question gives rise to altruistic motives. To date, no study has met this criterion. (Staub [1974] does not claim to have developed a measure of altruistic personality; rather, he characterizes the personality factor he assessed as a "prosocial orientation.") In an article entitled "Where Is the Altruism in the Altruistic Personality?" Batson et al. (1986) contend that the prosocial behavior of individuals who score high on the personality traits assessed by investigators such as Staub is not truly altruistic. Batson et al. show that although high-scoring individuals are more likely than low-scoring individuals to help a victim in distress when escape from the distressful situation is difficult, these "altruists" are not more likely to help when escape is easy. Batson et al. conclude,

the prosocial motivation was directed toward increasing the helper's own welfare rather than the welfare of the person in need. When it was relatively difficult to escape self-censure for failing to live up to one's self-image as a good, responsible, concerned person if one did not help, scores on these scales were positively correlated with helping. But when escape was relatively easy, the positive correlations vanished. (219)

Note that the validity of Batson et al.'s conclusion hinges on their definition of altruism. Batson et al. consider helping behaviors motivated by the avoidance of self-censure egoistic. Other investigators, (for example, Bar-Tal and Raviv 1982, 202) consider behaviors reinforced by such self-rewards to be altruistic.

## THE CASE STUDY APPROACH

A third approach to altruism involves case studies of individuals who have engaged in apparent acts of altruism. Investigators typically interview alleged altruists, and, in addition, may give them psychological tests and do background research on their lives. Case studies may involve single-act heroes (Blake 1978; Huston, Geis, and Wright 1976) or individuals who have devoted significant portions of their lives to helping others (McWilliams 1984; Oliner and Oliner 1988; Rosenhan 1970).

Case studies tend to be heavy on theoretical inference and light on empirical support. For example, Blake (1978) interprets the "altruistic suicide" of soldiers who smothered grenades in terms of Durkheim's conception of group cohesion. McWilliams (1984) interprets the altruism of five individuals who devoted their lives to humanitarian causes in terms of defenses such as identification with the victim and "dynamics" such as "the management of unconscious guilt and shame about hostility and greed" (193). Psychoanalysts tend to interpret altruistic personality in terms of the defense mechanism "altruistic surrender" (Kaplan 1984).

To support the contention that an individual possesses an altruistic personality, an investigator must establish that the motives underlying the prosocial behaviors the alleged altruist displays are genuinely altruistic. Let us examine the most comprehensive study on altruistic personality in the literature—a study based on the analysis of cases and other data—and determine how close it comes to meeting this condition.

Assisted by an international team of researchers, Oliner and Oliner (1988) sought out more than four hundred individuals who sheltered Jews in Europe during World War II ("rescuers"), and compared them to a group of 126 "nonrescuers," divided into those who actively resisted the Nazis and those who did not. Subjects were interviewed extensively about the circumstances surrounding their rescue behavior, and were asked to complete personality tests of social responsibility, internal-external orientation, self-esteem, and empathy. Finally, subjects were asked, in an altruism-checklist type of format, to identify the types of prosocial behavior they currently practiced. The self-reports of a substantial portion of the sample were checked against the reports of those they had rescued.

The Oliner and Oliner study improves on other approaches to altruistic personality in several ways. First, it employs a psychologically significant measure of altruism—a measure that occurred in a natural environment, usually involved considerable self-sacrifice and risk, rendered considerable gain to the recipient, was often repeated over many occasions, was characteristic of a lifestyle, and was directed toward members of a minority ethnic group. How different from making a phone call for a stranger, returning a lost wallet, giving a panhandler a quarter, or picking up spilled index cards! Second, the measure of altruism was buttressed by personality tests, background information, and a survey of current helping behavior. Third, the investigators were attentive to both personal and situational influences on helping.

On the basis of various quantitative and qualitative analyses of the data they collected, the Oliners conclude that different rescuers were guided by different types of motive. Although the most frequently attributed motive—an ethic of care or universal care— seems intrinsically altruistic, other self-attributed motives—external approval, hatred of the Nazis, and in some cases religion—do not seem to meet the Oliners' criteria for altruism. It is reassuring to note that the survivors who were interviewed also attributed their rescuers' behavior predominantly to care and universal care, though to a somewhat lower extent than the rescuers themselves.

Perhaps the major limitation of the Oliner and Oliner study was that both rescuers and survivors reported on events that occurred some four decades ago, yet the personality tests they took and the other types of helping behavior they reported were contemporary. Although the authors offer a wealth of data to support their conclusion that rescuers possessed altruistic personalities, virtually all the data involve inferences about what motivated behavior some forty years ago. Memory is notoriously reconstructive (Loftus 1979), and self-attributions of altruism tend to be self-serving (Gelfand and Hartmann 1982). Though the Jewish survivors tended to attribute the help they received to altruistic motives, these attributions may have been enhanced by the gratitude they felt. How ungrateful to attribute the behavior of someone who saved your life to a selfish motive! Finally, as acknowledged by the authors, it is difficult to draw causal inferences from their correlational data.

Case studies of lifestyle altruists counteract many of the problems with the behavioral consistency and psychometric approaches, but what they gain in qualitative assessment, they tend to lose in experimental control. Like the behavioral and psychometric approaches, most case studies fail to establish *why* helpers help—the source of the behavior and its underlying motives—and therefore the extent to which the help qualifies as altruistic.

### LIMITATIONS OF PAST APPROACHES TO ALTRUISTIC PERSONALITY: A SUMMARY

To summarize, we believe past approaches to altruistic personality are more or less limited conceptually for failing

1. to define altruism genotypically, in terms of an intrinsically altruistic internal motivational source that qualifies as a defining aspect of personality;
2. to supply a systematic basis for distinguishing among the different forms prosocial behavior or altruism may assume among people of the same and different ages;
3. to supply a basis for determining the adequacy of different forms of altruism; and
4. to account for the interaction between characteristics of people

and characteristics of situations in the determination of altruism.

In addition, past approaches tend to be limited methodologically for failing

1. to derive evidence of altruistic personality from naturally occurring, ecologically valid, and representative lifestyle patterns of behavior, and
2. to assess behavioral consistency in terms of its internal source.

## A DEVELOPMENTAL-INTERACTIONAL APPROACH TO ALTRUISTIC PERSONALITY

We turn now to an approach that, we submit, counteracts the limitations of the approaches we have reviewed—a developmental-interactional approach to altruistic personality. This approach is based on the assumption that the overriding cognitive orientations individuals acquire with development structure the patterns of altruistic behavior they display. Viewed developmentally, individuals' capacity for altruism, like, for example, their capacity to take the perspective of others or to behave morally (but unlike, for example, their activity level or level of introversion) undergoes a set of qualitative changes. The cognitive and affective structures and associated motivational orientations that define stages of development are the genotypic factors that give rise to different forms of altruism, and, indeed, to different conceptions of its nature and value. Although all forms of altruism have in common the goal or purpose of enhancing the welfare of another, the key components of altruism—self, other, cost, welfare—assume different meanings when conceptualized in terms of different cognitive structures. True or "pure" altruism is viewed as an ideal associated with the final stages of personal and social development.

The developmental-interactional approach to altruism we will advance builds upon the following fundamental assumptions of cognitive-developmental theory:

1. People's ways of understanding their physical and social worlds are organized in terms of cognitive structures that define stages of development. Cognitive structures provide overriding perspectives on events, interpretive frameworks, and modes of meaning making that guide information processing and organize behavior.

2. People normally pass through several stages of development during their lives in an invariant sequence, acquiring cognitive structures that enable them to interpret events in qualitatively different ways.
3. Each succeeding stage structure (overriding way of interpreting events) has a greater range of applicability and is more cognitively complex, more highly organized, and more adaptive than its predecessors.

These assumptions are not controversial in their general form. A spate of studies have documented developmental changes in conceptions of the physical world (Piaget 1971), the self (Loevinger 1976; Kegan 1982), social relations (Selman 1980), and morality (Colby and Kohlberg 1987). Such studies demonstrate that people not only acquire increasing quantities of knowledge with development—that adults know more things than children—but also that adults view the world in qualitatively different ways from children. For example, in Piaget's famous conservation task, young children think the quantity of liquid increases when poured from a short, fat container into a tall, thin container because it looks bigger, but older children understand that the quantity remains the same.

A central reason why advanced cognitive structures are more adequate (better organized and more adaptive) than less advanced cognitive structures is because they are more highly differentiated and integrated. For example, in conservation tasks, young children fail to differentiate the concept of tall from the concept of amount (in their world, things are "big" or "little"; "a lot" or "a little"); and they fail to maintain an integrated conception of amount across irrelevant changes in form. In addition, as emphasized by Piaget, young children fail to understand the integrative notion of reversibility (one could pour the liquid from the tall, thin beaker back to the short, fat beaker and see that the quantity was the same).

Our application of cognitive-developmental theory to altruism is based on the following five propositions:

1. The patterns of altruistic behavior displayed by people stem from and are shaped by the developmental stage structures they have acquired: the ways in which people construe themselves, others, and the social and moral relations between them give rise to the forms of altruism they display.

2. Different stage structures give rise to qualitatively different forms of altruism.
3. Each succeeding form of altruism meets the criterion of ideal or "pure" altruism—enhancing the welfare of others as an end in itself—more fully, exclusively, precisely, and effectively than its predecessors.
4. In contrast to highly constructivistic cognitive-developmental theorists such as Piaget and Kohlberg who assume people are "in" structurally homogeneous stages of development and therefore process all forms of information in a structurally equivalent way, we assume that individuals may process different types of information in different ways. In particular, we assume individuals retain old stage structures after new ones are acquired, and invoke them in certain circumstances.
5. The forms of altruism people display result from an interaction between the stage structures available to them and the demands and opportunities in the social and cultural contexts they create and encounter.

We turn now to an elaboration of each of these five propositions.

### From Stages of Development to Ideal Types of Altruism

The first proposition of the model, clearly central, states that stages structure altruism. But what stages? As pointed out by Snarey, Kohlberg, and Noam (1983), "nearly all structural theorists, to a greater or lesser degree, have suggested parallels between their own theory and the theories of others" (327). Several writers have aligned the stages of different theorists on the basis of parallels suggested by the theorists, age norms, empirically observed associations, and logical connections (see Daniels 1984; Fowler, 1984; Green and Haymes 1977; Kohlberg 1981, 1984; Loevinger 1976; Simpson 1976; Snarey 1986; Snarey, Kohlberg, and Noam 1983; Wilber 1981). Guided by this work, we aligned the stages we considered most relevant to altruism, and derived prototypic forms of altruism from the commonalities in their structure. Space does not permit a full explication of these commonalities (for that, see Krebs and Van Hesteren, in preparation), but the parallels among the stage descriptions of different theorists can be exemplified by considering the selected characterizations of Stage 3 summarized in table 6.1.

**Table 6.1**
Parallels in Different Theorists' Descriptions of Stage 3

---

*"Hard," Structure-based Parallels*

Piaget: *Early Formal Operations*
Formation of the inverse of the reciprocal; capacity to see relationships as simultaneously reciprocal; capacity to order triads of propositions or relations; beginning of reorientation from real to ideal.

Selman: *Third-person and Mutual Perspective Taking*
Individual realizes that both self and other can view each other mutually and simultaneously as subjects. Individual can step outside the two-person dyad and view the interaction from a third-person perspective.

Kohlberg: *Interpersonally Normative Morality*
The separate perspectives of individuals are coordinated into a third-person perspective, that of mutually trusting relationships among people. The justice operations are most clearly represented in Golden Rule role taking, which involves a second-order operation whereby concretely reciprocal exchanges are subjected to evaluation by reference to a superordinate or shared norm against which their fairness can be judged.

Haan: *Interactional-Interpersonal Morality*
Assimilation of self's interest to others' interests as the common interest; formulation of the self as a good, cooperating person among other good, cooperating persons.

Kegan: *The Interpersonal Self*
The capacity to coordinate one need system with another; enhanced empathic capacity and orientation to reciprocal obligation; others construed as being required to bring into being and to complete the self.

*"Soft," More Content-based Parallels*

Selman: *Intimate and Mutually Shared Friendships*
Friendships are seen as a basic means of developing mutual intimacy and mutual support.

Kohlberg: *Interpersonal Normative Morality*
Emphasis on being a good, altruistic, or prosocial role occupant and on good or bad motives as indicative of general personal morality; particularly concerned with maintaining interpersonal trust and social approval.

Loevinger: *Conformist Stage*
Perceiving self and other as conforming to external, socially approved norms, valuing of niceness, helpfulness, and cooperation.

Gilligan: *Goodness as Self-Sacrifice*
Moral judgment comes to rely on shared norms and expectations; survival is seen to depend on acceptance by others.

**Table 6.1**
Parallels in Different Theorists' Descriptions of Stage 3 (*cont.*)

Eisenberg: *Approval and Interpersonal Orientation*
Stereotyped images of good and bad persons and behaviors and/or
considerations of others' approval and acceptance in justifying prosocial or
nonhelping behaviors.

Maslow: *Love, Affection, and Belonging Orientation*
Strong need for affectionate relations with people in general.

When considering the relationships among the stages described
by different theorists, it is important to distinguish between the
conceptual parallels among them based on similar cognitive operations and orienting concerns and the empirical tendency for
people actually to be in isomorphic stages of development. Ideal
types of altruism may be derived logically from structural commonalities among parallel stages of development without implying
that people actually reach the parallel stages at the same time. We
will return to this issue when we discuss the fourth proposition of
our model.

*From Cognitive Structures to Altruistic Behavior.*   The primary functions of the cognitive structures that define stages of development
are to process information, interpret events, and endow phenomena with meaning. How do such meaning-making processes give
rise to altruistic behaviors? In our model, there are three main
routes. First, certain cognitive acquisitions are necessary, but not
sufficient, for certain forms of behavior. Second, interpretations of
events generate and structure affective states, which, in turn, give
rise to corresponding motives. Finally, people are motivated to
behave in ways that are consistent with their values and conceptions of themselves.

Space permits only a brief elaboration of this very complex issue.
First, you must know someone needs help before you will feel motivated to help him or her. As elaborated by Krebs and Russell
(1981), perspective taking is an important means of acquiring
knowledge about others' needs. Although perspective taking may
not be sufficient to induce altruism—an individual may perceive
that another needs help, yet not feel like helping—"the salient
recognition that a person needs help evokes in most people an

uncomfortable state akin to a lack of closure or a sense of cognitive inconsistency that presses for resolution. Helping is one way to resolve this type of cognitive discomfort" (Krebs and Russell 1981, 161).

Second, as elaborated by Hoffman (1982), stages of perspective taking structure the affective reactions intrinsic to empathy, which constitute motives for behavior. Knowing another person feels bad (or good) may make an observer feel bad (or good). Psychologists have no difficulty explaining people's tendency to enhance their own state of well-being (Wallach and Wallach 1983). As shown by Aronfreed (1968), Krebs (1975), and others, one way to make yourself feel good is to help someone with whom you are identified, and experience his or her pleasure or relief from pain vicariously.

Finally, and perhaps most importantly, the value people place on their conceptions of themselves as moral and altruistic people may induce behaviors that support these self-conceptions. Awareness of another's need and the sense that another should be helped are relatively impotent sources of action when dissociated from the self. We all know that millions of people are starving, and virtually everyone agrees that starving people should be helped, but this knowledge does not impel most of us to action because most of us do not feel responsible either for the plight of starving people or for alleviating it.

Theorists from different orientations have developed the general idea that behavior is structured by conceptions of self and ideal self. For example, from an information-processing approach, Markus (1983) suggests that self-schema contain motivational dispositions and behavioral strategies. More cognitive-developmentally, Blasi (1980, 1983, 1984) and Blasi and Oresick (1986) suggest that people behave morally in order to be true to their essential definitions of themselves. Cialdini et al. (1987) have shown that the affirmation of oneself as an altruistic person induces positive affect, and other researchers (e.g., Grusec 1982) have shown that inducing individuals to attribute their behavior to altruistic motives (i.e., to believe they are altruistic people) increases the probability of future altruistic behavior.

### A Developmental Typology of Altruism

The second proposition of our model asserts that different stage structures give rise to qualitatively different forms of altruism. The ideal types of altruism we derived from the aligned stages of relevant developmental theorists are outlined in table 6.2.

In presenting this typology of altruism, we must acknowledge a controversy surrounding the final stage—the pinnacle of the scheme. Strictly speaking, the principles of justice that define Stage 6 in schemes such as that of Kohlberg direct people to treat others fairly, not altruistically. For example, in distributing resources, principles of justice do not direct individuals to give others more than their share; they direct them to give others what they deserve (see Krebs 1982). Kohlberg and Power (1981) acknowledge this point, and suggest that some individuals may develop a Stage 7 orientation that is, in a sense, "beyond justice"—an "ethic of responsible universal love, service, or sacrifice—an ethic of supererogation" (349). In this sense, the apogee of altruism would seem to lie beyond Stage 6.

The general correspondence between our typology and those derived from other theoretical perspectives (see, for example, Bar-Tal and Raviv 1982; Oliner and Oliner 1988; Reykowski 1982) supplies a certain measure of concurrent validity for the scheme. However, our typology differs from those of other theorists in several important respects. Such differences should serve as the basis for research designed to evaluate the predictive ability of each typology. With this overview, we turn to the third proposition of our model, to a justification of the assumption that each form of altruism is more altruistic than its predecessor.

## Why the Types of Altruism That Stem from Advanced Stages Are More Altruistic Than the Types That Stem from Less Advanced Stages

What makes one form of prosocial behavior more altruistic than another form? Our answer to this question is, the extent to which it is (a) directed toward enhancing the welfare of others, and (b) performed as an end in itself. All behaviors produce a complex array of costs and benefits for self and others. The amount of altruism effectively engendered in an act can be viewed as a ratio between the net benefits (benefits minus costs) it produces for others and the net benefits it produces for self. As pointed out earlier, most psychological research on altruism defines benefit quantitatively and phenotypically—the amount of money donated, the number of index cards picked up, the time elapsed before inter-

**Table 6.2**

Forms of Altruism

---

### Undifferentiated Affective Responsiveness (Stage 0)

Survival-maintaining prosocial behaviors such as smiling and cooing are emitted reflexively in response to stimuli associated with the satisfaction of basic physiological needs. The self is undifferentiated from others. A global, undifferentiated tendency to feel overt signs of affect in others mediates primitive empathic reactions.

### Egocentric Accommodation (Stage 1)

*Egocentric accommodation* is oriented mainly to fulfilling safety and effectance needs. This form of behavior is responsive to external, situational demands, especially the demands of authorities, and to overt signs of distress in others (e.g., crying); it tends to be accommodating, physical, material, superficial, inappropriate, and egocentric (the individual gives others what he or she would want). Fulfilling requests, imitating adults, and behaving in ways that evoke positive reactions from others are prominent forms. Empathic responsiveness to the distress of others is aimed at relieving the self's discomfort. The central goals of *egocentric accommodation* are to do what one is supposed to, to ingratiate oneself to those in power, and to foster feelings of security.

### Instrumental Cooperation (Stage 2)

*Instrumental cooperation* is directed toward doing one's share in concrete exchanges with others. The currency is mainly material, and exchanges tend to be situationally specific and temporally constrained. This form of prosocial behavior is attentive to the subjective needs, intentions, and motives of others, but mainly as factors to be considered in exchanges. *Instrumental cooperation* may be compromising and cooperative. Tit for tat reciprocity is the proto typic form. The orientation is individualistic and pragmatic, but rule-governed and fair, accepting others' reciprocal right to maximize their gains. The central goal of *instrumental cooperation* is to give in order to get.

### Mutual Altruism (Stage 3)

*Mutual altruism* is sensitive to the audience of "generalized others" and aimed at fulfilling shared role obligations, avoiding social disapproval, sustaining a good reputation, upholding bonds of friendship, securing one's place in one's reference groups, conforming, and behaving in a socially acceptable manner. A consciousness of "we" overrides the sense of "me": self-interest is assimilated in shared interests and relationships. *Mutual altruism* tends to be idealistic and is guided by values such as trust, care, friendship, altruism, cooperation, loyalty, solidarity, intimacy, and a sense of belonging. It is oriented toward fulfilling the ongoing subjective needs of those to whom one is attached, within the bonds of propriety. A driving force behind mutual altruism is to sustain one's conception of oneself as a good person in the eyes of those with whom one identifies.

**Table 6.2**
Forms of Altruism (*cont.*)

### Conscientious Altruism (Stage 4)

*Conscientious altruism* is oriented toward fulfilling internalized, self-defining obligations to assist in maintaining the institutions of one's society even when such obligations violate the expectations of reference groups. This form of prosocial behavior is guided by an internal sense of social responsibility and conscience. *Conscientious altruism* is mediated by the desire to uphold the norms that guide self and others in doing their fair share to maintain the social system that fosters the welfare of its members (including oneself). It upholds the values of conscientiousness, responsibility, honor, and good citizenship, and is based on a realistic recognition of the complexity of self, others, and social relations. The central goal of *conscientious altruism* is to fulfill internalized social responsibilities.

### Autonomous Altruism (Stage 5)

The source of *autonomous altruism* is more internal than the sources of previous forms, based more in high order principles than in external laws, norms, or social conventions. This form of altruism is guided by internally held values such as upholding human dignity and equal rights, and maximizing benefits for all. It is based on a deep appreciation of individual differences, which mediates enhanced tolerance, and extends principles such as liberty, equality, and justice to all. *Autonomous altruism* is both more discriminating than earlier forms—proffered only when it upholds internalized values—and more universal, rendered impartially to others regardless of ethnic origin, nationality, and so on. The central goal of *autonomous altruism* is to uphold self-chosen, internalized utilitarian values.

### Integrated Altruism (Stage 6)

Because the self-other dichotomy is transcended when individuals' sense of self becomes fully integrated with their sense of humanity, the self's interests become integrated with the interests of others. Upholding the rights and ultimate welfare of all people, including oneself, entails upholding the principles underlying these values. Altruism is proactive and directed toward service to humanity (of which the self is a significant, yet relatively small aspect). Altruism is guided by humanitarian principles that prescribe that individuals give in accordance with their abilities and receive in accordance with their need. The inevitability of conflicts is recognized. Decisions are guided by self-consciously applied, procedurally oriented, just principles of mutual respect, impartiality, and fairness. The central goal of *integrated altruism* is to foster perfectly balanced and integrated social relations.

**Table 6.2**
Forms of Altruism (*cont.*)

---

*Universal Love (Stage 7)*

Altruism stems from a cosmic feeling of oneness with the universe, identification with the species and with the Ultimate, active compassion for a commonwealth of beings, a full sense of responsibility for the welfare and development of all people, especially the disadvantaged. "Stage 7" altruism is selfless, stemming from *agape*, an ethic of responsible universal love, service, and sacrifice that is extended to others without regard for merit. "Stage 7" altruism upholds the dignity of its recipients, freely giving up, perhaps not even considering, the self's just claims. The central goal of *universal love* is to mesh with an ultimately transformed and coordinated nonviolent world.

---

vening in an emergency—and it focuses exclusively on the welfare of the recipient. But the net benefits of an act also are a function of its quality and "purity." We propose that, relative to earlier stage structures, advanced stage structures give rise to the capacity and motivation to engage in (a) greater quantities of altruism, (b) forms of altruism that contribute more fully to the welfare of others, and (c) altruistic acts more purely directed toward the enhancement of the welfare of others.

Individuals motivated to behave altruistically can be viewed as facing a complex set of problems. Such individuals must determine whether others need or want help, whether potential recipients deserve to be helped, and who should render the assistance. When there is more than one person who needs help—and in the broadest sense there always is—aspiring altruists must decide how to allocate their altruism. After the decision to help is made, the altruist must decide what kind of help to render—which act or acts will enhance the welfare of recipients most fully. Finally, the altruist must be honest with himself or herself about the motivational pulls of various alternatives—what's in it for me?

We argue that the types of stage structure individuals invoke in altruism-evoking situations determine how they solve these problems. Individuals who possess sophisticated cognitive abilities (advanced stage structures) are better able to understand others' needs, to determine who deserves to be helped, to decide who is responsible for helping, and to figure out the most effective ways of helping than those with less sophisticated abilities; thus, they end up engaging in more altruistic forms of helping.

The general reason why advanced stages give rise to more adequate forms of altruism than earlier stages is because they are more highly differentiated and integrated. The processes of differentiation and integration act on individuals' conceptions of themselves, others, welfare, rights, and duties in ways that shape the quantity and quality of altruism. Indeed, the concept of quality implies exactness, fine tuning, and intricacy (differentiation), coordinated into meaningful and balanced forms (integration). More specifically, we contend that advanced (more highly differentiated and integrated) stage structures give rise to more altruistic motives and behaviors than earlier stage structures in six interrelated ways: (1) they enable individuals to understand the needs of others more fully, precisely, and deeply, (2) they mediate the distinction between self and other necessary for individuals to direct their altruism exclusively toward the needs of others, (3) they mediate an orientation toward an increasingly broad range of recipients, (4) they give rise to the insight necessary to enhance the welfare of others most fully and effectively, (5) they enable individuals to allocate their altruism most fairly to those who deserve it, and (6) they mitigate against denial and evasion of responsibility. These points are elaborated by Krebs and Van Hesteren (in preparation).

*On the Definition of Altruism.*   Trivers (1971) considers Stage 2 reciprocity altruistic, but most psychologists consider such behavior "instrumental." Bar-Tal and Raviv allow that altruists may "experience self-satisfaction or raised self-esteem as a result of the performance of the act" (1982, 202), but Batson et al. (1986) and Cialdini and Kenrick (1976) consider helping behavior that makes people feel good (about themselves) intrinsically egoistic, and Reykowski and Karylowski suggest that true altruism must spring from exocentric motives.

Viewing altruistic behavior developmentally supplies a basis for resolving such definitional differences. From a developmental perspective, egoism and altruism are not mutually exclusive traits, but two poles of a continuum marked on one end by an ideal conception of pure selfishness, and on the other by an ideal conception of pure altruism, neither of which may actually exist. Pure egoism entails behaving in a manner that serves only the self. Pure altruism entails voluntarily behaving in a manner exclusively directed toward the maximum enhancement of the welfare of others as an end in itself. The types of altruism outlined in table 6.2 all fall within the domain of altruistic behavior in the sense that they are all directed toward enhancing the welfare of another; however, each type is more altruistic than its predecessor because it meets the ideal of altruism more adequately. From our developmental perspective, helping in order to maintain a positive self-image (Stage 3) is more altruistic than helping in order to reciprocate a favor (Stage 2), but it is less altruistic than helping to uphold high-level moral principles (Stage 6).

This is not to say that the source of altruistic behavior is the only factor that needs be weighed in the calculus of altruism. Individuals who engage in large quantities of low-stage altruism might be said to behave more altruistically than individuals who engage in occasional acts of high-stage altruism. The net altruism displayed by an individual might best be viewed as some multiplicative function of the quantity and quality of the helping behaviors he or she displays (with quality defined by the stage structures from which the altruism stems).

### The Structural Consistency of Altruistic Behavior

In the fourth proposition, we turn to the interactional aspect of our model. To what extent do individuals actually manifest the ideal types of altruism outlined in table 6.2? For the sake of the theoretical elegance of our model, it would be nice if people developed as highly integrated wholes, and therefore displayed highly consistent patterns of behavior across social and cultural contexts, but with theorists such as Snarey, Kohlberg, and Noam (1983), we do not believe the evidence supports such an assumption.

This issue, of course, has been investigated empirically. Some investigators have reported significant disparity between development in different domains (see Turiel 1983); other investigators have observed a great deal of homogeneity across domains (see Lambert 1972); and still others have found that cognitive development is necessary but not sufficient for the development of perspective-taking skills, which in turn is necessary but not sufficient for moral development (see Walker 1986). Flavell (1982) reviews the evidence on the homogeneity of cognitive development, and concludes that there are some senses in which it is homogeneous and other senses in which it is heterogeneous.

Clearly, people do not change in every way all at once, but

equally clearly, people do not develop independently in every domain. Individuals may differ in the shape of the distribution of the stages they have acquired, both between and within domains. Those with constricted distributions may display considerable consistency in their behavior, whereas the behavior of those with flatter distributions may be significantly more variable (see Krebs et al. 1991).

### Person-Situation Interactions

The issue of between- and within-stage homogeneity is closely related to the question of the nature of the interaction between stage structures and situational factors in the determination of altruistic behavior. Strongly constructivistic theorists such as Kohlberg argue that individuals interpret virtually all issues in terms of their current developmental level. Other theorists (e.g., Damon 1977; Fischer 1983; Levine 1979; Rest 1983) advance more interactional positions. For example, Levine (1979) suggests that old stage structures are retained by individuals, and employed in situations that "pull" for them.

Evidence from our own research program and that of others gives rise to the final proposition of our model, that altruism results from an interaction between the stage structures available to people and the demands of the social and cultural contexts to which they are exposed (see Krebs et al. 1991, for a review of the evidence). The highest stages acquired by individuals set an upper limit on the stages available to them, and although abilities within and between domains tend to consolidate around a modal stage structure, individuals may "regress" to lower stages in situations that pull for lower-stage behavior. Altruism is both "pushed" out of people by internal stage structures and "pulled" out of people by altruism-evoking situations. In this sense, cross-situational consistency is in part defined by consistencies in the "pull" exerted by situations on cognitive structures (see Fredericksen 1972).

Situations differ in their power to elicit uniform behavior. In strong situations such as suddenly encountering someone who needs immediate, low-cost help, virtually everyone helps (see Piliavin et al. 1981). In weaker situations, more variance is controlled by between-person factors such as stages of development (see Snyder and Ickes 1985). Similarly, stage structures differ in their power to "construct" situations, with higher stages containing more constructive power than lower stages. In general, the behavior of individuals at low stages of development is more situational than the behavior of individuals at higher stages (see Kohlberg 1984); indeed an external, situational orientation is one of the defining characteristics of low stages of development.

To summarize, deriving ideal types of altruism logically from commonalities among equivalent stages in different developmental domains does not imply that development is highly homogeneous psychologically—that is, that individuals tend to be in isomorphic stages across domains—or that individuals will display only one type of altruism. Individuals differ in the homogeneity of their structural development, and altruism stems from an interaction between the stage structures available to people and the situations evoking them. Although it is unrealistic to expect a high degree of behavioral consistency across small samples of situations, individuals' dominant stage structures should determine the general form of their helping behavior across the wide ranges of situations they encounter in their everyday lives, especially those they choose or fashion. As shown by Epstein and O'Brien (1985), behavior tends to be "situationally specific and unstable at an individual-item level," but "general and stable at the aggregate level" (533) (see also Zeldin, Savin-Williams, and Small 1984).

## THE VALUE OF A DEVELOPMENTAL-INTERACTIONAL APPROACH

If a developmental-interactional approach to the study of altruistic personality has merit, it should be equipped to counteract the limitations of past approaches. We conclude by suggesting ways in which this is the case.

In a developmental approach, *altruism is defined genotypically*, in terms of the structures that define stages of development, not in terms of its phenotypic consequences. Prosocial behaviors that look identical from the outside—for example, inserting coins in a donation can—mean quite different things when they stem from different stage structures. A person who donates to charity out of a (Stage 4) sense of social responsibility is viewed as behaving more altruistically than a person who engages in exactly the same behavior to conform to the (Stage 3) expectations of an experimenter in a psychological experiment. Similarly, *the criteria of consistency for stage-based altruism lie in the defining characteristics of stages, not in the frequency of helping across different situations.* For example, at Stage 1, behavioral consistency would be defined in terms of avoiding punishment and obeying authority, at Stage 2 in terms of instrumental exchange, and so on.

The genotypic sources of altruism emphasized in our approach—cognitive structures—are more *broadly based and person defining* than personality traits. Unlike personality traits, which are assumed to compete with one another or to combine quantitatively for control over behavior, cognitive structures organize and integrate experience qualitatively. They determine the meaning and value individuals assign to events, and are integrally tied to individuals' views of themselves and others. Stages give rise to overriding motives and guiding orientations; traits supply more situationally specific refinements. For example, the personality trait need for approval would be expected to buttress altruism at Stage 3, whose defining structure places a positive value on meeting the expectations of others, but to oppose it at Stage 5 in situations where it is necessary to defy the expectations of a reference group to uphold the rights of an outsider.

As implied in the discussion of other issues, the developmental approach supplies *a basis for distinguishing among different types of altruism,* namely, in terms of the structures that define stages of cognitive, personal, social, and moral development. From this perspective, *children are expected to display different types of altruism from adults, and immature adults are expected to display the forms of altruism characteristic of children.* (See Poplawski [1986] for a typology of "adult altruism" that corresponds quite closely to the developmental types in table 6.2.)

The heart of the model advanced here lies in the proposition that *the forms of altruism that stem from relatively high stages of development are more adequate (more altruistic) than the forms of altruism that stem from lower stage structures.* In addition to the arguments advanced earlier, evidence of hierarchical inclusion, increasing differentiation and integration, the longitudinal tendency for people to go through stages in order, and other evidence advanced by stage theorists for their stage schemes constitute evidence for the increasing adequacy of the behaviors to which they give rise.

Finally, the developmental-interactional approach is *attentive to the dynamic interaction between stage structures and situations.* In-dividuals are not expected to display highly homogeneous, "pure" types of altruism; everyday experience demonstrates that they don't. Rather, the forms of altruism people display are expected to result from the interaction between the stage structures available to them and the types of situations they encounter and create.

The proper place to look for the behavioral manifestations of broadly based internal dispositions such as those reflected in stages of development is across comparably broadly based samples of behavior, not in specific responses to specific situations (especially situations unrepresentative of those people customarily encounter). This point is exemplified persuasively by Ajzen and Fishbein (1980) in their research on the relationship between attitudes and behavior. It is people's behavior in the situations they create, select, and define, not their forced-choice behavior in unnatural laboratory contexts, that reflect their cognitive structures, values, and orientations toward altruism.

Of course, it is more difficult to obtain ecologically valid samples of naturally occurring helping behavior than to assess isolated acts in a lab. Self-report measures are convenient, and they can be employed to assess lifestyle patterns of behavior, but, from a structural perspective, they should be more open ended and they should probe more deeply the motives that give rise to behaviors than the self-report tests customarily employed in research on altruism. In addition, self-reports should be validated against more objective measures such as ratings by friends, acquaintances, and colleagues, and naturalistic observations of behavior.

### CONCLUSION

In this chapter, we have argued that altruism is a product of the interaction between the ways in which individuals process information and the information they process. Individuals at all stages of development may perform altruistic acts, but they tend to do so for different reasons. One individual might rescue Jews because an authority tells him to; a second because she anticipates some payoff; a third because he empathizes with the Jews' plight; a sixth because she believes all people have a moral obligation to care for others in need. Although each of these acts may produce the same basic result, they vary in the extent to which they meet the ideal of altruism. To determine the degree of altruism in an act, we must identify its source and purpose. In the right place and the right time, everyone may engage in some form of altruism, but across places and across times, we would expect only those who have reached high stages of cognitive, affective, personal, and social development to display consistently the patterns of behavior others would consider truly altruistic.

## REFERENCES

Ajzen, I., and Fishbein, M. (1980). *Understanding attitudes and predicting social behavior.* Englewood Cliffs, NJ: Prentice-Hall.

Aronfreed, J. (1968). *Conduct and conscience.* New York: Academic Press.

Bar-Tal, D., and Raviv, A. (1982). A cognitive-learning model of helping behavior development: Possible implications and applications. In N. Eisenberg-Berg (Ed.), *The development of prosocial behavior.* New York: Academic Press.

Batson, D., Bolen, M., Cross, J., and Neuringer-Benefiel, H. (1986). Where is the altruism in the altruistic personality? *Journal of Personality and Social Psychology, 50,* 212–20.

Blake, J. (1978). Death by hand grenade: Altruistic suicide in combat. *Suicide and Life-Threatening Behavior, 8(1),* 46–59.

Blasi, A. (1980). Bridging moral cognition and moral action: A critical review of the literature. *Psychological Bulletin, 88,* 1–45.

––––– (1983). Bridging moral cognition and moral action: A theoretical view. *Developmental Review, 3,* 178–210.

––––– (1984). Moral identity: Its role in moral functioning. In W. M. Kurtines and J. L. Gewirtz (Eds.), *Morality, moral behavior, and moral development* (pp. 128–39). New York: Wiley.

Blasi, A., and Oresick, R. (1986). Emotions and cognitions in self-inconsistency. In D. J. Bearison and H. Zimiles (Eds.), *Thought and emotion: Developmental perspectives* (pp. 147–65). Hillsdale, NJ: Erlbaum.

Bowlby, J. (1969). *Attachment and loss* (Vol. I): *Attachment.* New York: Basic.

Bridgeman, D. (1983). Benevolent babies: Emergence of the social self. In D. Bridgeman (Ed.), *The nature of prosocial development* (pp. 95–111). New York: Academic Press.

Cialdini, R., and Kenrick, D. (1976). Altruism as hedonism: A social development perspective on the relationship of negative mood state and helping. *Journal of Personality and Social Psychology, 34,* 907–14.

Cialdini, R., Schaller, M., Houlihan, D., Arps, K., Fultz, J., and Beaman, A. (1987). Empathy-based helping: Is it selflessly or selfishly motivated? *Journal of Personality and Social Psychology, 52,* 749–58.

Colby, A., and Kohlberg, L. (Eds.) (1987). *The measurement of moral judgment.* (Vols. 1–2). Cambridge, MA: Cambridge University Press.

Damon, W. (1977). *The social world of the child.* San Francisco: Jossey-Bass.

Daniels, M. (1984). The relationship between moral development and self-actualization. *Journal of Moral Education, 13,* 25–30.

Deutsch, M. (1975). Equity, equality, and need: What determines which value will be used as the basis of distributive justice? *Journal of Social Issues, 31,* 137–50.

Eisenberg, N. (1982). The development of reasoning regarding prosocial behavior. In N. Eisenberg (Ed.), *The development of prosocial behavior* (pp. 219–49). New York: Academic Press.

Epstein, S., and O'Brien, E. (1985). The person-situation debate in historical and current perspective. *Psychological Bulletin, 98,* 513–37.

Fischer, K. (1983). Illuminating the processes of moral development. In A. Colby, L. Kohlberg, J. Gibbs, and M. Lieberman. A longitudinal study of moral judgment. *Monographs of the Society for Research in Child Development, 48* (Serial No. 200).

Flavell, J. (1982). On cognitive development. *Child Development, 53,* 1–10.

Fowler, J. (1984). *Becoming adult, becoming Christian: Adult development and Christian faith.* San Francisco: Harper & Row.

Fredericksen, N. (1972). Toward a taxonomy of situations. *American Psychologist, 27,* 114–24.

Gelfand, D., and Hartmann, D. (1982). Response consequences and attributions: Two contributors to prosocial behavior. In. N. Eisenberg (Ed.), *The development of prosocial behavior.* New York: Academic Press.

Gilligan, C. (1982). *In a different voice: Psychological theory and women's development.* Cambridge, MA: Harvard University Press.

Green, L., and Haymes, M. (1977). Motivational antecedents to maturity of moral judgment. *Motivation and Emotion, 1,* 165–79.

Grusec, J. (1982). The socialization of altruism. In N. Eisenberg (Ed.), *The development of prosocial behavior* (pp. 139–66). New York: Academic Press.

Haan, N. (1983). The interactional morality of everyday life. In N. Haan, R. Bellah, P. Rabinow, and W. Sullivan (Eds.), *Social science as moral inquiry* (pp. 218–50). New York: Columbia University Press.

Haan, N., Aerts, E., and Cooper, B. (1985). *On moral grounds: The search for practical morality.* New York: New York University Press.

Hay, D., and Rheingold, H. (1983). The early appearance of some valued social behaviors. In D. Bridgeman (Ed.), *The nature of prosocial development* (pp. 73–94). New York: Academic Press.

Higgins, A., Power, C., and Kohlberg, L. (1984). The relationship of moral atmosphere to judgments of responsibility. In W. Kurtines and J. Gewirtz (Eds.), *Morality, moral development, and moral behavior* (pp. 74–106). New York: Wiley.

Hoffman, M. (1982). Development of prosocial motivation: Empathy and guilt. In N. Eisenberg (Ed.), *The development of prosocial behavior* (pp. 281–313). New York: Academic Press.

Huston, T., Geis, G., and Wright, R. (1976). The angry samaritans. *Psychology Today, 85,* 61–64.

Kaplan, R. (1984). Empathy or altruistic surrender. *Dynamic Psychotherapy, 2,* 123–31.

Karylowski, J. (1984). Focus of attention and altruism: Endocentric and exocentric sources of altruistic behavior. In E. Staub, D. Bar-Tal, J. Karylowski, and J. Reykowski (Eds.), *Development and maintenance of prosocial behavior: International perspectives on positive morality* (pp. 139–54). New York: Plenum.

Kegan, R. (1982). *The evolving self: Problem and process in human development.* Cambridge, MA: Harvard University Press.

Kohlberg, L. (1981). *The philosophy of moral development: Moral stages and the idea of justice* (Vol. 1): *Essays on moral development*. San Francisco: Harper & Row.

—— (1984). *Essays on moral development* (Vol. 2): *The psychology of moral development*. New York: Harper & Row.

Kohlberg, L., and Power, C. (1981). Moral development, religious thinking, and the question of a seventh stage. In L. Kohlberg, *Essays on moral development* (Vol. 1): *The philosophy of moral development* (pp. 311–72). New York: Harper & Row.

Kohlberg, L., and Candee, D. (1984). The relationship of moral judgment to moral action. In L. Kohlberg (Ed.), *Essays on moral development* (Vol. 2): *The psychology of moral development* (pp. 498–581). New York: Harper & Row.

Krebs, D. (1975). Empathy and altruism. *Journal of Personality and Social Psychology, 32,* 1134–46.

—— (1982). Psychological approaches to altruism: An evaluation. *Ethics, 92,* 147–58.

—— (1991). Altruism and egoism: A false dichotomy? *Psychological Inquiry, 2,* 137–39.

Krebs, D., Denton, K., Carpendale, J., Vermeulen, S., Bartek, S., and Bush, A. (1989). The many faces of moral judgment. In M. A. Luszcz and T. Nettelbeck (Eds.), *Psychological development: Perspectives across the life-span* (pp. 97–105). Amsterdam: Elsevier Science Publishers.

Krebs, D., and Miller, D. (1985). Altruism and aggression. In G. Lindzey and E. Aronson (Eds.), *The handbook of social psychology* (Vol. II) (3rd Ed.) (pp. 1–71). New York: Random House.

Krebs, D., and Russell, C. (1981). Role-taking and altruism: When you put yourself in the shoes of another, will they carry you to their owner's aid? In J. P. Rushton and R. M. Sorrentino (Eds.), *Altruism and helping behavior: Social, personality, and developmental perspectives*. Hillsdale, NJ: Erlbaum.

Krebs, D., and Van Hesteren, F. (in preparation). The development of altruism.

Krebs, D., Vermeulen, S., Carpendale, J., and Denton, K. (1991). Structural and situational influences on moral judgment: The interaction between stage and dilemma. In W. Kurtines and J. Gewirtz (Eds.), *The handbook of moral behavior and development: Theory, research, and application*. Hillsdale, NJ: Erlbaum.

Lambert, H. (1972). *A comparison of Jane Loevinger's theory of ego development and Lawrence Kohlberg's theory of moral development*. Doctoral dissertation, University of Chicago.

Latané, B., and Darley, J. (1970). *The unresponsive bystander: Why doesn't he help?* New York: Appleton-Century-Crofts.

Leventhal, G. (1976). The distribution of rewards and resources in groups and organizations. In L. Berkowitz and E. Walster (Eds.), *Advances in experimental social psychology* (Vol. 9). New York: Academic Press.

Levine, C. (1979). Stage acquisition and stage use: An appraisal of stage displacement explanations of variation in moral reasoning. *Human Development, 22,* 145–64.

Loevinger, J. (1976). *Ego development*. San Francisco: Jossey-Bass.

Loftus, E. (1979). *Eyewitness testimony*. Cambridge, MA: Harvard University Press.

McWilliams, N. (1984). The psychology of the altruist. *Psychoanalytic Psychology, 1,* 193–213.

Markus, H. (1983). Self-knowledge: An expanded view. *Journal of Personality, 52,* 543–65.

Maslow, A. (1970). *Motivation and personality* (2nd Ed.). New York: Harper & Row.

Noam, G. (1988). The self, adult development, and the theory of biography and transformation. In D. K. Lapsley and F. C. Power (Eds.), *Self, ego, and identity: Integrative approaches* (pp. 3–29). New York: Springer-Verlag.

Oliner, S. P., and Oliner, P. M. (1988). *The altruistic personality: Rescuers of Jews in Nazi Europe.* New York: Free Press.

Piaget, J. (1932). *The moral judgment of the child.* London: Routledge and Kegan Paul.

———— (1971). The theory of stages and cognitive development. In D. G. Green and M. P. Ford (Eds.), *Measurement and Piaget.* New York: McGraw-Hill.

Piliavin, J., Dovidio, J., Gaertner, S., and Clark, R. III (1981). *Emergency intervention.* New York: Academic Press.

Poplawski, W. (1986). Adult altruism: Problems of terminology in prosocial behavior research. *Psychologia, 29,* 197–213.

Power, C., and Kohlberg, L. (1981). Faith, morality, and ego-development. In J. Fowler and A. Vergote (Eds.), *Toward moral and religious morality.* Morristown, NJ: Silver-Burdett.

Rest, J. (1983). Morality. In J. H. Flavell and E. Markman (Eds.), *Handbook of child psychology* (Vol. III) (4th Ed.) (pp. 556–629). New York: Wiley.

Reykowski, J. (1982). Development of prosocial motivation: A dialectic process. In N. Eisenberg (Ed.), *The development of prosocial behavior* (pp. 377–94). New York: Academic Press.

Romer, D., Gruder, C., and Lizzadro, T. (1986). A person-situation approach to altruistic behavior. *Journal of Personality and Social Psychology, 51,* 1001–12.

Rosenhan, D. (1970). The natural socialization of altruistic autonomy. In J. Macaulay and L. Berkowitz (Eds.), *Altruism and helping.* New York: Academic Press.

Rushton, J., Chrisjohn, R., and Fekken, G. (1981). The altruistic personality and the self-report altruism scale. *Personality and Individual Differences, 2,* 293–302.

Rushton, P. (1982). Altruism and society: A social learning perspective. *Ethics, 92(3),* 425–46.

Schwartz, S. (1977). Normative influences on altruism. In Berkowitz (Ed.), *Advances in experimental social psychology* (Vol. 10), (pp. 221–79). New York: Academic Press.

Selman, R. (1980). *The growth of interpersonal understanding.* New York: Academic Press.

Simpson, E. (1976). A wholistic approach to moral development and behavior. In T. Lickona (Ed.), *Moral development and behavior: Theory, research, and social issues* (pp. 159–70). New York: Holt, Rinehart & Wilson.

Snarey, J. (1985). Cross-cultural universality of social-moral development: A critical review of Kohlbergian research. *Psychological Bulletin, 97,* 202–32.

———— (1986). The relationship of social-moral development with cognitive and ego development. *Behavior Science Research, 20,* 132–46.

Snarey, J., Kohlberg, L., and Noam, G. (1983). Ego development in perspective: Structural stage, functional phase, and cultural age-period models. *Developmental Review, 3,* 303–38.

Snyder, M., and Ickes, W. (1985). Personality and social behavior. In G. Lindzey and E. Aronson (Eds.), *The handbook of social psychology* (3rd Ed.). New York: Random House.

Snyder, C., and Higgins, R. (1988). Excuses: Their effective role in the negotiation of reality. *Psychological Bulletin, 104,* 23–35.

Staub, E. (1974). Helping a distressed person: Social, personality, and stimulus determinants. In L. Berkowitz (Ed.), *Advances in experimental social psychology,* Vol. 7. New York: Academic Press.

——— (1984). Steps toward a comprehensive theory of moral conduct: Goal orientation, social behavior, kindness, and cruelty. In W. M. Kurtines and J. L. Gewirtz (Eds.), *Morality, moral development, and moral behavior: Basic issues in theory and research* (pp. 241–60). New York: Wiley.

Trivers, R. (1971). The evolution of reciprocal altruism. *Quarterly Review of Biology, 46(4),* 35–57.

Turiel, E. (1983). *The development of social knowledge: Morality and convention.* Cambridge: Cambridge University Press.

Walker, L. (1986). Experimental and cognitive sources of moral development in adulthood. *Human Development, 29,* 113–24.

Wallach, M., and Wallach, L. (1983). *Psychology's sanction for selfishness: The error of egoism in theory and therapy.* San Francisco: Freeman.

Werner, H., and Kaplan, B. (1963). *Symbol formation.* New York: Wiley.

Wilber, K. (1981). Ontogenetic development: Two fundamental patterns. *Journal of Transpersonal Psychology, 13,* 33–58.

Zeldin, R., Savin-Williams, R., and Small, S. (1984). Dimensions of prosocial behavior in adolescent males. *Journal of Social Psychology, 123(2),* 159–68.

# 7

# THE SELF IN MORAL AGENCY: TOWARD A THEORETICAL MODEL OF THE IDEAL ALTRUISTIC PERSONALITY

*Frank Van Hesteren*

In their chapter (this volume), Krebs and Van Hesteren outline a model of the development of altruistic personality based on a hierarchy of stage-based types of altruism. Within their developmental-interactional perspective, true, or pure, altruism is construed as an ideal associated with the final stages of personal and social development. Building upon this work, an attempt will be made in this chapter

1. to flesh out the description of the pinnacle of altruistic personality—the most highly developed, ideal type—in terms of the end-stage characteristics of a variety of developmental theories;
2. to explain the coordination and integration of these characteristics within the structure of personality;
3. to discuss the forces that drive development and integrate personality;
4. to explain the internal dynamics mediating between cognitive and affective structures and high-level altruistic behavior.

Individuals such as Mother Teresa and Albert Schweitzer are often regarded as being ideal exemplars of what it means to be altruistic. Regarding Schweitzer, Cousins (1985) has said, "No other person

The author would like to express his sincere appreciation to Dennis Krebs for his incisive commentary and helpful suggestions at various stages of the process involved in preparing this chapter.

of his time furnished more evidence of the possibilities of creative human development or the altruistic reach of an individual human being" (11). While it is commonly acknowledged that people like Albert Schweitzer and Mother Teresa possess unique personality characteristics that make them more inclined to display high quantities of high-quality altruism in a variety of situations than other types of people, few attempts have been made to arrive at a theoretical understanding of such ideal altruistic personalities. It is hoped that the model presented in this chapter will contribute to a better understanding of the inner motivational dynamics of such people.

## A PORTRAIT OF THE IDEAL ALTRUISTIC PERSONALITY

A point of departure in providing a portrait of the ideal altruistic personality will be the question, "What would an individual who had reached the end points of all forms of personal and social development be like and how would altruism be reflected in the makeup of such a person?" Proceeding in this manner will avoid the tendency inherent in the altruistic personality concept to suggest that altruism is *all* there is to personality and make it clear that an altruistic orientation is an integral aspect of a unified personality structure.

For the purposes of the model to be presented, it will be assumed that the cluster of personality characteristics identified by Maslow (1970) as being associated with self-actualization represents a hypothetical ideal of a person who has reached the final stages of development in all domains. In support of this position, it should be noted that a variety of developmental theorists have acknowledged the convergence of their higher stages with Maslow's self-actualization personality syndrome (e.g., Kegan 1982; Loevinger 1976). For example, in describing the "Integrated" stage of ego development, Loevinger (1976) suggests that "probably the best description of this stage is that of Maslow's Self-Actualizing person" (26). Maslow (1970) considered self-actualization to be a cohesive cluster of traits with a "common unity" (303) and found that an altruistic orientation was a highly salient, integral characteristic of the personalities of self-actualizing individuals.

Following Daniels (1984), it is assumed that "the processes of self-actualization and moral development may ... be simultaneous and equivalent" (28) and that, therefore, the end stages of a variety of developmental theories may be regarded as reflecting the moral maturity characteristics of self-actualizing people. Several theorists (Daniels 1984; Simpson 1976) have suggested that there are strong, clearly evident parallels between Maslow's (1970) level(s) of self-actualization and Stages Six and Seven of Kohlberg's theory of moral development. In this regard, Daniels (1984) maintains that "self-actualization is primarily a *moral* concept, and that Maslow may have selected his sample of self-actualizing people largely on the basis of their moral maturity" (29). It is maintained in the model that the final-stage characteristics of the developmental theories of Hoffman, Gilligan, and Kohlberg represent the qualities of moral maturity possessed by the self-actualizing person and serve to explain why he/she is altruistically oriented.

In what follows, the final-stage characteristics of the theorists identified above will be summarized and their relationship to altruism will be discussed. The portrait will then be rounded out by way of suggesting how these characteristics are integrated by, and within, the ideal altruistic personality.

Integral to the makeup of the ideal altruistic personality are advanced perspective-taking and empathic capacities (i.e., cognitive and affective structures) that make possible a relatively full, precise, and deep understanding of the needs of others (see Krebs and Van Hesteren, this volume). Highly developed people are capable of experiencing genuine "empathic concern" (see Batson 1987) and are able to have "empathy for another's general plight" (see Hoffman 1982). That is, they have a "conception of self and other as continuous persons with separate histories and identities" (Hoffman 1982) and a "generalized empathic distress capability" (Hoffman 1982) through which empathically aroused affect is joined with another's overall life situation.

Closely associated with the advanced empathic capabilities of the ideal altruistic personality is a moral orientation defined by principles of *care* (cf. Hoffman 1987). Gilligan (1979, 1982) has argued that moral maturity involves the invoking of a universal principle of "care-responsibility" and has suggested that within this orientation "the infliction of hurt is the centre of moral concern and is considered immoral whether or not it can otherwise be construed as fair" (Gilligan 1979, 442). Building upon this interpretation, it is assumed that the moral orientation of the ideal altruistic personality is identified with the phenomenon of *agape* (see Nygren 1982; Sorokin 1950), which is an "ethic of responsible universal love, service, or sacrifice—an ethic of supererogation" (Kohlberg and Power 1981, 349). It should be noted that an intimate relationship exists between principles of care and principles of justice (see Carter 1986; Kohlberg and Power 1981; Patterson 1977). Kohlberg and Power (1981) maintain that "although an ethic of *agape* goes beyond justice to supererogation, it still requires principles of fairness to resolve justice dilemmas" (352) and that "principles of reversible fairness are the only principles on which an ethic of *agape* could rest" (352). Regarding the relationship between justice and *agape*, Carter (1986) has argued that "it is *agape* that is the more fundamental and which enriches justice without rejecting its generally overwhelming claims" (83).

Having described the end-stage characteristics that serve to represent the qualities of moral maturity associated with the ideal altruistic personality, attention will now be given to briefly explaining how these characteristics give rise to, or increase the probability of, high-level altruism. First of all, sophisticated perspective-taking and empathic capacities make possible an in-depth understanding of others' needs. "The deeper one's understanding of the needs of others, the greater one's ability to be responsive to those needs, and the more one is able to offer high-quality altruism" (Krebs and Van Hesteren, this volume). Furthermore, the cognitive/affective structures that define universal principles of care give rise to moral imperatives that directly involve "promoting the welfare of others or preventing their harm or relieving the burden, hurt, or suffering (physical or psychological) of others" (Lyons 1983, 136). Generally speaking, individuals whose morality is defined by universal principles of justice and care are characteristically highly altruistic because an adherence to these principles results in a subordination of the self's individual lower-level interests to an orientation that involves a maximization of benefits for all (Krebs and Van Hesteren, forthcoming).

## THE INTEGRATION OF PERSONALITY

An attempt will now be made to explain how the highest-stage characteristics that portray the ideal altruistic personality are integrated within his/her personality structure. In what follows, two interrelated interpretations of the term "integration" will be used. In the first usage, the term will refer to the coordination of cognitive and affective considerations in the making of altruistic moral judgments on the part of the ideal altruistic personality. In the second usage, the term will refer to the organization, per se, of altruistic moral contents within the personality structure of the ideal altruistic personality. The ideas taken up in this section will constitute important reference points for the position taken up in subsequent sections that deal with the internal dynamics involved in moving from self-structures to altruistic behavior. It is important to keep in mind that the following discussion is based on the assumption that it is not unreasonable to assume that some individuals reach the final stages of development across all domains because the primary function of ego development is to integrate personality (see Noam, Kohlberg, and Snarey 1983).

In order to understand how the stage-derived characteristics of the ideal altruistic personality cohere as an integrated personality structure and how the internal dynamics of this type mediate altruistic behavior, an overarching concept of what it means to be a *knower* is needed (see Blasi 1988). While concepts like self, subject, person, and *knower* have traditionally been difficult to accommodate within the cognitive-developmental orientation (see Broughton 1981), recent neo-Piagetian theorizing about soft-structural developmental stages represents an attempt to account for them (e.g., Kegan 1982; Kohlberg, Levine, and Hewer 1983; Noam, Kohlberg, and Snarey 1983). Central to soft-structural interpretations of the self is the phenomenon of *personal meaning making* (see Kegan 1982). "Soft structural stages involve an ego or self consciously making meaning for itself. . . . The focus is on the self or ego viewed as some totality, or system of meaning, that confronts the world of the other" (Kohlberg, Levine, and Hewer 1983, 30).

Particularly central to the integrative functions of the self at high developmental levels is the capacity for post–formal operational thought and dialectical reflection (see Basseches 1980; Kramer 1983). The post–formal operational status of the ideal altruistic personality involves a capacity for self-consciously coordinating the cognitive and affective structures that constitute, or define, various personal and social developmental subdomains. In a post–formal operational theoretical context, the self is construed as a "unifying regulatory structure" (Edelstein and Noam 1982, 410) that encompasses intellectual, moral, and social dimensions of development. Particularly significant in relation to the model to be presented is the capacity of the self to mediate cognition and affect (see Edelstein and Noam 1982; Kegan 1982; Noam, Kohlberg, and Snarey 1983). In this regard, it is assumed that post–formal operational thought makes possible, or gives rise to, a *"relativistic ethics of responsibility"* (see Habermas 1990) that involves the coordination, or integration, of considerations of justice and considerations of care in the making of altruistic moral judgments in real-life situations. Such coordination of cognitive and affective considerations is possible at the post–formal operational level of functioning where reason represents one formal system that is consciously considered in relation to, and integrated or reconciled with, other possibly "mutually incompatible systems of knowledge" (Kramer 1983, 92).

It is assumed that the cognitive and affective high-stage structures that constitute, or define, the justice and care moral orientations give rise to conceptions of ideal self. For the purposes of the model, the moral contents represented by the justice and care orientations are understood to be integrated into the structure of personality by way of an ideal self-conception that Dabrowski (1964; Dabrowski, Kawczak, and Piechowski 1970) has called the "personality ideal."

Personality ideal is an individual standard against which one evaluates one's actual personality structure. It arises out of one's experience and development. Personality ideal is shaped autonomously and authentically, often in conflict and struggle with the prevalent ideals of society. It is a mental structure which is first intuitively conceived in its broad outline and which serves as the *empirical model for shaping one's own personality.* (Dabrowski, Kawczak, and Piechowski 1970, 175; emphasis added)

The "personality ideal" and its associated moral contents are considered, in turn, to be structured, or integrated, into personality by "self-schemata" (see Markus 1977, 1983). "Self-schemata are cognitive generalizations about the self, derived from past experience, that organize and guide the processing of self-related information contained in the individual's social experience" (Markus 1977, 64). Self-schemata are assumed to be located within the identity structure of the individual in the manner of what Kelly and his associates (see Kelly 1955; Stefan 1977) describe as *core personal constructs.* "Core constructs are those which govern a person's maintenance process—that is, those by which he maintains his identity and existence" (Kelly 1955, 482).

## THE "PERSONALITY IDEAL" AS A SHAPER OF
## DEVELOPMENT AND BEHAVIOR

Given the high priority assigned to the values associated with the justice and care orientations in the values hierarchy of the ideal altruistic personality, there is strong "conceptual support" (see Daniels 1988; Frick 1982) for altruism within his/her "personality ideal." According to Frick (1982), a major issue that arises in relation to Maslow's (1970) "hierarchy of needs" has to do with the idea that the so-called meta needs of the individual are biologically weaker than his/her "deficiency needs." That is, it is apparent that "individuals do not automatically seek to fulfill the meta needs of self-actualization when all prior deficiency needs have been satisfied" (Frick 1982, 40). Frick (1982) has suggested that the phenomenon of "conceptual support" can serve to begin to explain how development beyond the deficiency categories of Maslow's (1970) needs hierarchy occurs. According to Frick (1982),

as the power of biological control decreases, the importance of the conceptual and symbolic powers of the organism increases and assumes more and more prominence in ordering, promoting, and directing personal growth in accord with the self-actualizing trends of personality development. In other words, the higher in the motivational hierarchy we move, the more important a conceptual orientation becomes to our continued development.... The major hypothesis set forth here, therefore, is that continued striving for the fulfillment of the meta needs within the self-actualization process requires, in addition to prior gratifications, some *conceptual orientation or conceptual model toward one's own development.* (41; emphasis added)

In the model, the "personality ideal" represents a "conceptual model toward one's own development" and is considered to be a *shaper* of personality development. The cognitive structures that define the universal principles of justice and care are thought to provide "conceptual support" for altruism within the "personality ideal." It should be noted that what Schwartz (1977) has called "personal norms" and what Staub (1984a) has termed "personal goals" might be considered a kind of "conceptual support" for altruism since they represent conceptually based prosocial-altruistic standards that an individual uses as guides for personal conduct. Staub's (1984a) characterization of a "prosocial orientation" in terms of a three-dimensional "cognitive network" is particularly compatible with the way in which the phenomenon of "conceptual support" is being interpreted in the present model.

Dabrowski (1964; Dabrowski, Kawczak, and Piechowski 1970) considered "personality ideal" to be a "developmental dynamism" that becomes an increasingly pervasive moral motive force as a person progresses from Levels III and IV of his Theory of Positive Disintegration (i.e., the levels of Spontaneous and Organized Multi-Level Disintegration) to Level V, which is designated as the Level of Secondary Integration (see Hague 1986). As a high-level dynamism, the "personality ideal" is "postulated to be a shaper of development *and* behavior" (Dabrowski and Piechowski 1977, 76) and "the moving force of all that contributes to the full development of personality" (Dabrowski, Kawczak, and Piechowski 1970, 80). It shapes personality because it "causes the individual to be troubled by the gap between what . . . is and what . . . ought to be" (Hague 1987, 354). It should be noted in this regard that self-schemata embody not only ideas about the individual's current self-view but also ideas about "possible selves," that is, notions about the kind of person an individual "would very much like to become" (Markus and Nurius 1986, 954).

At high developmental levels, people are motivated, in a particularly powerful way, by what Dabrowski (Dabrowski, Kawczak, and Piechowski 1970) has called a "self-perfection instinct" and by what Puka (1983) has termed the "perfection principle" to close the gap between what "is" and what "ought to be." That is, they possess a strong tendency to strive toward actualization—to grow and develop and to fulfill their ideal selves. Such efforts to reduce "is-ought" discrepancies can be considered to occur on two interrelated levels. First, on the level of overall personality development (i.e., personality shaping), an individual may be motivated to close the gap between the kind of person he/she is and the kind of person he/she would be ideally. Second, on a specific behavioral level, an individual may be motivated to close the gap between the way he/she is behaving and the way he/she ought to be behaving.

## FROM SELF-STRUCTURES TO ALTRUISTIC BEHAVIOR

A theoretical model will now be presented in which an attempt is made to explain the internal dynamics involved in moving from self-structures to altruistic behavior. Each aspect of the model stems from, and is consistent with, the work of other theorists and particular emphasis is placed upon integrating aspects of cognitive-developmental theory with aspects of contemporary schema-information-processing theory.

Following are the basic presuppositions that undergird the model:

1. Stages of ego-development structure a sense of self that includes an ideal self or a "personality ideal."
2. At high stages, this sense of self is based on moral and behavioral standards that reflect the value of altruism: high-stage people view themselves as just, caring, and altruistic. These are important aspects of their identity.
3. The primary reason why such people behave altruistically is because they strive to behave in a manner that is consistent with their behavioral standards of altruism, morality, and self.
4. Important aspects of such self-consistency strivings are self-conscious comparison to standard processes, empathic processes, and the experience of anticipated existential guilt.

The first two elements of the model have been previously discussed. In what follows, an attempt will be made to explicate the general nature of the self-consistency striving processes engaged in by the ideal altruistic personality and to discuss two categories of internal dynamics that serve to further illuminate the self-consistency striving phenomenon.

The model of the ideal altruistic personality is based on the fundamental premise that individuals are motivated to behave in a manner consistent with their behavioral standards because they desire to uphold a sense of themselves as the kind of person they value. More specifically, it is assumed that at the core of the internal dynamics characterizing the ideal altruistic personality is a process of striving to behave in accordance with the moral obligations inherent in the "personality ideal."

Central to the fundamental premise underlying the model is the assumption that, at high developmental stages, self-consistency strivings, mediated by "responsibility judgments," increasingly come to characterize personality functioning in the moral domain (see Kohlberg and Candee 1984). According to Kohlberg and Candee (1984), "there is a monotonic increase in making judgments of responsibility consistent with deontic judgments of rightness as we move from stage to stage. This, in turn, means that there is a monotonic increase in the proportion of subjects acting 'morally' or in consistency with their deontic judgments made outside the situation" (57–58).

Blasi (1983, 1984) has interpreted the role of responsibility judgments and self-consistency strivings in a manner that is highly relevant to explaining the internal dynamics of the ideal altruistic personality. Blasi's (1983, 1984) self-model is an attempt to explore certain aspects of self-functioning that might serve to explain how, and under what conditions, a moral judgment leads to moral conduct. The basic contention in this model is that, in some instances at least, the outcome of making a moral judgment is a further judgment of responsibility in which the moral agent decides that he/she is obliged to engage in a morally positive action. Blasi (1984) suggests that the criteria for making such responsibility judgments "are related to the structure of one's self, or the essential definition of oneself" (129). Responsibility judgments are important because they tie abstract moral principles to the *self*—thus linking moral judgment and behavior.

The key to understanding how responsibility judgments contribute to moral behavior is the operation of self-consistency strivings. According to Blasi (1983), "The transition from a judgment of responsibility to action is supported dynamically by the tendency toward self-consistency, a central tendency in personality organization" (201). Self-consistency strivings and the responsibility dimension are inextricably associated with the concept of integrity. Blasi (1984) has explained the interrelatedness of these theoretical strands as follows:

The connection between moral identity and action is expressed through the concepts of responsibility (in the sense of strict obligation to act according to one's judgment) and integrity. These two concepts are closely related and derive their meaning from a view of moral action as an extension of the essential self into the domain of the possible, *of what is not but needs to be*, if the agent has to remain true to himself or herself. Responsibility, in this sense, stresses the self as a source of moral compulsion. Integrity, instead, emphasizes the idea of moral self-consistency, of intactness, and wholeness—all essential connotations of the self as a psychological organization. (132; emphasis added)

In the model, the "personality ideal," as previously described, is considered to be an aspect of the "essential definition of self" discussed by Blasi (1984). It is assumed that at high developmental levels one's "essential definition of self" has incorporated within it a concept of the person one would ideally like to be and that the motivation for self-consistency striving is not only to live up to the self that one is presently, but also to live up to the ideal self that one aspires to be. In this way, self-consistency strivings may be regarded as interacting with the "self-perfection instinct" (Dabrowski, Kawczak, and Piechowski 1970) in that they serve as a motive force not only in the direction of behaving in a manner consistent with one's actual, present self but *also* in the direction of behaving consistently with the self-ideal one regards oneself as having the potential to become. The "self-perfection instinct," therefore, functions *both* to develop, or shape, personality *and* to bridge the gap between self-structures and behavior.

In keeping with Blasi's (1983, 1984) interpretation of the concepts of responsibility and integrity, it is argued that the ideal altruistic personality (see Snyder and Kendzierski 1982) has a "believing means doing" orientation because the maintenance of a sense of moral personhood is contingent upon *consistently* having his/her beliefs, as these are represented in the "personality ideal," reflected in actual behavior. This "believing means doing" orientation is assumed to become particularly prominent at advanced developmental stages because it is only at these stages that an individual is powerfully disposed to make moral "responsibility attributions" that are in keeping with compelling, *highly internalized moral commands* (see Kohlberg and Candee 1984). According to Snyder and Kendzierski (1982), a "believing means doing" orientation results from the use of so-called relevance strategies that permit an individual to decide whether particular attitudes have important implications for his/her actions. Snyder and Kendzierski (1982) have described the relationship between "relevance strategies" and a "believing means doing" orientation in a way that is relevant to understanding how self-consistency strivings are involved in the generation of altruistic behavior.

We propose that relevance strategies will effectively enhance correspondence between attitude and behavior to the extent that they successfully induce individuals to adopt a "believing means doing" orientation to choosing their actions. This orientation effectively provides individuals with an "action structure"...or a "plan" (cf. Schank and Abelson 1977) for linking their attitudes and their behavior....It is as if an action structure mandates individuals to ask themselves the questions "Do I have a general attitude that is relevant to this specific situation?" and "What course of action does that attitude suggest that I pursue in this situation?", and then to instruct themselves, "If that is what my attitude says that I should do, then that is what I must do." (181)

Having discussed the general nature of the self-consistency strivings engaged in by the ideal altruistic personality in living up to the moral imperatives of the "personality ideal," particular attention will now be given to two categories of internal dynamics that serve to further explain such strivings.

### Self-Conscious Comparison to Behavioral Standard Processes

It is assumed in the model that self-conscious behavioral standard comparison processes are central to the self-consistency maintenance dynamics engaged in by the ideal altruistic personality in a situation where behaving altruistically is either a possibility or a necessity. Before discussing comparison to standard processes, per se, an attempt will be made to explain selected aspects of the behavioral standard activation process. In what follows, it will be argued that there are two reasons for a *heightened likelihood* that prosocial–altruistically oriented behavioral standards will be activated within the ideal altruistic personality in a potentially wide variety of situations.

First, the ideal altruistic personality is characteristically considered to have *ready access* to a rich and highly elaborated array of prosocial-altruistic constructs. The concept of construct accessibility (see Higgins and King 1981; Higgins, King, and Mavin 1982) is a particularly useful one in this context. According to Higgins and King (1981), "Construct accessibility is the readiness with which a stored construct is utilized in information-processing, that is, construct accessibility is concerned with stored constructs, their utilization in information-processing, and the likelihood of such utilization" (71). It is important to note that, according to Higgins, King, and Mavin (1982), the term "construct" is theoretically parallel to Markus's (1977) self-schema dimension. Utilizing the concept of construct accessibility, it is argued that prosocial-altruistic constructs (i.e., prosocial-altruistic self-schemata and the behavioral standards they contain) are particularly accessible to the ideal altruistic personality because of their central location within his/her identity structure. That is, prosocial-altruistic constructs have a high activation potential because of the central significance of altruism as a value and aspect of personal identity.

The second reason that prosocial–altruistically oriented behavioral standards have a high activation probability within the ideal altruistic personality has to do with the personal meaning that opportunities for behaving altruistically hold for him/her. Self-schemata at the core, or center, of an individual's identity structure are powerfully determinative of what kinds of life experiences and behavioral opportunities are valued and sought out. In the case of the ideal altruistic personality, the core-central self-schemata are comprised of prosocial-altruistic dimensions and so he/she tends to be particularly attuned to, or on the lookout for, situations of prosocial-altruistic relevance. This observational set is considered to directly increase the likelihood of prosocial–altruistically oriented behavioral standards being activated in situations where behaving altruistically is potential (see Rogers 1981). In the present model, then, the ideal altruistic personality is regarded as "maintaining a watching brief" (Rogers 1981, 208) for situations in which behavioral standards (i.e., those associated with the altruistic moral imperatives of the "personality ideal") might apply.

A substantial body of literature and research has accumulated that deals with comparison to standard processes as dimensions of self-regulation and with the role of self-awareness in reducing, or eliminating, discrepancies between present behavior and the behavior implicit in self-defining behavioral standards (Carver and Scheier 1981; Gibbons 1990; Wicklund 1982). Furthermore, research relative to self-awareness theory within a prosocial-altruistic context has tended, with reasonable consistency, to suggest that self-awareness is an important mediator of helping behavior (Duval, Duval, and Neely 1979; Gibbons and Wicklund 1982; Reykowski and Smolenska 1980). It should be noted that there has been a tendency in the research conducted to date to pay only minimal attention to, or to ignore rather completely, developmental considerations that might serve to moderate the self-awareness-helping relationship.

Wicklund (1982) has provided the following account of the self-consistency striving dynamics set in motion by the self-aware state:

Self-awareness theory views the self-focused condition as a state of motivation. The individual is said to engage in self-evaluation to the extent that attention is directed toward a within self-discrepancy, for instance a discrepancy between a moral principle and morally relevant actions....

As a motivational state, self-awareness is presumed to move an individual to close the gap between behaviors and ideals. The results should be attempted achievements, morally consistent behavior, and generally greater internal consistency where the self is involved. (213)

It should be noted that both Blasi (1983, 1984) and Wicklund (1982) maintain that people are motivated to behave consistently with personal standards and a sense of self. Wicklund's (1982) theory serves as a useful complement to Blasi's (1983, 1984) by emphasizing that feelings of responsibility involve self-awareness.

It is assumed in the model that the ideal altruistic personality has a characteristic high degree of self-awareness due to a personality dynamism that Dabrowski (Dabrowski, Kawczak, and Piechowski 1970) has termed *subject and object in oneself*, "which involves *constant objective and dynamic self-exploration*" (78; emphasis added). This heightened self-awareness means that he/she is conscious, in an *ongoing* way, of the prosocial-altruistic values (i.e., prosocial-altruistic constructs) that are integral to (i.e., at the core of) his/her personal identity. These values, as James (1982) would put it, occupy the "hot place" in his/her consciousness and are, therefore, readily accessible (cf. Markus and Nurius 1987). This heightened consciousness of prosocial–altruistically focused values and the strong tendency to strive for self-perfection relative to the moral content of the "personality ideal" contribute to an *habitual attunement* to discrepancies that may arise between present behavior and the morally responsible behavior required in a helping situation. It should be made clear that in the case of the ideal altruistic personality a discrepancy between present behavior and the behavior implicit in the "personality ideal" is not necessarily experienced as a negative state of affairs and that the primary response to a perceived behavioral discrepancy is not avoidance (cf. Buss 1980). Given his/her self-perfection orientation, he/she is regarded as tending to construe such discrepancies as opportunities for maintaining a sense of moral integrity by behaving in a morally responsible manner.

### Empathic Processes and the Experience of Anticipated Existential Guilt

Thus far, it has been suggested that self-conscious comparison to standard processes represents one category of internal dynamics that serves to explain, in part, the nature of the self-consistency strivings assumed to mediate between self-structures and altruistic behavior at the high developmental level characterizing the ideal altruistic personality. The focus will now shift to a second category of such internal dynamics having to do with empathic processes and the experience of anticipated existential guilt. Such processes are claimed to complement the self-conscious comparison to standard processes previously discussed. To reiterate, these two complementary categories of internal dynamics, taken together, are intended to provide a reasonably full account of the inner meaning-making dynamics of the ideal altruistic personality.

In the case of the ideal altruistic personality, altruistic behavior is assumed to be mediated through the *joint, or combined, influence* of "empathic concern" (Batson and Coke 1981), "category (principle) driven empathic affect" (Hoffman 1987, 1989), and anticipated existential guilt (Friedman 1988; Hoffman 1982). Following an explication of the general empathic processes engaged in by the ideal altruistic personality in the generation of altruistic behavior, attention will be given to the "category (principle) driven empathic affect" and anticipated existential guilt dimensions, which are particularly relevant to understanding the phenomenon of self-consistency striving.

*Empathic Processes Engaged in by the Ideal Altruistic Personality.* In the model, it is assumed that once the ideal altruistic personality experiences empathic arousal in a generalized, global manner, he/she is able to bring to bear on this relatively undifferentiated response high-stage perspective-taking structures that serve to further clarify the nature and extent of the need state of the other by providing more *information* about it. This line of thinking is consistent with that of Krebs and Russell (1981), who have pointed out with regard to perspective taking (role taking) that "the motivation intrinsic to this process is to gather information, to improve understanding, to enhance knowledge: not to behave altruistically" (160). Since the ideal altruistic personality brings to bear on an initial generalized, relatively undifferentiated empathic response a highly sophisticated capacity for acquiring a "cognitive sense of the other" (see Hoffman 1982), he/she is able to arrive at an optimally full and objective understanding of the other's need state. This enhanced understanding, in turn, is assumed to contribute to a heightening of (i.e., an increase in) empathic arousal (cf. Coke, Batson, and McDavis 1978). At the high developmental level characteristic of the ideal altruistic personality, such heightened empathic arousal is experienced as a sense of "empathic concern" that gives rise to high-quality altruism that has as its "ultimate goal" reducing the other's need rather than relieving one's own "personal distress" (see Batson 1987; Batson and Coke 1981).

The empathic processes described above have to do with the experience of empathic arousal and "empathic concern" as a result of responding to what Hoffman (1987) has termed "the immediate stimulus event," that is, cues from the situation and from the person in need of help. A complementary, or additional, source of empathic arousal is the phenomenon of "category (principle) driven empathic affect" (Hoffman 1986, 1987, 1989). Building upon contemporary schema-information processing concepts, particularly the concept of "schema-triggered affect" (see Fiske 1982), Hoffman (1987, 1989) has suggested that empathic affect can be associated with, and be released upon the activation of, moral principles. According to Hoffman (1987), "as a consequence of being coupled with empathic affect in moral encounters, a moral principle may be encoded and stored as an affectively charged representation—as a 'hot' cognition or category" (72). Hoffman (1987) has explained the processes involved in the triggering of principle-associated empathic affect and their relationship to prosocial behavior. Given the complexity of the processes under consideration and the importance of having them as fully and as accurately represented as possible, Hoffman (1987) will be quoted at some length.

A person's affective and cognitive responses in moral encounters are due not only to the immediate stimulus event . . . , but also to . . . the affectively charged moral principles that one's action and other aspects of the stimulus event may activate. The empathic affect elicited in moral encounters may thus have a stimulus driven component and a component driven by the activated, affectively charged principle. This may have important implications for prosocial action. In some situations, for example, the empathic affect elicited by the stimulus situation alone may be too weak, perhaps because of the paucity of relevant cues from victims, to override the egoistic motives that may also be operating. *But if one's caring principle were activated, its associated empathic affect might be released. This category driven component, alone or in combination with the stimulus driven component, may be powerful enough to extend the threshold needed to override the egoistic motives. Activating one's moral principles may thus provide an additional source of empathic affect, with a resulting increase in one's overall motivation for moral action.* The obverse side to this should also be mentioned. In some situations the empathic affect elicited by the stimulus event alone may be so intense that it produces the disruptive effects of "empathic overarousal" (Hoffman, 1978). In these cases, if one's caring principle were activated and the stimulus event assimilated to it, the category-driven component might reduce empathic affect intensity to a more manageable level. Thus the activation of an affectively charged moral principle may have a heightening or levelling effect and in general might function to stabilize one's level of empathic affect arousal in different situations. . . . *In sum, empathy may play a significant role in determining whether one becomes committed to a moral principle by giving the principle an affective base.* But once the principle is in place, activating it in future moral encounters may increase or decrease the intensity of one's empathic affective response. *Moral principles may thus make it more likely that moral conflict will lead to effective moral action.* (73; emphasis added)

Applying this line of thinking to the present model, it is maintained that the universal principles of justice and care, in the manner of an "affectively charged representation" or a "hot cognition" (Hoffman 1987, 72), have associated with them *high-quality* empathic affect. Furthermore, given their centrality within the identity structure of the ideal altruistic personality, these principles have a high activation potential. Hence it follows that the empathic affect schematically stored (associated) with these principles possesses a correspondingly high "triggering" propensity and that the ideal altruistic personality, therefore, experiences a high degree of "category (principle) driven empathic affect" in situations where behaving altruistically may be possible or required. As suggested by Hoffman (1987), such "category (principle) driven empathic affect" can serve to either increase empathic arousal or diminish it. *In either case, however, the result is a heightened likelihood of behaving in a self-consistent manner relative to the moral principles with which the empathic affect is associated.* That is, regardless of whether "category (principle) driven empathic affect" serves to increase empathic arousal in order to "override . . . egoistic motives" (Hoffman 1987, 73) or to reduce it in order to moderate the effects of empathic overarousal, the outcome is a strengthening of the motivation to behave in a manner consistent with one's self-defining moral principles.

*The Experience of Anticipated Existential Guilt.* The final phenomenon assumed to mediate altruistic behavior on the part of the ideal altruistic personality and to explain the nature of the self-consistency striving engaged in by him/her is the experience of anticipated existential guilt.

In the model, the phenomenon of existential guilt is interpreted in keeping with the views of Friedman (1988) and Hoffman (1982, 1983). Drawing on the writings of Martin Buber (1969), Friedman (1988) suggests that "existential guilt is an ontic interhuman reality" (29) that serves as an inducement to assuming *personal responsibility* for the manner in which one relates to others and the world. Hoffman (1982, 1983) has provided an account of existential guilt that usefully complements Friedman's (1988) interpretation and that illuminates how the experience of existential guilt gives rise to, or mediates, altruistic behavior. In what is intended to represent a speculative theoretical analysis, Hoffman (1982) maintains that the quality of empathy experienced by an individual is a function of the developmental maturity of his/her capacity to arrive at a "cognitive sense of the other." Within this theoretical framework, perspective-taking stages are assumed to structure affective responses in the form of empathy, and the affective state of empathy, in turn, is assumed to provide a motivational impetus for altruism in some contexts (see Hoffman 1982; Krebs and Russell 1981). Furthermore, it is assumed that low-level types of altruism are mediated by empathic reactions structured by low-level stages or types of perspective taking, which involve a fair amount of self-interest (i.e., helping to relieve empathically experienced distress in the self), but higher types are more differentiated and more exclusively directed to the needs of the other (cf. Batson 1987; Batson and Coke 1981; Krebs and Van Hesteren, this volume).

At the highest level of empathic functioning, designated by Hoffman (1982) as "empathy for another's general plight," an individual has a strong tendency to experience existential guilt, which "may result from the combination of empathic distress and awareness of being in a relative advantageous position with respect to the victim" (Hoffman 1983, 30). The experiencing of existential guilt, as interpreted in the present model, is assumed to lead the ideal altruistic personality to take personal responsibility for alleviating the distress of the person or group in a less privileged position. Hoffman (1982) has described how responsibility self-attributions may contribute to transforming empathic arousal into guilt:

Once aware of the identity of others beyond the immediate situation, one's empathic response to their general plight may be transformed into guilt if one feels responsible for their plight, or if one's attention shifts from their plight to the contrast between it and one's own relatively advantaged position. (303)

Hoffman (1982) goes on to suggest how, over the course of developmental maturation, guilt (including existential guilt) can become a motive force in its own right for prosocial behavior:

Although empathic distress is here viewed as a pre-requisite for the *development* [emphasis added] of guilt, it seems likely that guilt may become largely independent of its empathic origin....That is, guilt may become a part of all subsequent responses to another's distress, at least in situations in which one might have helped but did not. From then on, even as an innocent bystander, one may rarely experience empathic distress without some guilt. The line between empathic distress and guilt thus becomes very fine, and being an innocent bystander is a matter of degree. To the degree that one could have acted to help but did not, one may never feel totally innocent. *Empathy and guilt may thus be the quintessential prosocial motives* [emphasis added], since they may transform another's pain into one's own discomfort and make one feel partly responsible for the other's plight whether or not one has actually done anything to cause it. (303–4)

In the model, it is assumed that the ideal altruistic personality type's empathic response to the "other's general plight" (see Hoffman 1982) is transformed into guilt (i.e., existential guilt) since he/she is highly motivated (see Blasi 1983; Kohlberg and Candee 1984) to make responsibility self-attributions that are in keeping with the altruistic imperatives of the self-defining, universally applicable principles of justice and care embodied by the "personality ideal." The reasoning engaged in by the ideal altruistic personality in making such responsibility self-attributions might be as follows: "In light of my knowledge of the need state of this person in distress and my awareness of the discrepancy between my own relatively advantaged plight and the plight of the other, what do the moral principles that I have chosen to identify myself as a person demand of me in this situation?" The response to this question is, "If I am to continue to be able to live with myself, I must *behave* in a manner that is consistent with the altruistic demands of my self-defining moral principles. In other words, I must assume responsibility for responding to the need of the other in a way that is consistent with my 'personality ideal' if I am to maintain my sense of integrity as a moral person."

**SUMMARY AND CONCLUSION**

An attempt has been made in this chapter to provide a portrait of the ideal altruistic personality by characterizing him/her as a *knower* who engages in identifiable altruistic moral meaning-making processes in deciding to behave altruistically. Particular emphasis has been placed upon the internal processes that mediate between the self-structures that characterize the ideal altruistic personality and altruistic behavior. The theoretical model is intended to explain *why* the ideal altruistic personality is strongly disposed to engage in high quantities of high-quality altruism in a variety of situations and it provides an example of how taking developmental considerations into account can serve to address long-standing issues related to the so-called generality, or cross-situational behavioral consistency, phenomenon (cf. Krebs and Van Hesteren, this volume; Staub 1980). The model is also intended to be a response to a loud and persistent call within the area of prosocial-altruistic behavior for theory development and theoretical integration (see Krebs and Miller 1985; Staub 1984b).

Future research might involve the use of *qualitative* research methodologies to validate and refine the theoretical model (see Van Hesteren 1986). Particularly appropriate for the study of the kinds of complex altruistic moral decision-making processes identified in the model are phenomenological-hermeneutic approaches that are uniquely well suited to exploring various aspects of human agency such as self-consciousness, intentionality, and judgment (e.g., Giorgi 1985). It is encouraging to note what appears to be a growing readiness on the part of altruism researchers to rely upon the use of qualitative methodologies in their work. In recent years, the research reported by the Oliners (1988) in *The Altruistic Personality* stands out as a fine example of how a qualitative approach can result in the "discernment of a human face" (Konner 1982) in the study of altruism.

While it is hoped that the model presented in this chapter sheds some needed light on the inner dynamics of highly developed altruistic people, I do not intend to have the last word on the topic. Instead, I will defer to Thomas Merton (1981), who, in a book entitled *The Ascent to Truth,* seems to capture something of the essence of what all of this has been about.

Our nature imposes on us a certain pattern of development which we must follow if we are to fulfill our best capacities and achieve at least the partial happiness of being human. This pattern must be properly understood and worked out in all its essential elements. Otherwise, we fail. But it can be stated very simply, in a single sentence: *We must know the truth, and we must love the truth we know, and we must act according to the measure of our love.* (8)

## REFERENCES

Basseches, M. (1980). Dialectical schemata: A framework for the empirical study of dialectical thinking. *Human Development, 23,* 400–421.

Batson, C. D. (1987). Prosocial motivation: Is it ever truly altruistic? In L. Berkowitz (Ed.), *Advances in experimental social psychology* (Vol. 20, pp. 65–122). New York: Academic Press.

Batson, C. D., and Coke, J. S. (1981). Empathy: A source of altruistic motivation for helping? In J. P. Rushton and R. M. Sorrentino (Eds.), *Altruism and helping behavior: Social, personality, and developmental perspectives* (pp. 167–87). Hillsdale, NJ: Erlbaum.

Blasi, A. (1983). Moral cognition and moral action: A theoretical perspective. *Developmental Review, 3,* 178–210.

—————— (1984). Moral identity: Its role in moral functioning. In W. M. Kurtines and J. L. Gewirtz (Eds.), *Morality, moral behavior, and moral development* (pp. 128–39). New York: Wiley.

—————— (1988). Identity and the development of the self. In D. K. Lapsley and F. C. Power (Eds.), *Self, ego, and identity: Integrative approaches* (pp. 226–42). New York: Springer-Verlag.

Broughton, J. M. (1981). Piaget's structural developmental psychology: IV. Knowledge without a self and without history. *Human Development, 24,* 320–46.

Buber, M. (1969). *A believing humanism: Gleanings.* (M. S. Friedman, Ed. and Trans.). New York: Simon and Schuster.

Buss, A. M. (1980). *Self-consciousness and social anxiety.* San Fransisco: Freeman.

Carter, R. E. (1986). Beyond justice. *Journal of Moral Education, 16,* 83–98.

Carver, C. S., and Scheier, M. F. (1981). *Attention and self-regulation: A control-theory approach to human behavior.* New York: Springer-Verlag.

Coke, J. S., Batson, C. D., and McDavis, K. (1978). Empathic mediation of helping: A two stage model. *Journal of Personality and Social Psychology, 36,* 752–66.

Cousins, N. (1985). *Albert Schweitzer's mission: Healing and peace.* New York: Norton.

Dabrowski, K. (1964). *Positive disintegration.* Boston: Little-Brown.

Dabrowski, K., Kawczak, A., and Piechowski, M. M. (1970). *Mental growth through positive disintegration.* London: Gryf.

Dabrowski, K., and Piechowski, M. M. (1977). *Theory of levels of emotional devel-*

*opment.* Vol. 1, *Multilevelness and positive disintegration.* Oceanside, NY: Dabor Science Publications.

Daniels, M. (1984). The relationship between moral development and self-actualization. *Journal of Moral Education, 13* (1), 25–30.

———— (1988). The myth of self-actualization. *Journal of Humanistic Psychology, 28,* 7–38.

Duval, S., Duval, V.H., and Neely, R. (1979). Self-focus, felt responsibility, and helping behavior. *Journal of Personality and Social Psychology, 37,* 1769–78.

Edelstein, W., and Noam, G. (1982). Regulatory structures of the self and "postformal" stages in adulthood. *Human Development, 25,* 407–22.

Fiske, S.T. (1982). Schema-triggered affect: Applications to social perception. In M.S. Clarke and S.T. Fiske (Eds.), *Affect and cognition* (pp. 55–78). Hillsdale, NJ: Erlbaum.

Frick, W.B. (1982). Conceptual foundations of self-actualization: A contribution to motivation theory. *Journal of Humanistic Psychology, 22,* 33–52.

Friedman, M. (1988). The healing dialogue of psychotherapy. *Journal of Humanistic Psychology, 28,* 19–41.

Gibbons, F.X. (1990). Self-attention and behavior: A review and theoretical update. In M.P. Zanna (Ed.), *Advances in experimental social psychology* (Vol. 23, pp. 249–303). New York: Academic Press.

Gibbons, F.X., and Wicklund, R.A. (1982). Self-focused attention and helping behavior. *Journal of Personality and Social Psychology, 43,* 462–74.

Gilligan, C. (1979). Woman's place in man's life cycle. *Harvard Educational Review, 49,* 431–46.

————. (1982). *In a different voice: Psychological theory and women's development.* Cambridge, MA: Harvard University Press.

Giorgi, A. (Ed.). (1985). *Phenomenology and psychological research.* Pittsburgh, PA: Duquesne University Press.

Habermas, J. (1990). *Moral consciousness and communicative action.* (C. Lenhardt and S.W. Nicholson, Trans.). Cambridge, MA: MIT Press.

Hague, W.J. (1986). *New perspectives on religious and moral development.* Edmonton: University of Alberta Printing Services.

————. (1987). Moral Objectivity: Toward a new understanding of intuition. In W.J. Baker, L.P. Moss, H.V. Rappard, and H.J. Stam (Eds.), *Recent trends in theoretical psychology* (pp. 349–56). New York: Springer-Verlag.

Higgins, E.T., and King, G. (1981). Accessibility of social constructs: Information-processing consequences of individual and contextual variability. In N. Cantor and J.F. Kihlstrom (Eds.), *Personality, cognition, and social interaction* (pp. 69–121). Hillsdale, NJ: Erlbaum.

Higgins, E.T., King, G.A., and Mavin, G.H. (1982). Individual construct accessibility and subjective impressions and recall. *Journal of Personality and Social Psychology, 43,* 35–47.

Hoffman, M.L. (1978). Empathy, its development and prosocial implications. In C.B. Keasey (Ed.), *Nebraska symposium on motivation* (Vol. 25, pp. 169–218). Lincoln: University of Nebraska Press.

———— (1982). Development of prosocial motivation: Empathy and guilt. In N. Eisenberg (Ed.), *The development of prosocial behavior* (pp. 281–313). New York: Academic Press.

———— (1983). Empathy, guilt, and social cognition. In W.S. Overton (Ed.), *The *relationship between social and cognitive development* (pp. 1–52). Hillsdale, NJ: Erlbaum.

——— (1986). Affect, cognition, and motivation. In R.M. Sorrentino and E.T. Higgins (Eds.), *Handbook of motivation and cognition* (pp. 244–80). New York: Guilford.

——— (1987). The contribution of empathy to justice and moral judgment. In N. Eisenberg and J. Strayer (Eds.), *Empathy and its development* (pp. 47–80). New York: Cambridge University Press.

——— (1989). Empathy and prosocial activism. In N. Eisenberg, J. Reykowski, and E. Staub (Eds.), *Social and moral values: Individual and societal perspectives* (pp. 65–85). Hillsdale, NJ: Erlbaum.

James, W. (1982). *The varieties of religious experience.* (M.E. Marty, Ed.). New York: Penguin.

Kegan, R. (1982). *The evolving self: Problem and process in human development.* Cambridge, MA: Harvard University Press.

Kelly, G.A. (1955). *The psychology of personal constructs* (2 Vols.). New York: Norton.

Kohlberg, L., and Candee, D. (1984). The relationship of moral judgment to moral action. In W.M. Kurtines and J.L. Gewirtz (Eds.), *Morality, moral behavior, and moral development* (pp. 52–73). New York: Wiley.

Kohlberg, L., Levine, C., and Hewer, A. (1983). *Moral stages: A current formulation and a response to critics.* New York: Karger.

Kohlberg, L., and Power, C. (1981). Moral development, religious thinking, and the question of a seventh stage. In L. Kohlberg, *Essays on moral development.* Vol. 1, *The philosophy of moral development* (pp. 311–72). New York: Harper and Row.

Konner, M. (1982). *The tangled wing: Biological constraints on the human spirit.* New York: Holt, Rinehart, and Winston.

Kramer, D.A. (1983). Post-formal operations? A need for further conceptualization. *Human Development, 26,* 91–105.

Krebs, D.L., and Miller, D.T. (1985). Altruism and aggression. In G. Lindzey and E. Aronson (Eds.), *The handbook of social psychology.* (Vol. II, Third Edition) (pp. 1–71). New York: Random House.

Krebs, D., and Russell, C. (1981). Role-taking and altruism: When you put yourself in the shoes of another, will they take you to their owner's aid? In J.P. Rushton and R.M. Sorrentino (Eds.), *Altruism and helping behavior: Social, personality, and developmental perspectives* (pp. 141–65). Hillsdale, NJ: Erlbaum.

Krebs, D.L., and Van Hesteren, F. (forthcoming). The development of altruism.

Loevinger, J. (1976). *Ego development.* San Fransisco: Jossey-Bass.

Lyons, N.D. (1983). Two perspectives: On self, relationships, and morality. *Harvard Educational Review, 53,* 125–45.

Markus, H. (1977). Self-schemata and processing information about the self. *Journal of Personality and Social Psychology, 35,* 63–78.

——— (1983). Self-knowledge: An expanded view. *Journal of Personality, 52,* 543–65.

Markus, H., and Nurius, P. (1986). Possible selves. *American Psychologist, 41,* 954–69.

——— (1987). Possible selves: The interface between motivation and self-concept. In K. Yardley and T. Honess (Eds.), *Self and identity: Psychosocial perspectives* (pp. 157–72). New York: Wiley.

Maslow, A.H. (1970). *Motivation and personality* (Second Edition). New York: Harper and Row.

Merton, T. (1981). *The ascent to truth.* New York: Harcourt Brace Jovanovich.

Noam, G.G., Kohlberg, L., and Snarey, J. (1983). Steps toward a model of the self. In B. Lee and G.G. Noam (Eds.), *Developmental approaches to the self* (pp. 59–141). New York: Plenum.

Nygren, A. (1982). *Agape and eros.* (P.S. Watson, Trans.). Chicago: University of Chicago Press.

Oliner, S.P., and Oliner, P.M. (1988). *The altruistic personality.* New York: Free Press.

Patterson, B.E. (1977). *Reinhold Niebuhr.* Waco, TX: World Books.

Puka, B. (1983). Altruism and moral development. In D.L. Bridgman (Ed.), *The nature of prosocial development: Interdisciplinary theories and strategies* (pp. 185–204). New York: Academic Press.

Reykowski, J., and Smolenska, Z. (1980). Personality mechanisms of prosocial behavior. *Polish Psychological Bulletin, 11,* 219–30.

Rogers, T.B. (1981). A model of the self as an aspect of the human information processing system. In N. Cantor and J.F. Kihlstrom (Eds.), *Personality, cognition, and social interaction* (pp. 193–214). Hillsdale, NJ: Erlbaum.

Schank, R.C., and Abelson, R.P. (1977). *Scripts, plans, goals, and understanding: An inquiry into human knowledge structures.* Hillsdale, NJ: Erlbaum.

Schwartz, S.H. (1977). Normative influences on altruism. In L. Berkowitz (Ed.), *Advances in experimental social psychology* (Vol. 10, pp. 221–79). New York: Academic Press.

Simpson, E.L. (1976). A holistic approach to moral development and behavior. In T. Lickona (Ed.), *Moral development and behavior: Theory, research, and social issues* (pp. 159–70). New York: Holt, Rinehart, and Winston.

Snyder, M., and Kendzierski, D. (1982). Acting on one's attitudes: Procedures for linking attitudes and behavior. *Journal of Experimental Social Psychology, 18,* 165–83.

Sorokin, P.A. (1950). Love: Its aspects, production, transformation, and accumulation. In P.A. Sorokin (Ed.), *Explorations in altruistic love and behavior* (pp. 3–73). Boston: Beacon.

Staub, E. (1980). Social and prosocial behavior: Personal and situational influences and their interactions. In E. Staub (Ed.), *Personality: Basic aspects and current research* (pp. 236–94). Englewood Cliffs, NJ: Prentice-Hall.

—— (1984a). Steps toward a comprehensive theory of moral conduct: Goal orientation, social behavior, kindness, and cruelty. In W.M. Kurtines and J.L. Gerwitz (Eds.), *Morality, moral, behavior, and moral development* (pp. 241–60). New York: Wiley.

—— (1984b). Introduction: Status of the field, trends, issues, and tasks. In E. Staub, D. Bar-Tal, J. Karylowski, and J. Reykowski (Eds.), *Development and maintenance of prosocial behavior: International perspectives on positive morality* (pp. xxiii–xxvii). New York: Plenum.

Stefan, C. (1977). Core structure theory and implications. In D. Bannister (Ed.), *New perspectives in personal construct theory* (pp. 281–98). New York: Academic Press.

Van Hesteren, F. (1986). Counseling research in a different key: The promise of a human science perspective. *Canadian Journal of Counseling, 20,* 200–234.

Wicklund, R.A. (1982). How society uses self-awareness. In J. Suls (Ed.), *Psychological perspectives on the self* (Vol. 1, pp. 209–30). Hillsdale, NJ: Erlbaum.

# 8

# SELF, WE, AND OTHER(S): SCHEMATA, DISTINCTIVENESS, AND ALTRUISM

*Maria Jarymowicz*

## MECHANISMS OF ALTRUISTIC INVOLVEMENT: BASIC POSTULATES

Altruistic involvement is frequently explained by psychologists in terms of lack of psychological distance—cognitive and affective closeness—between self and others. On a cognitive level, psychological closeness is conceptualized as the degree of perceived similarity between a person and other people with regard to such qualities as age, social status, and personality. On an affective level, it relates to feelings of "we-ness" and group membership. A spate of studies has found that perception of similarity evokes positive attitudes and altruistic behavior (cf. Byrne 1969; Karylowski 1975; Reykowski 1979). In this chapter we will argue that altruistic involvement is based not only on perceived psychological closeness, but on other psychological mechanisms as well (cf. Schwartz 1970; Karylowski 1978; Reykowski 1979; Hoffman 1989), and that while perceived similarity may lead to some types of altruistic involvement, it may inhibit others.

It is possible to identify at least two types of altruistic involvement on the basis of self-other similarity. Both are based on lack of differentiation between self and other people, but they are related to different properties of the self-structure. The first type is based on an inability to differentiate self from others. Stemming from a low level of self-structure development, it implies an absence of personal standards of evaluation and internal sources of motivation and reinforcement. Altruistic involvement is regulated by external social factors, which entails dependence and/or conformity.

The second type of altruistic involvement is based on well-consolidated self-structures, indicating well-developed personal standards and internal mechanisms of regulation. In this case, when other people are perceived as similar, a process of personal standard generalization is evoked (cf. Reykowski 1979): perception of similarity stimulates processes by which personal standards are applied to others, which in turn induces people to treat "thy neighbor as thy self." In this case, altruistic involvement is accompanied by strong positive affective reactions, on the one hand, but by egocentricity on the other hand: others are treated like the self. This works fine when others are similar to the self, but perception of others who are different—perception of their internal states, expectations, needs, and goals—is inadequate. In other words, lack of me-we differentiation inhibits the process of taking the perspective of dissimilar others. In order to understand dissimilar people, one must differentiate what is good for himself or herself from what is good for others. This principle is derived from the Piagetian notion that self-other differentiation is a necessary condition for adopting a nonegocentric perspective. Altruistic involvement based on self-other differentiation and decentration is called exocentric involvement (Karylowski 1982b).

The research reported in the present chapter is based on the general assumption that taking others' perspectives is dependent on the differentiation of cognitive representations of the social world. The process of differentiation leads to the consolidation of qualitatively different cognitive schemata. Formation of distinct schemata is a necessary condition for decentration. In this framework, exocentric altruistic involvement may occur only if the self-schema is distinct from schemata representing others. This state is referred to as self-other cognitive schemata distinctiveness and self-distinctiveness. It implies that individuals with low self-distinctiveness (i.e., those whose self-schema is not distinct from their schemata of others) are not able to take the perspective of dissimilar others, and therefore are unable to experience exocentric altruistic involvement toward them. We turn now to empirical evidence collected in our laboratory that supports the framework proposed above.

## SELF-DISTINCTIVENESS AND EXOCENTRIC MANIFESTATIONS OF ALTRUISTIC INVOLVEMENT

### The Self-distinctiveness Notion and Its Operationalization

We define self-distinctiveness in terms of the distinctiveness of central (prototypical) attributes of the self-schema in relation to central (prototypical) attributes of the other(s)-schemata. Self-distinctiveness is assessed by way of the Social Perception Questionnaire. In this questionnaire, respondents are successively asked to concentrate on (a) others in general, (b) the we-category, and (c) the self. More specifically, respondents are asked to consider a list of seventy nouns describing different categories of human attributes (such as openness, religiousness, helpfulness, persistence, loyalty, elegance, and sense of duty) and to mark those that they "use frequently when thinking about other people." Subsequently, subjects are instructed to choose by circling among the marked items ten that they "use the most frequently." These ten items are considered to be prototypical attributes in others-schema.

Upon completion of the first part of the questionnaire, subjects are administered the second part, in which they are asked to focus on the we-category. First, they are requested to answer in a few sentences the following question: "Who are the people you label WE the most frequently?" Then they are instructed to repeat the procedure described previously for the category "others in general." This time the ten items they "use the most frequently" thinking about the we-category members are considered prototypical attributes of the we-schema. Finally, subjects are given the third part of the questionnaire, in which they are asked to center on the self. Again, they are instructed to choose ten items used "the most frequently" for the self-description. (In all parts of the questionnaire the same list of seventy nouns is presented.) These ten items are considered prototypical attributes of the self-schema.

On the basis of the three measures described above, it is possible to make various comparisons between the obtained sets of prototypical schemata attributes. We obtained two self-distinctiveness scores: one by comparing categories of attributes indicated as prototypical for the self with categories indicated as prototypical for others (SDo), and the other by comparing categories of attributes indicated as prototypical for the self with categories indicated as prototypical for the we (SDw). In addition, we obtained a we-distinctiveness score by comparing categories of attributes indicated as prototypical for the we and categories indicated as prototypical for others (WD). The scores consist of the number of different categories of attributes in the two compared sets.

## The Cognitive Differentiation-Exocentrism Hypothesis

On the basis of the general theoretical assumptions presented in the first section of this chapter, we expected that different levels of self-distinctiveness would be related to different mechanisms of altruistic involvement. Karylowski (1978, 1982b) distinguishes between two types of altruistic involvement that occur without expectation of external rewards and are related to internal reinforcements for altruistic activity—the endocentric and the exocentric type. Endocentric mechanisms operate when perception of another person's states stimulates the subject's centration on himself or herself, specifically on personal norms, which induce feelings of duty to help others, anticipation of guilt, and so on (see Schwartz 1970). This type of motivational state involves expectation of personal satisfaction. In contrast, exocentric mechanisms are related to centration on another person's states and expectations of his or her satisfaction. Personal goals are not considered at the beginning of the motivational process, but personal satisfaction may occur as a byproduct, as a consequence of perceiving positive change in another person's situation (cf. Jarymowicz 1979). Karylowski (1982a) argued that each type of altruistic involvement is related to a different set of relatively stable properties of personality.

Karylowski (1982a) presented a special technique to measure endocentrism versus exocentrism as an individual's dominant orientation and tendency to react in interpersonal contexts. Subjects are presented with descriptions of several situations in which an unknown person needs help. The subject is requested to indicate on a list of possible reactions how he or she would react. The list contains two categories of reactions: (a) endocentric, such as "I would feel bad if I did not help" (centration on personal states), and (b) exocentric, such as "I can imagine how badly he must have felt" (centration on partner's states). The difference between the number of each type of reaction indicated by a subject is treated as an index of his or her dominant type of altruistic involvement (endocentric or exocentric).

## STUDIES ON SELF-DISTINCTIVENESS AND ENDOCENTRIC VERSUS EXOCENTRIC ALTRUISM

We expected people with different levels of self-distinctiveness to differ in the tendency to react in non–self-related, exocentric ways (cf. Jarymowicz, forthcoming, a). In particular, we predicted that individuals with relatively low levels of self-distinctiveness would display less exocentric motivation than subjects with relatively high levels of self-distinctiveness. This hypothesis was verified in several studies (e.g., Szuster-Zbrojewicz 1988). In each study self-distinctiveness and endocentric versus exocentric reactions towards a partner were measured.

Kobuszewska (1989) provides an example of the described line of research. She used the self-distinctiveness measure and Karylowski's questionnaire. As shown in figure 8.1, Kobuszewska found that the lower subjects scored on self-distinctiveness, the higher the proportion of endocentric (self-related) justifications of help they supplied ($R^2 = .11$; $F(2, 117) = 5.63$, $p = .01$). Put another way, subjects with relatively low levels of self-distinctiveness supplied fewer exocentric justifications of altruistic involvement and more justifications of the endocentric type.

These results support the assumption that at least some degree of self-distinctiveness is necessary for decentration and exocentric involvement. At the same time, they raise another question. The implications of the studies seem to contradict two well-established premises based on empirical studies conducted in the framework of Tajfel's theory of social identity (Tajfel 1978), namely that weak me-we differentiation is related to high in-group involvement, and strong we-others differentiation leads to intergroup discrimination.

In the next sections we will argue that the present conception does not contradict Tajfel's theory. We will propose that, as Tajfel suggests, people with low self-distinctiveness may be extremely involved in their group, but only in a particular way.

### Me-We Distinctiveness and In-group Involvement

According to Tajfel, lack of cognitive me-we distinctiveness is related to strong emotional identification with reference groups, which in turn leads to manifestations of in-group involvement such as loyalty, effort in realization of common goals, etc. We, however,

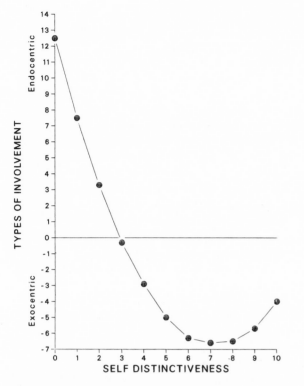

**Figure 8.1**
Endocentric versus exocentric involvement scores as a function of
degree of self-distinctiveness.

argue (on the basis of the previously presented theoretical conception and empirical findings) that this involvement occurs exclusively within an intergroup context. In contrast, in the context of
intragroup and interpersonal relations, another type of mechanism
plays a regulative role.

It is important to distinguish between myself as a representative
of the we-category and myself as an individual in interpersonal
relations. Different identity perspectives are stimulated in each
case: the former relates to social identity and the latter relates to
personal identity. As a consequence, different determinants of functioning are evoked (cf. Brown and Turner 1981). But before discussing this premise further, we will present empirical data

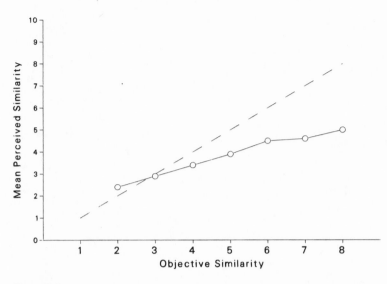

**Figure 8.2**
Mean perceived self-other similarity scores for traits at different levels
of objective similarity.

showing that lack of cognitive me-we distinctiveness is related to
personal identity problems that cause a particular type of in-group
involvement.

### The Similarity Underestimation Effect

In several studies on social comparison, we found a recurrent tendency for individuals to underestimate the degree of similarity
between themselves and others. In each study, subjects were asked
to describe themselves using a list of personality traits, then to
become acquainted with a "self-description," supposedly made by
another person, on the same list of traits. (Comparing both descriptions, we obtain an "objective similarity" score for each trait.)
Next, subjects were requested to assess the degree of self–target
person similarity on scales based on the same list of personality
traits as shown above. The relationship between perceived similarity and objective similarity is displayed in figure 8.2 (data from
Jarymowicz and Codol 1979).

As may be seen, the higher the objective similarity scores, the greater the degree of similarity underestimation. More specifically, there is no similarity underestimation at low levels of objective similarity, and the most similarity underestimation occurs at the highest levels of objective similarity. In general, we have found that the degree of underestimation may vary depending on the category of compared object. However, the effect occurs even when the object is defined as an attractive person or reference group (Jarymowicz 1987).

The results of our studies on similarity underestimation seem consistent with the results of Snyder's and Fromkin's study (cf. Snyder and Fromkin 1980) showing that when a person is confronted with information revealing very high similarity to others, he or she will attempt to create some distance. According to the authors' explanation, high degrees of similarity are aversive because they may cause identity problems. We assume that me-we and we-others cognitive differentiation plays a fundamental role in the process of personal and social identity formation (cf. Jarymowicz, forthcoming, b), and turn now to evidence supporting this assumption.

### Personal Identity Problems and Me-We-They Differentiation

Mandrosz-Wroblewska (1988) selected two groups of subjects (university students) who either declared that they had identity problems (group IP) or did not declare that they had identity problems (group NIP). After characterizing themselves in terms of the list of adjectives described above, subjects were asked to describe, with the same list of adjectives, in a very general and simple way, an unknown person presented by the experimenter (by a one-page description of a trivial event that supposedly happened to her "two weeks ago"). Then subjects were asked to estimate directly their degree of similarity to the target person. In one experimental condition the target person was presented as a student (a member of the we-category), and in another experimental condition the person was presented as a person twenty years older and from a peasant-worker social stratum (out-group member).

The results of this study revealed that in both the IP and NIP groups the degree of perceived similarity to another student was significantly higher than the degree of perceived similarity to the older peasant-worker. However, the relationship between the self-description and description of the target person was quite different

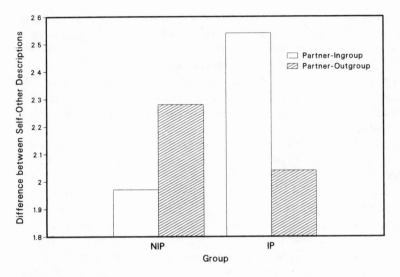

**Figure 8.3**
Mean difference between self and other descriptions in groups "without identity problems" (NIP) and "with identity problems" (IP).

in the two groups. The description of the unknown student (ingroup member) was significantly more similar to the self-descriptions of subjects with no identity problems than the description of an unknown peasant-worker, whereas subjects who declared identity problems described the we-category member (another student) as significantly more different from them than the peasant-worker! The data are shown in figure 8.3. The interaction shown in figure 8.3 was statistically significant. In contrast to the group without identity problems, the group with identity problems described the we-category member as less similar than the outgroup member to the self-description.

It should be emphasized that this (intuitively unexpected) result showing a stronger me-we than me-they differentiation (as measured in our study) was unconscious. On a conscious level, subjects' estimates of similarity between themselves and another student were higher than their estimates of similarity between themselves and a peasant-worker. The data in figure 8.3 are based on comparisons between self and other made by the experimenter.

These findings suggest that me-we differentiation is much more important than me-they differentiation for personal identity formation. This interpretation is consistent with some predictions from Festinger's classical theory of social comparison (cf. Festinger 1954). Specifically, according to Festinger, people prefer to compare themselves to similar others more than to dissimilar others because the former type of comparison is more useful for self-definition. As an implication of this assumption, we may expect that me-we comparisons are more useful and more important for identity formation than me-they comparisons. We may expect that the lack of self-we schemata distinctiveness, as related to identity problems, stimulates an unconscious tendency to search for differences. Fromkin has presented experimental data indicating that this tendency manifests itself on a cognitive as well as on a behavioral level of functioning. We may expect that it influences social behavior. For example, to resolve identity problems, individuals may search for ways in which they differ from others. Sometimes this process would be expected to produce so-called prosocial acts (to be recognized, visible, as shown by Codol 1979), but in other cases it may produce egocentric behavior.

**Desired Level of Mutual Control within Groups with Different Levels of Me-We Distinctiveness**

In one of our studies, we assessed the relationship between me-we-other distinctiveness and the degree of perceived and desired mutual control. We were particularly interested in people's desired level of control in within-group relations, and the relationship between desired level of own control over others to desired level of others' control over the self in me-we relationships. We expected that tendencies to control others and to resist control from them would be stronger among subjects with low self-distinctiveness than among subjects with high self-distinctiveness. Data on subjects with low, medium, and high self-distinctiveness are shown in figure 8.4 (the higher the mutual control score, the more imbalanced the equilibrium between a tendency to control others and to accept their control). As it may be seen, the higher self-distinctiveness (SDw), the lower the mutual control score ($F$ (2, 25) = 5.98, $p$ = .01)—that is, the higher the self-distinctiveness, the more balanced the equilibrium between the tendency to control other members of the we-category and to accept their control. The group with the lowest level of self-distinctiveness expressed the

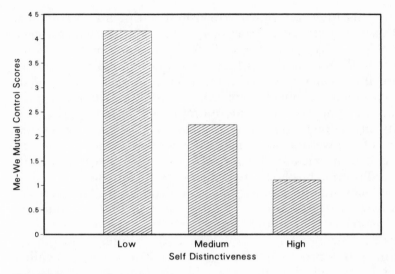

**Figure 8.4**
Mean me-we mutual control scores as a function of different levels of self-distinctiveness.

strongest motivation to control in-group members, relative to their motivation to accept control.

The results in figure 8.4 may be interpreted as suggesting that the higher the self-distinctiveness (here, self-we schemata distinctiveness), the greater the respect for the norm of reciprocity, which in this case is reflected in mutual control. The data may be viewed in the context of our theoretical framework as indicating that people with low self-distinctiveness are not able, in cognitive terms, to coordinate different social perspectives, and therefore are not sensitive to the norm of reciprocity. In addition, a motivational interpretation may be applied. Trouble stemming from the process of identity formation generates egocentricizing tension, decreasing the probability of exocentric involvement (cf. Reykowski 1979). In order to resolve the problem, individuals search for self-differentiation between me and we.

This assumption—that lack of me-we cognitive differentiation induces identity problems that motivate people to search for differences between themselves and others, and that the process may induce egocentric behavior—does not imply that people with low self-distinctiveness are not able to identify with their in-group goals, to be loyal and strongly involved. We argue that in such conditions the mechanisms of involvement are different (see opening section), and in some conditions personal problems inhibit exocentric motivation. In we-other contexts (i.e., of intergroup relations), a defensive tendency to maintain an identity based on the we-schema may occur. As a consequence, people with low levels of self-distinctiveness may be very loyal towards their own group, and low self-distinctiveness may lead to intergroup discrimination.

### Me-We Distinctiveness and Intergroup Relations

As shown by Brown and Turner (1981), principles of human behavior change as a function of personal versus social identity subsystems. Adopting a personal perspective (myself as an individual) or adopting a social perspective (myself as a representative of a reference group) induces different processes in in-group as well as in intergroup relations. The same person who orients to differences between self and others when centered on herself or himself may search for similarities when centered on in-group–out-group relationships. It is important to consider the implications of lack of self-we distinctiveness for intergroup relations: the differential treatment of in-group and out-group members.

### Feelings towards Out-Group Members

Some of our studies were designed to evaluate the assumption that the ability to coordinate different social perspectives is related to self-we schemata distinctiveness as a result of within-group comparison processes. We expected that me-we differentiation is a necessary condition for the ability to take the perspective of other social groups. Preliminary data from a field study were collected in Israel. In this study, young Israeli Jewish subjects (aged thirteen to seventeen) were requested to answer different questions concerning their reactions towards Israeli Arabs on measures tapping negativity/positivity of feelings, attribution of negative social traits, trust, social distance, and tendency to discriminate. Each subject estimated the extent to which he or she possessed characteristics typical of Jews (that is, for the we-category). A multiple regression showed that, as expected, the lower the me-we differentiation, the more negative the reactions towards the out-group members (Israeli Arabs).

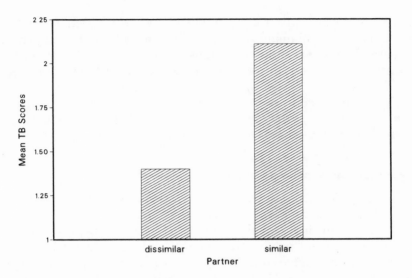

**Figure 8.5a**
Mean scores on tolerance of behaviors (TB) of dissimilar versus similar
partners in the low self-distinctiveness group.

### Attitudes towards Dissimilars

In another set of studies, we tested the hypothesis that subjects
with low levels of self-distinctiveness would display more positive
feelings towards a similar partner than towards a dissimilar one,
whereas subjects with relatively high levels of self-distinctiveness
would not display such a discrimination. In two experimental studies containing different operationalizations of each variable (cf.
Jarymowicz and Truszewski 1985; Krzemionka, forthcoming), we
obtained the same picture of the relationship between self-
distinctiveness, partner's similarity to the subject, and attitudes
towards the partner. The dependent variable in the first study was
tolerance for a partner's behavior and opinions, and the dependent
variable in the second study was feelings of attraction to a partner.
The results are shown in figures 8.5 and 8.6. In both studies, the
groups with low levels of self-distinctiveness obtained higher
scores on the measures of tolerance and partner's attractiveness
when making judgments about a similar partner than when making judgments about a dissimilar one. As shown on figure 8.6,
however, dissimilar and similar partners obtained equally positive

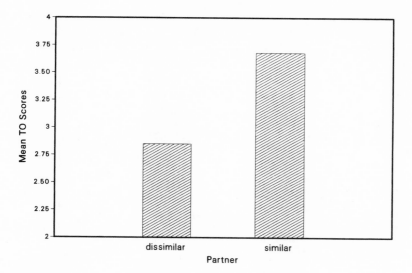

**Figure 8.5b**
Mean scores on tolerance of opinions (TO) of dissimilar versus similar
partners in the low self-distinctiveness group.

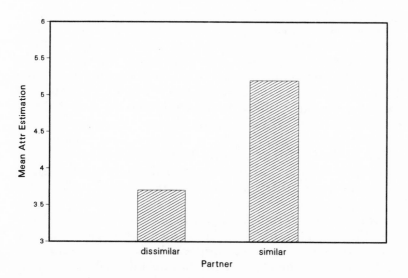

**Figure 8.5c**
Mean scores on attractiveness estimation (Attr) of dissimilar versus
similar partners in the low self-distinctiveness group.

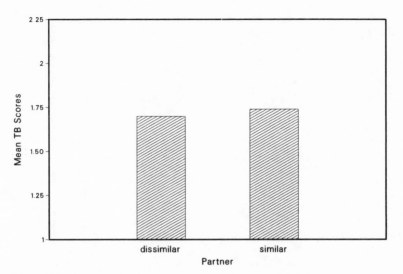

**Figure 8.6a**
Mean scores on tolerance of behaviors (TB) of dissimilar versus similar partners in the high self-distinctiveness group.

scores in the groups with high levels of self-distinctiveness (the differences were not significant). In the second study, a multiple regression showed that the attractiveness of a similar partner was not related to the level of self-distinctiveness, but the attractiveness of a dissimilar partner was negatively related to self-distinctiveness (the lower the self-distinctiveness, the lower the attractiveness ratings of the dissimilar partner). It should be emphasized that the latter effect pertained only to one index of distinctiveness—to the SDw scores, which refer to self-we distinctiveness ($R^2 = .34$, $F(9, 84) = 7.24$, $p = .0001$). Figure 8.7 shows that subjects with low self-distinctiveness estimated the attractiveness of a similar partner as higher than the attractiveness of a dissimilar partner, whereas subjects with high self-distinctiveness rated both partners as equally attractive.

The results of these studies suggest that a similar partner stimulates a relatively high level of liking among all subjects; people like those whom they view as similar. The results presented in figure 8.5 are consistent with the classic effect described by Byrne (1969): the higher the partner's similarity, the higher the partner's attractiveness. However, this effect did not occur in groups with high self-distinctiveness (see figure 8.6). Subjects in these groups

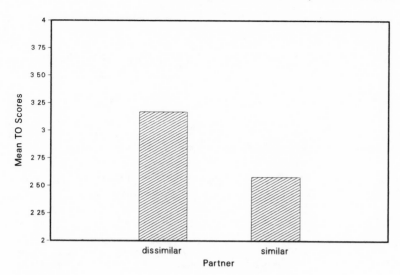

**Figure 8.6b**
Mean scores on tolerance of opinions (TO) of dissimilar versus similar
partners in the high self-distinctiveness group.

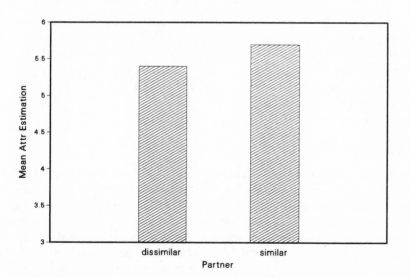

**Figure 8.6c**
Mean scores on attractiveness estimation (Attr) of dissimilar versus
similar partners in the high self-distinctiveness group.

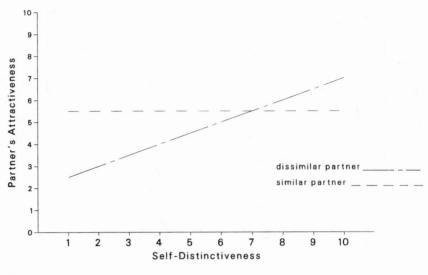

**Figure 8.7**
Partner's attractiveness as a function of degree of self-distinctiveness and self-partner similarity.

did not display the classic similar-dissimilar partner discrimination, suggesting that people with high self-we schemata distinctiveness do not employ self-related criteria for evaluating others. Indeed, as shown in figure 8.7, subjects with extremely high levels of self-distinctiveness appear to find dissimilar partners more attractive than similar partners.

## CONCLUSION

In summary, our research suggests that self-we-others cognitive schemata distinctiveness is related to some important prerequisites of altruistic involvement. First, in some conditions, lack of self-distinctiveness—for example, stemming from identity problems—seems to lead to egocentricizing tension that inhibits altruistic involvement. Second, in other conditions, lack of self-distinctiveness appears to lead to dependence and conformity. In such cases, altruistic involvement is based on external motivation, which does not occur without external influence. Third, low levels of self-distinctiveness appear to stimulate generalization of personal standards and the tendency to treat others from the self's perspective. Because generalization seems to be based on similarity of the other to the self, similar others evoke positive attitudes. Fourth, self-distinctiveness seems necessary for exocentric altruistic involvement, which requires the ability to decenter and take the perspective of others. Finally, self-we schemata distinctiveness seems necessary for taking the perspective of others from outside one's own group, implying that the probability of social discrimination is relatively low among people with high me-we differentiation. Lack of self-we distinctiveness leads to the defensive tendency to maintain an identity based on the we-others dichotomy, which is a source of prejudice and hostility.

## REFERENCES

Brown, R. J., and Turner, J. C. (1981). Interpersonal and intergroup behaviour. In J. C. Turner and H. Giles (Eds.), *Intergroup behaviour.* Blackwell.
Byrne, D. (1969). Attitudes and interpersonal attraction. In L. Berkowitz (Ed.), *Advances in experimental social psychology.* Academic Press.
Codol, J. P. (1979). *Semblables et differents. Recherches sur la quete de la similitude et de la difference sociale.* Université de Provence.
Festinger, K. (1954). A theory of social comparison processes. *Human Relations, 7,* 117–40.
Hoffman, M. (1989). Empathy and prosocial activity. In N. Eisenberg, J. Reykowski, and E. Staub (Eds.), *Social and moral values.* Erlbaum.
Jarymowicz, M. (1979). *Modyfikowanie wyobrazen dotyczacych Ja dla zwiekszania gotowosci do zachowan prospolecznych.* Ossolineum.
——— (1982). Odrebnosc obiektu porownan od innych a spostrzegane podobienstwo ja-obiekt. *Studia Psychologiczne, 2,* 59–72.
——— (1987). *Perceiving one's own individuality: The estimation and attractiveness of self-distinctness from others.* Wydawnictwa Uniwersytetu Warszawskiego.
——— (forthcoming, a). Proba konceptualizacji pojecia tozsamosc: Spostrzegana odrebnosc JA-INNI jako atrybut wlasnej tozsamosci. *Przeglad Psychologiczny.*
——— (forthcoming, b). Proba operacjonalizacji pojec tozsamosc spoleczna-tozsamosc osobista: Odrebnosc schematowa JA-MY-INNI jako atrybut tozsamosci. *Studia Psychologiczne.*
Jarymowicz, M., and Codol, J. P. (1979). Self-others similarity perception: Striving for diversity from other people. *Polish Psychological Bulletin, 10,* 41–48.
Jarymowicz, M., and Kwiatkowska, A. (1988). Atrybuty wlasnej tozsamosci: Cechy spostrzegane jako wspolne dla JA i INNYCH versus specyficznie wlasne. In M. Jarymowicz (Ed.), *Studia nad spostrzeganiem relacji JA-INNI: Tozsamosc, indywiduacja, przynaleznosc.* Ossolineum.
Jarymowicz, M., Sikorzynska A., and Waszuk, G. (1988). Poznawcze wyodrebnienie wlasnej osoby a funkcjonowanie spoleczne. In M. Jarymowicz (Ed.), *Studia nad*

*spostrzeganiem relacji Ja-Inni: Tozsamosc, indywiduacja, przynaleznosc.* Ossolineum.

Jarymowicz, M., and Truszewski, W. (1985). O tolerancyjnosci wobec podobnych i niepodobnych do Ja. *Przeglad Psychologiczny, 3*, 773–90.

Karylowski, J. (1975). *Z Badan nad mechanizmami pozytywnych ustosunkowan interpersonalnych.* Ossolineum.

———— (1978). O dwock typach mechanizmow regulacji czynnosci prospolecznych. Zaangazowanie osobiste versus zaangazowanie pozaosobiste. In J. Reykowski (Ed.), *Teoria osobowosci a zachowania prospoleczne.* Wydawnictwa IFIS PAN.

———— (1982a). *O dwoch typach altruizmu. Badania nad endo-i egzocentrycznymi zrodlami podejmowania bezinteresownych dzialan na rzecz innych ludzi.* Ossolineum.

———— (1982b). On the two types of altruistic behavior: Doing good to feel good versus to make the other feel good. In V. Derlega and J. Grzelak (Eds.), *Cooperation and helping behavior.* Academic Press.

Kobuszewska, E. (1989). *O dwoch typach altruizmu w warunkach deindywiduacji.* Unpublished Masters Thesis. University of Warsaw.

Krzemionka, D. (forthcoming). Poznawcze wyodrebnienie wlasnej osoby a atrakcyjnosc podobnych i niepodobnych do JA. *Studia Psychologiczne.*

Mandrosz-Wroblewska, J. (1988). Strategie redukowania problemow tozsamosciowych: Roznicowanie Ja-My i My-Oni. In M. Jarymowicz (Ed.), *Studia nad spostrzeganiem relacji Ja—Inni: Tozsamosc, indywiduacja, przynaleznosc.* Ossolineum.

Markus, H. (1977). Self-schemata and processing information about the self. *Journal of Personality and Social Psychology, 35*, 63–78.

Reykowski, J. (1979). *Motywacja, postawy prospoleczne, osobowosc.* PWN.

Schwartz, S. (1970). Moral decision-making and behavior. In J. R. Macaulay and L. Berkowitz (Eds.), *Altruism and helping behavior.* Academic Press.

Snyder, C. R., and Fromkin, H. L. (1980). *Uniqueness: The human pursuit of difference.* Plenum.

Szuster-Zbrojewicz, A. (1988). Z badan nad zwiazkami podobienstwa/odrebnosci Ja-Inni z gotowoscia do egzocentrycznego angazowania sie w sprawy pozaosobiste. In M. Jarymowicz (Ed.), *Studia nad spostrzeganiem relacji Ja-Inni: Tozsamosc, indywiduacja, przynaleznosc.* Ossolineum.

Tajfel, H. (1978). *Differentiation between social groups: Studies in social psychology of intergroup behavior.* Academic Press.

# 9

# MOTIVATIONS OF PEOPLE WHO HELPED JEWS SURVIVE THE NAZI OCCUPATION

*M. Zuzanna Smolenska and Janusz Reykowski*

One of the most intriguing questions for those who encounter acts that seem genuinely altruistic concerns their motivation. What could instigate some people to sacrifice not only their effort, time, and money, but also their lives, for other human beings? This is a question often asked by recipients of altruistic aid. In the present paper, we would like to discuss this issue on the basis of data collected in the framework of the Altruistic Personality Project— an extensive study of a large sample of people who helped Jews survive the Nazi occupation in Europe. The project was originated in the early eighties by Professor Samuel Oliner, who assembled a team of researchers from several countries—the USA, Poland, the Federal Republic of Germany, the Netherlands, France, and Italy.

The main goal of the Altruistic Personality Project was to determine the psychological characteristics of people involved in rescuing Jews, who could not have expected any material or other tangible reward. The essential feature of the behavior of such rescuers was its orientation toward the protection and maintenance of other people, in spite of the fact that such action entailed a grave threat to the individual involved and his or her close ones. In Poland, discovery of such activity by the Nazis was tantamount to a death sentence to the rescuer and to his or her family members. In Western countries—in France or in Holland, for example—rescuers risked internment in a concentration camp. It should be emphasized that such rescue behavior was not, as a rule, an impulsive response to an immediate situation, but rather an ongoing activity, carried out over a period of weeks, months, or years.

## METHODS OF RESEARCH

Selection of subjects was based upon documentation gathered by Jewish institutions. First, we obtained a list of people who had been decorated with the medal "Righteous among the Nations of the World," awarded by the Yad Vashem Institute in Jerusalem for help extended to Jews. In Poland we also received the names and addresses of rescuers from the Jewish Historical Institute.

The main instrument of the study was a questionnaire containing several dozens of items pertaining to the personal history of the rescuer and to the details of his or her rescuing activity. On this basis, it was possible to recreate in considerable detail what happened to the rescuers during the occupation, of what their rescue activity consisted, how long it lasted, what its scope was, and so on. In addition, the questionnaire contained a number of items dealing with the situation of respondents before and after the war. Finally, the rescuers were given several standard psychological tests (for a detailed description of all the instruments, see Oliner and Oliner 1988).

The data were collected in the course of an interview conducted by specially trained interviewers. Each interview lasted for several hours: the answers were written down by the interviewer and tape recorded. The design of the research consisted in comparing rescuers from different cultural settings, and comparing rescuers to people who were not involved in helping Jews. To this aim, two control groups were studied: "passive controls"—people living during the same period in the same neighborhood as rescuers who did not engage in any rescuing; and "active controls"—people involved in resistance against occupants, without helping Jews. The subjects from the control groups were studied by means of the same instruments as those used with rescuers.

## RECOGNITION OF THE NEEDS OF OTHERS:
## THE PREREQUISITE OF HELPING

It is commonly accepted that a precondition for undertaking any action on behalf of other people is recognition of their needs (Latane and Darley 1970; Schwartz 1977). Recognition of needs is the basis for goal setting, in this case for setting a prosocial goal (Staub 1980). We may leave aside the problem of accuracy of this recognition, focusing instead on the process through which prosocial goals are formed.

The recognition of need in another person is not always an easy task, to be sure. Even in cases where others' needs seem obvious—when their survival is at stake, when they are badly mistreated and deprived of their rights and possessions, for example—some observers may not recognize their needs. Studying our subjects' responses to questions designed to probe their reactions to the fate of persecuted Jews, we noticed that the vast majority of subjects from all groups was, more or less, aware of the stigmatization of Jews (e.g., they knew that Jews were compelled to wear the armband with the Star of David), expropriation of Jewish property (e.g., they had heard of or witnessed acts of expulsion of Jews from their homeplaces), physical abuse, and murders. But they differed in their reactions. Three different ways of reacting to this situation could be distinguished. First there were people (from the control groups) for whom this information was simply factual, stored in their memories as a record of (historical) events. It expanded their knowledge, but the concept of someone in need, apparently, was not salient in their interpretation of these events.

Another type of reaction consisted of emotional arousal (e.g., crying, agitation), feelings of compassion, horror, repulsion, and evaluative judgments (e.g., disapproval of the acts of persecution, moral contempt for the oppressors). Although quite common among the subjects from our control group, these reactions did not lead to the formation of a prosocial goal, and thus had practically no consequence as far as helping activity was concerned.

The third type of reaction was typical of those who rescued Jews. It consisted of interpretation of the situation as a kind of demand—recognition that other people are in need. It was the basis for the formation of a goal image—that is, a mental representation (or a concept) of a possible (not yet existing) state of affairs that is desirable for the subject, for example, recognition that a Jew needs a hiding place, false documents, food, or knowledge of a Catholic prayer. Since in this case the goals involve protection of other people's basic interests, we may call them prosocial.

The construction of a prosocial goal clearly requires certain intellectual capabilities. First, it requires the ability cognitively to transform the existing situation into another one. There were many people who, for different reasons, apparently were incapable of making such transformations. For them, the situation of persecuted Jews was a kind of horrifying spectacle: they were deeply moved by it, but they were not instigated to action. To be moved to action, they would have had to transform mentally the situation into one with action possibilities (i.e., they would have had to generate a goal image).

In some cases the formation of a prosocial goal was facilitated when the would-be rescuer was approached by a victim or his or her intermediaries who defined the need. Since the need was usually described in terms of the desired end state, the potential rescuer's task was reduced to finding concrete solutions for practical questions. It became, therefore, a problem-solving task (how to attain the end state) rather than a task that involved the generation of a goal image (providing, of course, that the individual accepted the goal).

Assuming an individual develops a cognitive representation of a possible state of affairs—an image of the situation in which the needs of a persecuted person are satisfied—the question arises, under what conditions can such an image acquire the potential for action control? We postulate that the action-control potential of the goal image stems from its affective content—from the fact that the goal image is charged with valence. But that raised another question—namely, where did the affective qualities of the goal image come from? Why did rescuers attach an affective meaning to outcomes oriented toward satisfying the needs of other people? Putting this question in other terms—what were the motives of rescuers?

## THE MOTIVES OF RESCUERS

The fact that another's misfortune can evoke affective reactions among witnesses is not at all surprising. It can be observed quite often in everyday life, and it has been documented by empirical research (Piliavin et al. 1981). It is, however, less obvious why and under what conditions such reactions can be transformed into action aimed at helping those in distress, especially if the action entails stress or grave threat to the actor, and requires great effort or other forms of self-sacrifice over extended periods of time.

In an attempt to get at the motivation of rescuers, we examined the following data: (a) self-reports of motives (answers to the question, "Now, can you summarize for me the main reasons why you became involved in this activity?"); (b) information about the conditions surrounding the initiation of rescuing, the forms of rescuing activity, and their termination; (c) the attitudes and behavior of rescuers' reference groups; (d) types of arguments the rescuers used when they met with opposition to or criticism of their activity; (e) forms of contact between rescuers and rescued persons; (f) the focus of attention of rescuers (as revealed in their account of their action and their relationships with other people, especially with rescued persons); (g) the role of other people in undertaking and sustaining the rescuing activity; and (h) behavior in various situations in which the interests of different people (including the rescuer, his or her close ones, the rescued persons, and other victims) were at stake. It should be emphasized that this set of data contains different kinds of information: self-report statements, information about situational factors that could instigate, facilitate, or inhibit altruistic behavior, information about cognitive and affective concomitants of rescuers' activities (especially in their crucial stages, such as during initiation, upon termination, and in encounter with major obstacles), and information about relationships with people who were involved in the activity.

We acknowledge that our data are insufficient to provide us in every case with information concerning all the above-mentioned issues. Nevertheless, all in all, our analysis of the data has convinced us that we have obtained a sufficient amount of information to reconstruct, in hypothetical form, the motivational structure underlying the rescue behavior of most of our subjects. On this basis, we were able to identify three major classes of motives that apparently instigated the rescuing—allocentric, normocentric, and axiological (Hoffman 1977, 1989; Reykowski 1982b, 1989).

*Allocentric motives* originate when attention is focused on the persecuted person or persons and his or her situation: under certain conditions (especially when directly exposed to the need of another person), there may be a kind of cognitive and/or affective "centration" on the fate of the person in need. Such centration seems to facilitate perspective taking and affective reactions such as empathy and compassion. It may lead to the arousal of a desire to do something to protect the needy person. Subjects to whom this motivational state was attributed tended to report, first, information related to the needs, situations, and emotional states of those they rescued. For example, when asked for their main reason for helping, they gave answers such as, "I knew they needed help. It was the most important" (R.101); "Those Jews came and cried, so what could we do? We didn't have a choice" (R.102); "Because we wanted to rescue her. We did not want her to be caught. We were sorry for her. We knew that if we sent her away she did not know where to go" (R.231); and, "When I saw a mother with a child, how could I refuse? The child made up my mind" (R.258).

*Normocentric motives* originate from the activation of a norm of helping. For some people, the mistreatment of Jews was relevant to the norms of "helpfulness," solidarity, etc. The norm could be interpreted in religious terms (e.g., the Christian prescription "love your neighbor") or in secular terms. The activation of such norms evokes a feeling of obligation to act: individuals are more or less aware that inaction will evoke feelings of guilt and remorse.

Feelings of obligation to observe a norm may be rooted in one of three sources: (a) the normative expectations of a reference group (e.g., family, church, political organizations), (b) an internalized sense of commitment to norms of the main socializing institutions (rescuers tended to refer either to religious institutions [to church] or to secular ones such as parental teachings and political organizations), or (c) the self-concept—some rescuers attributed feelings of obligations to their own "nature"—that is, the helping norm was regarded as the part of their self-identity; other rescuers defined themselves in terms of their social role or social belongingness, and believed that the role or social category assumes a particular form of conduct.

Note that the three sources of norms mentioned above differ with respect to the degree of internalization. In the first case, people seem to be directly dependent upon social definitions of the situation—their helping behavior depends upon social support (requests, approval, more or less continuous contact with others who do the same, or at least express their solidarity). In the second case, people act more or less independently, as long as they believe that the institution with which they are associated is approving their action. Hence, rescuing was more prevalent among church members who met in churches with appropriate spiritual reinforcement and among members of political parties that were against racial persecution. In the third case, people seem to be highly independent from any specific authority—their "normative compass" lies within themselves.

Good examples of normocentric motives are reflected in the following answers to questions about reasons for helping: "Because I was a Christian. It was our duty" (R.005); "I am a Christian and I want to do for Jesus what He wants us to do for the needy" (R.015); "I was raised with the philosophy that I should always help" (R.025).

*Axiological motives* originate from the actualization of moral principles such as "justice," "sanctity of human life," and so on. When an individual notices that his or her basic values are impinged upon, he or she may feel aroused in their defense. The reactions of such an individual are independent from the reactions of other people or any authority, since they are based upon his or her moral convictions. Axiological motives sensitize people to discrepancies between their principles and reality. The main goal of action is to reaffirm the principles. One cannot expect that his or her individual activity can stop injustice or prevent killing, but one can insure that the principles are kept alive as long as there are people who reaffirm them by their deeds.

It seems feasible to differentiate between two kinds of moral principles. One kind relates to the rules of distribution of goods, rights, and responsibilities—that is, to the rules of justice. The second kind pertains to concern for the well-being of others—that is, to the principle of care. There are major differences in the emotional consequences of these two kinds of motive. Justice motives tend to be associated with more impersonal, sometimes even cold, reactions. The person is likely to react with strong emotions (anger, hate) against those who attack the principle, but is less inclined to experience feelings toward the victim as an individual—rescuing or helping is a task the person imposes upon himself or herself as a natural implication of his or her principles. On the other hand, if the caring principle is operating, the person is likely to focus on the subjective states and reactions of the particular victim, and feelings of pity and solidarity with the needy are likely to be evoked. In this case, the tendency for kindness is dominant, while hate and indignation are less likely.

A defining characteristic of principles is their independence from external opinions and evaluations. Hence, actions guided by principles can be executed individually, on their own initiative. If other persons are involved, it is mainly for instrumental reasons rather than for psychological support or guidance. Principles also seem to differ from internalized norms in their origin: while internalized norms can be traced directly back to particular groups (authorities) who were the source of the norm, principles seem to develop, to a great extent, on the basis of individuals' own intellectual and moral efforts. Another difference between principles and internalized norms is related to the fact that, in the case of norms, there is a reference to certain groups or categories of people, such as religious groups, nations, professional groups or organizations and friends who, allegedly, espouse the same norms (normative system), whereas in the case of axiological motives, such a reference is lacking. If there were such a reference, it would comprise people who support (or adhere to) the same principles—in other words, adherence to the principles may play the primary role in determining association with others (while in the case of the normative orientation, it seems the other way around).

The following answers to the question about reasons for aiding Jews serve as examples of axiological motives—mainly those based on moral principles related to justice: "The reason is because each man is equal. We should all live....It was plain murder and I couldn't stand that. I would help a Mohammedan just as well as I did a Jew" (R.006); "The main reason is that I was a patriot. I was for my country. I was for law and order—the Germans robbed the people of their freedom....They took innocent people and I wanted to help" (R.201).

Summing up what was said about the three main categories of motives of altruistic helping, we can point out that they differ from each other with respect to the following characteristics:

*Instigating factors* (the aspects of the situation that tend to instigate the given motives). In the case of allocentric motives, direct exposure to a needy person, especially to his or her emotional reactions, is the most effective factor. In the case of normative motives, an appreciation of the fact that there is a normative demand appropriate to the given situation and that the demand is addressed to the subject is the strongest instigating factor. In the case of axiological motives, the primary factor is an interpretation of the situation as a violation of a principle espoused by the individual.

*Facilitating factors* (the conditions that contribute to or are necessary for sustaining an action controlled by the given motives). In the case of normocentric motives, an important role in the sustaining of rescuing action is played by moral support from other people, at least in the form of example. Such support is unnecessary in the case of axiological and allocentric motives. In the case of the latter, personal contacts with the needy person seem to play an important role in supporting the action.

*Affective concomitants of the helping action.* In the case of allo-centric motives, a personal feeling for the rescued people is typical, whereas in axiological and normocentric behavior, the feelings are more likely to be rather impersonal, focused on a norm or a principle (e.g., bad feelings that there is such injustice in the world).

*Typical forms of action.* In the case of allocentric motives, the action is most likely aimed at helping a particular person or group of people with whom an individual is in direct contact. In the case of axiological motives, the action may be directed toward a group of people with whom the individual has not had any direct contact. In the case of normocentric motives, the action of the rescuer is, very often, a kind of group task. The rescuer participates in an organization or in part of a social network involved in helping.

### RELATION AMONG MOTIVES

The three main categories of motives we have recognized in rescuers can be regarded as abstract (or ideal) types in the sense of the term proposed by Weber. We do not claim that the motives of any particular person fall exclusively in any of the three categories, but rather, we assume they fit to varying degrees. There are several reasons why we rarely come across motives of only one type— "pure" forms. First, rescuers may be guided by various mixtures of motives. Second, the motives of rescuers may change over time. For example, rescuing activity may begin under the influence of normative motives, but over time personal ties may develop between the rescuer and people who are rescued, and the latter may become important for their own sake. Personal contact appears to lead to the activation of allocentric motives, which supplement (or even replace) the original normative ones. The change might also affect the characteristics of the particular motive. Helping might stem originally from an emotional, empathic reaction to a direct cue, for example, seeing that someone is standing in the door begging for help. The initial reaction might be aimed only at the immediate needs of the person (for example, providing food and temporary shelter); however, following extended interaction, the rescuer might develop a much deeper insight into the fate of the victim and a much deeper appreciation for his or her basic needs.

Thus, the initial, simple sympathetic response might become transformed into a much more stable and much stronger motive.

Third, we must acknowledge that differences between motives are in certain cases not very clear, especially when motivational mechanisms achieve a high degree of generality. Two cases in point are worth considering. The first one concerns the similarity between a generalized allocentric orientation and axiological motives based upon the principle of caring. It is difficult to discriminate between people who have an all-embracing attitude toward other human beings—friends and strangers alike—based upon recognition and appreciation of their needs and interests, and those who develop an abstract principle of caring, in a sense defined by Gilligan as "the self-chosen principle of judgment that remains psychological in its concern with relationship and response but becomes universal in its condemnation of exploitation and hurt" (Gilligan 1982).

The second case of unclear demarcation between motives involves norms embedded in self-identity. Such norms, which are strongly internalized and have no apparent relationship to group membership, share many characteristics with principles. For example, both may generate motives that, apparently, can function without social support. However, norms embedded in self-identity seem to differ from principles because they are less abstract, they are not universal, and they are more closely connected to self-concept. One could argue that principles can function as superordinate concepts that prevail over the self.

There is an additional problem related to the classification of motives, a methodological one. In communication about motives and reasons for action, people use a limited repertoire of terms, which may differ enormously in meaning. Such differences may not be apparent because they stem from the deep structure of meaning. Thus, for example, a person who says that he or she behaved in a certain way for "God and country" may be using the phrase as a cliché for decorative purposes, as a kind of symbol that indicates the person's allegiance to a particular orientation ("God and country" was once a slogan of certain political groups in Poland), or to reflect an abstract principle that occupied a high position in the person's belief system. The same can be said about other concepts. For example, the term "justice" may be invoked to give a moral justification for an individual's or group's claim;

it may justify certain kinds of norms, such as harsh treatment to criminals or feeding the poor, or it may refer to a higher-order principle coordinating various perspectives and claims. Clearly, the words used by rescuers must be interpreted in the context of all that is known about them.

## CONCLUDING REMARKS

In closing, we would like to make two additional remarks. One concerns the relationship between the formation of a prosocial goal and undertaking the prosocial action. It should be stressed that the formation of a prosocial goal is not always a sufficient condition for helping. Analyzing our data, we have noticed that there were specific personal qualities that seemed to facilitate (or inhibit) helping action: one of them was ego strength, as manifested in a capability to withstand the stress related to dealing with the highly threatening and burdensome situations. Another personal quality was a kind of self-efficacy. Many, if not most of the rescuers were people who apparently believed in their own capability to cope with difficult life problems. Such beliefs appeared to help them assume responsibilities that were perceived by many others as overwhelming. We should stress, therefore, that one may not explain rescuing action by referring to the motivational processes alone.

Another remark concerns the motives of rescuers. Although we identified three major classes of other-oriented (prosocial) motives, we are not asserting that motives related to the personal needs of rescuers were completely absent. In fact, there are some indications that motives such as a desire for fame, need for excitement, need for nurturance, or need to establish a dominant position with respect to the helped person played some role. Taking into consideration all the circumstances surrounding the rescuing behavior, we claim that in most cases it was a secondary role. It is not possible to account for all the contingencies of rescuing actions by referring to self-oriented motives. The extensive body of data that may uphold this position can be found in the Oliners' book (Oliner and Oliner 1988). Our purpose here was simply to describe different patterns of motives intrinsically related to helping as they emerged from our analysis of the behavior of rescuers. We believe that they played a major role in undertaking the altruistic action.

## REFERENCES

Atkinson, J.W., and Birch, D. (1978). *Introduction to motivation.* New York: Van Nostrand.

Brown, R.J., and Turner, J.C. (1981). Interpersonal and intergroup behaviour. In J.C. Turner and H. Giles (Eds.), *Intergroup behaviour* (pp. 33–65). Oxford: Blackwell.

Eisenberg, N. (1986). *Altruistic emotion, cognition, and behavior.* Hillsdale, NJ: Erlbaum.

Gilligan, C. (1982). *In a different voice: Psychological theory and women's development.* Cambridge, Mass: Harvard University Press.

Hamilton, V. (1983). *The cognitive structures and processes of human motivation and personality.* Chichester: Wiley.

Hoffman, M. (1977). Empathy, its development and prosocial implications. In *Nebraska Symposium on Motivation* (Vol. 25). Lincoln: University of Nebraska Press.

——— (1982). Development of prosocial motivation: Empathy and guilt. In N. Eisenberg (Ed.), *Development of prosocial behavior* (pp. 281–313). Academic Press.

——— (1989). Empathy and prosocial activism. In N. Eisenberg, J. Reykowski, and E. Staub (Eds.), *Social and moral values: Individual and societal perspectives.* Hillsdale, NJ: Erlbaum.

Kelly, G.A. (1955). *The psychology of personal constructs.* New York: Norton.

Latane, B., and Darley, J.M. (1970). Social determinants of bystander intervention in emergencies. In J. Macaulay and L. Berkowitz (Eds.), *Altruism and helping behavior.* New York: Academic Press.

Markus, H. (1980). The self in thought and memory. In D.W. Wegner and R.R. Vallacher (Eds.), *The self in social psychology.* New York: Oxford University Press.

Oliner, S., and Oliner, P. (1988). *The altruistic personality: Rescuers of Jews in Nazi Europe.* New York: Free Press.

Piliavin, J., Dovidio, J.F., Gaertner, S.L., and Clark, R.D. III. (1981). *Emergency intervention.* New York: Academic Press.

Reykowski, J. (1982a). Social motivation. *Annual Review of Psychology, 33,* 123–55.

——— (1982b). Motivation of prosocial behavior. In V.J. Derlaga and J. Grzelak (Eds.), *Cooperation and helping behavior: Theories and research.* New York: Academic Press.

——— (1984). Spatial organization of a cognitive system and intrinsic prosocial motivation. In E. Staub, D. Bar-Tal, J. Karylowski, and J. Reykowski (Eds.), *Development and maintenance of prosocial behavior.* New York: Plenum.

——— (1989). Dimensions of development in moral values. In N. Eisenberg, J. Reykowski, and E. Staub (Eds.), *Social and moral values: Individual and societal perspectives.* Hillsdale, NJ: Erlbaum.

Schwartz, S.H. (1977). Normative influences on altruism. In L. Berkowitz (Ed.), *Advances in experimental social psychology* (Vol. 10). New York: Academic Press.

Staub, E. (1980). Social and prosocial behavior: Personal and situational influences and their interactions. In E. Staub (Ed.), *Personality: Basic aspects and current research.* Englewood Cliffs, NJ: Prentice-Hall.

Tajfel, H., Flamant, C., Bilig, M.C., and Bundy, R. (1971). Social categorization and intergroup behaviour. *European Journal of Social Psychology, 1,* 149–75.

Weiner, B., Russell, D., and Lerman, D. (1978). Affective consequences of causal ascription. In J.H. Harvey, W.J. Ickes, and R.F. Kidd (Eds.), *New directions in attribution research* (Vol. 2). Hillsdale, NJ: Erlbaum.

Zajonc, R.B. (1968). Cognitive theories in social psychology. In G. Lindzey and E. Aronson (Eds.), *The handbook of social psychology* (Vol. 1). Reading, MA: Addison-Wesley.

—— (1980). Feeling and thinking: Preferences need no inferences. *American Psychologist, 35,* 151–75.

# 10

# PREDICTING PROSOCIAL COMMITMENT IN DIFFERENT SOCIAL CONTEXTS

*Leo Montada*

Research on altruism is concerned with highly different predicaments and, consequently, with very different activities. Prosocial behavior may involve readiness to give away a small coin, donating bone marrow, helping a car driver with a flat tire, consoling people in pain and sorrow, or rescuing the politically persecuted. Schneider (1988) lists forty-four different actions used in empirical research on helping that are quite different with regard to costs incurred as well as riskiness.

It might be that all altruistic acts are based on a common facet of motivation and a common basic attitude toward other people in need. Some definitions of altruism state that the helper intends to benefit another; some add as constituents that the helper acts voluntarily and that he or she is not motivated to gain external rewards. However, we cannot expect that all the capabilities needed for effective helping, all motives, attitudes, and internal and external barriers against granting help, and all personal and social norms and responsibilities will be identical for all helping behaviors. Moreover, granting help as well as asking for and refusing help take place in social interactions and social contexts, making it necessary to consider the kind of relationship between the potential helper and the needy as well as the kind of social system both belong to, and so forth. Social contexts are very important in facilitating or preventing help. Experimental research on altruism in the laboratory rarely has taken the influence of social systems into account. Aspects of social systems such as role expectancies, status, norms, prejudices, solidarities, responsibilities, and so forth make it difficult to design experiments that are ecologically valid.

The studies reported in this chapter were concerned with two very different kinds of social relationships between potential helpers and the needy. In the first, the people needing help were not personally known to the subject; in the second, benefactor and recipient were involved in close relationships, namely that of adult daughters toward their mothers. The kind of relationship made a difference with respect to the motivation and structure of prosocial activities.

### STUDY I: MOTIVATION UNDERLYING PROSOCIAL COMMITMENTS TO THE DISADVANTAGED

There is poverty in all societies; there is child abuse and maltreatment of elderly people; there are seriously ill, bereaved, and handicapped people, battered women and crime victims, and politically persecuted refugees and emigrants seeking to escape economic privation. The reactions of people to the "fate" of those suffering such hardships range from prosocial commitment to indifference, derogation, and blame (Ryan 1971). Some individuals and groups fight for the entitlement of the disadvantaged; others oppose such prosocial overtures; and a rather passive majority assumedly believe it is a matter for the government, the churches, and so forth. The following questions were posed in this series of studies: What are the cognitive, emotional, and prosocial responses of relatively privileged subjects to the problems and needs of less fortunate people with whom the subjects are not personally acquainted? What are the predictors of prosocial commitment to various groups of disadvantaged people?

Data presented in this chapter were taken from a study concerned with unemployed people, poor people in developing countries, and foreign (Turkish) workers in Germany. These groups are only a small sample of people suffering hardships all over the world. We expected that emotional responses to the less fortunate would be a key to the analysis of motivations underlying prosocial (and nonprosocial) behavior. Among the various emotions people might experience when they confront individuals less fortunate than themselves, we assessed *sympathy for the needy, existential guilt, moral outrage, anger, fear of losing one's own advantages, con-*

*tentment with one's own better life,* and *hopelessness concerning the fate of the needy.* Three "prosocial" emotions expected to motivate prosocial actions—sympathy, existential guilt, and moral outrage—were contrasted with the four other emotions, which were expected to interfere with prosocial commitments.

As potential antecedents, we assessed a variety of variables, including *social attitudes* toward the less fortunate, *appraisals* of the causation and responsibility for the existence of disadvantages, appraisals of *injustice,* belief in a just world (Lerner 1980), and two principles of distributive justice—the equity principle and the need principle.

As potential consequences of the emotions, we assessed *attributions of responsibility to support the needy* to either oneself or to powerful others, and *readiness for prosocial commitment* to the disadvantaged. Several forms of prosocial commitment were distinguished: charitable ones, like spending money or joining a helping group, and more political ones, such as signing a petition demanding that political leaders do something to improve the lot of the disadvantaged, and participating in a demonstration for similar aims. We will first outline conceptualizations of these emotions on which we focused, and their expected differential impact on prosocial actions.

### Existential Guilt

Not everybody is able to feel happy about being the one who survived a disaster, was released from prison, was freed from repression, escaped persecutors, or lives on the sunny side of the world. Some of these "lucky" people experience feelings of guilt, as was observed, for example, in survivors from concentrations camps (Von Baeyer, Haefner, and Kisker 1964) and Hiroshima, and in those returning from Korean captivity (Lifton 1967).

Feelings of guilt are easy to understand in close relationships in which we consider the well-being of loved ones of equal or even greater importance than our own. Relative privilege is neither aimed at nor appreciated in these relationships. Sharing goods, or even giving more to loved ones is typical. To receive a relative privilege may be experienced as infringing on solidarity, love, or responsibility, and thus will not be enjoyed. We may well grant priority to a loved one if he or she were persecuted, helping even at the risk of our own life. But do we feel the same way toward people outside close relationships? What was assessed as existential guilt toward strangers in this study is merely a pale reflection of the guilt feelings some people may experience when close relatives or friends suffer. However, with reference to Hoffman (1976), we expected people to experience existential guilt vis-à-vis socially distant individuals and even strangers, when they did not feel that their own advantages were not deserved compared to the disadvantages of others, provided the others were perceived as needy, and they were not excluded subjectively from the potential helper's own community of responsibility (Deutsch 1985), in which members' entitlements are acknowledged not only on the basis of equity but also on the basis of their needs. Finally, perceiving a causal relationship between one's own advantages and the disadvantages of others, and, therefore, a kind of responsibility for the existence of their needs, was expected to contribute to the arousal of guilt feelings.

Those who perceive the differences between people as unjust acknowledge that the needy are entitled to receive support, and, consequently, are expected to favor reallocations of resources. But who considers the disadvantages of others unjust? Probably those who prefer the need principle. The nature of people's relationship to those who are needy partly determines which principle of distributive justice is perceived as adequate. As hypothesized by Deutsch (1985) and empirically corroborated in several studies (Schmitt and Montada 1982; for a review see Tornblom and Jonsson 1985), preferences for principles of justice depend on the social context: in a business context, competition is the dominant kind of relationship, and, therefore, the equity principle tends to be favored. In close relationships (friendship, family), the equality or the need principle is often considered more adequate. This way of thinking is not compatible with an illusionary belief in a just world that is defended by derogating victims and by blaming the disadvantaged for having self-inflicted their needs (Lerner 1980). As we know from several lines of research, responsibility for helping victims is warded off if their hardship is perceived as self-inflicted or deserved (Ryan 1971; Piliavin, Rodin, and Piliavin 1969; Ickes and Kidd 1976). Schwartz (1977) assumed that a tendency to deny responsibility arises when help is costly.

In a previous study (Montada, Schmitt, and Dalbert 1986), we demonstrated that existential guilt toward needy people is most prevalent in subjects who consider the need principle just, who consider the equity principle unjust, and who believe that they have at least some potential to contribute to a redistribution. Belief in a just world and denial of responsibility for the needy reduce the probability of feeling guilty.

## Moral Outrage Because of Unjust Disadvantages

Another emotion expected to motivate prosocial commitment is moral indignation or outrage. While existential guilt implies self-blame, moral outrage is directed toward someone else or to an institution perceived as having violated moral norms, human rights, or the entitlements of individuals. Many aggressive acts, many political protest movements, and many revolts and revolutions are motivated by moral outrage. Many of the riots by blacks were precipitated by a crime committed against a black by white people, a crime that was not prosecuted by the police and not brought to trial in a legal court (Lieberson and Silverman 1965). When open protest is dangerous because the adversary is powerful, moral outrage is combined with fear, which may result in (silent) hate (Montada and Boll 1988). When outrage overcomes fear, it may motivate the taking of risks. In totalitarian systems, it may motivate people to join resistance movements. Certainly, moral outrage motivates retaliation. Does it also motivate help and support to people who are unjustly in need?

Interpreting the observations by Keniston (1968) and Haan (1975) on the engagement of American youth in the civil rights movement and the movement to end the war in Vietnam during the 1960s, Hoffman (1976) suggested that many of the educated white students from middle-class families living in wealth and security were motivated by existential guilt feelings. If they were convinced that the majority culture or the government was to blame for the injustices toward the black population or the continuation of an unjust war in Vietnam, the motivation might also— or even more so—have been moral outrage.

Conceptually, the motivational impact of moral outrage on corrective helping is not unequivocal, because the focus of this emotion is less on the victim than on the perpetrator. Different categories of prosocial activity must be distinguished. Perhaps outrage primarily motivates retaliation, blame, or punishment toward the harmdoer, rather than support or help for the victim.

Yet, help has many faces. There is "downstream" helping, such as charity or rescuing people; there is "upstream" helping, focusing on prevention, and sometimes including efforts to change the social system or, at least, established policies. The latter form may involve opposing and blaming those who are perceived as being responsible for the existence of need and hardship, and this form, at least, could be motivated by moral outrage.

Opposing a powerful adversary also may offer a motivational basis for helping and rescuing victims, especially if there is no actual behavioral choice between retaliation against the perpetrator and support for the victims. In the case of socially disadvantaged people, one may ask what is preferred: directly supporting the needy or blaming those who are responsible and demanding that they support the needy. Both kinds of prosocial activity were assessed in the present study.

The antecedents and correlates of moral outrage were expected to be much the same as those for existential guilt, with one major exception: whereas guilt implies the attribution of responsibility to oneself for the existence of and for the remedy of others' needs, outrage implies the attribution of responsibility to others.

### Sympathy for the Disadvantaged

Conceptually, sympathy implies a concern for another person in which one shares his or her negative feelings. This concept and its operationalization correspond to Hoffman's concept of sympathetic distress and Batson's concept of empathy. Hoffman (1976) distinguished several levels in the development of empathy, ranging from an egocentric affection to a mature sympathetic distress, which is an other-centered concern based on a developed role-taking capacity enabling individuals to consider the problems and stressors of others within the framework of their life situation. Analyzing reactions to people in distress, Batson (e.g., Batson, Fultz, and Schoenrade 1987) distinguished between personal (unsympathetic) distress and empathy (distress resulting from a true concern for others) as two qualitatively distinct emotions with different motivational consequences.

Sympathy, as assessed in the present study, refers to compassionate perception of the needs or misery of others. However, sympathy does not seem to be "granted" to everybody in distress, and it does not seem to be granted in every situation. Again, as anticipated for existential guilt and moral outrage, social attitudes expressing social distance or closeness should be predictive; for example, it is not likely that we feel sympathy for adversaries or enemies.

In contrast to guilt and outrage, sympathy does not imply perceived injustice. However, if a bad fate were considered self-inflicted or deserved, this would interfere with the arousal of sympathy (see Piliavin, Rodin, and Piliavin 1969). Whether a character in a movie who is going to be hanged deserves this fate or not is crucial for our emotional response: we either react with sympathy for the "victim" and outrage toward his "murderers" or with moral satisfaction about the punishment of his crime. In the case of less fortunate people such as the unemployed, the perception of self-infliction may depend on beliefs and views of justice. The assumption of self-infliction may help defend an illusionary belief in a just world, and the equity principle may suggest that the misery is a just consequence of poor achievements. Thus, it was expected that sympathy would be less likely in subjects who score high on belief in a just world, on acceptance of the equity principle, and on appraisals of self-infliction, whereas perception of injustice and a positive view of the need principle might also be a breeding ground for sympathy just as for guilt and outrage.

What are the conceptual differences between sympathy and the other two prosocial emotions, and what are the differences in terms of their antecedents? Unlike existential guilt, sympathy neither implies a sense of responsibility to support the needy, nor does it presuppose the cognition of having violated a moral rule. Consequently, it was not expected that sympathy would be predicted by the variable perception of a (causal) relationship between one's own advantages and the needs of others. Unlike moral outrage, sympathy neither presupposes the acknowledgment that the needy are entitled to get support, nor does it involve blaming an agent or an agency for the existence and the remedy of needs. Unfortunately, neither of these variables was directly represented in the antecedents assessed in this study.

### Emotions Expected to Interfere with Prosocial Commitment

The other four emotions assessed were not expected to motivate prosocial or altruistic actions. Anger at the disadvantaged should occur when they are blamed for either having self-inflicted their fate or for not having tried hard enough to improve their situation.

Angry blame interferes with readiness to support and help. Expressions of contentment vis-à-vis people living in misery represent an egocentric view of one's own situation, made positive by downward comparison, not a concern for the needy. Fear of losing one's own advantages as a consequence of the misery of others also represents an egocentric concern. Although this kind of fear may motivate prosocial activities, such activities cannot be considered altruistically motivated. In the case of hopelessness concerning the future of the disadvantaged, any prosocial activity would be considered futile.

### Method

Methodological aspects are described very briefly. More comprehensive descriptions can be found in Montada and Schneider (1988, 1989).

*Subjects.* Eight hundred and sixty-five subjects took part in this study. The sample contained several subsamples who were privileged by education (university students), by wealth (people from wealthy neighborhoods and employers), or by social security (civil servants in tenured positions). Ages of subjects ranged from eighteen to eighty-six ($M = 36$). Fifty-nine percent of the sample was male, 41 percent female. Subjects with higher education were somewhat overrepresented (68 percent graduated from high school).

*Operationalization of Concepts.* Many of the core variables were assessed with the Existential Guilt Inventory (ESI) (Montada, Schmitt, and Dalbert 1986). In this inventory, respondents are confronted with written scenarios describing problems and needs of disadvantaged people. There are three scenarios for each of three groups of disadvantaged people (unemployed, foreign workers, poor people in the developing countries). The constructs assessed by the ESI include the following: (1) emotions: sympathy for the disadvantaged, existential guilt, outrage because of unjust differences, anger about the disadvantaged, contentment with one's own advantages, and hopelessness regarding an improvement in the lot of the needy; (2) cognitive appraisals of justice and responsibility: perceived injustice of differences, perception of a causal interrelatedness between one's own advantages and the disadvantages of the needy, perception of disadvantages as self-inflicted, perception of one's own advantages as justified and deserved, feelings of responsibility to act prosocially, and attribution of responsibility to act prosocially to powerful others or institutions.

Constructs were represented by statements that were rated on six-point scales expressing the degree to which the statements corresponded to the respondents' own feelings or cognitions. A nine-item scale was formulated for each construct (one item for each of the three scenarios for each of the three groups of disadvantaged people). Subjects' scores were their mean scores on these nine items. Usual procedures for testing homogeneity and reliability were applied to evaluate the quality of the scales. Further concepts were assessed with several newly developed scales, including a scale to measure Lerner's belief in a just world (Dalbert, Montada, and Schmitt 1987), scales to assess views on principles of distributive justice (especially the equity principle and the need principle), and two scales to measure attitudes toward the three groups of disadvantaged people in terms of attributing positive or negative traits to them. All scales had adequate homogeneity and consistency according to usual psychometric criteria.

Readiness for prosocial commitment also was assessed by items asking about willingness (1) to spend money, (2) to sign a petition addressed to the government, (3) to participate in a demonstration, and (4) to join an activity group. Each of these four types of prosocial activities was represented by two items for each of the three groups of disadvantaged people.

*Validity of Self-Report Data.* The validity of a subset of responses given by the subjects was tested by sampling external ratings of friends, acquaintances, or relatives. These external ratings correlated fairly highly with the subjects' answers (the self-reports) (e.g., correlations for six tested variables of the ESI varied between $r = .39$ and $r = .52$; $M = 46.7$), indicating that these answers indeed reflected a core of truth (Schneider et al. 1987).

*Longitudinal Replication.* The study was replicated with about half of the sample several months after the first wave of data collection. The replication was performed to explore (a) the stability of interindividual differences, (b) the stability of the relationships among variables, and (c) systematic changes. Overall, the stability of interindividual differences and relationships among variables

**Table 10.1**

Multiple Regression from Readiness to Prosocial Activities on Emotions, Existential Guilt, Moral Outrage, Sympathy, Anger, Fear, Contentment, and Hopelessness, Aggregated Across All Nine Situations for All Three Groups of Disadvantaged People ($N$ = 807)

| Predictors | rcrit | beta | b | Fb |
|---|---|---|---|---|
| Moral outrage | .53 | .41 | .36 | 135.99 |
| Existential guilt | .44 | .24 | .20 | 47.97 |
| Contentment | − .06 | − .10 | − .10 | 10.60 |
| Hopelessness | − .01 | − .10 | − .10 | 10.53 |
| (intercept) | | 2.57 | | |

multiple $R$ = .57; $R^2$ = .33; F*total* = 98.71; p*F* = .001

Adapted from Table V in Montada and Schneider (1989).

was high. Most of the correlations (zero-order as well as multiple) were higher in the replication study. Data reported here, however, were taken from the first wave.

### Results and Discussion: Motivation for Prosocial Commitment to the Disadvantaged—Sympathy or Morality?

The results of the study are presented and discussed mainly with respect to the motivation underlying prosocial commitment as it is indicated by emotional responses. Further aspects, such as the prediction of emotional responses and differences between groups with different demographic characteristics or political orientations, are mentioned only for the purpose of clarifying the meaning and the motivational impact of emotions.

Overall, 33 percent of the variance in prosocial commitment was accounted for by the emotions assessed (in the replication study, the quota was 40 percent). Table 10.1 shows the results for subjects over all four forms of prosocial commitment. Table 10.2 shows the results for each of these four forms separately. A closer look at the results reveals a somewhat surprising fact that may offer some new perspectives on prosocial commitment. The best predictor was not sympathy for the needy (only reaching significance for "spending money"), but, rather, moral outrage about the unjustness of differences between the privileged (the social stratum the subjects themselves belonged to) and the disadvantaged, followed by existential guilt because of one's own relative advantages.

**Table 10.2**

Multiple Regression from Different Forms of Prosocial Activities on the Emotions Guilt, Moral Outrage, Sympathy, Anger, Fear, Contentment, and Hopelessness Aggregated Across All Nine Items for All Three Groups of Disadvantaged People ($791 \leq N \leq 799$, Accepted Models $\text{p}_{\text{F}}b \leq .05$)

| Criterion | Predictors | rcrit | beta | b | Fb |
|---|---|---|---|---|---|
| **Spending money** | Moral outrage | .42 | .26 | .26 | 34.84 |
| | Existential guilt | .39 | .25 | .22 | 40.52 |
| | Hopelessness | − .04 | − .11 | − .13 | 10.71 |
| | Fear | − .05 | − .09 | − .10 | 7.20 |
| | Sympathy | .35 | .09 | .11 | 4.30 |
| | (intercept) | | | 2.80 | |
| | multiple $R = .49$; $R^2 = .24$; $F_{total} = 49.36$; $\text{p}_{\text{F}}total < .01$ | | | | |
| **Signing a petition** | Moral outrage | .50 | .39 | .44 | 114.79 |
| | Anger | − .28 | − .14 | − .15 | 18.67 |
| | Existential guilt | .38 | .15 | .15 | 16.31 |
| | Contentment | − .09 | − .08 | − .11 | 6.78 |
| | (intercept) | | | 2.43 | |
| | multiple $R = .54$; $R^2 = .30$; $F_{total} = 83.39$; $\text{p}_{\text{F}}total < .001$ | | | | |
| **Participation in a demonstration** | Moral outrage | .44 | .35 | .39 | 84.02 |
| | Contentment | − .13 | − .16 | − .21 | 26.54 |
| | Existential guilt | .33 | .14 | .15 | 13.18 |
| | Fear | .20 | .07 | .09 | 4.00 |
| | (intercept) | | | 2.67 | |
| | multiple $R = .48$; $R^2 = .23$; $F_{total} = 60.55$; $\text{p}_{\text{F}}total < .001$ | | | | |
| **Activity within a group** | Moral outrage | .38 | .26 | .28 | 45.24 |
| | Existential guilt | .35 | .20 | .20 | 25.21 |
| | Hopelessness | .01 | − .09 | − .12 | 6.93 |
| | Fear | .19 | .08 | .09 | 4.64 |
| | (intercept) | | | 2.27 | |
| | multiple $R = .43$; $R^2 = .19$; $F_{total} = 44.91$; $\text{p}_{\text{F}}total < .01$ | | | | |

Adapted from Table VI in Montada and Schneider (1989).

Negative contributions to the variance in prosocial commitment came from contentment with one's own advantages and hopelessness concerning the future fate of the needy (see table 10.1). When specific forms were used as criteria (table 10.2), fear of losing one's own advantages and anger about the disadvantaged also were among the significant predictors.

The negative effects of these emotions are easy to understand. Anger implies blaming the disadvantaged for having self-inflicted their problems, or for failing to exert enough effort to reduce them. Attributing responsibility to the disadvantaged for the existence and remedy of their needs interferes with assuming responsibility. Hopelessness concerning the future of the disadvantaged should paralyze any activity aimed at improving their lot. Contentment with one's own situation and fear of losing one's own advantages frequently reflects an egocentric justification of one's own advantages that interferes with acknowledging the needy's entitlement to support.

Fear of losing one's own advantages had a significant negative effect on spending money, but was positively related to two other forms of prosocial activity (table 10.2). This seemingly contradictory result may mean—as argued above—that fear of losing one's own advantages is not unambiguous with respect to the motivation underlying prosocial activities. While it basically represents an egocentric concern and not a concern for needy others, it may motivate activities in support of the needy with the ultimate goal of reducing the danger that huge disadvantages of others may lead to a destabilization of the social structure and thus jeopardize the subject's own situation.

Overall, the impact of the prosocial emotions was relatively high. The theoretically and practically most interesting finding was that moral outrage and guilt had much more impact than sympathy. This was a stable result, replicated longitudinally, and bivariate correlations between sympathy and readiness to prosocial commitment were strong, significant, and positive. This does not contradict the results of the multivariate analyses in which sympathy had low or insignificant effects (in the longitudinal replication, even negative effects) because both guilt ($r = .45$) and moral outrage ($r = .53$) were correlated with sympathy. Conceptually, it makes sense to assume that sympathy is a fertile soil, if not a prerequisite, for both of these emotions: it is doubtful we may feel existential guilt or outrage when we do not feel empathy for people suffering hardships. For instance, if our enemies suffer, we neither feel guilty nor outraged, but, rather, morally satisfied.

But guilt and outrage have other components. Conceptually, both imply (1) the perception that disadvantages are unjust and (2) attributions of responsibility for their existence and remedy. In the case of guilt, attributions are made to the subjects themselves;

in the case of outrage they are made to others who are held responsible. Conceptually, sympathy does not imply perceiving the needy to be entitled to obtain support, which does not contradict the assumption that perceiving injustice makes sympathy for the needy more likely. If acknowledging these entitlements contributes to the motivation underlying prosocial activities, this might explain why the predictive impact of guilt and outrage (1) included that of sympathy and (2) exceeded it. This also might be why sympathy did not contribute independently to the prediction of prosocial activities.

These conceptual differentiations between sympathy, existential guilt, and moral outrage could be tested only partially in this study. The predictor variables assessed and the zero-order correlations between the emotions were similar for all three prosocial emotions. However, since the predictors were correlated, multivariate analyses were more appropriate for identifying the differential associations. A comprehensive presentation of the results of these analyses would require considerable space. Only one table is presented showing the partial correlations of the three prosocial emotions with three responsibility-related variables (table 10.4). The interpretation, however, is based on an extended series of multivariate analyses (Montada and Schneider 1988, 1989).

In a path analysis with eleven predictors, controlling for social desirability (table 10.3), existential guilt was consistently related to (1) perceived injustice of the discrepancies between one's own advantages and the disadvantages of others, and (2) perception of a (causal) relationship between one's own advantages and the disadvantages of others (e.g., the poverty in the developing countries is also caused by the imbalances in prices for raw products and industrial products; or job sharing or giving up a second job would provide employment opportunities for others). This second variable represents the appraisal of one's responsibility for the existence of the unjust disadvantages of others. There were indirect effects mediated by these two predictors: endorsing the need principle in allocations was positively related to attitudes toward the disadvantaged, endorsing the equity principle and "belief in a just world" was negatively related. Existential guilt was strongly related to a sense of responsibility to support the needy.

It is easy to grasp the psychological meaning of existential guilt feelings suggested by this pattern of correlations: respondents reporting existential guilt perceive both the disadvantages of the

**Table 10.3**

Partial Correlations ($p < .01$), Social Desirability Partialed Out, between Emotional Responses and Several Categories of Predictors[1] ($N = 765$)

| Predictors | Emotions | | | | | | |
|---|---|---|---|---|---|---|---|
| | Existential Guilt | Moral Outrage | Sympathy | Anger | Fear of loss | Contentment | Hopelessness |
| *Appraisals of justice and responsibility* | | | | | | | |
| Perceived injustice of differences | .50 | .63 | .57 | -.40 | .13 | .12 | .06* |
| Perceived self-infliction of disadvantages | -.26 | -.34 | -.27 | .79 | .08* | .29 | .09 |
| Justification of own advantages | -.23 | -.27 | -.22 | .71 | .07* | .38 | .12 |
| Perceived interrelatedness of own advantages and disadvantages of others | .50 | .56 | .43 | -.36 | .31 | -.01** | .14 |
| Perceived own responsibility for help | .61 | .55 | .52 | -.02** | .15 | .13 | -.03** |
| Attribution of responsibility for help to powerful others | .23 | .43 | .39 | .04** | .26 | .19 | .21 |
| *Background variables* | | | | | | | |
| Belief in a just world, general | -.07 | -.15 | -.08* | .34 | -.04** | .18 | -.15 |
| Belief in a just world, specific | -.30 | -.40 | -.35 | .67 | -.04** | .16 | .02** |
| View of the equity principle | -.25 | -.36 | -.23 | .69 | -.01** | .28 | .10 |
| View of the need principle | .44 | .58 | .55 | -.33 | .17 | .00* | .09 |
| Positive attitudes toward the disadvantaged | .31 | .41 | .36 | -.35 | .05** | -.05** | -.02** |
| Negative attitudes toward the disadvantaged | -.20 | -.28 | -.28 | .51 | .08* | .15 | .07* |

* $.01 < p \leq .05$; ** $p > .05$

[1]Scale with items related to the three groups of disadvantaged addressed in this study.

**Table 10.4**

Partial Correlation Coefficients of the Three Prosocial Emotions
Existential Guilt, Sympathy, and Moral Outrage with Three
Responsibility Variables ($N$ = 818)

| | Causal Interrelatedness of Fates | Attribution of Responsibility for Supporting the Needy: | |
| --- | --- | --- | --- |
| | | To oneself | To powerful others |
| Existential guilt** | .26 | .43 | − .04* |
| Moral outrage** | .32 | .26 | .20 |
| Sympathy** | .02* | .16 | .20 |

* $p > .01$
**The other two prosocial emotions are partialed out.
Adapted from Table VIII in Montada and Schneider (1989).

needy and their own relative advantages as being related and as unjust. They tend to think that goods (wealth, security, jobs, and so forth) should be distributed according to the needs of the recipients, instead of merely following the equity principle, which means proportional to achievements and merits.

Invoking the need principle when confronted with disadvantaged people or victims means that these people are included in the community of those with whom the respondent is concerned and for whom he or she feels responsible. Enjoying huge advantages oneself is not without problems. The fact that positive attitudes toward the disadvantaged were included in the pattern of predictors of existential guilt supports this interpretation. Those who experience existential guilt feel responsible for supporting the needy.

The predictor pattern for moral outrage was very similar to that of existential guilt. The differences between the two emotions became obvious when the subjects were asked, "Who is responsible for improving the fate of the disadvantaged: the respondents themselves or powerful others?" While existential guilt was related only to the first alternative (subjects themselves felt responsible), moral outrage was related to both alternatives (see table 10.4), but much more weakly than guilt was to the first one. This corroborates the abovementioned view that outrage implies blaming others.

There was also considerable overlap between sympathy and the two other prosocial emotions in the pattern of predictors. In the conceptual analysis, sympathy was not assumed to be based on the acknowledgment of the entitlements of the needy, while both moral outrage and existential guilt were. Using the set of predictors assessed in this study, acknowledgment of the entitlements of the needy can be derived from (1) perceived injustice of disadvantages, (2) the need principle of justice, and (3) the perception of a (causal) relationship between one's own advantages and the disadvantages of others. While, empirically, sympathy was significantly related to the first and the second of these cognitive appraisals, it was not related to the third when partial correlations were considered (see table 10.4). This pattern supports the conceptual analysis.

In contrast to guilt and outrage, multiple regression analyses revealed that sympathy also was positively correlated with the equity principle. That seems somewhat contradictory, because arguments based on the equity principle may deny the entitlements of the needy, and this may interfere with prosocial commitment. With respect to responsibility for supporting the disadvantaged, sympathy was similar to outrage: both differed from guilt insofar as they were less strongly related to self-attributions of responsibility, and more strongly related to perceived responsibility of powerful others.

Moral outrage due to the unjust differences within and between societies was by far the best single predictor of prosocial commitments. This was especially true for political activities such as participation in a demonstration, signing a petition aimed at drawing attention to the fate of the disadvantaged, and blaming government and society for unjust policies. For the remaining two forms of political activity, the predictor weights were lower (table 10.2). In line with this evidence, members and supporters of the "Greens" in Germany—a left-wing protest party with a rather radical program of equality that supports needy and socially deprived people—scored significantly higher on moral outrage and readiness for political activities in favor of the disadvantaged than members and supporters of conservative parties.

The patterns of correlation among the three prosocial emotions within the network of variables included in this study do not offer a completely convincing explanation of why sympathy was less predictive of prosocial commitment than outrage. Yet, there are hints that sympathy does not imply the acknowledgment of entitlements of the needy.

On a conceptual level, it is easy to see how the three prosocial emotions differ in their impact on prosocial commitment. While guilt and outrage reflect the morality of a person, this is not necessarily the case for sympathy. Guilt and outrage are based on the notion that individuals feel that moral norms, which they experience as mandatory oughts, are being violated. Guilt is experienced when respondents themselves feel they have neglected their moral norms (at least by doing nothing to reduce injustice); outrage is experienced when another person or institution is blamed. Neglect of a moral ought is not a prerequisite for sympathy, even if blaming the needy and perceiving their hardship as deserved may interfere with the arousal of sympathy (Piliavin, Rodin, and Piliavin 1969).

The best interpretation of the findings in this study might be that prosocial commitment toward the disadvantaged was motivated primarily by the "moral" emotions outrage and guilt, which were more compelling than sympathy in motivating readiness to reduce injustice. Overall, justice-related variables (emotions, appraisals, need and equity principles, and belief in a just world) exert stronger effects on prosocial commitment than general positive and negative attitudes toward the needy.

These results will not necessarily generalize to other situations and contexts, such as when people have personal contact or are acquainted with the needy. One has to be especially cautious when generalizing to prosocial behavior in close relationships. In relationships that Melvin Lerner calls "identity relationships" (Lerner and Whitehead 1980), justice is not a salient issue. The well-being of a loved one is aimed at or appreciated without considering whether or not justice is maintained. Indeed, when justice becomes an issue in close relationships, the relationship may no longer be "very close." We have data on prosocial behavior in families showing that sympathy and love are significant motivators. We turn to this study now.

## STUDY II: PROSOCIAL COMMITMENTS IN CLOSE RELATIONSHIPS

This study investigated prosocial activities of adult children toward their parents (Cicirelli 1991; Schneewind forthcoming). To assure homogeneity of the sample, only adult daughters were included. We chose adult daughters because when a mother is living alone and needs care, her daughter usually assumes responsibility. This type of caretaking was one main interest in the study.

Although we were primarily interested in the analysis of caretaking for disabled mothers, we also included younger cohorts of daughters in the study whose mothers were not disabled, and who, consequently, were faced with quite different needs. Actually, a variety of prosocial activities in addition to caring and nursing a disabled mother were observed and analyzed. This was done to explore whether different needs and prosocial activities require different patterns of predictors. We can state in advance that although the dominant needs and desires of the old and young mothers varied quite considerably, the pattern of predictors was remarkably consistent across the age periods and across different categories of need-related activities. This makes it possible to present the results for the entire sample of respondents.

### Predictor Variables of Prosocial Commitment

A wide range of variables was assessed as predictors, including several known in social psychology as "determinants" of prosocial behavior, either in general (Bierhoff 1980) or within the context of the family (Schmitt and Gehle 1983). They belonged to the following categories:

1. traitlike variables: generalized empathy (Schmitt 1982), denial of responsibility (Schwartz 1977) (two scales assessing the tendency to refuse responsibility for elderly people in general):
2. social relations in the family: cohesion, control, and the quality of the daughter-mother dyad in the sense of mutual love (Cicirelli 1983);
3. past habitual prosocial activities toward the mother (Harris 1972; Bentler and Speckart 1979);
4. general attitudes toward prosocial behavior (Ajzen and Fishbein 1980; Benninghaus 1976);
5. normative beliefs, meaning personal norms, as understood by Schwartz (1977), of complying with specific desires and needs (Cicirelli 1983);
6. cognitive appraisals of the situation with respect to specific desires and needs: costs of complying (e.g., Lang and Brody 1983), legitimacy of the wishes of the mother (Langer and Abelson 1972), the subjective strength of a desire or a need, mother's costs when a daughter does not help or comply with specific desires (Piliavin, Piliavin, and Rodin 1975), the degree of perceived self-infliction of current needs by the mother herself

(Meyer and Mulherin 1980), and ability and opportunity to help and comply with mother's desires (Midlarsky 1971; Kuhl 1986);
7. anticipated costs, that is, costs the daughter expects in the case of noncompliance: anticipated guilt feelings (Rawlings 1970), anticipated blame or critique by significant others, and anticipated blame and critique by the mother.

### Method

*Subjects.* The sample consisted of 673 respondents taken from three birth cohorts of adult daughters twenty to twenty-five years, thirty to thirty-five years, forty-eight to fifty-three years) whose mothers were an average of twenty-seven years older than the daughters. The educational level of the sample was roughly representative of the population, and this was true for many other demographic attributes (e.g., married/not married, employed/not employed, rural/urban).

*Operationalization of Constructs.* The predictor variables listed above for Categories 1 and 2 were assessed by questionnaire scales that were newly developed with the exception of familial cohesion and familial control, which were measured with the German adaptation of the Moos scales (Engfer, Schneewind, and Hinderer 1977). The usual procedures of testing the homogeneity and internal consistency of the scales were applied. All scales mentioned in this chapter had adequate psychometric qualities. The predictor variables in Categories 3 to 7 were constructed as follows: from a list of thirty-four needs and desires a mother might have, subjects were required to select those five that were currently dominant. If an urgent desire or a strong need of her mother was not mentioned in the list, a daughter could include this within the five she was supposed to select as a replacement for one of the items on the list.

All scales in Categories 3 to 7 had five items, each of which was formulated individually with respect to each one of the five needs or desires of a mother selected by her daughter. These constructs were represented by stems of statements that were completed individually with reference to the selected needs and desires. These statements had to be rated on six-point scales. For instance, the construct "habitual prosocial activities in the past" (Category 3) was represented by five items, each one addressed to one of the five needs or desires selected individually. All items started with

the introductory phrase: "In the past—meaning up to today—I ..."
This phrase was completed with one of the five selected needs or
desires—for example, " ...have complied with my mother's desire
that I care for her when she is sick"—and had to be rated on a
scale with the poles frequently (1) and never (6).

One item for the variable "legitimacy of a need or desire" (Category 6) is given as a second example: "My mother's desire or need
for me to—e.g., take notice of her political views—is legitimate in
my eyes." This item had to be rated on a scale with the poles
absolutely (1) and not at all (6).

A last example represents anticipated guilt: "If I did not comply
with my mother's desire that I—e.g., help her with heavy chores
(like cleaning the house)—my conscience would bother me," rated
from extremely (1) to not at all (6).

Two measures of prosocial commitment were constructed in the
same way as the scales of Categories 3 to 7. First, respondents had
to rate their intention to act within the next few weeks with regard
to each of five needs and desires of the mothers that the daughters
had selected as the currently most urgent ones. Second, some weeks
later, the daughters had to rate the degree to which they actually
acted on each of the five needs or desires of the mother. Ratings
were made on six-point scales.

*Validity of the Self-Report Data.* The validity of the self-reports of
the respondents was tested via external ratings. Some of the mothers were asked to rate some key variables, including the actual
prosocial commitment of the daughter during the same time period
in which the daughter reported her behavior. The correlation between the self-reports of the daughters and the mothers on each
of the need-related activities concerning the behavior of the daughter ($r = .58$) seemed to justify confidence in the validity of self-
report data.

*Longitudinal Replication.* The questionnaire was given three times
at one-year intervals. This longitudinal replication is not reported
here. We point out only that the two longitudinal replications of
the data collection resulted in the same pattern of relationships
between variables as in the first data collection. This confirms the
reliability of the procedure.

**Table 10.5**

Regression from Prosocial Activities on Twenty-one Predictors (Including Aspects of Relationship, Traits, Habitual Behavior, Norms, Attitudes, Appraisals of the Predicament, Anticipated Guilt Feelings, and Critique in Case of Noncompliance) ($N = 496$; $\mathbf{p}Fb < .01$)

| Predictors | r | beta | b | Fb | $R^2$ |
|---|---|---|---|---|---|
| Habitual pros. behavior | .52 | .32 | .36 | 61.9 | |
| Abilities and opportunities | .43 | .24 | .33 | 42.1 | |
| Attitudes to pros. behavior | .46 | .18 | .20 | 19.9 | |
| Quality of relationship (love) | .31 | .13 | .14 | 12.7 | |
| Denial of responsibility | .11 | .10 | .12 | 8.9 | .41 |
| (intercept) | | | −.14 | | |

Adapted from Table I in Montada, Dalbert, and Schmitt (1988).

**Results and Discussion: Predicting Activities for the Benefit of the Mother—Oughts, Love, or a Matter of Course?**

The psychological predictors accounted for a significant portion of the variance in prosocial commitment for the benefit of the mother (tables 10.5 and 10.6). Since a large number of potential predictors was assessed, multivariate analyses (multiple regression and path analyses) were chosen. Some of the relevant results may be summed up as follows.

For predicting prosocial behavior, anticipated costs (in terms of time, money, interpersonal conflicts, postponing one's own interests) turned out to be unimportant in this familial context. This is in contrast to the results of experimental research on altruism toward needy people with whom helpers are not personally acquainted (Bierhoff 1980).

Normative orientations (subjects' moral norms) did not play an important, independent role: neither felt obligations (personal norms) to support the mother (or to comply with her wishes) nor anticipated guilt feelings for not acting prosocially contributed significantly to the prediction of actual prosocial actions.

The same was true for justice-related appraisals: neither the legitimacy of the mother's needs entitling her or not entitling her to receive the daughter's support (or to have the daughter comply with her desires), nor the mother's responsibility for the existence of her needs (their self-infliction) proved to be significant predictors.

**Table 10.6**
Regression from Intention to Act Prosocially on Twenty-one Predictors
(see head of table 10.5) ($N = 522$; **p**$Fb < .01$)

| Predictors | r | beta | b | Fb | R² |
|---|---|---|---|---|---|
| Desires are justified | .67 | .28 | .28 | 56.2 | |
| Personal norms | .59 | .16 | .11 | 16.7 | |
| Abilities and opportunities | .43 | .17 | .17 | 34.0 | |
| Anticipated guilt | .57 | .20 | .16 | 38.2 | |
| Attitudes to pros. behavior | .65 | .20 | .17 | 23.1 | |
| Needs are self-inflicted | − .43 | − .11 | .07 | 12.6 | .64 |
| (intercept) | | | .39 | | |

Adapted from Table III in Montada, Dalbert, and Schmitt (1988).

The variance of prosocial behavior was due mainly to the following five predictors:

1. the habitual prosocial activity of a daughter in favor of her mother in the past with respect to the five needs or desires selected;
2. the ability or opportunity of a daughter to act prosocially, again with respect to the five selected needs;
3. the general attitude of the daughter about whether or not it is generally right for a daughter to support her mother or to comply with her wishes (with respect to the five selected needs), reflecting a more general social norm of adequacy rather than a personally felt moral ought;
4. the quality of the relationship between mother and daughter, with the positive pole of the dimension simply meaning mutual love;
5. the absence of a general disposition to deny responsibility (for the elderly in general).

What does this pattern of predictors mean? The first three predictors may be interpreted as typical aspects of the daughter's social role in the dyad with her mother. Role-bound behavior is performed repeatedly over time (habitual prosocial behavior), the role holder is able to perform it (perceived own abilities and opportunities), and he or she believes that it is right to perform it (attitudes toward prosocial behavior). It is open to question whether this social role is imposed by social norms or whether it develops within the mother-daughter dyad. In the latter case, one could call it a "personal role."

The further two predictors were more motivational: the quality of the relationship (loving the mother) and the absence of a dispositional barrier in terms of a general traitlike tendency to deny responsibility.

These predictors outweighed the consideration of costs, own obligations, and just entitlements of the mother. The pattern of predictors does not seem to represent moral- or justice-related decision making, but rather a spontaneous expression of love as a matter of course resulting from the personal role of the daughters in relationship with their mothers. The assumption that the prosocial behavior of the daughters was not a matter of planful decision making may be corroborated by looking at the formation of "intentions" to act prosocially in the future. As mentioned above, some weeks before the subjects were asked what they actually had done for the benefit of their mothers, they were asked what they intended to do. Though uttered intentions were rather good predictors of actual actions—when "intention to act prosocially" was added to the predictor set it gained the highest weight of all predictors, increasing the explained variance from .41 to .47 (Montada, Schneider, and Reichle 1988)—they were far from being perfect. Thus, daughters did on occasion change their intentions.

Interestingly, intentions were predicted by a different set of variables than actual prosocial behavior, as can be seen by comparing table 10.6 and table 10.7. Prediction of intentions was best based on the following variables:

1. the rating of the legitimacy of the desires of the mother, implying that the mothers are entitled to receive support or to have their daughters comply;
2. (negatively) the perception that mothers' needs are self-inflicted, implying that the mothers are not entitled to support;
3. felt obligation (representing personal norms) and anticipated guilt feelings in case of not acting prosocially.

These justice- and morality-related predictors were supplemented by the following two predictors that also predicted actual prosocial behavior: the appraisal of having abilities and opportunities to support the mother and the attitude that, in general, it is all right for a daughter to act that way.

In summary, compared to actual prosocial activities, intentions to behave prosocially seem to be more a matter of reasoned decision making in which personal norms and justice-related appraisals of the situation are considered. Actual behavior may follow the intentions, but it does not necessarily have to. It is often a "matter of course," not a consequence of moral decision making, when daughters—and we tend to generalize to all people—behave prosocially in close relationships.

**CONCLUSION**

The thesis of this chapter—that the motivation underlying pro-social activities varies with the social context and the relationships between the potential helper and the needy—was empirically cor-roborated by two studies, one of them on prosocial activities in behalf of different groups of disadvantaged people who are not personally known, and the other on prosocial commitments in the family. In the first case, moral norms of justice played an important role: perceived injustice and perceived responsibilities for injustice led to feelings of either guilt or moral outrage. Both of these emo-tions disposed individuals to prosocial action, whereas sympathy for the needy did not contribute much to this disposition.

In the second case, considerations of justice and entitlements and personally experienced moral oughts and responsibilities (per-sonal norms in the sense of Schwartz 1977) were largely irrelevant to the prediction of actual prosocial commitment. They were pre-dictive only of the intention to act prosocially. Actual prosocial behavior seemed to be motivated by love (sympathy) alone, and it seems to be realized in terms of an individual's role in the rela-tionship to the needy person (the mother)—a role the helper (the daughter) endorses.

The cases presented here indicate how cautious we must be with generalizations from one situation to another, in which different helpers act in different social systems, in which different excuses and justifications for refusing help are offered, in which help re-quires different abilities, and so forth.

In conclusion, I would like to note that these studies suggest that focusing emotional responses on victims or on the needy may be useful in understanding and predicting prosocial actions. From a philosophical point of view, Blum (1980) makes this point very convincingly. Many different emotions dispose individuals or in-terfere with prosocial activities. This is well known, and there is a lot of empirical support for it (Rosenhan et al. 1982). This study features two relatively neglected emotions—existential guilt and moral outrage. Both are key concepts in ethics as well as in the psychology of morality. These emotions seemed to be based authentically on subjectively important oughts from which a subject does not tolerate deviations. Turning to the second study, I would like to note that prosocial activities not only require motives or oughts but also abilities and opportunities. Perceived abilities and habitual prosocial behavior turn out to be better predictors than moral oughts or moral motives in some situations (e.g., Kuhl 1986). Consequently, promoting prosocial activities requires not only the development of altruistic attitudes and motives and norms, but also the cultivation of ability to act correspondingly.

**REFERENCES**

Ajzen, I., and Fishbein, M. (1980). *Understanding attitudes and predicting social behavior*. Englewood Cliffs, NJ: Prentice Hall.

Batson, C.D., Fultz, J., and Schoenrade, P.A. (1987). Distress and empathy: Two qualitatively distinct vicarious emotions with different motivational consequences. *Journal of Personality, 55*, 19–39.

Benninghaus, H. (1976). *Ergebnisse und Perspektiven der Einstellungs-Verhaltens-Forschung*. Meisenheim: Hain.

Bentler, P.M., and Speckart, G. (1979). Models of attitude-behavior relations. *Psychological Review, 86*, 452–64.

Bierhoff, H.W. (1980). *Hilfreiches Verhalten: Soziale Einflüsse und pedagogische Implikationen*. Darmstadt: Steinkopff.

Blum, L.A. (1980). *Friendship, altruism, and morality*. London: Routledge and Kegan Paul.

Cicirelli, V.G. (1983). Adult children's attachment and helping behavior to elderly parents: A path model. *Journal of Marriage and the Family, 45*, 815–25.

——— (1991). Adult children's help to aging parents: Attachment and altruism. In Montada, L., and Bierhoff, H.W. (Eds.), *Altruism in Social Systems*. Toronto: Hogrefe.

Dalbert, C., Montada, L., and Schmitt, M. (1987). Glaube an eine gerechte Welt als Motiv: Validierungskorrelate zweier Skalen. *Psychologische Beiträge, 29*, 596–615.

Deutsch, M. (1985). *Distributive justice: A social psychological perspective*. New Haven: Yale University Press.

Engfer, A., Schneewind, K.A., and Hinderer, J. (1977). Die Familien-Klima-Skalen (FKS). Ein Fragebogen zur Erhebung perzipierter Familienumwelten nach R.H. Moos. *Arbeitsbericht Nr. 16 aus dem EKB-Projekt*. Munich: Universität München.

Haan, N. (1975). Hypothetical and actual moral reasoning in a situation of civil disobedience. *Journal of Personality and Social Psychology, 32*, 255–70.

Harris, B. (1972). The effects of performing one altruistic act on the likelihood of performing another. *Journal of Social Psychology, 88*, 65–73.

Hoffman, M.L. (1976). Empathy, role-taking, guilt, and development of altruistic motives. In Lickona, T. (Ed.), *Moral development and behavior.* New York: Holt, Rinehart & Winston. Pp. 124–43.

Ickes, W.J., and Kidd, R.F. (1976). An attributional analysis of helping behavior. In Harvey, D.I., Ickes, W.J., and Kidd, R.F. (Eds.), *New directions in attributional research. Vol. 1.* Hillsdale, N.J.: Erlbaum. Pp. 311–34.

Keniston, K. (1968). *Young radicals: Notes on committed youth.* New York: Harcourt, Brace and World.

Kuhl, U. (1986). *Selbstsicherheit und prosoziales Handeln.* Munich: Profil Verlag.

Lang, A.M., and Brody, E.M. (1983). Characteristics of middle-aged daughters and help to their elderly mothers. *Journal of Marriage and the Family, 45,* 193–202.

Langer, E.J., and Abelson, R.P. (1972). The semantics of asking a favor: How to succeed in getting help without really trying. *Journal of Personality and Social Psychology, 24,* 26–32.

Lerner, M.J. (1980). *The belief in a just world: A fundamental delusion.* New York: Plenum.

Lerner, M.J., and Whitehead, L.A. (1980). Verfahrensgerechtigkeit aus der Sicht der Gerechtigkeitsmotiv-Theorie. In Mikula, G. (Ed.), *Gerechtigkeit und soziale Interaktion.* Bern: Huber. Pp. 251–300.

Lieberson, S., and Silverman, R.A. (1965). The precipitants and underlying conditions of race riots. *American Sociological Review, 30,* 887–98.

Lifton, R.J. (1967). *Death in life: Survivors of Hiroshima.* New York: Random House.

Meyer, M.P., and Mulherin, A. (1980). From attribution to helping. *Journal of Personality and Social Psychology, 39,* 201–10.

Midlarsky, E. (1971). Aiding under stress: The effects of competence, dependency, visibility, and fatalism. *Journal of Personality, 39,* 132–49.

Montada, L., and Boll, T. (1988). Auslösung und Dämpfung von Feindseligkeit. Bundesministerium der Verteidigung P II 4 (Ed.), *Untersuchungen des Psychologischen Dienstes der Bundeswehr, 23,* 43–144.

Montada, L., Dalbert, C., and Schmitt, M. (1988). Ist prosoziales Handeln im Kontext Familie abhangig von situationalen, personalen oder systemischen Faktoren? In Bierhoff, H.W., and Montada, L. (Eds.), *Altruismus—Bedingungen der Hilfsbereitschaft.* Göttingen: Hogrefe. Pp. 179–205.

Montada, L., Schmitt, M., and Dalbert, C. (1986). Thinking about justice and dealing with one's own privileges: A study of existential guilt. In Bierhoff, H.W., Cohen, R., and Greenberg, J. (Eds.), *Justice in social relations.* New York: Plenum. Pp. 125–43.

Montada, L., and Schneider, A. (1988). Justice and emotional reactions to victims. *E.S.—Bericht Nr. 7 ( = Berichte aus der Arbeitsgruppe "Verantwortung, Gerechtigkeit, Moral" Nr. 47).* Trier: Universität Trier.

——— (1989). Coping mit Problemen sozial Schwacher: Annotierte Ergebenistabellen. *E.S.–Bericht Nr. 9 ( = Berichte aus der Arbeitsgruppe "Verantwortung, Gerechtigkeit, Moral" Nr. 52).* Trier: Universität Trier.

Montada, L., Schneider, A., and Reichle, B. (1988). Emotionen und Hilfsbereitschaft. In Bierhoff, H.W. and Montada, L. (Eds.), *Altruismus—Bedingungen der Hilfsbereitschaft.* Göttingen: Hogrefe. Pp. 130–53.

Piliavin, I.M., Piliavin, J.A., and Rodin, J. (1975). Costs, diffusion, and the stigmatized victim. *Journal of Personality and Social Psychology, 32*, 429–38.

Piliavin, J., Rodin, J., and Piliavin, I. (1969). Good samaritanism: An underground phenomenon? *Journal of Personality and Social Psychology, 13*, 289–99.

Rawlings, E.I. (1970). Reactive guilt and anticipatory guilt in altruistic behavior. In Macaulay, J., and Berkowitz, L. (Eds.), *Altruism and helping behavior*. New York: Academic Press. Pp. 163–77.

Rosenhan, D.L., Salovey, P., Karylowski, J., and Hargis, K. (1982). Emotion and altruism. In Rushton, J.P., and Sorrentino, R.M. (Eds.), *Altruism and helping behavior*. Hillsdale, NJ: Erlbaum. Pp. 234–50.

Ryan, W. (1971). *Blaming the victim*. New York: Pantheon.

Schmitt, M. (1982). Empathie: Konzepte, Entwicklung, Quantifizierung. *P.I.V.— Bericht Nr. 5 (= Berichte aus der Arbeitsgruppe "Verantwortung, Gerechtigkeit, Moral" Nr. 12)*. Trier: Universität Trier.

Schmitt, M., and Gehle, H. (1983). Interpersonale Verantwortlichkeit erwachsener Töchter ihren Müttern gegenüber: Verantwortlichkeitsnormen, Hilfeleistungen, und ihre Korrelate–ein Überblick über die Literatur. *P.I.V.—Bericht Nr. 10 (= Berichte aus der Arbeitsgruppe "Verantwortung, Gerechtigkeit, Moral" Nr. 17)*. Trier: Universität Trier.

Schmitt, M., and Montada, L. (1982). Determinanten erlebter Gerechtigkeit. *Zeitschrift fur Sozialpsycholgie, 13*, 32–44.

Schneewind, K.A. (forthcoming). Familiennals intime Beziehungssysteme. In Schmidt-Denter, U. and Manz, W. (Eds.), *Entwicklung und Erziehung im okopsychologischen Kontext*. Munich: Reinhardt.

Schneider, A., Meissner, A., Montada, L., and Reichle, B. (1987). Validierung von Selbstberichten über Fremdratings. *E.S.—Bericht Nr. 5 (= Berichte aus der Arbeitsgruppe "Verantwortung, Gerechtigkeit, Moral" Nr. 41)*. Trier: Universität Trier.

Schneider, H.D. (1988). Helfen als Problemloserprozess. In Bierhoff, H.W., and Montada, L. (Eds.), *Altruismus—Bedingungen der Hilfsbereitschaft*. Göttingen: Hogrefe. Pp. 7–35.

Schwartz, S.H. (1977). Normative influences on altruism. In Berkowitz, L. (Ed.), *Advances in experimental social psychology, Vol. 10*. New York: Academic Press. Pp. 221–79.

Tornblom, K.Y., and Jonsson, D.R. (1985). Subrules of the equality and contribution principles: Their perceived fairness in distribution and retribution. *Social Psychology Quarterly, 48*, 249–61.

Von Baeyer, W.R., Haefner, H., and Kisker, K.P. (1964). *Psychiatrie der Verfolgten*. Berlin: Springer.

**11**

# HELPING IN LATE LIFE

*Elizabeth Midlarsky*

## INTRODUCTION

This is a chapter about altruism and helping in late life. Helping is used here as a general term referring to all instances in which one individual comes to the aid of another. Altruism, on the other hand, is viewed as a subcategory of helping, in which the behavior is voluntary—and is motivated by concern for others rather than by the anticipation of rewards.

What do we know about altruism and helping in older adults? In the literature of gerontology, burgeoning in response to the recent, dramatic increases in longevity, the importance of helping is often cited. Pairing of the two terms "aging" and "helping" typically evokes the image of help giving that flows from the young to the old. Indeed, the proportion of aged persons is often represented by the dependency ratio, defined as the "ratio of the combination of persons over 65 plus children under 15 to those in the working age population" (Hendricks and Hendricks 1981, 61). This ratio is generally interpreted as an objective means for expressing "numerical relationships between the 'productive' and dependent components of a population" (Adamchak and Friedmann 1983, 321).

It is therefore not surprising, perhaps, that the predominant

Work on this Chapter was supported by grants awarded by the AARP Andrus Foundation and the National Institute on Aging (AGO6535). The author wishes to acknowledge the intellectual support of Eva Kahana and Mary Elizabeth Hannah, and the valuable contributions of Robin Corley.

emphasis in the social science literature has been on service needs of older adults, and the societal response to those needs (Cape 1978; Exton-Smith and Evans 1977; Frankfather, Smith, and Caro 1981; George 1987; Kahana and Felton 1977; Lawton, Moss, and Grimes 1985). At the same time that one group of gerontologists emphasizes passivity and dependency, a second group emphasizes autonomy and personal control. For this second group, healthy, maximally functioning older adults are viewed as having the capacity to avert dependency at least to some extent, and to maintain independence—a cherished goal in today's society (Cohler 1983; Dean, Hickey, and Holstein 1986; Gould 1972). Indeed, autonomy has been described as a hallmark of adult development (Giele 1980). At the highest levels of functioning, the elderly may be involved in networks of relationships in which they give as well as receive help (Breytspraak, Halpert, and Olson 1985; Morgan 1976; Payne and Bull 1985). Only rarely is the possibility of altruism, or nonreciprocal helping, given serious consideration (Kahana, Midlarsky, and Kahana 1987).

There is, however, an irony inherent in the focus on old age as a period in which help is received or exchanged, but rarely emitted for the sake of others. If, as other contributors to this volume contend, the capacity for altruism generally increases with development, shouldn't we expect the elderly to manifest the most altruism? The view of old age as a period of dependency and self-absorption, devoid of yearnings to be altruistic, bespeaks a highly negative view at best.

Ultimately, however, speculations and suppositions must be put to empirical test. The goal of this chapter is therefore to describe a program of research that was designed to investigate the degree to which older adults help others, the nature of the helping, and the consequences of the participation in contributory roles.

## CROSS-AGE COMPARISONS OF HELPING: NATURALISTIC-EXPERIMENTAL RESEARCH

The first of the studies in this domain, conducted with such associates as Eva Kahana, Mary Elizabeth Hannah, and Robin Corley, was designed to investigate the functional form of the relationship between age and altruism. In considering human interaction, we sometimes appear to assume that altruism is or, from a societal perspective, *should* be a product of development. "Mature" individuals, willing to put aside their own needs, at least at times, to consider the rights and needs of others are vital contributors to a civilized society. But does such "maturity" reach its apex at forty? At fifty-five? At eighty? At least some self-report measures of helping—which include items inquiring how often one has helped older persons shovel snow or cross the street—seem to assume that the young help, and the old receive help. Are all old people needy recipients in today's society (Brickman et al. 1982), or do they emit helping responses? If older adults do help others, with what degree of frequency does the helping occur, compared to younger persons? Specifically, it was the question of relative frequency that the first set of studies addressed.

The studies of the relationships between age and helping were undertaken in a research climate in which the preponderance of psychological investigations in this domain are small-scale experiments, looking at when and why children, adolescents, and, occasionally, young adults help others (cf. Krebs and Miller 1985; Midlarsky and Hannah 1985). In most of the research, helping is studied in the psychology laboratory—an artificial and unfamiliar setting for human behavior. The widespread reliance on laboratory experimentation has had the great virtue of facilitating causal interpretation of factors eliciting or maintaining altruism under controlled conditions. On the other hand, laboratory research has limited ecological validity, so that there is always the danger that even the most sophisticated research on altruism may provide little information about the prevalence of helping and altruism outside of the psychologist's laboratory (Dovidio 1984).

Review of the literature uncovered few studies addressing the question of relative frequency of helping at different ages. This is not to say that no relevant research has been conducted (Brickman et al. 1982; Eron 1987; Rushton et al. 1986). There was, however, a paucity of studies in which (1) direct observation was made of the actual frequencies and amounts of helping in real-life settings (see Latane and Darley 1970; Rheingold, Hay, and West 1976; Strayer, Wareing, and Rushton 1979); (2) helping was observed in people of varying ages (Midlarsky and Kahana 1983). No studies could be found in which helping by people of different ages was studied in identical situations. Our research was designed to directly observe real-life helping by persons of diverse ages. Although in vivo settings were employed, great care was exercised in order to assure situational equivalence across age groups. In planning these studies we also took cognizance of the possibility that altruism and helping are of at least two kinds—sharing of one's resources or "wealth" (in the form of time, money, effort), and sharing of a burden of pain, difficulty, or adversity (as in rescue attempts) (Midlarsky 1968). Because of the possibility that the relative frequency by older and younger persons would vary with the type of helping, separate lines of investigation were conducted.

### Donation Behavior

Investigators of donations, or generosity, have tended to find a linear relationship between age and helping, generally upholding the prediction that helping increases with age (Barnett, King, and Howard 1979; Midlarsky and Hannah 1985). However, these developmental studies have typically included respondents no older than late adolescents.

From the existing literature, two competing hypotheses—of a curvilinear versus a linear functional form—emerged concerning the relationship between altruism and age, when the span of ages is extended to include late life. The prediction of a curvilinear relationship is based on empirical findings of an increase in donations with age in the early years, in combination with theoretical positions in the field of gerontology. For some gerontologists, a special joy of the later years of life can be autonomy—the freedom, at last, from social obligations and expectations (Cohler 1983). In contrast to Cohler's (1983) emphasis on the motivating force of autonomy, other theorists argue that the most salient characteristic of late life, just as in early life, is dependency (Baltes et al. 1983). The social exchange position also predicts decreased helping in late life, at least in situations in which the "justice rule" prevails. As Dowd (1980) writes, older adults as a group have "invested their lives in society. . . . Yet their rewards, in terms of income, prestige or autonomy fall far below our usual definitions of proportionality" (598). The implication is that because of perceived unfairness, older adults would no longer be motivated to help others. Taken together, then, we find a composite view in which, following a period in early life in which relatively little concern is expressed for the welfare of others, individuals become increasingly generous—concomitant with decreases in dependency. Late life becomes, once again, a period of relatively little concern for others because of the focus on one's own need for autonomy, enhanced dependency, or a consciousness of inequitable treatment.

Militating against the curvilinear hypothesis, however, are theoretical perspectives positing that vital involvement in the social world, in which *caring* is a central element, is required for successful adaptation in old age (Erikson, Erikson, and Kivnick 1986). There is also evidence that altruistic behavior and motives may exhibit a linear increase from middle to later adulthood. In a cross-sectional study of 572 pairs of twins, from nineteen to sixty years of age, paper-and-pencil measures of altruism, empathy, and nurturance increased with age (Rushton et al. 1986).

In an effort to explore donation behavior across the life span, and to determine whether the relationship between age and donations is linear or curvilinear, two experiments were performed in randomly selected shopping malls and parks, known to be frequented by individuals of diverse ages. In both experiments, people had the opportunity to donate to a fund for infants with birth defects (Midlarsky and Hannah 1989).

In the first study, the standard situation included posters with pictures of sad or crying infants and their parents. Over a two-week period, a young woman in her twenties set up a small table near the posters and invited donations, on a randomized schedule. Behavior was observed during numerous time slots by one solicitor and three research assistants at each site.

Results of this study indicated that there was an increase in numbers donating from the youngest ages (5–14 years: 32%), through the early adult years (25–34 years: 59%), a plateau in the middle-adult years (35–64: 73%), a rise at age 65 (65–74: 93%), followed by a decrease in the 75 + age group. Ryan's (1960) procedure for pairwise comparison in chi square yielded the finding that more people 15–24 years of age donated than did those 5–14 years of age ($p < .001$ for all comparisons). The three groups from 35 to 64 years of age donated significantly more frequently than did all of the younger groups ($p < .001$), but did not differ significantly from one another. In addition, more individuals 65 to 74 years of age donated than did those in any other group studied here. Fewer of the oldest group, aged 75 and above, donated than did those in the 65- to 74-year age group. Nevertheless, more people in the oldest group donated than did those in any of the under–65 age groups who were exposed to the charitable appeal ($p < .001$ for all comparisons). Analysis of var-

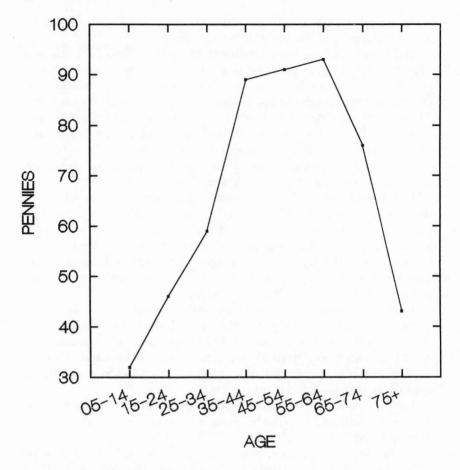

**Figure 11.1**
Response by age to solicitation for donations to a fund for infants with
birth defects. (*Note:* Mean donations are given in pennies.)

iance of *amounts* donated yielded a significant main effect for
donor age ($F$ (7,2700) = 194.13, $p$ < .001), and eta squared cal-
culated on age indicated that this effect accounted for 41% of
the variance. Figure 11.1 depicts the relationship between age
and amounts donated.

As figure 11.1 suggests, amounts donated showed a linear trend from ages 5–14 through ages 35–44, followed by a plateau until the age of 65, at which time there was a significant decline. Results of Newman-Keuls tests indicated that all of the mean differences were significant (at $p < .01$ and $p < .001$) with the exception of the three groups of adults in the 35- to 64-year age range. The youngest respondents, 5–15 years of age, donated the smallest amounts, followed by the oldest group, 75 years of age and over ($p < .01$). The mean amount donated by the young-old, 65–74 years of age, was significantly greater than the means for the groups ranging from 5–15 through 55–64, and for the oldest old (all significant at $p < .001$). However, although the young-old were the most frequent donors, on the average they donated significantly less money than did all three groups of adults in the 35- to 64-year age range. Because of the possibility that amounts donated may have reflected differential financial resources across the life span—wherein donations were more costly for older adults—a second experiment was conducted.

The second experiment addressed the question of whether the relationship between age and amounts donated was due to a decline in perceived financial resources, and a concomitant increase in costs of donating for the elderly, rather than a disinclination to give. The donation task in the second experiment required time and effort, rather than actual funds. In this study, people approaching the donation table saw a two-lever device, rather than a donation canister. Each person approaching the machine was told that if he or she wanted to help the infants with birth defects, then he or she should operate the lever labeled "for the children." For each pull of that lever, five cents would be donated to the fund by local merchants.

The second, or "neutral" lever was included to clarify the meaning of the experimental results. One possibility, in a study using a novel apparatus, is that a response to "gadgetorial seduction," and not an altruistic impulse, may predispose the lever pulls. What makes a lever pull or any other motoric response altruistic is the motive. Thus, the neutral lever—for which no explanation was given to the study participants—was introduced to reduce the ambiguity about what caused the responses that were observed.

Results of the second experiment indicated that the *numbers* of people donating at the various ages were very similar to the numbers in the first experiment, with more older persons than younger persons proffering help. As in Study 1, using pairwise mean comparisons, evidence was found for a linear increase in numbers of persons donating with age. Results also indicated that the numbers donating in each age group, the age trends, and the significance levels were virtually identical in the two studies, with one exception. Although a larger proportion of young-old individuals, 65–74 years of age (92%), donated in comparison with the oldest adults, ages 75 and above (87%), the difference between the two oldest groups failed to reach significance.

The relationship between age and amount donated, with donations defined in terms of lever pulls, is depicted in figure 11.2. ANOVA of amount donated resulted in $F$ (7, 2681) = 611.08, $p$ < .001 for donor age. Eta squared indicated that 58% of the variance was explained by donor age. Newman-Keuls tests provided evidence of a steady increase in amounts donated, with each age group donating more than the group below it in age, and with the oldest respondents (75 years and above) donating most. All of the age groups differed significantly from one another, with the exception of those aged 35–44, 45–54, and 55–64, which once again were not significantly different from one another in amounts donated.

Pulls of the neutral lever—which was included to eliminate the argument that the motoric response used as the dependent variable was based primarily on the novelty of the donation task—were extremely rare. Numbers of neutral lever pulls ranged from a mean of 1.16 for the highest responders (i.e., the youngest individuals, 5–14 years of age) to a mean of zero for both the 65–74 and the 75+ age groups. Indeed, the oldest people in the study were the only respondents who entirely ignored this lever.

Hence, in Study 2 the relationship between age and helping was maintained and the highest donations were given by the oldest adults. These results were obtained in the context of a procedure wherein the attempt was made to equate the costs of helping across age groups as much as possible. The methodology included the use of a donation task that was novel for all recipients, and the selection of times (weekends) and places (parks, malls, and shopping centers) in which the people studied were generally at leisure. In sum, the results of the two experiments taken together indicate that generosity may increase throughout life, particularly when resources for helping are available.

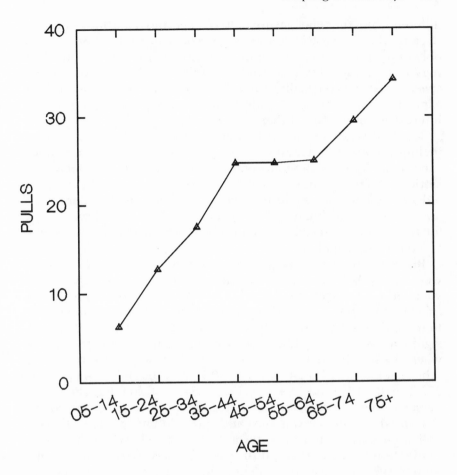

**Figure 11.2**
Motoric response by age to solicitation for donation to a fund for
infants with birth defects. (*Note:* Mean donations are in lever pulls.)

**Rescue**

A second line of investigations was then designed to explore the
relationship between age and rescue behavior among persons in
the adolescent (age eighteen) to late-life age range. The principal
rationale underlying this research was to evaluate the possibility
that the relationship between age and rescue behavior may be

different than the relationship between age and donation behavior. Because the decrease in resources and consequent increase in costs of helping associated with aging may be even more pronounced in regard to rescue, in which two facets of responding—strength and speed—may be markedly diminished (Kausler 1982), our initial expectation was that the elderly would manifest *lower* rates of interest in rescue than other age groups.

The first study began with announcements of first aid classes, including thorough training in emergency intervention techniques such as CPR. These announcements were made in a diversity of settings to insure that similar numbers of younger (18–64) and older (65 +) people would be exposed to them. Independent variables included the financial cost of the classes (no cost, three dollars for the course materials, or ten dollars), and transportation (provided or not provided).

Results indicated that persons between the age of 64 and 75 were more likely to sign up for and attend such classes than were younger adults aged 18–24, ($\chi^2$ (1) = 46.1, $p < .001$) and 25–34 ($\chi^2$ (1) = 109.03, $p < .001$) but not significantly more apt to participate than were people aged 35–64 ($\chi^2$ (1) = 1.07, $p < .05$). Also, significantly more middle-aged persons signed up for the course when the fee was ten dollars, in comparison with all three of the other age groups: 18–24 ($\chi^2$ (1) = 36.95, $p < .001$), 25–34 ($\chi^2$ (1) = 25.72, $p < .001$), and 65 + ($\chi^2$ (1) = 8.54, $p < .01$). For the oldest persons, there were no significant differences between the condition in which the fee was zero and three dollars ($\chi^2$ (1) < 1). Verbalizations supported the interpretation that there was sufficient motivation to incur a cost, if the cost was perceived as affordable. Among the youngest respondents, the monetary cost was an important factor. Of the 18–24-year-olds signing up for the course, 58% responded when no fee was charged, 30% in the condition in which the fee was three dollars, and 12% when the fee was ten dollars: $\chi^2$ (2) = 43.33, $p < .001$. In regard to transportation, older adults were disproportionately represented in the condition in which transportation was provided: $\chi^2$ (1) = 254.89, $p < .001$. No effect was obtained for transportation in the other age groups ($\chi^2$ (1) < 1 for each age group).

Results of a followup questionnaire determined that the oldest adults, 78% of whom were fully or partially retired from paid employment, had lower perceived financial resources (Liang, et al. 1980), and were less likely to have a means of transportation readily accessible, than people in the other three age groups. In order to obtain an estimate of cost in the form of time expenditure, respondents were asked about perceived time available for this activity. All of the participants, including the oldest individuals, responded by saying that their time was at a premium, but that the activity was valuable enough to be undertaken. No age differences were found in perceptions about available time.

All of the people who enrolled were also asked their motives for wanting to participate. Younger persons expressed a wide range of motives, from interest in the subject matter (35%) to desire to obtain a new skill (74%), curiosity (54%), perceived need to fulfill a career-related or educational objective (36%), interest in filling some spare time (27%), and desire to learn how better to help others (34%). Elderly persons gave less diverse motives for their interest. The great majority (85%) expressed a strong desire to be effective helpers in situations involving health emergencies. In regard to the CPR component of the program, the most frequent type of spontaneous comment by older adults (62%) was "Who knows! If I learn to do this right, I may be able to save a life!"

In a continuation of this research, respondents were categorized into three age groups: younger adults (18–34), middle-aged adults (35–64), and older adults (65 +). One-half of those enrolling were given the course of instruction, and one-half engaged in a series of value clarification exercises, which was described to them as a necessary prerequisite to the actual first aid course. Participants in both conditions were exposed, on an individual basis, to a staged emergency requiring quick response to a need for medical help by a 30-year-old woman. Data from this investigation are summarized in table 11.1. Results indicated that significantly fewer of the older adults attempted to help than either people in the 18–34 age range ($\chi^2$ (1) = 10.73, $p < .01$) or people 65 years of age and older ($\chi^2$ (1) = 18.52, $p < .001$). Within the group of elderly participants, older persons in the first aid course were more likely to help than those who had not taken it ($\chi^2$ (1) = 7.81, $p < .01$). In contrast, neither younger persons nor middle-aged persons completing the first aid course were more likely to help than were those who had not received the first aid training ($\chi^2$ (1) < 1 for both comparisons).

The effectiveness of the help provided—defined as the degree of appropriateness and accuracy of the skills that were employed—were then examined. As the data in table 11.1 indicate, trained older persons were more likely to be *effective* helpers, both in com-

**Table 11.1**

Numbers, Percentages, and Effectiveness of Rescue Attempts by Participant Age and Completion of First-Aid Course

| | First Aid Course | | | | | |
| | Completed | | | Not Completed | | |
| *Age of Respondent* | *N* | *%* | *Effectiveness* | *N* | *%* | *Effectiveness* |
|---|---|---|---|---|---|---|
| 18–34 | 91 | 83 | 121 | 93 | 85 | 76 |
| 35–64 | 97 | 88 | 110 | 95 | 86 | 74 |
| 65+ | 87 | 79 | 162 | 67 | 61 | 71 |

Note: Each of the six groups included 110 respondents. The effectiveness scores are based on a weighted combination of ratings of the appropriateness and accuracy of methods used to intervene. Further information about their derivation is available from the author.

parison with older people who were not yet trained, and with both trained and untrained younger people ($p < .01$ for all comparisons). Since measures of effective helping reflected the knowledge of helping skills and strategies learned in the first aid course, the older adults appeared to be good students, indeed. As memory researchers have found, the performance of older adults on tasks designed to assess memory is improved when the material is meaningful, when they are motivated, and when the tasks are performed in the context of a naturalistic situation rather than the artificial environment of the experimental laboratory (Hartley, Harker, and Walsh 1980; Hultsch 1974; Light 1991).

This study demonstrates that when faced with the need for physical intervention, older people may be less apt to offer assistance than younger people. On the other hand, more older adults attended a CPR class when the class was made accessible and affordable. The primary motive expressed for attending the class was, for most older adults, the desire to help others rather than a desire for self-improvement or satisfaction of their curiosity. The fact that the number of helping attempts was increased among the older participants completing the first aid class, and not among the younger or middle-aged adults, may reflect a lower initial level of perceived competence to respond in an emergency among older adults. An important effect of the training may have been to disinhibit helping by increasing both actual and perceived competence. It is interesting to note that younger trained helpers are not more effective than older trained helpers. Indeed, they may be somewhat less motivated to help, as indicated by their overrepresentation as participants in the no-fee group.

## SURVEY RESEARCH ON HELPING BY THE ELDERLY

Experimental studies have the advantage of permitting the direct observation of behavior under controlled conditions. However, issues of sampling may be less rigorously addressed than they are in surveys of broader populations. Encouraged by the results of the experimental studies in natural settings—which revealed the importance and likelihood of helping in the elderly—investigations of the incidence, prevalence, and meaning of help giving in the lives of the elderly were undertaken. The following is an example of one of the surveys that was conducted.

In this initial, exploratory-descriptive study, the sampling sites were age-homogeneous apartments in the Detroit metropolitan area. Residents of these apartments have typically moved from a house or apartment in an age-heterogeneous setting. In their new apartment, they continue to live independently in the community, but support services are more accessible than in age-heterogeneous settings. The total sample consisted of 117 respondents, representing a broad spectrum of socioeconomic status and cultural and religious backgrounds. The age range was 62 to 100, with a mean of 75.6 and a standard deviation of eight years. Slightly over two-thirds (67%) were female, and 23% were male. Data were collected through lengthy, in-depth interviews.

Results of this survey revealed that helping behaviors were perceived by respondents to be both prevalent and salient. Sixty-seven percent of respondents reported providing a great deal of help to others during the previous year, and the vast majority (81%) reported spending at least some of their time helping others.

Helping also was valued by the elderly, with everyone in the sample considering helping to be an important activity in their lives. Sixty percent viewed helping as very important. When asked whether their current helping was more, less, or the same amount as it was earlier in their lives, 49% reported maintaining earlier levels, 39% reported some decline, and 18% reported that they now provide increased amounts of help. A significantly greater number of the oldest old (80+) reported a decrease in helping with age than did the younger old (62–79): $\chi^2$ (3) = 62.1, $p < .001$. When asked about the recipients of their help giving, 88% primarily help neighbors, 85% reported helping friends, and 71% said that they help members of their families. These results indicate that older people may typically provide assistance to several groups within their social context rather than limiting their helping to any one group.

In order to determine the types of helping in which older adults currently engage, we employed a modified version of the Self-Report Altruism Scale (Rushton, Chrisjohn, and Fekken 1981) (See table 11.2). This scale presents diverse types of helping acts, and asks respondents about the frequency with which they were emitted during the past year. The three helping acts in which the largest percentages of respondents engaged once or more than once during the year are holding the elevator door for someone (91.4%), giving emotional support (90.5%), and donating money to charity (88%). The three helping acts engaged in by the smallest percentages of respondents are donating blood (2.6%), lending a stranger an item of value (16.3%), and helping an acquaintance move households (27.4%).

Respondents were also asked whether they found that helping others was a positive or rewarding experience. All said that helping brought its own rewards, at least to some extent. Specific intrinsic and/or allocentric rewards included inner satisfaction (2.8%), vicarious reinforcement based on perceptions of benefits experienced by the recipient (13%), a sense of usefulness (12%) or competence (16%) derived from knowledge of positive outcomes for the other (12%), and a sense of meaning based upon the fulfillment of religious or moral obligations (16%). One 86-year-old woman eloquently stated that helping others "confirms one's own existence and integration."

A small number of respondents (3%) reported extrinsic rewards as the salient ones in helping behavior—and these respondents themselves were generally older or more needy than most. Specific forms of direct reciprocity were expected by fourteen (12%), and material payments were mentioned by one. Acknowledgment by others, gratitude, and a good reputation among one's peers were noted by two respondents as comprising the rewards of helping others.

These findings provide an indication of the importance of altruistic motives for self-reported helping by older people. The self-reports of the elderly indicate that they, at least, believed that they helped others because of the beneficial outcomes for the recipient or because of the psychological benefits to themselves rather than because of less altruistic rewards such as tangible forms of reciprocal helping, money, or recognition. There are, of course, limi-

**Table 11.2**

Percentages of Respondents Reporting Diverse Helping Behaviors

| Item | Never | Once | Response More than once | Often | Very often | Summary (Once or More) |
|---|---|---|---|---|---|---|
| Looked in on Sick | 17.1 | 0 | 34.2 | 24.8 | 23.9 | 82.9 |
| Gave Directions | 17.9 | 2.6 | 35.0 | 27.4 | 17.1 | 82.1 |
| Made Change | 26.5 | .9 | 35.0 | 29.1 | 8.5 | 73.0 |
| Money to Charity | 12.0 | 6.8 | 31.6 | 30.8 | 18.8 | 88.0 |
| Money to Someone | 40.9 | 11.3 | 37.4 | 8.7 | 1.7 | 59.1 |
| Goods to Charity | 25.6 | 15.4 | 35.9 | 11.1 | 12.0 | 74.4 |
| Volunteer Work for Charity | 51.3 | 3.4 | 19.7 | 6.8 | 18.8 | 48.7 |
| Gave Blood | 97.4 | 1.7 | .9 | — | — | 2.6 |
| Carried Belongings | 31.6 | 5.1 | 35.9 | 18.8 | 8.5 | 68.3 |
| Held Elevator | 8.5 | 1.7 | 14.5 | 44.4 | 30.8 | 91.4 |
| Let Ahead on Line | 24.8 | .9 | 39.8 | 20.4 | 14.2 | 75.3 |
| Gave Lift in Car | 42.9 | 3.8 | 12.4 | 21.9 | 19.0 | 57.1 |
| Pointed out Undercharge | 67.3 | 11.5 | 17.7 | 3.5 | — | 32.7 |
| Lent Stranger Item of Value | 83.6 | 1.7 | 9.5 | 3.4 | 1.7 | 16.3 |
| Bought Card from Charity | 39.3 | 18.8 | 25.6 | 9.4 | 6.8 | 60.6 |
| Helped with Chores | 69.8 | 6.0 | 17.2 | 2.6 | 4.3 | 30.1 |
| Looked after Things | 54.3 | 11.2 | 18.1 | 11.2 | 5.2 | 45.7 |
| Helped Handicapped Cross Street | 40.5 | 4.3 | 30.2 | 16.4 | 8.6 | 59.5 |
| Offered Seat | 58.8 | 7.0 | 26.3 | 4.4 | 3.5 | 72.7 |
| Helped Acquaintance Move | 72.6 | 9.7 | 17.7 | — | — | 27.4 |
| Looked in on Friend or Neighbor | 18.1 | 4.3 | 23.3 | 24.1 | 30.2 | 81.9 |
| Gave Advice to Friend | 25.9 | 5.2 | 31.0 | 19.8 | 18.1 | 74.1 |
| Picked up Things at Store | 25.2 | 2.6 | 27.8 | 27.0 | 17.4 | 74.8 |
| Babysat Free | 67.5 | 2.6 | 17.1 | 6.0 | 6.8 | 32.5 |
| Helped Neighbor w/ Chores | 56.9 | 5.2 | 19.8 | 9.5 | 8.6 | 43.1 |
| Gave Emotional Support | 9.5 | 5.2 | 33.6 | 29.3 | 22.4 | 90.5 |

tations to the study based on the fact that a self-report methodology was used. If the self-attributions are valid, however, they raise questions about the universal applicability of an exchange model of helping to elderly providers of help (Blau 1964; Dowd 1980; Kahana, Midlarsky, and Kahana 1987).

## EXPERIMENTAL INVESTIGATION OF THE EFFECT OF HELPING ON PSYCHOSOCIAL WELL-BEING

In addition to exploring the nature and prevalence of helping by the elderly, the survey research projects examined the effects on older adults' helping of personal and situational variables found to be associated with altruism among younger people. As predicted, personality variables such as empathy (Mehrabian and Epstein 1972), social responsibility (Berkowitz and Lutterman 1968), locus of control (Rotter 1966), and prosocial moral judgment (Eisenberg-Berg and Hand 1979) were significant predictors of helping in samples of older adults (e.g., Midlarsky, Kahana, and Corley 1986a, 1986b, 1987).

In designing the survey, we also postulated that participation in helping should be a significant predictor of psychosocial well-being among older adults. On the basis of factor analyses, the conception of well-being includes several dimensions, including self-esteem and the sense of social integration (cf. Midlarsky, Kahana, and Corley 1986a). In regard to one aspect of well-being—self-esteem—the idea that helping may benefit the helpers by augmenting feelings of usefulness and militating against perceptions of the self as helpless and dependent has been termed the "helper-therapy principle" (Riessman 1976, 41). Older people are often on the receiving end of help far more so than they were earlier in life—a state of affairs that may produce stress (Karuza et al. 1983). Wentowski (1981) found that even when older people have become frail and need assistance from others, those who continue to serve as helpers maintain higher levels of self-esteem than those not helping. Just as people who are always on the receiving end of help experience declines in their self-esteem as a result of social comparisons with others (Gergen 1977), helping enhances the sense of relative efficacy and productiveness. Other investigators have postulated, and provided a modicum of evidence, that helping others enhances social integration with others (the converse of loneliness) (Midlarsky and Kahana 1983).

Results of the interview projects provided support for the hypothesized links between helping and dimensions of well-being. Thus, for example, self-reported helping predicted self-esteem, and was the single most important predictor of subjective social integration. However, this research consisted of the application of regression analyses to cross-sectional data, so that the direction of causation could not be directly ascertained.

An experimental study was therefore performed to clarify the direction of causation. Our goal was to intervene in such a way as to promote an increase in helping, and then to determine the effects both of the intervention and of self-reported helping on subsequent indices of well-being. The intervention was the provision of information about helping opportunities.

The decision to provide information about helping opportunities as the intervention came from the finding of a significant association between perceived opportunities and helping in the cross-sectional surveys. Because the surveys employed a cross-sectional methodology, it was unclear whether knowledge of opportunities triggered helping, whether altruistic people perceived more opportunities, or whether a third set of factors cause both the perception of opportunities and helpfulness. Our choice of volunteering as the form of helping upon which to focus the intervention effort was based on findings of our own and of other investigators that relatively small percentages of the elderly regularly engage in volunteer work (estimates range from 7 percent to 22 percent), but that many additional older persons actively express interest in becoming so involved (Harris 1975; Payne 1977). Those who do serve as volunteers indicated that their helping fills a role vacuum (Chambre 1984), and often that they are helping more now than they ever have. They report that as a result of responding to perceived helping opportunities, they feel that their lives are meaningful.

The basic premise of the experimental study, then, was that the provision of information about volunteer opportunities should result in an increase in helping behavior and that important benefits would then accrue not only to the recipient of services by the elderly, but also to the older helper (Midlarsky 1989). The study was designed to capitalize on the fact that we had already interviewed a total of 517 older persons across two survey projects to determine the extent of their helping and well-being. The availability of pretested people permitted the use of the powerful Solomon Four-Group Design, which has the advantage of maximizing both internal and external validity.

The four experimental groups were formed in the following way. First, we randomly selected a group of sixty people from the 517 interviewed in the prior survey research projects. These sixty people are referred to as the pretested group. We then formed a group of sixty additional people by drawing a random sample from the population from which the pretested group had been drawn. One-half of the pretested individuals and one-half of the newly selected older adults received the experimental intervention. After a lapse of six months, participants in all four groups were interviewed for the second time. The sampling procedure yielded 120 people, 30 in each of the four groups. They ranged in age from 68 to 100, with an average age of 80 years. Of the respondents, 73% were female and 27% were male. (The ratio of females to males corresponds to the availability of community-dwelling older men and women who are competent and willing to provide informed consent.) This sample was demographically comparable to the samples in our prior research, and there were no significant differences among the four study groups in regard to demographic variables. The experimental intervention consisted of the provision of personalized, in-depth information about volunteer opportunities. A personalized brochure was assembled for each individual participant, based on information obtained in an initial telephone contact. The brochure included a description of several volunteer opportunities that were carefully matched to the respondents' interests and talents. The names and numbers of coordinators also were provided, and participants were exhorted about the need for volunteers and helpers throughout the community. Results of this investigation indicated that the intervention ($F$ (1,116) = 8.71, $p < .001$, $\eta^2 = .06$.), the pretest, in which prior helping was discussed in depth ($F$ (1,116) = 13.74, $p < .001$, $\eta^2 = .09$), and their interaction ($F$ (1,116) = 7.54, $p < .01$, $\eta^2 = .05$) significantly affected perceived opportunities. Those who were exposed to the intervention reported increased knowledge (62.4%), enhanced sensitivity to helping opportunities (83.2%), and satisfaction (82%).

The effect of the intervention on both volunteering and on overall helping was significant and had a more powerful explanatory effect than did the pretest. That is, analysis of variance of self-reported volunteering yielded significant effects for the pretest ($F$ (1,116) = 4.53, $p < .05$, $\eta^2 = .03$) and for the intervention ($F$ (1,116) = 20.95, $p < .0001$, $\eta^2 = .14$). Analysis of self-reported helping yielded significant effects of the pretest ($F$ (1,116) = 10.75, $p < .01$, $\eta^2 = .06$) and for the intervention ($F$ (1,116) = 43.78, $p < .0001$, $\eta^2 = .24$). In regard to overall helping, the pretest

**Table 11.3**
Predictors of Self-Esteem

| Predictor variable | $R^2$ increment | Standardized regression coefficient | F |
|---|---|---|---|
| Volunteering | .21 | .33 | 29.41* |
| Neighbor help | .07 | .31 | 21.19* |
| Family help | .00 | −.05 | 14.14* |

Note: $R^2$ = .28
*$p$ < .0001

**Table 11.4**
Predictors of Subjective Social Integration

| Predictor variable | $R^2$ increment | Standardized regression coefficient | F |
|---|---|---|---|
| Volunteering | .09 | .26 | 5.27* |
| Child help | .01 | −.09 | 2.91 |
| Neighbor | .02 | .20 | 2.30 |
| Family help | .01 | −.11 | 1.80 |

Note: $R^2$ = .12
*$p$ < .05

significantly augmented the efficacy of the intervention in its effect on helping and volunteering. That is, for the interactive effect of the pretest and the intervention on overall helping ($F$ (1,116) = 9.30, $p$ < .01, $\eta^2$ = .05). In addition, the intervention unexpectedly had a significant, direct effect on self-esteem. Many of the respondents reported being gratified and reassured regarding their potential usefulness, when "so much trouble" was taken to inform them that their efforts were a valuable resource for their community.

The effects of volunteering and helping on the two indices of well-being discussed above—self-esteem and subjective social integration—were examined through hierarchical multiple regression analyses. The results are presented in tables 11.3 and 11.4.

Examination of tables 11.3 and 11.4 shows that volunteering emerged as the strongest predictor of both self-esteem and subjective social integration in the current investigation. The implication of this finding is that volunteering to serve the needs of others—a form of social participation that is acutely needed within American society—benefits the older volunteer in important ways.

Another form of helping that greatly benefits the older person is that which appears to spring from altruistic motives. In the studies reported here, a group of helpers were identified who also were characterized by high scores on the personality variables associated with altruism and helping in younger individuals, such as social responsibility and empathy. Further analysis of the protocols for these individuals indicated that they apparently participated in more helping, and helping that was more costly and long-term than did individuals who scored lower on measures of those characteristics (Midlarsky and Kahana, forthcoming). Individuals scoring high on measures of altruistic predispositions also stated more other-centered motives for helping. While their *reasons* for helping centered on the needs of others, it was they who were more likely to show increases in well-being as their self-reported rates of helping increased.

## CONCLUSION

We are living in an era of unprecedented expansion of our population of elders—a trend that is likely to continue for several decades. Older people are undoubtedly affected by health concerns, and by the existence of a paucity of services to meet their growing catalog of needs. However, an unrelieved focus on the older adult as unilateral recipient of help, victimized by the accretion of the years, is damaging both to the individual and to the society that is expected to carry the increased burden.

The series of investigations reported here is based on a model whose basic premise is that helping can be a form of coping (Midlarsky 1991), particularly when the individual faces possible decrements in self-esteem as a result of growing vulnerability and the loss of roles such as parent of dependent children and employed worker—both of which may put the individual in a position in which help is often sought and valued.

The most well-meaning among us may overlook the very human and powerful need to serve others that for at least some of the elderly is a corollary of maturity. The inadvertent failure to recognize altruistic motivation for what it is may result in adverse sequelae both for the would-be older benefactor and for the recipient (see Rosen, Mickler, and Spiers 1986). Recognition of the resource value of the "third age" may ultimately benefit both society and the elderly themselves.

## REFERENCES

Adamchak, D. J., and Friedmann, E. A. (1983). Societal aging and generational dependency relationships. *Research on Aging, 5,* 319–38.

Adams, B. N. (1968). *Kinship in an urban setting.* N.Y.: Markham.

Baltes, M., Honn, S., Barton, E., Orzech, M., and Lago, D. (1983). On the social ecology, dependency, and independence in elderly nursing home residents. *Journal of Gerontology, 2,* 18–24.

Baltes, P., Smith, J., Saudinger, M., and Saworka, D. (1990). Wisdom. In M. Perlmutter (Ed.), *Late-life potential.* N.Y.: Springer.

Barnett, M., King, L., and Howard, J. (1979). Inducing affect about self or other. *Developmental Psychology, 15,* 164–67.

Berkowitz, L., and Lutterman, K. (1968). The traditionally socially responsible personality. *Public Opinion Quarterly, 32,* 169–85.

Blau, P. M. (1964). *Exchange and power in social life.* N.Y.: Wiley.

Breytspraak, L., Halpert, B., and Olson, P. (1985). The voluntary organization as a support system in the aging process. In W. A. Peterson and J. Quadragno (Eds.), *Social bonds in later life.* Beverly Hills, Cal.: Sage, 273–86.

Brickman, P., Rabinowitz, V., Karuza, J., Jr., Coates, D., Cohn, E., and Kidder, L. (1982). Models of helping and coping. *American Psychologist, 37,* 368–87.

Butler, R. (1975). *Why survive?* N.Y.: Harper & Row.

Campbell, D. T., and Stanley, J. C. (1963). *Experimental and quasi-experimental designs for research.* Chicago: Rand-McNally.

Cape, R. (1978). *Aging: Its complex management.* Hagerstown, Md.: Harper & Row.

Chambre, S. M. (1984). Is volunteering a substitute for role loss in old age? *Gerontologist, 24* (3), 272–98.

Cicero, M. T. (1773). *Cato.* London: Dodsley.

Cohler, B. (1983). Autonomy and interdependence in the family of adulthood. *Gerontologist, 23* (1), 33–39.

Dean, K., Hickey, T., and Holstein, B. E. (1986). *Self-care and health in old age.* London: Croom-Helm.

Dovidio, J. F. (1984). Helping behavior and altruism. *Advances in experimental social psychology,* vol. 17. New York: Academic Press, 361–427.

Dowd, J. (1980). Exchange rates and old people. *Journal of Gerontology, 35,* 596–602.

Eisenberg-Berg, N., and Hand, M. (1979). The relationship of preschoolers' reasoning about prosocial moral conflict to prosocial behavior. *Child Development, 50,* 356–63.

Erikson, E., Erikson, M., and Kivnick, H. (1986). *Vital involvement in old age.* N.Y.: Norton.

Eron, L. (1987). The development of aggressive behavior from the perspective of a developing behaviorism. *American Psychologist, 42,* 435–42.

Exton-Smith, A., and Evans, J. (Eds.) (1977). *Care of the elderly.* N.Y.: Grune & Stratton.

Frankfather, D., Smith, M., and Caro, F. (1981). *Family care of the elderly.* Lexington, Mass.: Heath.

George, L. (1987). Non-familial support for older persons. In G. Lesnoff-Caravaglia (Ed.), *Handbook of applied gerontology.* N.Y.: Human Sciences Press, 310–40.

Gergen, K. J. (1977). The social construction of self-knowledge. In T. Mischel (Ed.), *The self.* Oxford: Blackwell.

Giele, J. (1980). Adulthood as transcendence of age and sex. In N. Smelser and E. Erikson (Eds.), *Themes of love and work in adulthood.* Cambridge, Mass.: Harvard University Press.

Gould, R. L. (1972). The phases of adult life. *American Journal of Psychiatry, 129,* 521–31.

Harris, L. (1975). *The myth and reality of aging in America.* Washington, D.C.: National Council on Aging.

Hartley, J., Harker, J.D., and Walsh, D. A. (1980). Contemporary issues and new directions in adult development of learning and memory. In L. Poon (Ed.), *Aging in the 1980s: Psychological issues.* Washington, D.C.: American Psychological Association.

Hendricks, J., and Hendricks, C. (1981). *Aging in mass society.* 2nd ed. Cambridge, Mass.: Winthrop.

Holliday, S., Burnaby, B., and Chandler, M. (1986). *Wisdom.* N.Y.: Karger.

Hultsch, D. F. (1974). Learning to love in adulthood. *Journal of Gerontology, 29,* 302–8.

Jung, C. (1971). The stages of life. (Trans. R. Hull). In J. Campbell (Ed.), *The portable Jung.* N.Y.: Viking.

Kahana, E., and Felton, B. (1977). Social context and personal needs. *Journal of Social Issues, 33,* 56–74.

Kahana, E., Midlarsky, E., and Kahana, B. (1987). Beyond dependency, autonomy, and exchange. *Social Justice Research, 1* (4), 439–59.

Karuza, J., Coates, D., Cohn, E., Kidder, L., and Rabinowitz, V. C. (1983). Responsibility and helping. *Academic Psychology Bulletin, 5* (2), 183–94.

Kausler, D. (1982). *Experimental psychology and human aging.* N.Y.: Wiley.

Krebs, D., and Miller, D. (1985). Altruism and aggression. In G. Lindzey and E. Aronson (Eds.), *The handbook of social psychology* (3rd ed.). Reading, Mass.: Addison-Wesley.

Latane, B., and Darley, J. M. (1970). *The unresponsive bystander.* N.Y.: Appleton-Century-Crofts.

Lawton, M., Moss, M., and Grimes, M. (1985). The changing service needs of older tenants in planned housing. *Gerontologist, 25,* 258–64.

Liang, J., Dvorkin, K., Kahana, E., and Mazian, F. (1980). Social integration and morale. *Journal of Gerontology, 35* (5), 746–57.

Light, L. (1991). Memory and aging. *Annual Review of Psychology, 42,* 333–76.

Mehrabian, A., and Epstein, N. (1972). A measure of emotional empathy. *Journal of Personality, 40,* 525–43.

Midlarsky, E. (1968). Aiding responses. *Merrill-Palmer Quarterly, 14,* 229–60.

—— (1989). *Helping and volunteering by the elderly.* Presented at the Gerontological Society of America, November, Minneapolis, Minn.

—— (1991). Helping as coping. In M. Clark (Ed.), *Prosocial behavior. Review of Personality and Social Psychology.* Newbury Park, Cal.: Sage, 238–64.

Midlarsky, E., and Hannah, M. (1985). Competence, reticence, and helping by children and adolescents. *Developmental Psychology, 21,* 531–41.

—— (1989). The generous elderly. *Psychology and Aging, 49* (3), 346–51.

Midlarsky, E., and Kahana, E. (1983). Helping by the elderly. In M. Kleiman (Ed.),

*Interdisciplinary topics in gerontology*, vol. 17. Basel, Switzerland: Karger, 10–24.

—— (forthcoming). *For the sake of others*. Newbury Park, Cal.: Sage.

Midlarsky, E., Kahana, E., and Corley, R. (1986a). Personal and situational influences on late life helping. *Humboldt Journal of Social Relations, 13* (1 & 2), 217–33.

—— (1986b). *Altruistic moral judgment among the elderly*. Paper presented at the Gerontological Society of America, November, Chicago, Illinois.

—— (1987). *Altruist or hedonist?* Paper presented at the American Psychological Association, New York, N.Y.

Morgan, L. A. (1976). A re-examination of widowhood and morale. *Journal of Gerontology, 31*, 687–95.

Munnichs, J. M. A. (1976). *Dependency or interdependency in old age*. The Hague: Nijhoff.

Munsterberg, H. (1983). *The crown of life*. San Diego, Cal.: Harcourt Brace Jovanovich.

Payne, B. P. (1977). The older volunteer. *Gerontologist, 17*, 355–61.

Payne, B., and Bull, C. N. (1985). The older volunteer. In W. A. Peterson and J. Quadagno (Eds.), *Social bonds in late life*. Beverly Hills, Cal.: Sage, 251–72.

Rheingold, H., Hay, D., and West, M. (1976). Sharing in the second year of life. *Child Development, 47*, 1148–58.

Riegel, K. (1977). The dialectics of time. In N. Datan & H. Reese (Eds.), *Life-span developmental psychology*. New York.: Academic Press.

Riessman, F. (1976). How does self-help work? *Social Policy, 7*, 41–45.

Rosen, S., Mickler, S., and Spiers, C. (1986). The spurned philanthropist. *Humboldt Journal of Social Relations, 13* (1 & 2), 145–58.

Rotter, J. B. (1966). Generalized expectancies for internal versus external control of reinforcement. *Psychological Monographs, 80*, 1–28.

Rushton, J., Chrisjohn, R., and Fekken, G. (1981). The altruistic personality and the self-report altruism scale. *Personality and Individual Differences, 2*, 293–302.

Rushton, J., Fuller, D., Neale, M., Nias, D., and Eysenck, J. (1986). Altruism and aggression. *Journal of Personality and Social Psychology, 50*, 1192–98.

Ryan, T. (1960). Significance tests for multiple comparisons of proportions of variance and other statistics. *Psychogical Bulletin, 57*, 318–28.

Scheier, C., and Geller, S. (1979). Analysis of random effects in modeling studies. *Child Development, 50*, 752–57.

Strayer, F., Wareing, S., and Rushton, J. (1979). Social constraints on naturally occurring preschool altruism. *Ethology and Sociobiology, 1*, 3–11.

Wentowski, G. J. (1981). Reciprocity and the coping strategies of older people. *Gerontologist, 21*, 600–609.

# PART FIVE

# EMBRACING THE "OUTSIDER"

*Edited by Lawrence Baron*

# INTRODUCTION

*Lawrence Baron*

In situations where the dangers facing a person or group are the result of state-sanctioned policies, individual and collective attempts to aid those in peril have broad political and sociological implications. The historical context of this kind of rescue determines the risks involved in helping the victims and how legitimate their persecution seems to the general population. In turn, these factors affect the incidence of rescue, first by providing common positive or negative reasons either for protecting or abandoning those in need, and second by facilitating or inhibiting rescue based on the perceived and real dangers it might entail. Moreover, the prevailing values within a particular society or subculture influence the motivations that rescuers cite to explain their behavior. Finally, how one defines an act of altruism relates to the historical conditions and national or regional culture in which its occurs.

Richard Hovannisian's pioneering chapter about Turks who saved the lives of Armenians during the Genocide of 1915 attests to the culturally relative meaning of altruism. He documents many cases of Turks who acted upon a variety of humanitarian motives, but observes that these motives often were commingled with what appear to us today as less-than-noble ulterior motives such as the adoption of children by barren couples, the conversion of the rescued to Islam, and the exploitation of the rescued for their labor. Nevertheless, he discerns shades of altruism among these motives. Regarding the employment of the rescued Armenians, Hovannisian reminds us "to look at rural societies and realize that even in the most humanitarian of families, labor is a way of life for all family members." Similarly, in the minds of devout Turkish

Moslems, the conversions of the rescued were "good deeds essential to the physical and spiritual well-being of their new wards." Finally, Hovannisian compares the risks run by the Turkish rescuers to those of gentiles who saved Jews during the Holocaust to note that the former "had little to fear in case of exposure" since the goal of their government was the Turkification of the Armenians and not their racial extermination, as was the case during the Jewish Holocaust.

Lawrence Baron's chapter tries to identify what was distinctively Dutch about the motivations of Dutch rescuers of Jews during the German occupation. Despite Holland's tradition of religious tolerance, the Jews suffered higher numerical and proportional losses there than in other West European nations under Nazi rule. Baron attributes this to a variety of causes: Holland's location and topography, the repressive regime imposed on the Dutch, the crushing of early opposition to Nazi anti-Semitism, the compliance of the Dutch civil service and Jewish officials in the administration of racist policies, and the time lag between the first deportations and the development of a national rescue network. Once that network was operational, however, rescuing Jews became an integral part of resistance activities, unlike in countries like Poland, where Jews were never fully accepted as fellow citizens and political anti-Semitism was much stronger. Baron contends that the frequency of rescuers saving Jews whom they already knew was probably higher in Holland than in many other nations as a result of the higher degree of Jewish integration in Dutch society. He attributes the pronounced philo-Semitism among Dutch Calvinists who rescued Jews for theological reasons to Calvinism's relatively positive views of Jews and Judaism and to the political role Dutch Calvinism had played in its country's history.

By contrast the historical circumstances in wartime Poland were far less conducive to the mass rescue of Jews. There the Nazi regime brutally wielded its power to implement the "Final Solution" and enslave and terrorize the native gentile population. Even though some factions within the Polish resistance defended the Jews, others refused to do so, reflecting the virulent anti-Semitism pervading many Polish Catholic and nationalistic movements. The Polish nuns depicted in Ewa Kurek-Lesik's article not only jeopardized their convents and lives to hide Jewish children, but also frequently had to "suppress this anti-Semitism, or rise above it in the name of a higher ideal." "Motivated by a Christian duty towards others and by their fidelity to the ideals" expressed in their religious vows, they focused on the humanity and suffering of their wards and overlooked their Jewishness. The distrust between Polish Catholics and Jews was symbolized by the controversy over whether to christen the Jewish children being hidden in the convents. While many nuns felt baptism was essential for concealing the real identity of these children, orthodox Jews suspected the nuns of trying to convert their children permanently and preferred their children to be martyrs for their faith rather than apostates.

Rachel Hertz-Lazarowitz firmly roots the altruistic and political evolution of Dov Yirmiya in Israeli political culture. Dov hailed from a pioneering Zionist family and identified with the socialism of the Mapam party. Although he fought for his country's independence and security, he also recognized that Israel's victories had resulted in injustices against the Palestinians, who either lost their homes and lived as refugees in neighboring countries or encountered official discrimination if they stayed as citizens in Israel. His revulsion over what he witnessed during the 1982 Lebanon War heightened his empathy for their plight and prompted his political intervention on their behalf. Thus, he organized volunteer relief services for them, while simultaneously supporting a call for Israeli soldiers to refuse military service in the Occupied Territories. Hertz-Lazarowitz argues that the trauma of the Holocaust and Israel's struggle for survival have created a culture where there is "a close proximity between personal and collective boundaries." Thus, Dov's altruistic response to the suffering of the Palestinians could not be confined to remedial acts of charity and led to political activism to change the policies he believed were the source of their ordeal. She adds that his actions and views have been expressed in dramatic terms because he self-consciously plays a role on the political stage of his country. As in all of the selections in this section, the highly personal decision to embrace the despised other in his or her hour of need has public causes and repercussions.

# 12

# THE QUESTION OF ALTRUISM DURING THE ARMENIAN GENOCIDE OF 1915

*Richard G. Hovannisian*

Intervention and altruism during the Armenian Genocide of 1915 is a subject that has received little attention. Although many survivors have related incidents of external intervention that saved their lives, these episodes have always been parts of much larger stories of cruelty, suffering, trauma, and seemingly miraculous personal escape from the fate that befell most Armenians in the Ottoman or Turkish Empire during World War I. In the aftermath of the Armenian Genocide, the survivors, barred from returning home, scattered around the world, while the perpetrator regime and all successive Turkish governments engaged in unrelenting campaigns of denial and rationalization. These developments have discouraged investigations into the degree to which altruism may have been manifested during the most disruptive and irreparable catastrophe in the three-thousand-year history of the Armenian people. In many ways, therefore, this study is a first attempt to assess and categorize the primary motivations for and frequency of intervention.

What must be stated at the outset is that seeking instances of altruism in a genocide should not and cannot obviate the enormity of the crime and its consequences. Identifying episodes of apparent kindness in the midst of the destruction of a people may afford some solace and provide some affirmation about inherent goodness, but it should not disguise the fact that for every case of intervention in the Armenian Genocide there were thousands of cases of participation in or approval of the measures applied. In fact, the proportion of public involvement was very high. The hundreds of thousands of Armenians in the deportation caravans were fair game to all who would attack them to strip them of their last few possessions, to abduct pretty girls and children, or to vent their killing rage upon the victims, often as previously arranged by the ruling Young Turk dictatorship and its Special Organization (Teshkilat-i Mahsuse), whose responsibility it was to oversee the deportations—that is, the process of annihilation. The Special Organization used as agents of death and destruction hardened criminals who were purposefully released from prison, predatory tribes that were incited to wait in ambush for the deportee caravans as they passed through narrow gorges and defiles or approached river crossings, and Muslim refugees (*muhajirs*) from the Balkans, who were encouraged to wreak vengeance on the Armenian Christians and occupy the towns and villages that they were forced to abandon.

Although the Armenian Genocide of 1915 and the Holocaust of World War II took place at different times and under different circumstances, there were nonetheless some striking similarities:

· Perpetuation of genocide under the cover of an international war, thus minimizing the possibility of foreign intervention.
· Conception of the plan by a monolithic and xenophobic clique.
· Espousal of an ideology giving purpose and justification to exclusivism and intolerance toward elements resisting or deemed unworthy of assimilation.
· Imposition of strict party discipline and secrecy during the period of preparation.
· Formation of extralegal special armed forces to ensure rigorous execution of the operation.
· Provocation of public hostility toward the victim group and ascription to it of the very excesses to which it would be subjected.
· Certainty of the vulnerability of the targeted group, as demonstrated in the Armenian case by the previous massacres of 1894–1896 and 1909.
· Exploitation of advances in mechanization and communication to achieve unprecedented means for control, coordination, and thoroughness.
· Use of positive and negative sanctions, such as promotions and the incentive to loot or, conversely, dismissal and punishment of

recalcitrant officials and intimidation of persons who might be inclined to harbor members of the victim group.

In the search for altruism during the Armenian Genocide, there are, in contrast to Holocaust research, some insurmountable barriers. Because most of those who intervened on behalf of Armenians in 1915 were at the time already mature adults, usually between forty and sixty years of age, none of them is still alive. There is no way, therefore, to question them about their motivations, upbringing, or character, and to develop reliable profiles of them. It is extremely difficult to interview their children and grandchildren in the face of continuous official Turkish denials of the genocide. Hence, we must rely almost entirely on information provided by the survivors themselves, most of whom were children in 1915.

Because of the politics surrounding the Armenian Genocide, the expulsion of the survivors, uncompensated confiscation of Armenian goods and properties, and the abiding bitterness and trauma of the survivors and their progeny, virtually no contact occurred between the survivors after their rescue and resettlement and those who had intervened on their behalf. Moreover, in a significant number of cases it would be difficult or impossible, in the best of circumstances, to identify those who intervened, since they did so along the deportation routes for periods lasting from a few minutes to a day and remain nameless.

As a child in the San Joaquin Valley of California, I was often present when women who had survived the genocide would gather to exchange stories of deportation and suffering. These exchanges were perhaps the only therapy that this generation of survivors was afforded. The women had been subjected to prolonged punishment, for, unlike most of the male population, they were not killed outright within a few days' march of their homes. Rather, they were driven for weeks and months toward the deserts, becoming personal witnesses and victims to the cruelest tortures and evils that humans could devise.

Yet, running through many of the stories were unfamiliar names that were not Armenian, names that were recited with a certain reverence, names that I later learned included honorific titles such as *bey, agha, effendi,* indicative of high status in a Turkic society. A Zia Bey, Haji Effendi, or Mehmed Agha had intervened, and that act has been critical to the survival of the storyteller.

The interventions were not seen as final rescue or emancipation—that came only after World War I, when American and other relief agencies joined in Armenian efforts to seek out and rescue surviving women and children. The outside intercession was nonetheless central and critical to the ultimate rescue. Thus, the stream of consciousness regarding intervention has always been part of survivor lore, yet never the subject for study or analysis.

## THE ORAL HISTORY SAMPLE

This study is based on data derived from 527 oral history interviews with Armenian survivors (see table 12.1). The interviews have been conducted over the past twenty years as part of a course in Armenian oral history at the University of California, Los Angeles (UCLA). A little explanation is in order. Keenly aware of the rapid disappearance of the survivor generation and with it the loss of first-hand accounts and valuable information about life before and during the cataclysm, I introduced a university course on oral history. For it I devised or adapted questions relating to the Armenian experience in the Ottoman Empire—home life, schools and professions, customs and holidays, social structures, intercommunity and intracommunity relations, and then the deportations and massacres, means of self-preservation, and finally rescue and relocation.

The questionnaire devised as a guide to the interviewer does not include direct questions about external intervention. This information has, by and large, been volunteered by the interviewees. Nonetheless, intervention is so important in the stories of the survivors that it may be safely assumed that nearly all such cases have been noted. Other qualifiers must be added. To date, only a few of the 527 interviews, more than 90% of which are in the Armenian language, have been transcribed, as the emphasis has been on the collection process. In the preparation of this study, I have relied on the written interview summaries filed by the interviewers in order to identify cases of probable intervention. From those summaries, 183 cases or 34.7% of the total of 527 interviews were deemed to include information on intervention. These figures should be regarded as minimal, because it is likely that some cases of intervention were not noted in the student summaries.

Of the 183 interviewees who reported instances of intervention, ninety-six (52.5%) were males and eighty-seven (47.5%) were fe-

**Table 12.1a**

## UCLA Armenian Oral History Project Summary of Interviews

|  | *Actual Number* | *Percent of Total* |
|---|---|---|
| Total Number of Oral History Interviews | 527 | 100.0 |
| Number of Interviews in Which Intervention Indicated | 183 | 34.7 |
| Gender of Survivors |  |  |
| Male | 96 | 52.5 |
| Female | 87 | 47.5 |
| Age Groups of Survivors in the Year 1915 |  |  |
| 1–5  (born after 1910, before 1915) | 7 | 3.8 |
| 6–10 (born after 1905, before 1910) | 71 | 38.8 |
| 11–15 (born after 1900, before 1905) | 56 | 30.6 |
| 16–20 (born after 1895, before 1900) | 37 | 20.2 |
| 21–25 (born after 1890, before 1895) | 11 | 6.0 |
| 26–30 (born after 1885, before 1890) | 1 | 0.6 |
| Total | 183 | 100.0 |
| Place of Origin of Survivors |  |  |
| Bitlis | 6 | 3.3 |
| Diarbekir (Dikranagerd) | 6 | 3.3 |
| Erzerum (Garin) | 25 | 13.7 |
| Harput (Kharpert) | 43 | 23.6 |
| Sivas (Sepastia) | 22 | 12.1 |
| Van | 1 | 0.6 |
| Cilicia | 34 | 18.7 |
| Other Regions | 45 | 24.7 |
| Total | 182 | 100.0 |
| Total Number of Interventions | 233 |  |
| Number of Rescuers Identified |  |  |
| Male | 206 | 92.4 |
| Female | 17 | 7.6 |
| Total | 223 | 100.0 |
| Ethnic Origin of Rescuers Identified |  |  |
| Turk | 147 | 65.9 |
| Arab | 39 | 17.5 |
| Kurd | 29 | 13.0 |
| Assyrian | 3 | 1.4 |
| American | 2 | 0.9 |
| Circassian | 2 | 0.9 |
| Dane | 1 | 0.4 |
| Total | 223 | 100.0 |

**Table 12.1b**

UCLA Armenian Oral History Project Summary of Interviews

|  | *Actual Number* | *Percent of Total* |
|---|---|---|
| Socioeconomic Status of Rescuers Identified |  |  |
| Peasant | 76 | 38.0 |
| Notable (mostly rural) | 35 | 17.5 |
| Government official | 35 | 17.5 |
| Soldier or gendarme | 33 | 16.5 |
| Merchant | 21 | 10.5 |
| Total | 200 | 100.0 |
| Length of Intervention |  |  |
| Day(s) | 43 | 27.2 |
| Month(s) | 20 | 12.7 |
| Year(s) | 95 | 60.1 |
| Total | 158 | 100.0 |
| Number of Persons Affected by Intervention |  |  |
| One | 110 | 49.1 |
| More than one | 114 | 50.9 |
| Total | 224 | 100.0 |
| Intervention Initiated by |  |  |
| Victim | 64 | 31.4 |
| Rescuer | 140 | 68.6 |
| Total | 204 | 100.0 |
| Intervention Based on |  |  |
| Prior acquaintance | 53 | 24.8 |
| No prior acquaintance | 161 | 75.2 |
| Total | 214 | 100.0 |
| Primary Motivation for Intervention |  |  |
| Economic (see breakdown below) | 102 | 43.8 |
| Piety | 10 | 4.3 |
| Missionary/Christian | 1 | 0.4 |
| Humanitarian | 120 | 51.5 |
| Total | 233 | 100.0 |
| Breakdown of Economic Motivation |  |  |
| Bribes | 26 | 25.5 |
| Professional/artisan | 19 | 18.6 |
| Home/field labor | 57 | 55.9 |
| Total | 102 | 100.0 |

males. In listening to these selected 183 interviews, I tried to determine the place of origin and age of the interviewees, the ethnic identity and social and economic status of the interveners, and the motives for the interventions. I looked particularly for cases in which humanitarian or altruistic motivations were clearly dominant. Obviously, it is difficult to make determinations relating to the motives for intervention or to develop sociopsychological profiles of the personalities involved. Not only is it impossible to speak to the principals themselves, but the survivors' explanations come more than half a century after the fact and may be colored or conditioned by time or by the stories of others.

Nearly three-quarters of this group of respondents were fifteen years old or younger in 1915. Of the 183 survivors who mentioned intervention, seventy-one (38.8%) were six to ten years old, fifty-six (30.6%) were eleven to fifteen years old, and seven (3.8%) were one to five years old. Only thirty-seven (20.2%) were sixteen to twenty years old, and the number of those twenty-one to twenty-five years old drops sharply to eleven (6.0%). These statistics are not a true reflection of the ratio of survival, since many in the older age groups who experienced intervention are no longer living to tell about it. Nor do the 183 persons who experienced intervention, out of a total of 527 survivor interviews, reflect the actual proportion of interventions when measured against all deportees; the ratio applies to the proportion of interventions only among deportees who survived. When compared with the total number of Armenian deportees in 1915, the incidence of intervention drops drastically.

The 183 survivors collectively experienced 233 interventions. Of the 233 incidents identified, 206 (92.4%) were initiated by males, while only seventeen (7.6%) were initiated by females. These figures reflect the sheltered position of women in traditional Islamic societies, yet it is clear that women played a key role vis-à-vis the Armenian survivors once they had been brought into the Muslim households. In half the cases (49.1%), the intervention affected only one person, but in the other half (50.9%) two or more persons were saved. In only a third (31.4%) of the cases was the intervention initiated or requested by the victims, and in just a quarter of them (24.8%) was intercession based on prior acquaintance or friendship. As far as can be determined from the interviews, the ethnic origins of the interveners were Turkish, 147 (65.9%), Arab, thirty-nine (17.5%), Kurdish, twenty-nine (13%), and Assyrian, Circassian,

Danish, and American collectively forming eight (3.6%). From other sources, it is learned that along the Black Sea coast and elsewhere some Armenians were initially sheltered by Greek families, although this was usually temporary because of the vulnerability of the Greeks themselves.

Based on socioeconomic classes or professions, two hundred of those who intervened have been identified as follows: peasant or villager, seventy-six (38.0%); notable (mostly rural), thirty-five (17.5%); government official, thirty-five (17.5%); soldier or gendarme, thirty-three (16.5%); merchant, twenty-one (10.5%). The duration of the intervention, in 158 identifiable cases, was as follows: day or days, forty-three (27.2%), month or months, twenty (12.7%), year or years, ninety-five (60.1%).

The 183 survivors came from all parts of the Ottoman Empire, including the European districts near the capital city, Constantinople or Istanbul. Some came from the Armenian quarters and villages in the Turkish heartlands of western and central Anatolia, and many originated in the region of Cilicia, which lies at the northeastern tip of the Mediterranean Sea and is relatively close to the Syrian deserts, the destination of most deportees. By the time caravans from other Armenian provinces reached Cilicia, they had already been greatly decimated. Those caravans came primarily from the six eastern provinces, known as Turkish Armenia or Western Armenia, and including Erzerum (Garin), Van, Bitlis, Diarbekir (Dikranagerd), Harput (Kharpert), and Sivas (Sepastia). The provinces of Van, Erzerum, and Bitlis were closest to the Persian and Russian frontiers, and nearly all Armenians from these regions either fled abroad or were massacred outright without regard to age or sex. Of those who were deported, few survived because of the great distances that had to be traversed to the desert and the organized ambushes and other perils en route. Ironically, although some of the worst massacres took place in the province of Kharpert, which an American eyewitness labeled "slaughterhouse province," a large number of women and children there escaped deportation through religious conversion and adoption by Muslim households. Of the 183 survivors, forty-three came from that large province.

## THE QUESTION OF MOTIVATION

The most problematic aspect of this study is the qualification and quantification of the motives of those who intervened. There are a few clear-cut cases of sexual exploitation, bribery, forced labor, piety or moral sentiment, and adoption by childless couples. I have shown the cause of most cases of intervention to be humanitarian, but if altruism means that there is no profit motive or gain for the intervener, then the majority of those cases would have to be reclassified or discarded. There is no doubt that humanitarian motives were present and strong, and some cases give not the least hint of anything but humanitarian sentiment. But there are far more instances in which presumed humanitarian intervention includes home or field labor by the person rescued, conversion to Islam and Turkification, or adoption. These may not have been the initial motives for intervention, but labor, conversion, and adoption are recurrent factors in many instances of intervention classified as humanitarian. Yet before discarding these cases, one must look at rural societies and realize that even in the most humanitarian of families, labor is a way of life for all family members.

There are cases, of course, when it becomes clear that the intervention was made in order to acquire economic benefit. Children, in particular, were a cheap source of labor, and the testimonies of the survivors bear this out. For the researcher, however, arbitrary decisions have to be made as to whether to classify a particular case as humanitarian, even when some labor is involved, or to classify it as economic, even when those for whom the survivor worked were kind and humane. Multiple motivations were often present at the same time, yet based on the definitions of altruism used in studies of the Holocaust, a significant number of cases that I have termed as humanitarian intervention would have to be disqualified.

One other point should be mentioned that may weigh against altruism. Once the main waves of deportation and massacre of Armenians had swept over all the Armenian communities—that is, by the end of 1915—many of the stragglers or survivors could be taken in or adopted quite openly on condition that they convert to and profess Islam. Unlike the Holocaust, therefore, at certain places and at certain times there was little or no risk in having persons born as Armenians in a household. This point underscores a significant difference between the Young Turk perpetrators of the Armenian Genocide and the Nazi perpetrators of the Holocaust. The Young Turks were extreme nationalists, but they were not racists in the Nazi sense. They wanted to create a Turkic empire and eliminate all obstacles to the realization of that goal. The Turks had absorbed subject peoples for centuries, and the continued absorption of powerless and defenseless Armenians did not jeopardize the fulfillment of this objective. On the contrary, in some areas Armenian children were gathered into orphanages to be "Turkified." Hence, while many Muslims who took in Armenian women and children must be regarded as performing humanitarian deeds, on the whole they had little to fear in case of exposure.

## SEXUAL EXPLOITATION

The major categories of motivation that I have listed are economic, religious, and humanitarian. A few fall outside these categories and may be termed exploitative. Many women survivors have used euphemisms to imply sexual abuse, whether witnessed or experienced. This is a very sensitive issue, and few have had the courage of Satenig (b. 1901), from the region of Nicomedia or Izmid in western Anatolia, who confided to a female interviewer,

I saw the man had his eye on me. His wife was in Constantinople. I submitted to that man. Do you understand, I have not told this to anyone. It is the first time that I am revealing it. I submitted. And how did he look after me, do you know? Just like his wife. He was careful not to show it to anyone, so many guests would come. I submitted. He looked after me. He named me "Samie."

When nine-year-old Trfanda Godabashian (b. 1906) of Kharpert was being deported, a Turkish woman offered to save her if she would marry her son. Infuriated by the girl's refusal, the woman gave her son a knife to kill Trfanda, but just then another Turk on horseback rescued her and took her home along with another Armenian youngster.

Flor Proudian (b. 1901) of Kharpert says,

They came and took me. Supposedly there was a Turkish boy who had seen and wanted me. I said, "It is impossible for me to become a Turk." I went up the steps and rolled down, saying, "I will not become a Turk and I'll die here," but it did no good. Two women came, two Turks. They grabbed my arms and are taking me. I am shouting and screaming, saying, "I won't become a Turk," but they pay no heed. They took me and put me in their house, saying, "You are going to stay here now. Although you are young, our son is also young."

## THE ECONOMIC FACTOR

Economic motives for intervention are dominant in 102 (43.8%) of the 233 instances of intervention. Of these 102, twenty-six (25.5%) were for bribes, nineteen (18.6%) for professional skills, and fifty-seven (55.9%) for domestic and field labor. The cases of bribery are the most clear-cut for economic profit, with nearly all of these involving Turkish officials, gendarmes, and soldiers, and usually being of short duration. Bribes were used to get exemption from or to postpone deportation, to receive provisions or favors en route, or to be sent, at a critical juncture on the road to Syria, toward the relative safety of Aleppo rather than to almost certain death in the desert around Deir-el-Zor. City dwellers usually had more resources with which to attempt bribery, but even so only a small percentage of those who used bribes actually managed to survive.

Serop Chiloyan (b. 1903) of Kharpert recalls that his father paid a Turkish agha, or notable, to protect his family. Nonetheless, several family members were deported and the rest were forced to work the lands of the agha. Richard Kaloustian (b. 1901) of the Arabkir region of Kharpert notes that his father, like other rich Armenians, knew the chief of police and repeatedly gave him bribes, but eventually the family was deported. Yet perhaps the delay had spared them from the ferocious massacres to which the first caravans were subjected. Anna Torigian (b. 1906) from one of the villages of Kharpert was saved by a Turk whose shop was next to that of her father. After receiving payment, the neighbor helped store all of the family's merchandise and offered to keep Anna. She was saved in this way, while the rest of the family was deported.

Baghdasar Bourjikian (b. 1903), Vahe Churukian (b. 1906), and Beatrice Ashkharian (b. 1902), all of Kessab, were able to avoid deportation to Deir-el-Zor through the bribes paid by their families. On the road of exile from their native Hadjin, Gassia Kahayan's family bribed the gendarmes to send them towards Urfa rather than to Deir-el-Zor. Samuel Kadorian (b. 1907) also reached Urfa from his native Kharpert through bribes his mother paid a guard. Yervant Cholakian (b. 1907) of Hadjin was able to reach Aleppo through his father's bribes. In Aintab, the father of Ohannes Karamanougian (b. 1906) repeatedly paid city officials and gendarmes to exempt his family, but a new governor later refused to spare them and all were deported. Marie Aprahamian (b. 1901) of Aintab, whose family eventually reached Port Said, emphasizes that the possibility of survival was much higher if one had a lot of money. In all these and similar cases, the profit motive involves almost exclusively Turkish soldiers, gendarmes, and officials who intervened in exchange for payment. Buying their way out of immediate deportation spared some Armenians, but their survival was by no means guaranteed, for they still faced starvation, dehydration, epidemic, and recapture by other Turkish gendarmes.

The nineteen cases of escape ascribed to professional or special skills constitute only 8.1% of the 233 interventions in this study. Garegin Sahakian (b. 1895) of Marash was saved at Berejik, along with his relatives, because Turks who needed an ironsmith took them to Hromkla. They remained there until 1918, when they had to flee because of a new, intolerant *kaimakam*, or district governor. The family of Armenouhi Sousamaian (b. 1900) of Urgup in Caesarea province was deported to Syria, but because her father was able to repair the mill at Rakka, the family was allowed to stay there for the duration of the war. Max Tangarian (b. 1898) of Bursa was taken in with his family by a baker in Konia to make bread for the Turkish army. Makrouhi Sahatjian (b. 1897) of Erzerum was in a deportation caravan when she arrived with her sister in Suruj, where the two girls were taken in as seamstresses for the wife of a Turkish official.

Garabed Merjanian (b. 1904) of Marash was en route to the desert when an unexpected intervention occurred:

When we arrived at Meskene, one of my father's old customers said, "Mr. Panos, the deportation officer has a bad toothache," and he took my father. Father returned two hours later. He had treated the teeth and made the officer well. At that time the Armenian caravan was leaving Meskene, and my father asked to rejoin it. But the officer said, "Are you crazy! They are going to death, and you want your family to join them?" My father was a barber and understood dentistry. So the Turkish military official arranged for us to remain in Meskene for a year.

Beatrice Kitabdjian (b. 1907) of Aintab describes her father as "something like a real estate agent" in the government:

He was highly literate. The Turkish effendis told him to stay and to inventory all the houses, properties, and lands of the Armenians. For that reason my father remained. The effendis liked him very much. They told him to stay in their village, a half-hour from Aintab. And it happened that way. He stayed there, and we remained in our home in Aintab.

Of the interventions for economic purposes, domestic and field labor and herding are the reasons most commonly given. The majority of these rescues were not devoid of humanitarian components. The survivors frequently attest to the fact that they were not mistreated and express gratitude that the intervention spared their lives. Only a few are as resentful as Anoush Shirinian (b. 1898) of Caesarea, who saved her daughter from a Turkish abductor with the help of a Kurdish woman. The Kurd then took mother and daughter to a Turkish household, where for four years, "we were forced to work like slaves." Anoush, whose name was changed to Jamileh, was eventually thrown out. Vertaim Sarkissian (b. 1906) of Yozgat was rescued by a Turkish woman after having been left alone for three days among the bodies of her massacred townspeople. She was taken to the village of Bektash, where she became a servant in a Turkish household. Siroon Tashjian (b. 1907) of Kharpert was given away by her mother to a Kurdish woman for safekeeping. She lived with the family for four years and did all kinds of work, forgetting her Armenian identity until her rescue after the war. Lloyd Kafesjian (b. 1910) of Tamzara, Sivas province, was taken in with his mother and sister by an affluent Turk, in whose household all three served. Later, Lloyd was given to an elderly Turkish woman, for whom he ran errands and tended garden. Kourken Handjian (b. 1907) of Erzinjan, Erzerum province, extols the Turk who sheltered him and his mother and put them to work. "He was a very kind man, a very kind man, because he had quite a few Armenian servants in his home." Rebecca Doramdjian (b. 1907) of Urfa, on the other hand, says that she served in several Muslim households, in some places treated kindly and in other places badly.

Some survivors show great pride in their labor. Vartan Misserian (b. 1902) of Sivas, for example, relates the following story:

> I remained in a Turkish family for ten or twelve years.... The Turks issued an order that all who were keeping Armenians must give them up. The man comforted me, saying not to be afraid, as he would not turn me over to the Turkish gendarmes. He had some land and he sent me there, and I hid there for a time until the police were gone. There I grazed their animals, and then, when I was able to do quite a bit of work, I can say, putting my hand on my conscience, that I provided for that household, because the man didn't look after the house very much but was always gambling. I would go to the fields of others and help in the harvest, and

with the money I earned provide for our house. The man's mother continued to look after me like my own mother.

Quite a few of the survivors were taken in by Arabs for herding and field labor. Artin Kopooshian (b. 1906) of Adana was given shelter by an Arab as he lagged behind the caravan and thereafter tended sheep. Garabed Aroushian (b. 1905) of Severeg, Diarbekir province, became a camel herder for an Arab after losing his family on the way to Deir-el-Zor. Hovnan Dostourian (b. 1907) of Yarasa was given to an Arab as a servant and stayed with him for four or five years. When the war was over and he was rescued, Hovnan ran away from the orphanage to return to his Arab family.

Nearly all of these testimonies show that even as small children the survivors were expected to work. It bears repeating that the family in rural societies is a unit of economic production, and descriptions of Armenian family life before the genocide demonstrate that children often helped in tending the livestock, working the fields, and cooking, weaving, and other household chores. Thus, the outside parties had something to gain from the extra help afforded by the free labor of the Armenian children, but in most cases they treated the youngsters decently and provided them with food, clothing, and shelter.

## RELIGIOUS MOTIVATION

Religion and piety figure in many of the interviews. In cases of economic or humanitarian motives for intercession, there are frequent references to conversion, Muslim customs and attitudes, and "Turkification." Still, only ten (4.3%) cases of intervention seem to have been based foremost on religion. Of these, two or three entail pious opposition to the persecution of Armenians, whereas more often the rescue and conversion of Armenians were seen as good deeds essential to the physical and spiritual well-being of their new wards. Exemplifying the first group is the episode related by Vahram Morookian (b. 1900) of Everek:

A Turkish *molla*, bearded, who was very friendly to the Armenians—no matter that the Turkish government did not want anyone to help us and declared that no Turks should protect an Armenian—this man nevertheless, with several others who shared his views, considered it an obligation to lead us as far as Tarsus so that nothing would happen to us on the way.

Religious sentiment may also have affected the situation at Zonguldak, where, according to Hagop Adayamanian (b. 1896), the *kaimakam*, a pious man, was on good terms with the Armenian priest and saved six hundred people by persuading his superiors to spare them. In this category, too, are individuals such as the Arab family that rescued Siranoush Husinian (b. 1905) of Urfa and took her for medical treatment to Mardin, exclaiming repeatedly, "Whoever did this to you, God will punish them."

Piety as a motive for converting Armenians runs throughout the accounts. Vartouhi Boghosian (b. 1905) of St. Stepanos explains that the Arab woman who was like a foster mother to her for three years wanted her to convert for her own good. "If you are a Muslim, you will go to heaven, but if you convert to Islam from Christianity, then you will go to a heaven ten times greater." Haroutiun Kevorkian (b. 1903) of Charsanjak, Kharpert province, asserts that he was kept by a Kurd because "in the Muslim faith whoever frees a person and converts him will receive great rewards in heaven. If you change your religion, whatever sins you have committed will be forgiven. They named me Husein."

In written testimony, Aram Haigaz (b. 1900) of Shabin-Karahisar, Sivas province, states that his mother urged him to convert to Islam and find a way to escape from the deportation caravan. A group of Turkish women gave him the *selevat* oath of profession and then took him to their sheikh, who awaited permission from a higher authority to adopt the boy. Aram was converted and renamed Muslim. His sheikh was warm and caring, and also provided shelter for an Armenian woman, who was very sick, and her two children. But because the woman had resisted conversion to Islam, upon her death the Kurds refused to accord her a burial and rolled her body down a hill. Her two children were then converted, renamed, and adopted.

Only one case has been found in which the outside party discouraged Armenians from converting. Hovaness Basmajian (b. 1909) of Kessab fled with his brother and two sisters from Damascus to an Arab village, where the brother served as assistant to a shoemaker, for which he received a gold piece each month. Hovaness remembers the villagers as extremely generous people. The shoemaker was exceptional in that he told the Armenian brothers and sisters that it would be wrong for them to renounce their Christ for Muhammad.

The broad grey zone in assigning a primary motivation in cases where there is overlap is evidenced in the story of Grigor Ookhtentz (b. 1909) of Sivrihisar:

My brother and I were adopted by Turks, in the direction of Chai. After we stayed there five or six months, they asked us to become Muslims, because there were no longer any Armenians. They were all dead and gone.

I knew Turkish and could speak it, but then I forgot how to speak Armenian. Thus, they changed our religion and named me Hasan, and my brother, Mahmed. We stayed with those families until 1918. I was a servant with Khalil Ibrahim, but he looked after me well, as he had no other children. The place where my brother stayed was worse.

Shukry Kopushian (b. 1901) of Hadjin lived among the Arabs for seventeen years, grazing sheep:

They were Muslims and I had to become a Muslim with them, having to pray according to their religion. We learned it and performed the *namaz* [prayers].

Cut off from the outside world, Shukry married an Arab girl and had two children before he learned quite by chance that his sister was alive. Joining her in Beirut, he remarried and resumed an Armenian life.

There were also instances of government-sponsored conversion. Haroutiun Tabakian (b. 1907) of Hadjin states that his brother bribed an Arab to guide the boy to the safety of Aleppo. Once there, however, Haroutiun and three hundred other orphans were taken by train at night to Balekesir in Anatolia. Turkish officials gathered the orphans in the Armenian church there and began teaching them Turkish. All were converted to Islam. Haroutiun ran away and never found out what happened to the other children.

## HUMANITARIAN MOTIVATION

The humanitarian factor shows up in at least three-quarters of all the interventions and was the primary motivation in 120 (51.5%) of the total of 233 incidents reported. It is in this category that acts of altruism are found. Sometimes it was the Turkish or Kurdish neighbors of Armenians who intervened selflessly. Previous friendship was an important though not overriding factor in humanitarian intervention. Where there was no previous acquaintance, the sheltering of helpless women and children was regarded as both humanitarian and pious, especially since many of the children were converted and adopted. In their own altruism, many converted Armenians tried to help other Armenians. Examples of incidents involving both previous and no previous acquaintance will illustrate the strength of humanitarian sentiment among the small segment of the population that was moved to intervene.

### Prior Acquaintance

Prior acquaintance was instrumental in saving a caravan of thirty-five hundred deportees. Missak Parseghian (b. 1895) of Aintab explains that when they reached a town between Hama and Homs in Syria, the *kaimakam*, who was a native of Aintab, recognized them and helped them very much. "He was a Turk by the name of Mahmed Agha. There were loads of good Turks who saved the lives of Armenians."

Intervention took place more often on a personal level. Arsen Magdessian (b. 1903) of Yozgat recalls,

My mother fell on her knees before Tahir Agha. Even though he was a Turk, Tahir's eyes brimmed with tears. He said, "Get up, my daughter. Whoever has caused this, may both eyes be blinded." He turned to his brother and said, "Khurshud, you need a son. They are to be pitied. We have eaten much bread from their hands. Take this boy." Khurshud said, "This boy is clean. I shall take him."

Nazar Nazarian (b. 1904) of Aintab declares, "Mustafa was a good man. My mother sent me to him because my father knew him. He kept me with him until the end of the war and did not tell anyone in the village that I was an Armenian." Yeghisapet Terzian (b. 1895) and Tavrez Tatevosian (b. 1903) were working in their villages of Tadem and Bazmashen, Kharpert province, when they were warned by familiar Turks from neighboring villages of impending danger and were able to go into hiding while most of the villages of the province were emptied and the population set out on the death marches.

Zabel Apelian (b. 1907) of Diarbekir was rescued by an army officer known to the family. During the deportations, her mother implored the officer to take Zabel and her sister to his family in Mardin. Since the sisters kept crying and asking for their mother, the officer went back looking for the woman and found her near death in a ditch. In her interview, Zabel relates the joy she and her sister felt when their mother was brought to join them.

The family of Aram Kilichjian (b. 1903) of Kirshehir and some other fellow townspeople were for unexplained reasons brought back from the deportation route to their homes, already nothing more than heaps of rubble. Yet that night several neighboring Turkish families brought soup so that the children could eat. Aram's brother was in the Turkish army and his commander took special interest in the Kilichjian family. The episode includes humanitarian, religious, and coercive aspects, all at once:

My brother's commander, Zia Bey, whose word the Turks respected, came and said, "Give this boy to me." When the man saw that my mother and sister didn't want to give me up, he summoned a Turk he knew, gave him a donkey, and told my mother, "Go with him and see what they are doing to young Armenians." My mother went to the place called Giulasar and saw that many Armenians had died there and were being ripped apart by vultures. Finally, my mother was persuaded and delivered me to that man. Zia Bey took me to his family in his village. They were not my mother and father, but the people loved me and looked after me. . . . The man had a grown daughter, who would take me in her lap and cuddle me.

After a month, I saw that there was a commotion in the house and that preparations were being made. . . . I thought it was something like a wedding. It was a circumcision ceremony for Zia Bey's son. They came and found me, too, and tried to circumcise me at the same time. I fled to the garden and hid, but they came and found me and did it to me. Afterwards, Zia Bey's son lay on one side of the room and I lay on the other—but the man liked me very much. And they gave me the name Said.

It was a time of famine. . . . There was a bread that was called "vasika" bread. One room of this man's house was filled with flour. This man's wife, whom I called *abla* [auntie], would say, "Get up and take these breads to your mother and family." In those difficult days our family was well fed. That woman was very good and liked to help. If I say she was better than my mother, believe me. . . . The woman and her daughters would get cloth from their store and sew clothes for my mother and sisters, who by that time had been Islamicized at the urgings of the family that had taken me. My sisters had married Turkish boys. Naturally my mother wept and said, "I'll die but I won't become a Turk." Zia Bey said, "Don't cry, no one will take your religion from you, but I want you on the surface to show yourself to be Turkish, so that they won't kill you.

In one of the few interviews conducted in English, Henry Vartanian (b. 1906) of Zara, province of Sivas or Sepastia, talks about Ali Effendi, who had operated a mill with Henry's father:

My father was well recognized in government circles. He had a friend by the name of Ali Effendi. . . . He is a Turk, but a beautiful man. A man with

a soul.... The systematic exile and genocide began. Ali Effendi said that
he has to bring us from Zara, because it was too dangerous there. One of
his wives was vacationing and her house was empty. So, he said, "I will
take you to that house." We were six children and my mother. Ali Effendi
told us specifically not to make our presence in his wife's house detected.
"I don't want any Turk or anyone in the area to know that you are here."
He used to lock the door and go to his work. He would bring us food and
then lock up and go. He kept us there for three months.

Intervention based on friendship had limits. Henry continues by
saying that orders came from Istanbul a second time for the Armenians to be deported. Ali Effendi came to Mrs. Vartanian:

He said, "I don't want to hand you over to the government. But," he said,
"there is only one way in order that I don't get hurt. I know," he said,
"that this is not right, but this is a necessity." He said, "You should change
your religion." My mother is mad. She says, "No! Ali Effendi."

I tell you, he was a wonderful man. He said, "Well, I don't blame you.
I would have felt the same way. But let me give you a little advice....
Remember that if I hand you over to the government they will exile you
immediately and once you cross the bridge at the outskirts of the city they
will kill your children in front of your eyes, and a Turk will take you as
a wife, because that is permitted by law. I don't want my best friend's
family to be killed." He said, "You in your heart be, remain a Christian,
but outwardly you accept the Muslim religion. This way you can survive.
One of these days the war will be over, and then you can go back to your
religion."

I guess my mother realized the danger and decided that the best thing
to do was to change our religion. Ali Effendi managed to help us in that.
We were given Muslim names, and we became *donmes*.

### No Prior Acquaintance

Three-quarters of the interventions were by individuals previously
unknown to the survivors. As in cases based on prior acquaintance,
adoption and conversion often accompanied the humanitarian
acts. Children were deprived of a sense of personhood as they were
given away, shared, or moved from one home to another. It was
extremely traumatic to be picked out of a crowd for adoption and
to be separated from parents and siblings. Christine Avakian (b.
1903) of Adana complains, "It was like we were a piece of furniture
or some object." Children were no better than "pets or senseless
creatures." On the deportation route at Killis, Christine's father

entrusted his two daughters to a Kurd, who kept one and gave the other to his brother. Despite her bitterness, Christine goes on to speak affectionately about her Kurdish "mama" and "papa." By and large, the survivors intermix their tears over the loss of parents and siblings with praise for their adoptive Muslim parents, this even as they express seething resentment against the Turkish government and even against the Turkish people collectively.

Missak Shiroyan (b. 1901) of Erzerum states that by the time his deportation caravan reached Kharpert most of the people in it had already died:

Turkish officials came to gather the children. They collected as many of us as there were. They brought us to Mezre and put us into a house, of course one that had belonged to an Armenian. Their purpose was to save our lives and to Islamicize us. They began to take Armenian children and pass them out to Turks and Kurds. They adopted me as their child and named me Fayek, a Turkish name. The family that adopted me was a man and wife, the man at least sixty or sixty-five. I was a cute little boy at the time. They had no children, and I must say that they pampered me like their own child.

Also deported from Erzerum, Manoushag Meserlian (b. 1907) reminisces, "They cared for us very well, be it food or clothing. Of course, however much, they didn't look after us like their own children. They tried to Islamicize me and I think they named me Fatum."

Aghavni Mazmanian (b. 1895) of Sivas relates that while she was being deported,

A Turk came to me and said, "I shall find a good place for you. Don't cry." He was a Turk from Malatia, but he was a very good man. He had seven Armenian orphans in his home. He went and found another Turk. "Khalil," he said, "this kid is to be pitied. Take her to your home." My *agha* was like a saint, and my *khanum* [his wife] was very kind. They cared for me like a mother and father.

Speaking in English, Virginia Oghigian (b. 1908), also of Sivas, points to the conflict that often arose when, after the war, relatives came to rescue children adopted by Muslim families:

I was given away to a Turkish woman who took me to her house. So my younger brother and I were taken to this home to become their children. They changed our names and gave us Turkish names. My name was Shahseda. In this Turkish home, we had to follow Turkish rules. Girls had to cover their faces when speaking or spoken to. There were about five Armenian orphans in the house.

Oh well, one day my mother finally came to see me and to take me with her. She told me very bad things about what had happened to Armenians. She took me by the arm and wanted me to pay attention to what she was saying. I didn't listen, because I was mad at her, since she had left me alone for so long. I didn't want to talk to her.

Arshaluis Setrakian (b. 1912) of Gurun, Sivas province, recalls,

They were a large family, and I would help care for the little ones. I think I stayed there two years. I liked that home very much, because they looked after me, food and drink were plentiful. This was the home of a very rich man.... In the evenings they, together with several other wealthy households, would pass out bread to Armenian refugees. When my mother came to retrieve me, it was very difficult. It was with wails and tears that I was separated [from my adopted family].

Among the cases that come closest to altruism, the following may be taken as representative examples. Vartan Melidonian (b. 1899) of Erzinjan, Erzerum province, straggled into Kharpert after weeks of torment:

All members of my family had died, and I was the only one left alive, but I was wounded in several places. I set out and entered a village. A Turk told me to follow him. He took me to his home and then brought yogurt, bread, cream. I could not eat it. My stomach had dried up and nothing would go down. All I wanted was to die and join my parents. They took me to the barn and covered me. I stayed with that Turk until 1922. The Turk, Hasan Effendi, was wealthy and gave me a home in his village, Adav. The man had four children, and he looked after me like one of them.

Mary Ishkhanian (b. 1909) of Malatia, Kharpert province, was taken in by a woman who had eight sons. During the first few days. Mary cried incessantly. Annoyed by the wailing, one of the sons shouted, "Shut up, *gavoor* [infidel]." The woman slapped her grown son and warned him never again to address the girl in that debasing way. Mary lived happily in that household for three years.

The family of Haig Setrakian (b. 1902) of Konia found shelter in Tarsus for four years:

I must say that we encountered good people. In Tarsus we found a house. The landlord was a Turk who worked in the military. Every two days, the town crier would pass through the streets calling upon anyone harboring Armenians to turn them over to the government. This man, no matter what, did not lay a hand on us. We hid in a place dug into the ground, and until the end this man did not lay a hand on us. In this way we passed very difficult days.

Finally, there are many instances of Armenians, albeit converted to Islam and given new Turkish identities, trying to help other Armenians. Sirvart Chadirjian (b. 1899) of Kerasond, for example, was forcibly married to a Turkish soldier. He was kind to her and helped her assist other Armenian women to escape. After Haroutiun Kevorkian of Charsanjak had been converted and renamed Husein, he did not forget his origins:

When a caravan of Armenians passed through our village, I was able to save a woman. I took her to my agha's house and there she stayed with us as a servant for a year and a half. On another occasion, I found an Armenian boy. It is shameful to say but the Turks had sodomized him. I got him and brought him to our house and gave him my bed. I was now able to free whomever I could. I was now a dyed-in-the-wool Muslim. I was all of fourteen years old at the time.

**CONCLUSION**

Several conclusions may be drawn from this investigation. Any study of altruism during the Armenian Genocide of 1915 is bound to be problematic for several reasons. Foremost among them are the total absence of those who intervened and the inaccessibility of their family members or others who may have had information passed down and who could cast light on the personalities of the interveners. The unwillingness of all Turkish governments since World War I to face up to the genocide is a major hindrance to scholarly inquiry and compounds the difficulties. The main source of information, therefore, is to be found in the accounts of survivors, and the present study is based on 527 taped survivor interviews in the Armenian Oral History Collection at UCLA. They are, however, general interviews and have no specific focus on intervention. These limitations notwithstanding, the statistics and categories that have emerged from the 183 interviews that mention intervention are significant, because the sample is a large one.

The most obvious conclusion is that in the extreme situation caused by the genocidal policies of the Young Turk rulers of the Ottoman Empire, there were numerous individuals, families, and even entire villages that were moved to intervene. Without such intercession, many Armenians could not have survived the death and destruction that surrounded them and lived to tell their stories.

Varied motives for intervention appear in the 183 selected interviews. Sometimes they are simple and straightforward—people acting as if instinctively on emotions of empathy, sympathy, piety, and concern. These emotions in some instances were reserved only for friends and neighbors, but more often they extended to anyone in acute distress. At other times, the motives overlap and are more complex. Humanitarian factors, for example, are evident in many instances of economic motivation; on the other hand, humanitarian intercession often brought economic or other benefits to the intervener. It is for this reason that I have used the term "altruism" sparingly, since a strict application would disqualify many whose primary motivation is listed as humanitarian.

Further study may allow some refinement of the categories of motivation and help to broaden our understanding of the subject. It would be helpful, for example, to assess the risk, burden, and cost of harboring Armenians. Serious moral issues also need to be addressed. How, for example, should one view the childless couple, or the family with no male children, who rescued, converted, and adopted Armenian infants and youngsters and loved and provided for them, even as they did everything possible to make them forget their ethnic and religious origins? To what degree were humanitarian and altruistic motives compromised in the attempts by adoptive parents to prevent the return of these children after the collapse of the Young Turk regime and the end of World War I? A comparative approach would undoubtedly be useful in making these determinations, inasmuch as a significant corpus of relevant materials has already been developed on the Holocaust.

Finally, it is hoped that additional studies may begin to break down stereotypes and show that even in the extreme circumstances of 1915, there were many Turks, Kurds, and others who opposed the persecution of the Armenians. The testimony of the victims attests to the fact that kindness and solace were manifest amid the cruelty and suffering, and that the human spirit was never fully extinguished.

The end of denial by the Turkish government, together with a repudiation and renunciation of the genocidal policies of the Young Turk regime, would go a long way in alleviating the continuing

Armenian trauma. Such a positive change could open the way to a possible rapprochement that would honor the memory of the victims of genocide and make some form of compensation while allowing for due recognition of those Turks and others who intervened during the most extreme situation in the long history of the Armenian people.

# 13

# THE DUTCHNESS OF DUTCH RESCUERS:
# THE NATIONAL DIMENSION OF ALTRUISM

*Lawrence Baron*

Shortly before her arrest in 1944, Anne Frank reacted to rumors about Dutch gentiles turning against the Jews by writing the following entry in her diary: "I hope one thing only, and that is that this hatred of the Jews will be a passing thing, that the Dutch will show what they are after all, and that they will never totter and lose their sense of right."[1] The minority of Dutch men and women who rescued Jews like the Franks clearly lived up to the high expectations Anne had for her fellow citizens. Yet was their moral courage derived from something distinctive in Dutch culture and history that prevented them from condoning Nazi anti-Semitism and prompted them to save Jews from deportation and death? Or did it stem primarily from idiosyncratic factors in the backgrounds, personalities, traits, and values of the rescuers themselves?

The existing literature on the rescue and rescuers of Jews during the Holocaust has not provided answers to these questions. Although historians have analyzed specific national conditions and traditions to explain why mass Jewish rescue occurred in countries like Bulgaria, Denmark, and Italy, they have avoided speculating about the motivations of individual rescuers because the documentary evidence on which their research is based does not reveal such personal information.[2] Conversely, psychologists and sociologists who have conducted systematic interviews of surviving rescuers have focused on identifying the recurring patterns of psychosocial variables that fostered and sustained their decisions

to help persecuted Jews.[3] This second kind of approach understandably has not examined the interaction between the subjective
determinants of the rescuers' behavior and the objective cultural
and political context that influenced it.[4]

In this chapter I will narrate and analyze several case studies
of Dutch rescuers who were interviewed for the Altruistic Personality Project by me or other members of its research team.[5] Drawing on the project's database both for Holland and Poland, as well
as on other scholarly works about the rescue and rescuers of Jews
in various countries, I will delineate how the themes raised in their
interviews typified political, religious, and social forces that
shaped the history of the Netherlands before and during the German occupation. By doing so, I will identify some of the connections between public milieu and private motivations that inspired
Dutch gentiles to shield Jews from the Nazis and native collaborators during World War II at the risk of their own lives.

To place the actions and attitudes of the Dutch rescuers in a
broader perspective, let me begin with an overview of the history
of Jewish-Christian relations and the course of the Holocaust in
the Netherlands. The near annihilation of Dutch Jewry by the Nazis
appears to be a paradox in light of Holland's long national tradition
of religious tolerance and civic equality. The Dutch war of independence against Spain in the 1560s and 1570s inaugurated this
tradition through its rejection of the introduction of the Catholic
Inquisition in Holland and the weakening of both state and religious authority during that struggle. The permission to settle and
worship that many Dutch cities granted to Jewish immigrants in
the following century represented a byproduct of efforts to avert
further intra-Christian bloodshed, as well as an economic decision
to enhance local mercantile growth.[6] From then on, Dutch Jews
never became the target of the sort of anti-Semitic riots that spo-
radically erupted throughout Europe. In 1796 the French Revolutionary Army invaded Holland and granted equal rights to all
citizens regardless of their religious affiliation. After the defeat of
Napoleon, the Netherlands retained this principle in its constitu-
tion in contrast to the revocation of Jewish emancipation by other
nations that had been conquered by France. This enabled Dutch
Jews to gain entry and acceptance into most sectors of the economic and political life of Holland in the nineteenth and twentieth
centuries.[7]

Although the Dutch population was not immune to fascist and

anti-Semitic ideas in the 1930s, their popular appeal remained limited to a small minority. The precipitous drop in the volume of foreign trade and industrial production and the resulting sharp rise in unemployment provided the tinder for extremist firebrands like Anton Mussert of the National Socialist Movement of the Netherlands (hereafter, abbreviated as the NSB). Mussert attacked the inefficiency of parliamentary government and the divisive parochialism of Dutch political parties for causing the economic crisis and failing to surmount it. His call for an authoritarian corporate state and an imperialistic foreign policy attracted almost 8 percent of the votes in the provincial elections of 1935. Initially, Mussert distinguished between "nationally minded Dutchmen of Jewish race," who even qualified for membership in the NSB, and unassimilated orthodox and East European Jews, who never could be Dutch citizens. In the wake of Germany's diplomatic successes between 1936 and 1939, elements within the NSB led by Rost van Tonningen advocated Nazi ideology and racist anti-Semitism. Faced with pressure from the pro-Nazi wing of his party, Mussert drafted a proposal in 1938 for establishing a Jewish "homeland" in South America where European Jews would be resettled. The NSB's closer identification with the Third Reich and anti-Semitism diminished its electoral support. By 1939, the party received less than 4 percent of the votes in the provincial elections.[8] Nevertheless, the influx of twenty-five thousand Jewish refugees from Austria, Germany, and Poland during the 1930s generated some anti-Semitic resentment among the Dutch. While Dutch Jews remained unscathed by this development, it led to a government decision in 1939 to intern German Jewish refugees at Westerbork who had entered the country illegally or could not support themselves, rather than granting them permanent asylum.[9]

The rapid German victory over the Netherlands in May of 1940 transformed what had seemed like a secure haven for Jews into a perilous hell. Bordering on heavily patrolled waters, other occupied countries, and Germany itself, the location of Holland made escape difficult and dangerous. The easily blocked network of bridges and canals, the flat terrain, the lack of forests, and the high population density handicapped the attempts of those trying to evade or resist the Nazis. The concentration of 60 percent of Dutch Jewry in Amsterdam facilitated the enforcement of Nazi anti-Semitic policies, especially the deportations of Jews. As Raul Hilberg has observed, "It was as though the Dutch Jews had already been placed in a natural trap."[10]

Since Hitler valued Holland for economic, military, and racial reasons, he subjected it to tighter SS and Nazi party control than other occupied Western European countries. He viewed the Dutch as fellow Aryans whose state would someday be absorbed into Germany once it was purified of Jewish and other harmful influences. Moreover, Holland's location at the mouths of the Rhine and Maas Rivers, its fertile farmlands, fine harbors, and North Sea coastline that could serve as a jumping-off point for invading England made the country economically and strategically crucial to Germany's war effort. Thus, Hitler decided against putting Holland under military rule and instead appointed SS General Artur Seyss-Inquart as Reichskommissar to head a civilian administration similar to the one Germany had installed in Norway. Hanns Rauter, the SS security and police chief, took his orders directly from Himmler. The Nazi party exerted its ideological influence over Holland through Special Affairs Commissioner Fritz Schmidt, who was in charge of propaganda and political education.[11] To gain some perspective on the extent of Nazi power in Holland, it should be noted that five thousand German police were stationed there compared to three thousand in France, even though the latter was much bigger in size and population and harbored twice as many Jews.[12]

Breaking initial promises that Nazi ideology would not be imposed on Holland, Germany disenfranchised, impoverished, and registered Dutch Jewry by enacting increasingly restrictive discriminatory measures against the Jews during the first two years of the occupation. Relying primarily on bureaucratic and legal means rather than on force, the Nazis hoped to avoid offending Dutch sensibilities and provoking resistance. Since this phase of anti-Semitic measures occurred when German rule was still relatively tolerable for most Dutch gentiles, they tended to dissociate themselves from the ordeal that the Jews were undergoing. In the autumn of 1940, Dutch civil servants were ordered to fill out forms indicating if their grandparents were Jewish or Aryan. This "Aryan attestation" served as the basis for dismissing all Jews holding government positions in November. Around the same time Jewish-owned businesses were identified for eventual transfer to German owners. In January of 1941 Jews were ordered to register with the authorities. This information enabled the government to bar them from most public places, jobs, and social activities. The marking of the Jews climaxed in April 1942 when they were compelled to wear a yellow star inscribed with "Jood" (Jew) on their outer clothing.[13]

The bureaucratic identification of the Jews and their economic and political exclusion from Dutch society expedited their subsequent concentration and deportation. This process began in early 1942 when unemployed Jews were ordered to report to labor camps and Dutch Jews living in the provinces were evacuated to Jewish neighborhoods in Amsterdam. Then groups of Jews were relocated to the transit camps at Vugt and Westerbork. From there, the first trains loaded with Jews departed in mid-July for the extermination camps of Auschwitz and Sobibor. Within a year, seventy-seven thousand Jews had been deported. By the time the transports were halted in September of 1944, an additional thirty thousand Jews had been taken to those death camps or to Bergen-Belsen and Theresienstadt. Only fifty-two hundred of all of the deported Jews managed to survive their ordeal. Another eight thousand Jews, who had tried to hide in Holland, were apprehended and executed by the Germans during the occupation. All told, almost 80 percent of Holland's 140,000 Jews perished in the Holocaust. Thus, it sustained a greater loss of Jewish lives both numerically and proportionally than any other occupied country in Western Europe![14]

Although the primary blame for this catastrophe rests with Germany, some responsibility for it lies directly with Dutch collaborators. Following Holland's defeat, the two wings of the NSB competed for the favor of the Nazi authorities. Mussert believed Dutch support for Germany's war effort would be paid back by the establishment of an enlarged sovereign Dutch state led by him and closely allied with a Nazi-dominated "League of Germanic Peoples." Van Tonningen conversely shared the SS goal of integrating a racially purified Holland into the "Greater German Reich." This split in the NSB weakened its leverage with the Germans, who played one faction against the other to ensure its complicity. The lure of power swelled the NSB's membership to one hundred thousand people. From its ranks, Germany recruited about one-third of Holland's mayors and municipal civil servants to enforce Nazi policies at the local level. Over twenty-two thousand Dutchmen enlisted in the Waffen-SS to fight for Germany abroad, and twelve thousand joined the WA, the Dutch stormtroopers who terrorized and informed on political and racial enemies at home. Nevertheless, no more than 1.25 percent of the Dutch population belonged to the NSB. Its acts of treason discredited it in the eyes of most Dutch citizens.[15]

Until Germany's military hold on the European continent began to weaken in early 1943, a broad segment of the Dutch population and civil service engaged in more acceptable forms of accommodation to Nazi power. In the immediate wake of Holland's defeat, several respected Dutch leaders created the Netherlands Union to rally the nation's political parties behind a program of national corporative reconstruction and loyal relations towards Germany. Although Seyss-Inquart banned this organization in late 1941, the Netherlands Union attracted eight hundred thousand members, nearly one-sixth of the adult population, with its timid attempt to reassert Dutch sovereignty while simultaneously deferring to foreign domination.[16] The secretaries-general, the senior Dutch officials who remained at their posts when the Dutch queen and cabinet went into exile, administered Nazi policies, fearing the drastic consequences of disobedience. Under the provisions of a 1937 government directive, these functionaries were expected to cooperate with an occupying power if they believed that doing so brought more benefits than harm to the general welfare of their country. Offended by the harshness of Nazi laws against the Jews, the secretaries-general often lodged formal protests, but then agreed to implement these laws to avoid German reprisals against the Dutch people and the Nazification of the bureaucracy. It was not until May of 1943 that the government-in-exile explicitly prohibited "all cooperation" in the enforcement of anti-Jewish measures. By then, the efficient participation of Dutch officials in the expatriation, expropriation, and expulsion of Dutch Jewry had aided the Germans substantially and had lent a semblance of legitimacy to blatantly discriminatory policies.[17]

The Jewish Council pursued a similar strategy of defensive acquiescence. Appointed by the Germans in February 1941 to disarm Jews who had defended themselves against WA stormtroopers, the council consisted of prominent Dutch Jews who served as the official conduit between the regime and the Jewish community. Its members felt that Jewish compliance with Nazi decrees might mitigate the severity of future policies and justify the retention of deportation exemptions for Jews employed by the council or the Germans. By publishing a newspaper informing the Jews about each anti-Semitic decree, the council, in effect, insulated Dutch gentiles from these alarming developments.[18] Moreover, the apparent willingness of the council to preside over the segregation of its own community may not have seemed so unusual to Dutch gentiles accustomed to the *verzuiling,* or "pillarization" of Dutch society into separate political and social subcultures based on a person's affiliation with a particular Christian denomination or with secular liberal and Socialist movements.[19] The Jewish Council also inadvertently helped select which Jews were sent to Westerbork by determining who received exemption permits for working on behalf of the Germans. Although the number of these permits steadily dwindled from thirty-five thousand in July 1942 to none by September 1943, the competitive scramble to obtain them preserved the illusion that the Germans would not deport all the Jews.[20] Once the deportations began, the credibility of the council declined. Thereafter, 80 percent of the Jews refused to report for internment at Westerbork, necessitating the dispatch of special police squads to capture them.[21]

The first overt demonstration of Dutch solidarity with the Jews came too early to help them. At the end of February of 1941, Communist-led workers in Amsterdam mounted a general strike to protest the brutal arrest of 425 Jews whom the Germans deported to Mauthausen in retaliation for the murder of an NSB stormtrooper. This impressive demonstration of support for the Jews prompted the Germans to impose a state of siege, kill several strikers, and imprison one hundred strike leaders. The ruthless suppression of the strike dealt a severe blow to the nascent Communist resistance movement and symbolized a graphic warning to less politicized Dutch citizens about the fate of those who opposed Nazism. Its chilling effect on underground activity in the next two years was reinforced by the German practice of taking and frequently executing Dutch hostages to quell any native discontent with specific occupation policies.[22]

When the deportations of Jews began in mid-1942, Germany's exploitation of Holland's economy and labor force remained at a relatively tolerable level for the rest of the population. Suffering the strains of defeats at Stalingrad and North Africa in the winter of 1942/1943, Germany tightened its control over Holland in the first half of 1943 by ordering male university students to sign loyalty oaths and agree to work six months in Germany after graduating, attempting to intern three hundred thousand Dutch army veterans, and requiring all men between the ages of eighteen and thirty-five to register for forced labor in Germany. This triggered a series of Dutch strikes in April and May of that year. The need to assist all those refusing to comply with new demands enlarged and eventually unified the local groups that had started to emerge in the previous year to aid both gentile and Jewish "divers," as such fugitives were called. The National Organization for Assistance to Divers, known as the LO, did not amalgamate these ideologically and religiously diverse groups into a national rescue network until August 1943. By then over eighty thousand Jews had been deported. Of the three hundred thousand people hidden by the LO, twenty-four thousand were Jews, and sixteen thousand of them survived the war without falling into German hands. The rescue of this remnant was a significant accomplishment considering the deprivation and repression of the Dutch during the last two years of the war, particularly in the "hunger winter" of 1944–1945, when thousands died from the food embargo that Germany imposed on Western Holland to break a Dutch railroad strike. Nevertheless, the chances of a Jew finding a family to hide him or her were worse than those of a Dutch gentile.[23]

The experience of the LO, however, indicates that anti-Nazi resistance often translated into assistance for the Jews. People angered by German oppression found one outlet for their resentment in Jewish relief work. Such resistance followed a timetable set by the evolution of the harshness of German measures against Dutch citizens as a whole. Thus, it tragically lagged behind the Nazi schedule for the deportation of the Jews.

This gradual transition from initial resignation to German rule to active opposition against it and its anti-Semitic policies is typified by the story of the van Lennep family. They resented German rule from the beginning of the occupation and knew about Nazi persecution of the Jews through experiences that their son Nicholas had. When he visited Germany just after Kristallnacht, he had been shocked by what he heard and saw there. In 1942, he returned to the student boarding house where he was living in Amsterdam to discover that it had been sealed off and its Jewish owners had been arrested. To get back his confiscated belongings, Nicholas had to undergo Gestapo interrogation about why he had chosen to rent a room from Jews. The next year Nicholas refused to sign the student oath of obedience to German law and its accompanying pledge to work six months in Germany following his graduation. Since the punishment for not signing was immediate conscription for such labor, he joined the underground, where he served as a courier for the Allies and a distributor of food ration stamps and false identity papers to other fugitives from Nazism. Several months later, he returned home to learn that his parents had built a hiding place for him in a crawl space under a closet. When a friend subsequently asked Mrs. van Lennep to hide her Jewish husband, Mrs. van Lennep consented to the request. For the remainder of the war, the Jewish man resided with the family, retreating to the crawl space whenever there was any threat of being caught.[24]

Despite their dislike of the occupation and their awareness of the plight of the Jews, the van Lenneps refrained from taking any action until Nazi rule threatened to harm their son. By aiding him, these law-abiding citizens crossed the mental threshold separating passive discontent from active opposition. Their first venture into clandestine activity gave them the courage to rescue the Jewish man and made sheltering him more feasible because they now had a hiding place and could procure additional food and advance warnings about imminent police raids on their home through their son's contacts with the underground.

Resistance-rescuers like the van Lenneps recognized that the Dutch struggle against the Germans included saving the Jews. Such rescuers tend to cite German crimes like the bombing of Rotterdam, reprisal executions of members of the underground, and the conscription of Dutch men for forced labor, in addition to Nazi anti-Semitism, as reasons why they helped Jews. Their grievances against the occupation predisposed them to accede to underground or individual requests to aid Jewish fugitives. Forty-two percent of the Dutch rescuers in the Altruistic Personality Project's sample belonged to resistance groups whose political orientation covered the ideological spectrum from religious conservatives to Marxist radicals. This indicates that there was a broad consensus within the Dutch resistance to save Jews as part of the national struggle against Germany.[25]

To be sure, this linkage of resistance to rescue was not confined to Holland. In Denmark, where the attempt to deport the Jews followed after the Nazi imposition of a state of emergency in 1943, the collective rescue of almost all the Jews residing there was synchronized and synonymous with the general rebellion against Germany.[26] The French reaction to the persecution of the Jews paralleled that of the Dutch. During the first two years of the occupation, the majority of the population either endorsed or tolerated Vichy's anti-Semitic policies, anticipating that its collaboration would keep Germany from occupying Southern France and thus shield the French from direct Nazi rule. When this hope was dashed by the German takeover of the South in November of 1942 and the conscription of French labor in 1943, resistance against the Nazis and support for the Jews became more common.[27]

On the other hand, the solidarity of anti-German resistance movements with Jews was not axiomatic in countries where political anti-Semitism had been strong before the war. In her book on Polish rescuers, Nechama Tec reports that 50 percent of the rescuers in her sample participated in the underground and 55 percent considered their efforts to save Jews a protest against Germany. Though she cites several instances of anti-Semites and right-wingers who helped Jews, she notes that most of the rescuers adhering to particular political ideologies were Socialists or Communists.[28] In contrast to countries where the civic equality of the Jews was widely accepted before the outbreak of World War II, the debate over whether to extend support to the Jews as part of the resistance against the Germans was an issue that divided, rather than united, the Polish underground.[29]

A second category of Dutch rescuers was motivated primarily by bonds of affection, friendship, or loyalty to the Jew or Jews they saved. Louisa Scholten was a housewife in the city of Groningen. Although her husband worked for the underground locating hiding places for Jews, he never involved her in this risky undertaking. But Louisa was drawn into similar covert activities by her concern for a Jewish man who rented a room in her home. When he was ordered to report to a German labor camp in 1941, she tried in vain to convince him not to comply and to remain at her house. A year later she became more alarmed about his safety when she went to Westerbork Transit Camp to bring clothing to relatives of his who had been interned there. Meanwhile, the Jewish man escaped from the Germans and belatedly accepted Louisa's offer of sanctuary. He then invited one of his brothers to join him and live in the secure hiding place the Scholtens had built in their house by installing a false wall in an upstairs bedroom. In the course of the war, two other Jews found refuge behind this phony wall. Three months before the end of the war, the SS raided the Scholtens' residence and killed Louisa's husband and Jewish friend. In the tumult Louisa fled on foot and went into hiding for the rest of the war.

Louisa's story illustrates how positive personal relationships with Jews predisposed some gentiles to help these Jews. Her case is remarkable because her adult experiences with Jews enabled her to overcome a childhood aversion to them. Her father had been embittered by what he perceived as unscrupulous business transactions on the part of Jewish competitors and taught his daughter that all Jews were greedy materialists. During the Depression, Louisa had trouble finding a job and in desperation applied for a secretarial position for which she was unqualified. The Jewish owner of the company hired her with the stipulation that she learn shorthand within three months. She worked for him for eleven years and always was well treated. After the German invasion, she quit her job to protest the Aryanization of his company. Her former employer generously granted her three months' severance pay. Louisa's wartime protection of Jews originated from the gratitude she felt towards a group of people who had been kind to her in the past and whose persecution seemed unwarranted in the present. Throughout her interview, she made comments that revealed this sort of reasoning: "All my life has been crossed with Jewish people. I don't know why. That's the way it is sometimes." "I couldn't say no when Jews asked me to help."[30] Louisa's case also demonstrates that the decision to rescue Jews often was a cumulative process, beginning with aiding a friend and subsequently extending protection to his or her relatives and friends, and even to strangers.

It should come as no surprise that feelings of mutual appreciation, friendship, love, and responsibility sometimes withstood the Nazi campaign to break the bonds between gentiles and Jews. People are more likely to help others they already have an attachment to than total strangers. The Altruistic Personality Project's overall sample of rescuers indicates that around twice as many rescuers as bystanders had Jewish coworkers, employees, employers, or friends before the war.[31] Attachment rescuers from Holland rarely explain their actions in terms of the protection of the constitutional rights of Dutch nationals. Instead, abstract principles of law usually appear to have mattered less to them than the personal relationships they had developed with Jews. Of course, the frequency of these relationships was a byproduct of Jewish social integration, which, in turn, had been fostered by Dutch democratic values. When the Altruistic Personality Project begins to analyze its data on a comparative national basis, I suspect that the national incidence of rescuers who cite previous personal attachments to Jews as their reason for initially helping Jews will be correlated directly to the degree of acceptance Jews had achieved in each country. For example, the percentage of Dutch rescuers attributing their rescue of Jews to friendship appears to be considerably higher than among the Polish rescuers in the project's interview pool or Nechama Tec's study.[32]

In this regard, it is worth remembering that the story of Anne Frank and her family is a story of friendships that endured the strain of Nazi terror. Miep Gies's recent memoir depicts a scenario of rescue that is similar in some respects to the tale told by Louisa Scholten. Miep also had been unemployed during the Depression and appreciated the chance to work that Otto Frank had given her then. She soon became both his trusted employee and close friend and regularly socialized with his family and the German Jewish emigrants who often gathered at the Frank home. Thus, Miep gladly joined Frank's other friends and colleagues, Koophuis and Kraler, in creating a haven in the attic of the building that housed Frank's business. Included among those who found sanctuary there were Mr. van Dann, her coworker from Frank's company, and Mr. Dussel, a refugee she met through the Franks who had become her dentist. Furthermore, Miep and her husband also felt obliged to locate hiding places for their Jewish landlady and her two grandchildren.[33]

The third, and most distinctively Dutch category of rescuer consists of pious Dutch Calvinists who helped Jews primarily for theological reasons. Let me draw on two such cases that epitomize this type of devout activism. In early 1942 a friend beseeched Theresa Wytema to hide a four-year-old Jewish girl who had been abandoned by her mother. Theresa persuaded her husband Martin to hide the child by reminding him of the parable of the good Samaritan. Soon the Wytemas' home became a temporary haven for anyone hunted by the Germans. On most nights, there were twelve strangers in addition to the Wytemas' own six children sleeping in their six-room house. Martin and Theresa insisted that only people who would be difficult to place in other safe houses, like pregnant women and handicapped individuals, could stay with them for prolonged periods or the duration of the war. During the occupation, the Wytemas harbored approximately 450 persons, the majority of whom were Jews.[34]

Arie van Mansum was a twenty-year-old who lived with his parents in Maastricht in 1940. During the 1930s, he had met German Jewish refugees who had been helped by his church. By 1942, his church youth group transformed itself into a secret placement agency for Jews trying to evade the Nazis. As a traveling salesman, Arie had a credible alibi for traversing the countryside to identify and persuade trustworthy local families to hide Jews. Once when a Dutch couple agreed to hide a Jewish widow, but not her baby son, Arie decided to keep the child in his own home. Several months later the same scenario was repeated with another Jewish infant. The Germans arrested Arie and imprisoned him for the last eighteen months of the war. Fortunately, his sister carried on his work, and both have been honored as "Righteous Gentiles" by Yad Vashem.[35]

When probed about their motives, rescuers like Theresa and Arie attribute their decisions to hide Jews primarily to their Dutch Calvinist upbringing and faith. Theresa fondly reminisced about how her father had inspired her own faith through both his words and deeds. His emphasis on living an ethical life had been gleaned from the Jewish and Christian bibles. True to his credo, he also housed Jews when Theresa's home was under surveillance. Theresa constantly quoted scripture to justify her participation in such dangerous activities. An analysis of her testimony reveals three prominent themes. First, she repeatedly stressed that Christians had an obligation to save God's chosen people with comments like this: "I think it is one of the privileges that I have to tell others the faithfulness of my Father in Heaven who protects his people. God wanted to protect Israel in the first place." In the same vein, she remembered telling the first Jewish girl whom she saved that "God will never destroy the Jewish people, and nobody on earth ever will do that because God made that promise. We have accepted our Messiah—Jesus Christ. Your father Isaac is my father Isaac. Your father Abraham is my father Abraham." Second, Theresa considered it her Christian duty to minister to the needs of the persecuted as Jesus had done. As she put it, "When you are a Christian, you see the world differently. You see it like Jesus sees it. You see the need. The Jews were his people, and his people were in need." Finally, her Calvinist stress on predestination inclined her to view every opportunity to rescue Jews as divinely ordained. This imbued her with courage in the most harrowing circumstances. When she learned that the mother of the abandoned Jewish girl had assured her child that "Christians would help her," Theresa felt that she had been destined to fulfill this mission of mercy. She and her husband countered their fears of the risks they ran by reciting the ninety-first psalm: "He that dwelleth in the secret place of the Most High, shall abide under the shadow of the Almighty. ... Under his wings shalt thou trust."[36]

Arie highlighted similar themes in his interview. He remembered the piety of his parents and especially the biblical lessons they had taught him. The prominence of the Old Testament in their household was evidenced by Arie's pronounced philo-Semitism. Several times he noted that the Jews were God's chosen people, and that without Judaism, there could be no Christianity. Arie also disputed the infamous charge that the Jews had been guilty of killing Christ. To him, Christ clearly had died for everybody's sins, and blaming the Jews was a convenient way for many Christians to evade the evil within themselves. Although Arie admitted that he was scared to death of the Germans, he persisted in his activities out of the consciousness that it was the Christian thing to do. Biblical analogies to the plight of the Jews strengthened this conviction. For example, when the danger arose that members of his congregation were not secretive enough about the Jewish rescue ring, the pastor preached a sermon about what the consequences would have been if the handmaidens of Pharaoh's daughter had revealed that she had adopted the Jewish baby who had been plucked from the bulrushes.[37]

The religious reasoning evidenced by Arie and Theresa bears the distinct imprint of Dutch Calvinism. The Dutch Reformed Church originally had been forged in the independence struggle against Spanish and Catholic domination in the sixteenth century. As a result, it had developed a theological justification for revolt against sacrilegious tyranny that became an article of faith in its earliest confession of beliefs. The fusion of conservative Calvinist values and Dutch nationalism was formalized in the nineteenth century with the creation of the Antirevolutionary party and the Christian Historical Union, both of which opposed liberal secularism, Socialist radicalism, and Catholic sectarianism. Most of the religious rescuers I have interviewed were members of one of these two parties and associated their religious convictions with political action.[38]

The Protestant theologian Clark Williamson has observed that Calvinism has tended to take a "more benevolent attitude toward Jews, owing to its higher view of the Hebrew bible and the place of Law in Christian life, and to Calvin's claim that the old and new covenants are identical in substance, differing only in form."[39] To be sure, the Calvinist tradition also propagated the negative Christian views of the Jews and Judaism. The biblical literalism of the Dutch Reformed tradition did perpetuate the anti-Judaic themes of the New Testament, providing a religious rationalization for not helping the Jews during the Holocaust. The conservatism of Dutch Calvinist political parties often associated the Jews with the hated secularizing movements of Marxism and liberalism and justified the alignment of Dutch civic and social life along Christian lines. Moreover, the doctrine of predestination just as easily could be invoked to rationalize passivity, on the assumption that the persecution of the Jews was their divine punishment.[40] Yet the strong Calvinist identification with the Jews as the "Chosen People" and their role in fulfilling God's purpose in history could provide a countervailing positive image of the Jews.[41] As one Calvinist rescuer told me, "We have a special feeling for the Jewish people."[42] In this regard, it is theologically significant that approximately one-third of the rescuers in the Altruistic Personality Project sample belonged to the more traditional Christian Reformed Churches that had seceded from the Dutch Reformed Church in the nineteenth century as a protest against its progressive liberalization.[43] Even though members of these schismatic churches constituted only 8 percent of the Dutch population, they accounted for 25 percent of the rescues of Jews in Holland, according to the estimates of most scholars.[44] The disproportionate representation of congregants from these churches in Jewish rescue efforts and the motivations such rescuers ascribe to their activities serve as graphic testimony to the power of their Dutch Calvinist piety and faith.

An analysis of the lives of such religious rescuers also clarifies the mutual interaction between personality development and social environment. These people derived their morality and habits of helping others from their parents and congregations. They grew up in close, strict families that were deeply involved in their churches. Thus, their religious subculture reinforced the beliefs and behaviors taught by their parents. During the occupation, these local congregations often became centers of rescue and resistance, providing a support network that facilitated individual participation in activities that may have otherwise appeared too risky. Sometimes, lay people led these movements; at other times ministers organized reluctant and scared congregants.[45] The results of organized religious rescue networks could be impressive. In Nieuwlande, hundreds of Jews were saved when a Calvinist activist named Johannes Post mobilized the villagers to operate a rescue ring out of the town church. Interestingly, Post had overcome his own prejudices against Jews for the sake of defending higher patriotic and religious ideals. Yad Vashem has taken the unprecedented step of honoring the entire town collectively, as well as individually recognizing its 202 residents as "Righteous Gentiles."[46]

The Calvinist rescuers often cite clergymen or Christian politicians as role models who stiffened their own determination to oppose the Nazis. Theresa, for example, greatly admired such underground leaders and professed her steadfast adherence to the principles of her political party, the Christian Historical Union, by declaring, "They followed the bible; they followed the scripture; and for us that was enough."[47] Like the majority of the Dutch population, the leadership of the Calvinist churches initially tried to reach an accommodation with the Germans, but then started issuing protests that became stronger as Nazi policies increasingly infringed on their beliefs. Furthermore, they were pressured by the dissident Calvinist theologians who formed the Lunteren Group to take a more forthright stand against the Germans. In July of 1942 the Inter-Church Consultation, an alliance of Dutch Protestant and Catholic churches, threatened to read from their pulpits a statement denouncing the Jewish deportations if the Germans did not desist from this policy. The Nazis responded by offering to spare Jewish converts to Christianity if the protest would not be read. Although the mainstream Dutch Reformed Church accepted this bargain, the Christian Reformed Churches and Catholic Church refused to do so. One hundred Jewish Catholics were immediately deported to Auschwitz as a reprisal.[48] The interviews with Calvinist rescuers demonstrate that they felt they had the blessings of their church leaders, even when this was not always the case. Regrettably, there are too few Dutch Catholics in the Altruistic Personality

Project's interview pool to provide a meaningful comparison with their Calvinist counterparts.

Comparing religiously motivated Dutch rescuers, however, with Polish rescuers motivated by Catholic beliefs reveals striking national religious differences. Such Polish Catholics ascribe their behavior to the more general Christian ethical commandment to "love thy neighbor" rather than to a respect for God's chosen people, the ethics of the prophets, or the approval of their national religious leaders.[49] Ewa Kurek-Lesik's recent study of Polish nuns who saved Jewish children shows that they often were following the orders of their superiors, who conceived of monastic service as helping all of humankind in the quest to deserve eternal salvation. In this case, however, the head of each convent was acting on her own moral decisions rather than obeying a policy set by the church hierarchy.[50] According to Nechama Tec, most Polish Catholic rescuers of Jews operated without any directive from their clergymen and responded to their own independent interpretation of what Catholicism required them to do in this situation.[51]

Many of the Dutch who failed to aid Jews during the German occupation probably had backgrounds and personality profiles similar to those of the rescuers I have analyzed here. I surmise that concern for their families, fear of Nazi reprisals, and personal pragmatism, among other reasons, inhibited people who initially may have sympathized with the plight of the Jews from acting on those feelings. As one Dutch historian observed after the war, "One felt sorry for the Jews and congratulated oneself on not being one of them. People gradually got used to Jews having the worst of it."[52]

Thus, it was left to their more courageous counterparts to pay homage to what was best in Holland's heritage. It is telling that so few of the Dutch rescuers can be classified as socially marginal like the Polish rescuers in Nechama Tec's sample.[53] Since positive attitudes towards Jews represented a prewar consensus in Dutch public opinion, the rescuers of Jews stemmed more from the mainstream of Dutch society than from its margins. Their aid to the Jews represented a normative altruism in keeping with typical Dutch values and was akin to the sort of altruism exhibited by the Danes and the Italians.[54] For the resistance-rescuers, the past integration of Dutch Jewry made it imperative to save Jews since they were an integral part of the national community. Others felt personally compelled to shield Jewish acquaintances and friends from harm's way. The Calvinist rescuers acted on beliefs and through organizations that had deep roots in the soil of Dutch history. None of them ever tottered or lost their sense of right, as Anne Frank had feared. No one portrayed their humane legacy better than Anne herself when she noted, "Although others may show heroism in the war or against the Germans, our helpers display heroism in their cheerfulness and affection."[55]

## NOTES

1. Anne Frank, *The Diary of a Young Girl*, trans. B. M. Mooyaart-Doubleday (New York, 1953), p. 212.
2. For example, see Frederick Barry Chary, *The Bulgarian Jews and the Final Solution, 1940–1944* (Pittsburgh, 1972); Leni Yahil, *The Rescue of Danish Jewry* (Philadelphia, 1969); Susan Zuccotti, *The Italians and the Holocaust: Persecution, Rescue, and Survival* (New York, 1987).
3. Lawrence Baron, "The Holocaust and Human Decency: A Review of Research on the Rescue of Jews in Nazi-Occupied Europe," *Humboldt Journal of Social Relations*, XIII:1–2 (Fall/Winter and Spring/Summer 1985–1986), pp. 237–51.
4. Helen Fein, "Good People versus Dirty Work: Helping Jews Evade the Holocaust," *Contemporary Sociology*, XVIII:2 (March 1989), pp. 192–93. See Samuel P. Oliner and Pearl M. Oliner, *The Altruistic Personality: Rescuers of Jews in Nazi Europe* (New York, 1988).
5. Lawrence Baron, "The Dynamics of Decency: Dutch Rescuers of Jews during the Holocaust," in Ed. Michael R. Marrus, *The Nazi Holocaust*, Vol.5 (Westport, Ct., 1989).
6. John Edwards, *The Jews in Christian Europe, 1400–1700* (London and New York, 1988), pp. 93–104; Jonathan Israel, *European Jewry in the Age of Mercantilism, 1550–1750* (Oxford, 1985).
7. Judith C. E. Belinfante, *Joods Historisch Museum* (Haarlem, 1978), pp. 62–83.
8. Gerhard Hirschfeld, *Nazi Rule and Dutch Collaboration: The Netherlands under German Occupation, 1940–1945*, trans. Louise Willmot (Hamburg, New York, and Oxford, 1988), pp. 242–66.
9. Bob Moore, "Jewish Refugees in the Netherlands, 1933–1940," *Leo Baeck Institute Year Book*, XXIX (1984), pp. 73–101; Bob Moore, *Refugees from Nazi Germany in the Netherlands* (Dordrecht, 1986); Dan Michman, "The Committee for Jewish Refugees in Holland, 1933–1940," *Yad Vashem Studies*, XIV (1981), pp. 205–32.
10. Raul Hilberg, *The Destruction of the European Jews*, Vol.2 (New York, 1985), p. 570; Jacob Presser, *The Destruction of the Dutch Jews* (New York, 1969), pp. 7–9; Leni Yahil, "Methods of Persecution: A Comparison of the 'Final Solution' in Holland and Denmark," *Scripta Hierosolymitana*, XXIII (1972), p. 283.
11. Hirschfeld, pp. 12–54; Konrad Kwiet, *Reichskommissariat Niederlande* (Stuttgart, 1968); Louis de Jong, *Het Koninkrijk der Nederlanden tijdens de Tweede Wereldoorlog*, 13 Volumes (The Hague, 1969–1988); Werner Warmbrunn, *The Dutch under German Occupation, 1940–1945* (Stanford, 1963), pp. 25–42.
12. J. C. H. Blom, "The Persecution of the Jews in the Netherlands: A Comparative

Western European Perspective," *European History Quarterly*, XIX:3 (July 1989), pp. 338–39. Blom's more nuanced explanation for the extent of Jewish victimization in Holland is more factually correct and convincing than the accusatory one of Judith Miller, *One, by One, by One* (New York, 1990), pp. 93–111.

13. Presser, pp. 7–94; Henry Mason, "Testing Human Bonds within Nations: Jews in the Occupied Netherlands," *Political Science Quarterly*, IC:2 (Summer 1984), pp. 317–25; Jozeph Michman, "The Netherlands," *Encyclopedia of the Holocaust*, Volume 3 (New York, 1990), pp. 1045–57.

14. Presser, pp. 94–213; Helen Fein, *Accounting for Genocide: National Responses and Jewish Victimization during the Holocaust* (New York, 1979), pp. 262–89; Walter Laqueur, *The Terrible Secret: Suppression of the Truth About Hitler's "Final Solution"* (New York, 1982), pp. 149–56; Mason, pp. 316, 325–37.

15. Hirschfeld, pp. 266–310; for a depiction of the ostracism of NSB members during the occupation, see the novel by Evert Hartman, *War without Friends*, trans. Patricia Crampton (New York, 1982).

16. Hirschfeld, pp. 55–86; M. L. Smith, "Neither Resistance nor Collaboration: Historians and the Problem of the 'Netherlandse Unie,'" *History*, LXXII: 235 (June 1987), pp. 251–78; Warmbrunn, pp. 133–36.

17. Hirschfeld, pp. 132–84. For the text of the 1943 radio message from the exile government to Dutch civil servants working under the German occupation, see Werner Rings, *Life with the Enemy: Collaboration and Resistance in Hitler's Europe, 1939–1945*, trans. J. Maxwell Brownjohn (New York, 1982), pp. 323–25.

18. Mason, p. 332; Yahil, "Methods," pp. 290–91.

19. Blom, pp. 345–46; William Z. Shetter, *The Pillars of Society: Six Centuries of Civilization in the Netherlands* (The Hague, 1971); John P. Williams, "Netherlands' Foreign Policy as a Reflection of Its Political System," in Ed. William H. Fletcher, *Papers from the First Interdisciplinary Conference on Netherlandic Studies* (Lanham, Md., 1985), pp. 191–86; J. P. Kruyt, *Verzuiling* (Zaandijk, 1959).

20. Presser, pp. 25–277.

21. Joseph Michman, "The Controversial Stand of the Joodse Raad in the Netherlands: Lodewijk Visser's Struggle," *Yad Vashem Studies*, X (1974), pp. 9–68; Mason, pp. 332–35; Presser, pp. 278–96.

22. Henry L. Mason, *Mass Demonstrations against Foreign Regimes* (New Orleans, 1966), pp. 4–7, 20–22, 35–36, 47–48, 60–61, 72–76; B. A. Sijes, *De Februari-Starking* (The Hague, 1954).

23. Warmbrunn, pp. 112–18, 185–220; Louis de Jong, "Help to People in Hiding," *Delta: A Review of Arts, Life, and Thought in the Netherlands*, VIII:1 (Spring 1965), pp. 37–79. For a series of biographical sketches of Dutch rescuers, see Andre Stein, *Quiet Heroes: True Stories of the Rescue of Jews by Christians in Nazi-Occupied Holland* (New York, 1988).

24. Interview of Nicholas van Lennep by Lawrence Baron and Theodore Linn, January 13, 1984. The transcripts of these interviews are on file with the Altruistic Personality Project, Department of Sociology, Humboldt State University. The rescuers' names have been changed here to protect their confidentiality.

25. Altruistic Personality Project Data Base, VE 15, VE 15A. Themes of resistance

are often mixed with other motivations. See Interview of Gretje D. by Lawrence Baron, October 30, 1984; Interview of Louisa S. by Ellen Land-Weber, July 2, 1984.

26. Harold Flender, *Rescue in Denmark* (New York, 1964); Ed. Leo Goldberger, *The Rescue of the Danish Jews: Moral Courage under Stress* (New York, 1987); Yahil, "Methods," pp. 279–300; Yahil, *The Rescue*.

27. Michael R. Marrus and Robert O. Paxton, "The Nazis and the Jews in Occupied Western Europe," *Journal of Modern History*, LIV (December 1982), pp. 687–714.

28. Nechama Tec, *When Light Pierced the Darkness: Christian Rescuers of Jews in Nazi-Occupied Poland* (New York, 1986), pp. 120–28, 226. Sixty percent of the Polish rescuers who expressed a political preference were Communists and Socialists; another 30 percent identified with the Social Democrats or Peasants' party.

29. For accounts of the relations between Poles and Jews during the German occupation, see Yisrael Gutman, *The Jews of Warsaw, 1939–1943* (Sussex, 1982), pp. 250–67; Richard C. Lukas, *The Forgotten Holocaust: The Poles under German Occupation, 1939–1944* (Lexington, 1986), pp. 121–51.

30. Interview of Louisa Scholten by Ellen Land-Weber, July 2, 1984.

31. Oliner and Oliner, pp. 115, 184–86, 275, 304–5, 312, 320.

32. Tec, pp. 129–36, 187–88, 227, 233; Altruistic Personality Project Data Base, VE18. An initial screening of the Altruistic Personality Project's data on Dutch rescuers yields only fragmentary results on this issue. Only 17 percent of the sample indicated whether they rescued Jewish friends or not. Of those, however, 57 percent said they helped rescue close Jewish friends. Only 37 percent of the Polish rescuers in Tec's sample listed friendship as their motivation for helping Jews.

33. Miep Gies with Alison Leslie Gold, *Anne Frank Remembered: The Story of the Woman Who Helped to Hide the Frank Family* (New York, 1987); "The Reminiscences of Victor Kugler—the Mr. Kraler of Anne Frank's Diary," *Yad Vashem Studies*, XIII (1979), pp. 353–85.

34. Interview of Theresa Wytema by Ellen Land-Weber, June 23, 1984.

35. Interview with Arie van Mansum by Lawrence Baron and Theodore Linn, October 22, 1983.

36. Theresa Wytema Interview.

37. Arie van Mansum Interview.

38. Walter Lagerweg, "The History of Calvinism in the Netherlands," in Ed. John H. Bratt, *The Rise and Development of Calvinism* (Grand Rapids, 1968), pp. 63–102; Pieter de Jong, "Responses of the Churches in the Netherlands to the Nazi Occupation," in Ed. Michael D. Ryan, *Human Responses to the Holocaust: Perpetrators and Victims, Bystanders and Resisters* (New York, 1981), pp. 128–29; W. Robert Godfrey, "Calvin and Calvinism in the Netherlands," in Ed. W. Stanford Reid, *John Calvin: His Influence in the Western World* (Grand Rapids, 1982), pp. 95–120; Ralph C. Hancock, *Calvin and the Foundations of Modern Politics* (Ithaca and London, 1989). Corrie ten Boom exemplifies how this pious Calvinism inspired the rescue of Jews. See Corrie ten Boom, *The Hiding Place* (New York, 1974).

39. Clark M. Williamson, *Has God Rejected His People: Anti-Judaism in the Christian*

*Church* (Nashville, 1982), pp. 102–3; Solomon Rappaport, *Jew and Gentile: The Philo-Semitic Aspect* (New York, 1980), pp. 103–4

40. Salo Baron, "John Calvin and the Jews," in *Harry A. Wolfson Jubilee Volume* (Jerusalem, 1965), pp. 141–58; Alice L. Eckhardt, "The Reformation and the Jews," *Shofar*, VII:4 (Summer 1989), pp. 35–39; Mary Potter Engel, "Calvin and the Jews: A Textual Puzzle," *Princeton Seminary Bulletin*, Supplementary Issue 1 (1990), pp. 106–23; Jacob van Gelderen, "Protestantism and the Jews in Nineteenth-Century Holland," *Dutch Jewish History*, II (1989), pp. 323–26. In a talk presented in San Diego on January 17, 1990, Cornelius Suijk, the International Director of the Anne Frank Foundation, recalled that some of the devout Calvinists he approached to help Jews during the occupation declined because they felt the ordeal of the Jews was God's will.

41. Louis de Jong, "Jews and Non-Jews in Nazi-Occupied Holland," in Ed. Max Beloff, *On the Track of Tyranny* (London, 1960), pp. 139–41; Joseph Michman, "Some Reflections on the Dutch Churches and the Jews," in Eds. Otto Dov Kulka and Paul R. Mendes-Flohr, *Judaism and Christianity under the Impact of National Socialism* (Jerusalem, 1987), pp. 349–51; Pieter de Jong, pp. 128–29; B. A. Sijes, "Several Observations concerning the Position of the Jews in Occupied Holand during World War II," in Eds. Yisrael Gutman and Ephraim Zuroff, *Rescue Attempts during the Holocaust* (Jerusalem, 1978), pp. 528–29. The postwar impact of the Holocaust on Dutch Calvinism reveals this ambivalence towards the Jews as "the Chosen People" and the unredeemed who rejected Christ as the Messiah and remain to be converted. See the excellent article by Jacobus Schoneveld, "The Dutch Protestant Churches' Changing Attitudes towards the Jewish People in the Twentieth Century," *Dutch Jewish History*, II (1989), pp. 337–69.

42. Interview of Ruth de J. by Lawrence Baron and Theodore Linn, Sept. 18, 1985.

43. Altruistic Personality Project Data Base, VB18, VB18A, VB28, VB28A, VC8, VC8A. Since the tables for the religious affiliation of the rescuers are incomplete, my estimate is based on the religious affiliation of the rescuers' parents. This finding may confirm the curvilinear relationship between religious beliefs, the degree of one's church commitment, and the extent of one's prejudice towards outsiders. See Rob Eisinga, Albert Felling, and Jan Peters, "Religious Belief, Church Involvement, and Ethnocentrism in the Netherlands," *Journal for the Scientific Study of Religion*, XXIX:1 (March 1990), pp. 54–75.

44. Mason, "Testing," p. 331; Michman, "Some Reflections," p. 350.

45. Douglas Huneke, "A Study of Christians Who Rescued Jews during the Nazi Era," *Humboldt Journal of Social Relations*, IX:1 (Fall/Winter 1981/1982), p. 145.

46. Jacob Boas, "Research Plan for *Nieuwlande, a Righteous Town*" (undated); Louis de Jong, "Jews and Non-Jews," p. 151.

47. Interview of Theresa Wytema.

48. Pieter de Jong, pp. 121–41; H. C. Touw, "The Resistance of the Netherlands Church," *The Annals of the American Academy of Political and Social Science*, 245 (May 1946), pp. 149–61; Michman, "Some Reflections," pp. 349–51; Ger van Roon, "The Dutch Protestants, the Third Reich, and the Persecution of the Jews," in Eds. Kulka and Mendes-Flohr, *Judaism and Christianity under the Impact of National Socialism* (Jerusalem, 1987), pp. 341–47; Warmbrunn, pp. 156–64.

49. See the article by Zusanna Smolenska in this volume.
50. See the article by Ewa Kurek-Lesik in this volume; and Ewa Kurek-Lesik, "The Conditions of Admittance and the Social Background of Jewish Children Saved by Women's Religious Orders in Poland from 1939–1945," *Polin: A Journal of Polish-Jewish Studies*, III, pp. 244–75.
51. Tec, pp. 137–49.
52. R. Rijksen quoted in Presser, p. 325.
53. Tec, 150–54.
54. Zuccotti, p. 323. Zuccotti questions whether the marginality theory can be applied to Italian rescuers.
55. Frank, p. 130.

# 14

# THE ROLE OF POLISH NUNS IN THE
# RESCUE OF JEWS, 1939–1945

*Ewa Kurek-Lesik*

If we look at it from a certain perspective, the history of humankind can appear to be predominantly a history of evil. It can be seen as generally a struggle for power: to rule, to impose one's religion or ideology on an enemy, or to conquer more territory. Such conflicts can understandably result in war, blood, tears, and humiliation. Indeed, it can be suggested that countries either inflicted suffering on their foes or endured the suffering inflicted on them. The history of Poland and of the nations living within its borders may not seem to be significantly different from this general pattern. Polish territories were the center of Nazi atrocities during World War II. Here the Germans killed three million Polish Jews and three million Polish gentiles. Yet Auschwitz, that factory of death, provided Father Maximilian Kolbe a living example of selfless love, a living example of one person sacrificing his or her life for another. Moreover, near the town of Tarnów is the grave of Otto Schimek, a German soldier who chose to die rather than to murder innocent people. How many other selfless people were there in Poland during World War II? Memoirs and records from those years document that there were many others, including Polish nuns, who aided Polish Jews and their children, who would otherwise have been doomed to die in the Holocaust.

To talk about the hiding of Jews in Polish convents during World War II is fraught with problems. One is the lack of records due to the fact that the rescue of Jews and their children in Poland was carried out clandestinely. Obviously, the nuns would not record their activities. After the war, political conditions and the pressure of day-to-day work for the sisters, as well as their own attitudes, were not conducive to the task of completing the archives with notes or statements about wartime activities. The Jews themselves left the convents and scattered throughout Poland and to the four corners of the world. They were rarely able, and perhaps not willing, to visit the places where they had spent their wartime years. Therefore, I had to recover this lost history as best I could by traveling in Poland, Israel, and America to collect information.

To rescue Jews was a dangerous activity for Polish nuns. If caught they would have paid for it with their lives. Neither cassock, habit, nor bishop's mitre provided protection from the penalty of death for such a transgression. For example, records show that at least two sisters of the Order of the Immaculate Conception and eight Sisters of Charity were executed by the Germans for their participation in helping Jews and their children.

Before the outbreak of World War II, there were eighty-five orders of nuns in Poland, consisting of seventy-four orders or congregations of active sisters, and eleven contemplative orders. Numerically, there were over twenty thousand nuns in Poland at the time. My research shows that about 62 percent of the eighty-five religious communities of women in Poland were engaged in helping Jews during the war. The opportunities for nuns to engage in rescue work were limited during the occupation by German policies towards the Roman Catholic Church. These policies differed significantly in various parts of Poland. Nuns who were situated in parts of the country incorporated into the Reich in October 1939 were not able to do anything. They were interned in prisons and labor camps, relocated, or went into hiding. Nuns who were in the areas occupied by the Soviet Union until June 1941 were forced to work and not allowed to wear their religious garb. In sum, almost the only nuns in a position to help Jews during the war lived in the convents in the General Government. For this reason, my information relates primarily to nuns' activities in this geographical area.

The most active were the nuns located in Warsaw and its environs. In the capital city alone, twenty-three houses hid Jewish children and forty-one other houses did so on the outskirts of the city. These figures are not definitive, of course. They are, however, the product of information received from nuns themselves and from Jews who were rescued by nuns. There is today no way of ascertaining the actual number of children rescued by orphanages and boarding schools. Nevertheless, it seems that the number of children saved was at least fifteen hundred. How many more there may have been will probably always remain a mystery.

My research focuses on the rescuing of Jewish children. However, the data I have collected indicates that more adult Jews were rescued than were Jewish children. This is because almost all of the convents hiding Jewish children also saved adult Jews. Surely, in comparison with the three million Polish Jews who were murdered, the number of those saved in the convents is ridiculously small. Did Polish nuns do all they could to save Polish Jews? Wladislaw Bartoszewski, who was devoted to the cause of saving Jews, answered a similar question in the following way: "During the war in Poland to do all one could for the murdered Jews meant to die for them, and I am alive."

However, each of the Polish nuns who saved Jewish life had to be prepared for the possibility that she would have to pay with her own life for disregarding the German ban on helping the Jews. When I asked one of the nuns if she had been afraid of death, she answered, "Of course I was afraid; everybody was. But it was the war and so many people were dying. One must die for something; it might as well be a Jew." This answer is simultaneously banal and profound. It must be remembered that Polish nuns were probably neither less nor more anti-Semitic than the whole of the Polish society. A great majority of nuns came from average Polish families. Some of them would bring into the convents stereotyped, often negative images of Jews.

When I asked Polish writer Jan Dobraczynski, who cooperated with convents in saving about three hundred children from the Warsaw ghetto, why he did so, he told me, "I come from nationalist circles, often charged with anti-Semitism. Why did I save Jewish children? Because they were children, because they were people. I would save any man in danger of death, and a child—every child— is particularly dear to me. This is what my Catholic religion orders me to do."

The above quotation typifies many others and proves that anti-Semitism did not matter as much when it came to saving Jews in convents. A persecuted Jew somehow stopped being a Jew and became simply a man, woman, or child in need of help. The Polish nuns were motivated by a Christian duty towards others and by their fidelity to the ideals that they were pledged to do so in a special way by their vows. This is what a nun from one of the Warsaw houses, sister Maria Ena, said:

I won't forget the conference of sister Wanda Garczynska. It was 1942–1943. The school in Kazimierzowska Street had been closed. The SS was based in a huge block opposite our house, where the RGO kitchen for the needy was open and functioning almost without a break. The people, too, came in a constant stream—children, young people, adults with canisters for soup. Only for soup? For everything. Kazimierzowska pulsated with life—from the nursery to the university. Amongst this hive of activity there were also Jewesses, with red, curly hair, freckled, with prominent ears and unusual eyes. These obviously were Jews. There could be no mistake. It was well known that concealing a Jew meant the death sentence.

The sisters knew that other orders had already been warned and searched. So she hid nothing, withheld nothing, and she called us together. She began the conference by reading a fragment of the Gospel of St. John, verses 3–17. She explained that she did not wish to jeopardize the house, the sisters, the community. She knew what could be awaiting us. There was no thought of self. She knew: you should love one another as I have loved you. How? So that He gave His life.

I lowered my head. I did not dare look at the other sisters. We had to decide. If we said one word, openly, honestly admitted to fear for our skins, our own lives, the lives of so many sisters, the community. . . . Was it prudent to risk it for a few Jewish families? It was our decision whether or not Jews hiding with us would have to leave.

There was silence.

No one stirred. Not a single breath. We were ready. We would not give up the Jewish children. We would rather die, all of us. The silence was overwhelming—we did not look at each other. The sister was sitting with closed eyes, her hands folded over the Gospel. She was no doubt praying.

We got up. We did not even pray together as we normally did. We went to the chapel. We felt light and joyful, though very grave. We were ready.

A communal decision was not taken in every convent as in the case above. Mostly, it was a sole decision, taken by the Mother Superior of a given convent. But it always flowed from the most important Christian commandment, from the commandment of love.

The Polish nuns faced death for reasons other than hiding Jews. They also could be executed for hiding priests and underground activists wanted by the Gestapo, for active cooperation with guerrillas and underground organizations, as well as for a great many other "offenses" against the German law. They not only saved Jewish children, but also Polish, Ukrainian, Gypsy, and even German children, towards the end of the war. If they distributed soup, they distributed it among all the hungry people without asking who they were. If they dressed a guerrilla's wounds, they did not ask him to which political side he belonged. This is why saving Jews and Jewish children should first of all be seen in the broader context of monastic service to humanity.

It is true that the call to save Jews was a completely new task for sisters in Poland. This task gave rise to numerous controversies and misunderstandings fueled further by the sharp clash of the Jewish and Christian religions over the centuries.

These religious controversies arose mainly over the cases of saving Jewish children, and the intensity of the conflicts depended directly on the degree of religious fervor on both sides. Many Jewish communities, imperiled by the Holocaust, accepted that life-and-death stakes justified the subordination of religious norms to save lives. They adopted the position that a little baptismal water would not harm Jewish children in the long run if it helped them survive the war. On the other hand, more orthodox Jewish communities believed that in the name of Kiddush Hashem the Jewish children should rather die than break the most sacred of the Jewish commandments. This attitude had a special significance both for the course of saving Jewish children in convents and for its scale. The famous Jewish historian, Ringelblum, recorded that it was Jewish orthodox opposition that turned down the offer made by church circles to save children from the Warsaw ghetto in 1942. It also became a future source of the accusation that the convents wanted to convert the Jewish children they rescued (Ringelblum 1983).

I have a feeling that this charge cannot be proven. It is true that often, in order to save the life, a Jewish child was christened at a certain moment. Baptism, in such cases, was an indispensable prerequisite for successfully hiding the children, but it was never an aim in itself.

For example, in Szymanów

when a group of [Jewish] children made their First Confession, one of the girls, when she was led into the sacristy where the confessional was, suddenly burst out crying. She told the priest, who tried to comfort her most warmly, that when her father was leaving her and her younger brother on the "Aryan" side, counting on their rescue, he forbid her, under oath, to reveal to anybody that they had not been already christened. Realizing that she was going to Holy Communion, and she would commit sacrilege, proved to be too heavy a burden to be carried by a nine-year-old girl. The nuns, informed by the priest about this situation, christened the girl, keeping it secret from other children with whom she went to Communion. (Bartoszewski and Lewin 1969)

The baptism of the girl was necessary so that she could, for the reason of her own safety, go to Holy Communion and not raise anybody's suspicions. The nuns had a choice: in full consciousness to allow a sacrilege, or to christen the child, against the Judaic faith. The dilemma was not for human beings to solve and so they acted according to the rules of their own religion.

The circumstances of christening the Jewish girl described above illustrate one of numerous dilemmas faced by Polish nuns hiding Jewish children during the last war. Throughout Poland, the nuns' attitude towards baptism varied greatly and ranged from the conviction that all the children living in the convent should be christened, to the opinion that was expressed by a nun when she said to a child asking to be christened "pray to the Jewish God and we shall pray to Lord Jesus—when we pray together, perhaps we'll survive the war" (related by rescued person).

The motivation for saving children in convents is most fully defined by those who were rescued. Saved by the Order of the Resurrection nuns a young Jewish boy said after the war, "It is just hard to believe what subterfuges the sisters used to make my stay with them possible, especially in the winter and autumn, and even to make it more pleasant. This is what charity flowing from God's love can do." The mother of a saved Jewish child wrote from the United States to a nun whom she had found after a long search:

I have a strange feeling. It seems to me that I have found one of my own sisters again. You are as close to my heart as if you were my own sister; for who else gave us so many proofs of devotion, of understanding our misery, and of human feelings? I always vividly remember the moment when soon after the war I came to the convent to express my gratitude for saving my child and to leave the money which we still had after the war. Dear Sister Ludwika, our guardian Angel, told me then: "Keep this money for the Germans have taken everything from you. But whenever somebody will need help in his life, please help him." I have kept these words in memory and they have been a holy commandment for me. I have tried to help whenever I could, and when people thanked me, I told them the story of sister Ludwika's deed and of her request.

Maria Klein, who was saved in Przemysl, recently has written from Israel: "My leaving the nuns was only physical. Spiritually I always try to live in such a way that I could look into their eyes with a clear conscience."

"To know what is just and to be just is the same thing," proclaimed Socrates. In this statement there is a deep, everlasting truth. Humanity has always needed examples of the proper way of behavior. It needs it today too. It needs people who are just in the Socratic sense—contemporary altruists. This is why history about forgotten instances of altruism is of great importance. It can serve the world by illustrating models of behavior that are worth emulating. It points the way to the highest ideals of humanity: to good and love. Undoubtedly, the Polish nuns who risked their own lives to save the lives of other people during the last war are role models of altruism for both Jews and gentiles alike.

## BIBLIOGRAPHY

Wladystaw Bartoszewski and Zofia Lewin, eds. *Righteous among Nations. How Poles Helped the Jews, 1939–1945*. London: Earlscourt, 1969.
———, eds. *The Samaritans: Heroes of the Holocaust*. New York: Twayne, 1970.
———, eds. *Ten jest z ojczwzny mojej* (He is of my fatherland). Krakow, 1967. P. 807.
N. Blumethal. *Materialy z czasow okupacji Niemieckiej w Polsce*. Centralna Zydowska Komisja Historyczna w Polsce, 1946.
E. Chodzinski. "Pomoc Zydom udzielana prezez konspiracyjne Biuro Falszywych Dokmentow w okresie okupacji Hitlerowskiej" (Help offered to Jews during the occupation by the underground office of illegal documents). *Biuletyn Zydowskiego Instytutu Historycznego* 75 (1970): 129–32.
T. Czarnowski. Pomoc ludnosci Zydowskiej przez pracownikow wydzialu ludnosci zarzadu M. St. Warszawy w okresie okupacji, 1939–1945 (Help offered Jews by employees of the Warsaw population department during the occupation). *Builetyn Zydowskiego Instytutu Historycznego* 75 (1970): 119–28.
Samuel P. Oliner and Pearl M. Oliner. *The Altrustic Personality: Rescuers of Jews in Nazi Europe*. New York: Free Press, 1988.
T. Prekerowa. *Konspiracyjna rada pomocy, Zydom w Warzawie, 1942–1945* (Illegal help to Jews in Warsaw). Warszawa: Panstwowy Instytut Wydawniczy, 1982.
Emmanuel Ringelblum. *Kronika Getta Warszawskiego* (Notes from the Warsaw Ghetto). Warszawa, 1983. P. 391.
Waclaw Zajaczkowski. *Martyrs of Charity*. Washington, D.C.: St. Maximilian Kolbe Foundation, 1988.

# 15

# POLITICAL ALTRUISM: A CASE STUDY

*Rachel Hertz-Lazarowitz*

## INTRODUCTION

The present chapter is a case study of Dov Yirmiya, a man who can best be described as a political altruist. Yirmiya's life is best characterized by his altruistic deeds carried out within the Israeli political context. Dov has been described as a "pessimistic do-gooder" and an "Arab lover," tying together the public-political and personal-altruistic facets of his personality.

The chapter is comprised of five sections: The first, "Dov Yirmiya: A Life Story," recounts the major events in Yirmiya's life. The second part, "Personal versus Public Dimensions of Altruism," describes Dov's altruistic actions during the Lebanon War (June 1982–end 1983). The third part, "The Crystallization of a Political-Altruist," portrays Yirmiya's construction of his altruistic and political self. The fourth section, "Reflections and Interpretations," is based on an introspective conversation with Dov. The fifth section, "A Theoretical Summary of a Political-Altruist," is a conceptualization of a political altruist that describes Yirmiya as an activist who functions between personal and collective boundaries. This section suggests the contribution of this work to the field of altruism and personality.

## I. DOV YIRMIYA: A LIFE STORY

Dov Yirmiya was born in 1914 in the *moshava* (settlement) of Beit-Gan near Yavniel. In 1920, his family moved to Nahalal, the first *moshav,* and established a farm. Dov's childhood was shaped by his life in Nahalal, and the daily hardships of being the son of a farming family (*Halutzim-Haklaim*). To be a farmer in those years (1920) was the realization of the Zionist dream, and working the land (*Adama*) was the highest mission. However, this task entailed considerable hardship for Dov's family.

Although Dov's father and mother were committed to the idea of becoming pioneers (*Halutzim*), they were not prepared for this destiny. Dov's mother grew up in a middle-class family and was a student of pharmacology in Russia. Dov's father moved to Palestine for two reasons. The first was to escape and find refuge from the Russian *Okhranka* (Secret Police) that was after him for his revolutionary activities. Secondly, his family wanted him to study engineering at the Technion in Haifa. While Dov's mother was a Zionist, his father was a cosmopolitan Socialist. Dov's parents had opposite personalities and approaches to their duties and commitments in life.

Upon deciding to become a farmer, Dov's mother devoted all her life to the farm (*Meshek*) in Nahalal. She was a woman of firm responsibility and commitment to her duty, working eighteen hours a day to earn some extra money in order to balance the family budget. Rooted in his revolutionary youth, Dov's father possessed a certain penchant for adventure, mixed with bohemian tendencies. Of his own accord, he embraced farming as a way of life upon his arrival in Palestine in 1910, although he was sent by his family to study engineering at the Technion. He passed on his extensive knowledge of farming as well as his skill and love of toiling the soil to Dov, who from childhood worked on the farm and became a devout farmer himself.

However, the difficult economic conditions of the time inflicted their farm with unusual misfortune. Consequently, the farm incurred considerable debts. Dov's father was forced to seek work elsewhere in order to defray those debts, leaving his wife with Dov, who was still a young boy, to operate the farm. Following the economic blows that befell them, Dov's parents' marriage went astray.

His parents separated in 1937 but never divorced. His father joined Kibbutz Beit-Alpha and was an outstanding and devoted farmer until he reached the age of eighty. Dov's father died at the age of ninety-two in full command of his body and mind. Torn between these two strong people, Dov recalls that he was always "his mother's son." He identified with her and worked hard to help her. But at the same time Dov was attracted to his father's extensive knowledge of farming, music, art, literature, and politics, as well as his value system. Dov himself had a talent for music, and his father encouraged him to pursue this. He remembers that his father was the one who taught him about socialism, justice, and the importance of developing friendly relationships with their Arab neighbors in the Izrael Valley. Dov maintained a close relationship with each of his parents separately, until they passed away. (She lived with Dov during the last years of her life.) His mother was, according to his definition, "a perfectionist who set very high standards." Without doubt, his strong values of commitment, duty, and hard work were influenced by her.

Overall, Dov's personality combines this sense of devotion and commitment with certain theatrical traits, a combination that gives him a special charm. Dov left the farm in 1934 because he wanted to study music in Tel-Aviv. His mother sold the farm in 1939, and moved to Hadera, where she became the director of an agricultural training school for young women (Meshek H'poa'lot).

In 1929, Yirmiya joined the Haganah. In 1934, while studying music in Tel-Aviv, he joined the "Hashomer Hatzair," a leftist youth movement that taught its members the ideology of communal, Socialist way of life and encouraged them to materialize this ideology by founding new *kibbutzim*. In 1938, with a group of youth from this movement, Dov founded Kibbutz Eilon in the Western Galilee. He participated in the Battle of Hanita, and was later appointed commander of Eilon. During World War II, Dov served in a unit of the Palestinian Transport Corps in the British army, operating in the Middle Eastern and North African fronts, and in the Allied forces invasion of Italy. When the war was over, he helped the Palyam (Palmach Naval Corps) smuggle the remnants of the Holocaust survivors into Palestine. In 1948, Dov joined the Israeli Defense Forces (IDF), and during the War of Independence served as a company commander and a battalion second in command, participating in battles in the Eastern and Western Galilee, and in the conquest of Nazareth. After the war, he continued to serve in the army, eventually reaching the rank of colonel (*Aluf-Mishne*).

Dov retired from active service in the IDF in 1958, and became a member of Kibbutz Sarid, where he worked in agriculture and taught Hebrew to new immigrants. An active member of Mapam, the Socialist left party, Dov was an activist in the struggle for equality for the Israeli Arabs and participated in actions against the military rule over the Arab minority. Dov saw the continuation of military rule beyond the end of the War of Independence as a political act designed to oppress, and discriminate against, the Arab minority in Israel. Already in 1948, he had refused to accept the position of military governor of the Galilee that he had been offered at the time. Following his retirement from IDF active service in 1958, he engaged in a continuous political struggle against the military rule until its dissolution in 1966.

In 1965, he became one of the founders of the northern district Nature Reserve Authority (NRA), where he worked until he retired in 1979. During this time, he vociferously objected to the establishment of the Green Patrol as a section of the NRA. Yirmiya accused the NRA director, General Yaffe, who had been Dov's friend since adolescence, of initiating the Green Patrol as a private militia for the harassment of the Bedouins under the pretext of "nature conservancy." He assailed the Green Patrol for driving away Bedouin shepherds from lands in the Galilee and the Negev and for confiscating their herds.

During the 1967 war, Dov volunteered for service and was appointed defense commander of the town of Kiryat-Shmonah, and since then has served in the reserves on a voluntary basis. In 1974, following the PLO attack on Ma'alot, he established the Civil Guard Unit in his present home in the town of Nahariya in the Western Galilee, and was its first commander. In this capacity, he personally fought a terrorist group that attacked and killed a mother and her two children in a residence near his home. The civil guard unit (Hamishmar Ha'ezrahi) he established was the first in the country, and has served as a model for the National Civil Guard system.

During the Littani campaign in 1978, Dov served as an officer in a military rule unit, which was named the Unit for Civilian Aid for political reasons. During the Lebanon War, he served once again in the same unit. At that time, he kept a daily diary of his activities and of the events he witnessed in Lebanon. The diary was published as a book entitled *My War Diary* in 1983. Several chapters describing the tragedy of Palestinian refugees and the actions and behavior of the IDF were published earlier, in July of 1982, in an Israeli newspaper. Following their publication, Dov was expelled from the army in August of the same year. After his expulsion from the army, Dov devoted all of his time to helping the Palestinian refugees in Lebanon. Details of this period are described in the second part of the present chapter. Yirmiya's effort to aid the refugees and publicize their plight was recognized in December 1983, when he was granted the Emil Grinzweig Award (named after the "Peace Now" activist who had been killed by a grenade thrown by a right-wing Jew) as man of the year for his work for human rights. The award is granted by the Civil Rights Association in Israel. The money was donated to a kindergarten of the Arab el Cammane Bedouin tribe.

Until the Lebanon War, Dov's actions had fallen within the legitimate boundaries of Israeli society. Although Dov's life was interwoven with two different missions, one being the actualization of a Jewish homeland and the other being the pursuit of Jewish-Arab coexistence and reconciliation, there always seemed to be a balance between the two. Most of the documentation about the man reflects this message: he was a "bleeding-heart" Jew who strongly believed in the vision and mission of a Jewish-Zionist homeland. Since the Lebanon War, all of Dov's activities have been centered on the Jewish-Arab relationship, with a special emphasis on the plight of the Palestinians and their vantage point. Consequently, from 1983 to 1989, Dov became a very controversial figure in the Israeli-Jewish society.

Among his activities in recent years, Dov served as a liaison for the American Jewish volunteers of "Interns for Peace." This organization, founded in the U.S., brought together community workers from Israel (both Jews and Arabs) and from the U.S. The volunteers worked on educational and recreational projects in neighboring Arab and Jewish communities in order to promote understanding and coexistence. Dov's role in this project was to prepare the American volunteers for their assignment in the Arab villages. Subsequently, he served, together with an Arab colleague, as a secretary of Reshet (Network). The function of this organization was to coordinate all voluntary educational and community-oriented groups in Israel promoting Jewish-Arab understanding.

In the summer of 1984, following Kahane's election to the Knesset, Dov resigned from his position in Reshet in order to devote himself full-time to work for the Jewish-Arab Committee against Racism and for Coexistence. Together with Maruan Dwairi of Nazareth, Dov became the coordinator of this organization, where he was active for almost two years. Wherever Kahane organized a demonstration, usually a highly provocative one, Dov and the committee members held a counterdemonstration. Once Kahane's platform was recognized as racist and he was no longer able to be reelected to the Knesset, the committee dissolved. During these two years, Dov experienced physical violence for the first time. While demonstrating in Jerusalem against Kahane in February of 1986, he was badly beaten by a few "Magav" (border police) soldiers, and spent a month in bed.

In 1987, Yirmiya joined a delegation that traveled to meet with PLO representatives in Romania. The government and the general public bitterly attacked the Jewish group invited to attend this first meeting with the PLO. Of all the Jews that attended the meetings, Dov was the only Ashkenazi Jew who could speak, read, and write Arabic fluently. Upon their return, the secretariat members of the delegation were tried, fined, and sentenced to a six-month prison term. With the outbreak of the Intifada in December 1987, Dov was deeply troubled. In his view, it was the realization of the bleak future he had feared so much, and the danger of the moral destruction of the Israeli society. What he saw and experienced in the Lebanon War had grown to become infinitely more frightening.

A man of action, Dov and two other Jewish young men established the "Red Line" movement, Jews and Arabs against the occupation. The "Red line" launched a four-day peace march from the Galilee to Jerusalem as an immediate response to the IDF treatment of the Intifada and the continued occupation. It was the first movement, of Jews and Arabs, that protested the IDF handling of the Intifada and the continued occupation that had led to it. For Dov, the occupation was, and still is, the root of all evil. It was Dov, his fifty years of personal contacts with Arabs in the Galilee, his reputation for political involvement, peace seeking, and benevolent activities, that made this group unique. The movement is still active to this day. The Intifada has worried Dov and made him more pessimistic than ever before. His focus is on protest activities within the green lines, and on rendering material and moral support to the Palestinians in the occupied territories. Yirmiya, in the shadow of the Intifada, has emerged as one of the country's leading advocates of sarvanut (conscientious objection) to serve in the territories. Yirmiya was interrogated by the police for his active support of this dissident movement.

In the early 1980s, Yirmiya had a well-publicized correspondence with the veteran "Sarvan," Gadi Elgazi. Elgazi refused to serve in occupied Lebanon and was sentenced to prison. Dov comments, "At that time, I argued against this, believing that it was better that people with a conscience would serve in order to moderate and curb IDF behavior there. Now, I know that Elgazi was right. The soldiers must refuse to serve as part of the occupying forces of thuggery and repression" (*Jerusalem Post Magazine*, June 24, 1988; for the sarvanut movement in Israel, see Linn 1989; Linn 1988).

Dov continues to be in frequent contact with his many Arab friends, acquaintances, and admirers. In a recent interview, he told me that he works with children in a Bedouin settlement in the Galilee on Mount Cammane. Yirmiya has been the driving force behind fund raising for the kindergarten that for four years has been the only facility for 3–6-year-old children of the Arab Sawaed tribe. Since the midsixties, the government has been cajoling and pushing the Arab Cammane to get off the mountain and settle in a nearby *wadi*. The tribe has resisted the attempted transfer; some of their lands have been expropriated or seized and several houses have been destroyed by bulldozers. The government's refusal to grant official recognition to the Arab Cammane sites has resulted in a denial of all basic services to the village. As a result, Yirmiya decided to help operate a kindergarten and is there at least once every two weeks. "You cannot imagine the joy I have in seeing those kids in the kindergarten that I am helping operate. I take my accordion, and I teach them to sing and dance 'Hevenu Shalom Alechem' [We brought peace on you]. They are my kids, their families are my families, and they call me Sidna Dov [Grandpa Dov]. Sometimes, not realizing that I am a Jew, they sing anti-Jewish songs that they heard on the radio, at which point Bedouin teachers would use the occasion to tell them that I am a Jew ..., emphasizing the absurdity of the songs and of the stereotype of the Israeli Jew."

## II. THE PERSONAL VERSUS PUBLIC DIMENSIONS OF ALTRUISM

In analyzing Dov Yirmiya's actions and activities, a consistent pattern emerges from his early adulthood as a young commander in the 1948 War of Independence to the summer of 1989. Yirmiya's way is to actively pursue two roads, two main paths. One involves altruistic actions according to the traditional definition of helping people in need, sharing resources with them (Bar-Tal 1985–1986; Staub 1978; Eisenberg 1986), and even more so, taking personal risks in order to rescue people (Oliner and Oliner 1988). The second entails public and political actions: organizing and playing a role in political groups, writing articles and letters to newspaper editors, organizing demonstrations, publishing a book, and lecturing in public. In other words, it means working not only for the "people" but also for the "cause."

It seems that as an altruistic person, Yirmiya seeks meaningful and personal relationships with people in need. He pursues the personal, face-to-face contact and interaction with human beings who are facing crisis, under stress, or in danger; it may be a family denied its right to build its home on their land in the Galilee, an Arab threatened to be expelled from his job, a Bedouin who needs certain contacts to obtain travel documents, or a Russian immigrant who needs furniture. In all these (real) cases, Dov is there to help.

Yet, as a political persona, Yirmiya is neither naive nor just a "good Samaritan." He has an extraordinary sense of awareness and understanding that society in general, and powerful people in particular, are significant players in enhancing or depriving the masses and the individuals of their needs. Consequently, throughout his entire life, Yirmiya has been fighting powerful key figures in Israeli society such as Dayan, Kenig, Yaffe, Sharon, and others. For this he paid dearly. He has never been "one of the boys," nor a powerful political figure. He has never been awarded money, status, fame, or approval by the authorities. His power and strength stem from his conviction that he himself is indeed moral, right, clean, and uncorrupted by money, power, majority consent, or favoritism. Today, at the age of seventy-five, he is one of the living symbols of Israel in its ideal form. He lives modestly, in a nearly spartan fashion, dresses in the 1948 battledress fashion, and devotes all his energy to causes in which he believes.

In the history of this man's life, which includes five decades of toiling for coexistence between Jews and Arabs, the period of the Lebanon War clearly illustrates the two dimensions of altruism: personal and public. When the IDF invaded Lebanon in June 1982, Dov was called to serve in his unit. Having lived almost all of his adult life in the Galilee, and having dedicated a good share of his life to its defense, he knew from the start that "Operation Peace for the Galilee," as this was intentionally labeled by the Likud government, was totally unnecessary and unjustified. His wife, Menuha (the daughter of Yaffe, the founding family of Nahalal and a prominent figure in the *Halutzim* generation) implored him not to go. She said, "After all, you are against this war, you do not have to go because of your age." Despite his initial objection to the war, Dov decided to serve so that he would be able to help victims of Israeli aggression, and was at the age of sixty-eight the oldest soldier to serve in the Lebanon War.

Dov was emotionally torn by the inner conflict involved in joining an evil system in order to minimize the suffering of others. He maintained the belief that even in an unpleasant situation a person as an individual can do significant good. Such feelings occur frequently among altruistic people (Staub 1984). In many of his writings during and after the war, Yirmiya continually returns to the fact that he joined the "Operation," even though he knew it was fundamentally wrong. In a lecture he gave in December 1984 at the Forum, one of the most respected platforms at Tel-Aviv University, he openly criticized Israel's actions. "The Lebanon War— from the moral and diplomatic viewpoints as well as from the way it had been waged—is the result of Herut leaders' delusions of grandeur; as such, it found its classic expression in the rhetoric of one of the greatest demagogues in Jewish history, Menachem Begin. He, and the terrifying creature he fostered, launched the IDF on a crusade combining the Star of David and the Phalangist cross, according to a scenario that only a sick imagination could have dreamt up. The crusade failed, and the unholy alliance was doomed before it even began.... Only an army whose commanders were devoid of all restraint of conscience and morality, immersed in nationalism and racism, could have ignored its human responsibility and obligation according to the law of nations, in its handling of noncombatant populations in conquered territories—as indeed the IDF has done in this war" (see also Schiff and Yaari 1984).

Yirmiya's verbal and writing style is, as can be seen here, very dramatic. Most of his writings have the flavor of drama. He adds, "the description is ruthless—reality was much more so. This realization is exceedingly hard for someone like myself, who spent his entire life assuring a safe refuge for his sisters and brothers, in absolute faith that my country would be democratic." Later in the same lecture, he pointed out that not all is black:

Throughout this insane war, despite the prevailing spirit of hatred and revenge promoted by the political leaders and high command, there were thousands of soldiers and officers who fought and behaved in a humanitarian way.... They looked at the other side and saw not only the enemy, but also human beings. They distinguished between soldiers and children, between enemy outposts and private homes, and between an unavoidable fighting and a cruel revenge for its own sake. Such was the case of a young paratroop officer at the infamous Place de la Mer in Sidon. Covered with dust, his eyes burning from sleepless nights, facing thousands of detainees, mostly women, children, and elderly, he recognized me and ran toward me shouting: "Dov, do something for these people! Look how they are parched in the sun, thirsty, and hungry. How can you, the military authorities, stand this? How did we become such a cruel army? Yesterday I was fighting in En-Hilwe, and my friend was killed next to me. But I cannot stand this cruelty of ours anymore. We have already divided the little water and food we had, but it was just a drop in the bucket compared to what they need. Please bring at least some drinking water, do something!"

This was what Dov had encountered in the Lebanon War. He saw tens of thousands of refugees, mostly women, children, and elderly people, suffering under horrible conditions, totally dependent on the good, albeit missing, will of the IDF. He left his home town Nahariya, determined to write everything he saw and encountered each day. His political self documented people, events, interactions, decisions, thoughts, and reflections. That notebook became *My War Diary*, a personal and a political document, which was cited in *Ha'aretz* by one book reviewer as the most important book of 1983. Why did Dov write this book? As he put it, "What I saw, experienced, and learned during my tour of duty could not remain my own private property. It was my obligation as a human being, a Jew, a Zionist, and as a soldier in the IDF, to present this information to the public."

Yirmiya's main assignment during the Lebanon War was within the Civil Aid Unit, which meant assisting the civilian noncombatant population in burying its dead, renewing water and electricity supplies, distributing food, supplying medical services, finding shelter for families whose homes were destroyed, and getting children back to school. Those most affected by the war were the Palestinians. Most of the men either fled or were held in camps because they were considered PLO members. In the midst of the wrought political situation in Lebanon, the Palestinians were endangered by all ethnic and religious groups. In many cases, the IDF was their only source of security and means of survival.

Dov was in the Lebanon combat zone for only twenty-five days, and wrote seventy pages in the evenings after his tireless work helping the civilian population. In his diary, Dov bitterly criticizes the Israeli government's policy toward the Palestinian civilians. He documents how high-ranking officers and others in supervisory positions disrupted him and his unit in their effort to help. He describes the daily indifference to human needs. He cites acts and places where various things could have been done to ease people's suffering but were not. In Dov's view, this was intentional. Yirmiya believes that the purpose here was to deny the refugees help in order to coerce them into abandoning their camps and fleeing to the North. He had perpetual conflicts with Israeli figures about his programs and activities. They regarded him as an "Arab-lover" and resented his eagerness to help restore civilian life in the war zone. Dov had particularly bitter conflicts with General Maymon, the military governor of the area.

When the first chapter was published during the war, it moved the country and its consciousness. Dov started to look for informal, personal ways to furnish the refugees with basic necessities such as food, water, clothes, tents, and medicine. He knocked on many doors, wrote to the newspapers and to numerous politicians, called upon friends, organizations, and factories for support. He was the only individual to organize the Israeli-Arab community to help their people, the Palestinians in Lebanon. The results of these intense efforts were indeed remarkable. During the war itself, with the help of family and friends, Dov organized Emergency Aid; clothes, food, and medications were collected from Jews and Arabs in the Galilee. These supplies were transported personally by Dov to Lebanon, and with the help of local people in Lebanon, distributed to those in need. The man devoted himself completely to his work. He was moved, shocked, even horrified by what he saw. The drive to help and rescue was Yirmiya's prime motivation in the twenty-five days he spent on his tour of duty in Lebanon.

Following his activities in Lebanon, from June 6 to July 1, his talks in Israel after his return from reserve duty, and the publication of chapters of his diary in an Israeli newspaper in July of 1982, Dov was expelled from the army on August 5, 1982. He only discovered this decision during a meeting of his military unit when a summary of previous tours of duty was provided in preparation for the next tour of duty planned for August 10. In a personal letter, handed to him by his commander, Dov was severely criticized for the chapters of the diary published in *Hotam* (July 1982). The commander's letter described the situation in Lebanon from the point of view of the IDF, justifying the destruction in the Palestinian camps with the claim that the terrorists had scattered among the civilian population. He wrote to Dov, "I sensed, while reading your diary, not only the smell of friendship for the Arabs but for the terrorists as well."

For Yirmiya, this was a most painful moment. In a very degrading way, the IDF had brought a fascinating career of a man to an end. This was not an ordinary citizen, but rather one who, in almost fifty years of service in the military and security forces, was loyal both to his country and to his own human values and beliefs.

But Yirmiya's unqualified decision was to continue his work for the people in Lebanon. After the publication of excerpts from his diary, he became a very controversial figure, occupying center stage. He formed a new organization: Citizens for Humanitarian Aid (CHA) in Lebanon. This was the only voluntary organization that Jews and Arabs formed in cooperation during the Lebanon War.

The organization was active for about fifteen months, until October 1983. During this period, Dov and other activists in the organization went back and forth from the Galilee to Lebanon, encountering hardship and danger. They managed to raise funds and to provide essential help to the Palestinian noncombatant population. Within months, after gathering contributions from kibbutzim, Arab villages, and individuals from all over the country, the CHA committee sent the refugees seventy tons of clothing, including forty-five hundred pairs of children boots, bed covers, food, medication, and supplies. In addition, the committee raised fifty thousand U.S. dollars with which they bought and delivered ten prefabricated houses to the school in Sidon's Ein Hilwe camp, which had been flattened by IDF bombardments. Dov continued his work until it was impossible to get back to the people: "Then came the guerrilla war and the Israeli evacuation."

The initiation of the committee's activities was inspired by Dov's personal altruistic dimension. Reading his diary, one can sense the care and empathy that characterize all of his activities. The political outcome of Dov's activity in Lebanon was the writing and, eventually, the publication of his diary as a book. Today, in the era of the Intifada, unfortunately, clashes with Palestinians, injury, and death have become daily occurrences. Many of the IDF's activities are controversial within the Israeli society. Dov's book, published in 1983, can be seen today as a raging prophecy. It was the first book that described the ugly side of the IDF; it was written by a man who grew within the army, and who crushed the myth of "the purity of arms of the IDF" and of Israeli wars as always unavoidable wars. This book was the first to claim that it is not the image of the Israelis but, rather, the real people and their actions that should be the focus of concern. The book was attacked, repudiated, and criticized by numerous IDF and public figures of the Israeli establishment. Furthermore, Yirmiya was personally attacked as an enemy of Israel and described as a man who suffers from the very old Jewish malady: *self-hatred.* On the other hand, it raised positive and encouraging reactions from many first-rank journalists in daily newspapers and weekly magazines. Similar reactions were expressed by many members of the Knesset, public figures of the Left-Camp, and numerous other readers.

While the political impact of the book is yet to be studied, there is no doubt that it precedes a number of related and significant events. The most dramatic ones were Begin's resignation and self-exile, the beginning of the sarvanut (Linn 1989), and the Yesh-Gvul (There is a limit) movement. Since the Lebanon War, there has been growing support of conscientious objectors—that is, those soldiers who refuse, on moral grounds, to serve in the occupied territories. The book also preceded the rise of Kahane and his group, and the bipolarization of Israeli society. In 1983, three editions of the book appeared in Hebrew and Arabic in Israel. It was then translated into English and published by South End Press in Boston (1983), and by Pluto Press in London (1984). In 1986, the book was translated from English to Italian, and the English version was translated into Arabic and published in Beirut in 1987 and in Israel in 1988. All royalties were donated to the organizations in which Dov is active.

Dov had always perceived himself as a man of action and not a man of words. The Lebanon War and his political orientation led him to become an author and to publish a book; his political self documented his personal altruistic self. This combination became a very powerful personal testimony.

### III. THE CRYSTALLIZATION OF A POLITICAL ALTRUIST

Reviewing the files that Dov Yirmiya has been collecting for many years was like entering into and searching among the many layers of his soul. While reading the material, I kept wondering how it must have felt to have seen a published ad about his own death on April 26, 1948, and then, a day later, the announcement that he was alive but badly wounded. What did it feel like to reread the debates, letters of protest he wrote engulfed by surging emotions, when some of those referred to are already dead? What is his reaction when he reads dramatic claims for socialism and the belief that Stalin was the *sun of the nation* when he does not believe in it any longer? Over the years, Dov has collected hundreds of newspaper clips, primarily documenting his activities, letters to the editors, and public speeches in Hebrew, English, and Arabic, as if awaiting his biography to be written one day.

Reviewing the titles that other writers had ascribed to him, it became very clear that this man was perceived as a unique and rare individual who has become increasingly scarce in our society. Truly altruistic people are a rare species (Staub 1978; Rushton 1980; Oliner and Oliner 1988) in any society, and due to Israel's relatively small size, Dov had attracted a great deal of attention. The titles of the many articles written by different journalists at various times consistently reflect the two facets of the man, the *activist* military man and the *dreamer-passionate*, empathic human being. For example, Tom Segev of *Ha'aretz* entitled his article *The Good Soul from Nahariya*. Paraphrasing Brecht's play *The Good Soul* [*Woman*] *of Szechwan*, Segev wrote, "Dov Yirmiya is breaking the last taboo; he might be sentenced for advocating *sarvanut*. Yirmiya, a farmer, a soldier and a musician, the man with a thousand battles could be exceptional story material." As for his personality, Segev continued, "He hates the slogan 'shooting and crying,' he shoots and thinks; old-young, charming and generous, he always fights for his principles and always pays for it." He concluded the article with, "I tried to convince him to write the story of his life, but Yirmiya said that there are more important things he had to do" (*Ha'aretz*, March 3, 1988).

Dov refers to his first "shoot and think" incident during the War of Independence (1948), when he was confronted with a moral dilemma of whether or not to overlook a war crime that one of his officers, a close friend, had committed. This young man killed thirty-five Arab civilians who had previously surrendered. After painful deliberations, Dov decided to report the incident, thereby initiating the only military court-martial for such a crime during that war. The officer was sentenced to a seven-year prison term but was pardoned shortly thereafter.

Avishai Grossman from *Al Hamishmar* (Mapam daily newspaper) referred to Yirmiya as an officer and a gentleman, and entitled his article "Alone on the Red Line" (July 6, 1988). The political magazine *New Outlook* of August 1987 described him as "an exemplary model to all peace and justice seekers between nations." In the consciousness section of the magazine, the article entitled "Dov Kishot," playing a pun on the literary figure of Don Quixote, depicted the wars Dov waged against people whom he perceived as being destructive to the cause of Jewish-Arab coexistence. In one case, Dov opposed the nomination of General David Maymon as commissioner of the prisons in Israel because this was the man responsible for the IDF handling of the civilian population in the Lebanon War. He was the man who said that "Yirmiya will not set foot on Lebanese soil again" and was behind Yirmiya's expulsion from the army. Yirmiya felt that it was a disastrous decision to put a man with such an anti-Arab ideology in charge of the prisons in Israel because so many of the inmates were Arabs (*Monitin*, December 1988). The personal attack against Maymon is only one example of Yirmiya's personal crusades against those whom he perceived to be detrimental to Jewish-Arab coexistence, and particularly, those treating Arabs in an unjust and discriminating way.

Most of the time, Yirmiya realized that his was a lost battle, but this realization never prevented him from speaking his mind, nor did it attenuate his defiance. He confronted his long-time friend and boss, the late Avraham Yoffe, director of the National Park Service, under whose leadership the Green Patrol banished Arabs from their grazing land. Another target for his offensive was Israel Kenig, former commissioner of the Ministry of the Interior, who was in charge of Arab affairs in northern Israel. For years, Dov vociferously opposed Kenig's policy and actions and viewed him as a major source of evil. Lastly, Dov condemned Ariel Sharon for his politics and actions in the Lebanon War.

Dov is never reluctant to voice his opinions with Jews and Arabs alike. His writing style has always been prophetic and full of conviction. In a dramatic manner, Dov expresses his thoughts in black and white. He never conceals his emotions and involvement. At the same time, he has a very charming and humble disposition.

Reviewing his files, I read many letters to the editor and short articles sent to newspapers and returned to him with one excuse or another as to why the newspaper declined to publish the material. Even when published, his writings have been sometimes revised and subdued. Yet, Dov has not been discouraged from continuing his struggle against injustice. The articles written about him never neglected to mention the fact that he had been a high-ranking officer in the IDF. One can recall that Yirmiya completed his service as a career officer in 1958, and yet in *The Jerusalem Post* of May 1988, the article reads, "Colonel admits to urging soldiers to refuse to serve in the territories." The adjectives colonel (*Sgan-Aluf*) and ex-officer have always been associated with his name and activities. Indeed, in Israel one's army rank is usually associated with the person. This is particularly evident in the case of high-ranking officers, mainly generals, who hold prominent public positions as civilians. In Dov's case, it was usually noted in order to emphasize his criticism of the IDF and his involvement in the peace camp.

One of the best descriptions of Yirmiya was written by Menachem Golan in *Maar'iv* on October 8, 1982. The article, titled "Persona non Grata," evokes an emotional and painful reaction to Yirmiya's expulsion from the army. This was still a time when Yirmiya refrained from openly attacking the IDF. Golan quotes Yirmiya as saying, "Yes, I will volunteer in the future, and will ask to serve in the IDF wherever it goes. It is my army and my country, and no one will take them from me. I gave them my whole life." Note, however, that since the Intifada broke out, Yirmiya has no longer abided by his own words.

Between 1967 and 1979 Dov documented the bulk of his activities himself. There were only a few clippings from 1967 to 1978, but since 1979 his files have grown to include hundreds of documents. Dov's explanation as to this discrepancy was that only after his retirement in 1978–1979 did he find the time to write so many letters and responses to the press, and to organize his files. However, knowing Dov, I think that consciously or unconsciously he is more at peace with the last ten to twenty years of his life than with the years prior to 1970. After talking with Dov, I was under the impression that he is restructuring his own vision of his life.

Another issue relevant to Dov's emergence as a political activist is his political affiliation. All his life Dov declared himself a member of Mapam, at one time the most leftist Socialist-Zionist party.

In the thirties and forties, Mapam was very dogmatic and in line with Russian ideology. Yet, the party could not be considered Communist because of its particular Zionist ideology that espoused the vision of a binational Jewish-Arab state based on the principles of parity. Like many leftists of this era, Dov was torn between the utopian ideas of justice, equality, and social rights of the Socialist ideology, which are still important to him, and the sharp and bitter disillusionment with reality. Dov remained formally and ritualistically loyal to Mapam, but he frowns upon its loss of direction. His disappointment with the party led him to search for alternative modes of operation outside the narrow and confining party line, focusing on practical Jewish-Arab cooperation as delineated throughout this chapter.

## IV. REFLECTIONS AND INTERPRETATIONS

I have known Dov since 1963. Listening to him and observing his actions, I am amazed at the intensity of his emotional experiences, the extent of his responsiveness to other human beings, and the profundity of his concern with significant issues. These qualities have surfaced repeatedly in Dov's actions. At the age of seventy-five, Dov views his life in its entirety as consistent with his beliefs and values. Even when he fought the Arabs in 1948, he claims that he always believed in the right of the two nations to exist.

While attempting to clarify a few points, I asked Yirmiya what he perceives to be the most important things he has done in his life. His answer came somewhat unexpectedly. For him the fact that he was a farmer, a man who toiled the land, sowing and reaping, was very important. As he put it, "I was always in touch with my body and soul as a child at Ba'it Gan, and a farmer in Nahalal from 1920 to 1938." The second most significant thing, in Dov's opinion, is the fact that he lived on a kibbutz, the most utopian socialist way of life, and the most unique form of life the Israeli society has created (Talmon-Garber 1970). I found this answer to reflect Dov's close affinity to the most central and sacred values and visions of the Jewish-Zionist movement—the revival of the land and the creation of a just society on the *kibbutz.*

When I asked Yirmiya what he was most disappointed about at this stage of his life, he replied in a philosophical way: "the body [organism] wears out, and the rest is down hill. I cannot stop thinking about how short life is." He added, "I am disappointed with the fact that a single lifetime is too short to realize the fulfillment and attainment of one's truly most valued ideas. When I reflect on what happened to socialism and communism, and the transformation of Zionism in the twentieth century, I think that there is no future or hope for mankind. Many have told me that I am a pessimist, and I think that indeed I am."

In his usual dramatic tone Dov went on.

You asked me why I continue to do what I do and why I am still so active. The answer is very complicated. First of all, it is the lust for life, to be alive. If you refrain from doing things in which you believe, you may indeed shorten the process [of life]. I do all of those things for Arabs because they are the underdogs. They suffer from the fact that we attained our dream and they did not. I was always attracted to them and to their lifestyle. As a child in Nahalal, I truly thought about them as my brothers, and *always* believed that Zionism would benefit *them* as well. With all my heart I believed that we would learn what we could from each other, and that after 1947, two states would eventually be created here, one for them and one for us. I learned their language, their culture, and their ways of life. I was *not* the only one to hold these beliefs; many of the *Halutzim*, while defending Jewish communities against Arab attacks in times of bloody uprising of the Arabs against the British and their Zionist proteges, still believed in future coexistence of Jews and Arabs in this country.

As a youngster, Dov said he was also very attracted to communism, and to the Socialist-Zionist ideology. He felt confident that communism would solve all nationalistic conflicts, including ours. He concluded that "it was only later, when all the horrors of Stalin were uncovered, that I finally detached myself from the Communist ideology although I still think that some elements of it are truthful. This disappointment just added to my pessimistic view of human nature."

Yirmiya ponders whether he really is biased and partial towards the Arabs, as even his wife says he sometimes is. Indeed, it looks as if he has more Arab friends than Jewish ones, at least in the political realm. Dov admits that he is not able to analyze his motives, and that some probably stem from his childhood, family structure, and relationships. "But I do know one thing," he adds, "I feel an *obligation* to work for the Arab cause because the great majority of Jews *do not*. That's why I stand in the stead of one hundred thousand Jews who do not lift a finger to help the Arabs in their plight. Perhaps others *feel* the way I do but *do nothing* about it. What I am doing is in my name as well as theirs."

Analyzing the years that have passed since 1948, Dov thinks that Israeli Jews have committed many immoral acts toward the Arabs. Dov says he feels the guilt of Israel's actions. He internalized ideas and writings of authors like Dostoevsky and Tolstoy, as well as his father and his admired and beloved schoolteacher. He hates nationalism, when it means superiority of people and nations over others. Yirmiya made it clear that he never adopted the main Jewish ideology that Jews are "the chosen people," a view he holds in no small measure due to this father's way of thinking. He never revered people because they were Jewish nor considered himself unique because he was one.

I feel that Jewish-Arab coexistence is the most crucial issue in our own existence as people and as a nation. If we do not learn to do the fair and just thing, which is to recognize the right of the Palestinians to realize their national, cultural, and individual independence, I am convinced that we will not be able to maintain ours either. This idea motivates me to do everything I can in order to prevent the moral, and eventually, the physical destruction of our dream as a people.

I asked Yirmiya why he has always been working in the periphery of the political realm and why he has never pushed himself to become a central political figure, within Mapam, the party with which he has been affiliated. Why is he a Don Quixote type? Yirmiya's answer was twofold. First of all, he had come to recognize that even Mapam does not respond seriously enough when it comes to the Arab issue, and he had found many contradictions, even hypocrisy, in their ideology and actions. He said he could not join Rakach, which is the Communist party, because of his painful disillusionment with Russia, and because of the party's dogmatism. However, he did not reject their *people* as individuals when they joined in activities against racism or for aid in Lebanon. On the contrary, Yirmiya always succeeded in assembling people from diverse organizations, parties, and groups, who would not otherwise talk to each other, let alone cooperate in a political activity.

Secondly, the reason why Yirmiya never assumed the role of political leadership is tied to his own self-perception as a man not molded to become a politician. He thinks very modestly about himself. Yirmiya definitely recognizes his talents in motivating and mobilizing people but thinks he lacks the intellectual scope needed to become a national leader.

Yirmiya reflects on his life with modesty, uncertainty, searching for answers. He sees many of his one-time partners in action, soldiers under his command, friends, and acquaintances who now belong to the establishment, occupying significant positions and enjoying their accompanying and derived benefits. Nevertheless, Yirmiya deeply despises them for not remaining loyal and truthful to the ideals they once held, at the time when both they and the state were young and pure.

Yet, Dov is aware of the fact that his activities have endowed him with status, reputation, and the admiration of those people and groups he values, although they sometimes oppose the way in which he tries to enact his ideas. At the end of our conversation, he said,

You ask what drives me. Aren't we all driven by fear of a dog, fear of darkness, fear of a bullet, fear of death and mortality? I know that what I demand of others, I first demand of myself. I *was* frightened when I was beaten, interrogated by the police, or when I participated in radical activities that could invoke violent reactions. Yet, at these times, I felt as if I were again a commander in the War of 1948, leading the troops and calling, "follow me." Sometimes I expect that there are hundreds of people behind me, but in fact, there may be only a few, or I may even be alone.

## V. A THEORETICAL SUMMARY OF A POLITICAL ALTRUIST

Reviewing the literature on altruism, one finds a growing body of literature that describes helping and virtuous behavior of individuals in times of catastrophe, such as the Holocaust era. These are individuals who saved the lives of others at a high risk to themselves. Much of this literature attempts to characterize the personality of the rescuers (see Oliner and Oliner 1988; London 1970; Huneke 1985–1986; Wundheiler 1985–1986). On the other hand, there is a vast body of literature that describes political activists in various settings. One example is the book on *Jews, Christians, and the New Left* (Rothman and Lichter 1982). These analyses usually focus on puzzling questions: what makes those people be who they are? What is the interface of personality and ideology? Usually, the answers are found within the theoretical framework of deepset aspects of intrapsychic functioning and family relations. Other analyses are based on sociopsychological theoretical concepts such as social marginality (London 1970).

Dov's life combines the altruist and political activist in a way that unfolds a different type of altruist, not described or discussed earlier in the literature. In certain respects, Dov cannot be analyzed merely according to the profile of the altruist-rescuer who saved the lives of Jews during an era of homicide on a scale never before imagined (Kohn 1989). Neither can he be analyzed *only* according to psychological profiles of a political activist. Dov conforms to the definition of an altruist (see Eisenberg 1986, 210) as "a person whose behavior is motivated by (1) empathy, (2) self-evaluative emotions associated with specific internalized moral values and norms and one's responsibility to act in accordance with these values or norms, (3) cognitions concerning those values, and . . . (4) cognitions and accompanying affect . . . related to self-evaluation vis-à-vis one's moral self-image" (Eisenberg 1986, 210). Dov's life has focused on helping a group of people, in this case the Arabs, and for almost fifty years, he did so in various ways. He has, in many respects, a one-track mind, devoting most of his energy to the issues he had cognitively decided were fundamental.

In order to understand Dov's life in a theoretical framework, I draw on concepts of personality boundaries within the unique Israeli context (Shalit 1987). I will also draw on action theories, since I view Dov as an action-oriented altruist. Action in the Israeli context means politics, and politics for Dov is affected by Marxism, which also shaped the basic concepts of action theory (see Von Cranach and Harré 1982). Included in the action theory are some social-drama concepts in which Dov is the actor; he is fully aware of the stage, role, text, and impact of his actions, and uses it to rewrite or restage some of the scenes in the Jewish-Arab drama (Harré 1979).

When analyzing Dov's personality, it is essential to understand that the Israeli existential condition is unique. As suggested by Shalit (1987), the Israeli represents a person who is the product of close proximity between personal and collective boundaries (375). There is always a deep sense of anxiety and fear of extinction— fear of both physical and national extinction. The syndrome, characterized by Holocaust survivors, is intensified by tens of millions of Arabs who continue to threaten the existence of the Israeli Jews. The role of that anxiety in the collective boundaries of the Israeli Jews, and Jews everywhere, affects pragmatic politics in Israel (Kelman 1987). The post-Holocaust syndrome is a perpetual element of daily life here, just like the air we breathe and the streets we walk.

This unique setting has a profound impact on many Israelis, and in this context, Dov represents the majority. In 1948, the newly born fragile nation was forced to fight for its existence; an individual's personal boundaries were in full accordance with the necessity to change the geographical borders—that is, to establish a geographical region for the collective Jewish nation (Shalit 1987). This necessity led to a war that had a traumatic outcome for the Arabs. At that time, in 1948, we Israelis, including Dov, as well as the rest of the world, thought that that war and the change in geographical borders were inevitable outcomes of what was believed to be a *moral* act. Subsequent wars—Sinai (1956), Six-Day (1967), Littani operation (1978), and Lebanon (1982)—led many people to experience a dissonance between the personal and the collective boundaries.

Gradually, these changes made people like Dov question the legitimacy of Israel's acts, and the morality of its policies, and recognize the injustices inherent in the continuous flux in our collective self. Dov's inner self came to be in bitter and painful conflict with his collective self. For Dov, both the Littani operation and the Lebanon War were somewhat of a traumatic recurrence of the 1948 war. He again encountered the *people* the Palestinians, who were exiled in 1948. From his personal entries in his diary, it is evident that he could not separate the 1982 events from those in 1948. He became increasingly distressed and disturbed by what he saw; the same people and their offspring were still there, suffering and being denied their basic human rights. Yirmiya's analysis of the situation implies that the Israeli government was still treating these people as terrorists. It is my hypothesis that many conflicts that Yirmiya had experienced earlier turned into anger and rage in Lebanon. His ability to analyze sociopolitical processes within a Marxist frame of thinking, and his strong sense of morality and justice, led Dov to become a *Sarvan* (a conscientious objector), commending the morality of refusing to serve in the occupied territories.

Due to the proximity between individual and social processes in Israel, everyone takes a position on the current sociopolitical situation. Dov's position is described in this chapter as a unique combination of a political, collective, as well as a personal, altruistic self. Thus, the fact that Yirmiya's most outstanding actions occurred in Lebanon indicates that he was driven by guilt and shame for the collective Israeli society, who had again expanded its geographic borders and harmed the Palestinians. Dov expresses this very clearly when he says that he acts not only for himself but also for a hundred thousand Jews who do not share his views and concerns and do not extend their help to those in need.

An analysis of human behavior according to a social drama model (Harré 1979) has shed light on the Jewish-Arab conflict (Hertz-Lazarowitz 1988). According to this analysis, Yirmiya is a key actor in a drama that results directly from a troubled socio-political reality; this drama has been playing on our region's stage for over one hundred years, and for Dov, almost seventy years. With heightened awareness and great determination, he decides on the roles, texts, and stages on which he will perform. As Dov's life unfolds, it resembles a fascinating drama with many theatrical features. At different phases, Yirmiya has made some dramatic moves, for example, breaking the "taboo" of speaking with members of the PLO, traveling to Romania, and meeting with "delegitimized others" (Bar-Tal 1988). His style of speaking and writing is theatrical. He still dresses and behaves much like the 1948 Israelis (Elon 1972). He was proclaimed dead and is still alive. He has led a grandiose life story laced with love, hate, jealousy, devotion, and unexpected turns that marked his personal as well as his public self. On the one hand, he plays the prophet, and on the other, the cohen who does the holy work (*Avodat Kodesh*). Von Cranach and Harré (1982) view action as serving to maintain the actor's self by adapting to the demands of his environment (76) (see also Eisenberg 1986, 26–29).

Mario Von Cranach and Harré (1982) introduced the term *action* in the following manner: "Our key concept is that of action (*Handlen*, in Hebrew; *Peula, Bizua*). By that we mean a type of behavior that is, at least partially, consciously directed towards a planned and intentional goal. The word 'conscious' is intended to express the fact that the subjective experiences, accessible to the doer himself, and related to the action, are associated with the objective performance of the action; the action is represented in a cognitive manner . . . we do not expect all parts of action to be conscious" (16–17).

Dov represents a man of action and perceives himself as such. The fact that he directs all his actions toward being a political altruist, concerned with the Palestinian/Arabs' plight, may be the result of his own self-reflection and cognitive analysis that have gradually shaped his political thinking. The Israeli sociopolitical drama is forever changing, which no doubt impacts the processes of thought and action.

Certain psychological theories teach us that individuals may displace their own conflicts on the political level. This chapter describes a complex man engulfed by both internal and external conflicts, who nevertheless maintains his basic value system and integrity. It is yet to be determined which theory best explains the man. In my opinion, Dov is a highly emotional person with a strong drive to promote justice and equality in society as a whole. He is blessed with a tremendous ability to organize and activate people. Consciously or unconsciously, he decided to work for what he thinks is the *most crucial* issue facing the state of Israel, which is the coexistence of Jews and Arabs, and to do so *not* through *large* organizations such as political parties, but through small, mobile, and dynamic organizations that are immune to corruption.

Thus, the profile of the man and the evolution of his political altruism may be characterized by the following elements: Dov works for and with people, mainly Arab and pro-Arab Jews. His relationships with those people are long-term. He continues to be a close, reliable friend who is there, ready to help. Dov mobilizes himself and others to participate in ad hoc activities dealing with crucial, traumatic, and acute problems. Those activities are performed in small organizations that open new paths for addressing acute problems. Some of these activities have been subsequently adapted and extended by political parties or well-established organizations, such as actions against the military rule and the Green Patrol, his establishment of the Committee against Racism and the "Red Line"—Jews and Arabs against occupation—and, more recently, his participation in the delegation to Romania to meet the PLO. Yirmiya, in his action, was ahead of the people and of his time. It took the Israeli society years to get to the *same* point that he had reached much earlier.

On a personal level, Dov manifests most of the characteristics of an altruist: empathy, the ability to assume the perspective of another person or group of people, the concern for the needs and plight of others, and the natural ability to extend himself to others. He thinks of helping as the proper thing to do, without viewing it as an outstanding act; he feels he does what has to be done.

Yirmiya wants his life to be purposeful and is forever examining himself. He is aware of mortality and frightened by it on an existential-philosophical level. For observers like myself and for others with whom I talked about Yirmiya, he is becoming increasingly critical (some say extremely so) of Israeli society and the Zionist dream, but still dreams and fights for its moral actualization.

Moral beliefs are central to Dov's actions and thinking. Each and every day, he combines his caring commitment to *people* with his commitment to abstract *principles* of justice, equality, moral conduct, and humanism.

## ACKNOWLEDGMENTS

Thanks are extended to Dov Yirmiya for being (as he is always) empathic, emotional, logical, and sharing. Ms. Anat Frankel made significant contributions to this work through her insights and suggestions. Sharon Nazariyan and Jennifer Friedman assisted greatly in preparing this manuscript, and lastly, thanks are due to Tamar Zelniker for her excellent and inspiring editing of the manuscript.

## REFERENCES

Bar-Tal, D. (1985/86). Altruistic motivation to help: Definition, utility, and operationalization. *Humboldt Journal of Social Relations 13*, 1–2, 3–15.

—— (1988). Delegitimizing relations between Israeli Jews and Palestinians: A social psychological analysis. In J.E. Hofman, et al., *Arab-Jewish Relations in Israel*. Bristol, In.: Wyndham Hall Press, 217–49.

Ben-Zion Zitrin (1986). Dov Kishot, Ha'Naziv Ha'yadua. *Monitin*, December.

Eisenberg, N. (1986). *Altruistic emotions, cognition, and behavior*, Hillsdale, N.J.: Erlbaum.

Elon, A. (1972). *The Israelis: Founders and sons*. New York: Holt, Rinehart, and Winston.

Grossman, A. (1988). Alone in the red line. *Al-Hamishmar*, July 6.

Harré, R. (1979). *Social being*. Oxford: Blackwell.

Hertz-Lazarowitz, R. (1988). Conflict on campus: A social drama perspective. In J.E. Hofman et al., *Arab-Jewish relations in Israel*. Bristol, In.: Wyndham Hall Press.

Huneke, D.K. (1985/86). The lessons of Herman Grabe's life: The origins of a moral person. *Humboldt Journal of Social Relations 13*, 1–2, 320–32.

Kelman, H.C. (1987). The political psychology of the Israeli-Palestinian conflict: How can we overcome the barriers to a negotiated solution? *Political Psychology, 8*, 3, 347–65.

Kohn, A. (1989). Evidence for a moral tradition. *Psychology Today*, January–February, 72–73 (Reviewing Oliner, S., and Oliner, P. book *The altruistic personality: Rescuers of Jews in Nazi Europe*).

Linn, R. (1988). Moral judgment in extreme social contexts: Soldiers who refuse to fight and physicians who strike? *Journal of Applied Social Psychology 18*, 13, 1149–70.

———. (1989). *Not shooting and not crying*. Westport, Conn.: Greenwood.

London, P. (1970). The rescuers: Motivational hypotheses about Christians who saved Jews from the Nazis. In J. Macaulay and L. Berkowitz, *Altruism and helping behavior: Social psychological studies of some antecedents and consequences*. New York: Academic Press.

Morris, B., Jermiad (1988). *Jerusalem Post Magazine*, June 24.

Oliner, S., and Oliner, P. (1988). *The altruistic personality: Rescuers of Jews in Nazi Europe*. New York: Free Press.

Rothman, S., and Lichter R. (1982). *Roots of radicalism: Jews, Christians, and the new left*. New York: Oxford University Press.

Rushton, J.P. (1980). *Altruism, socialization, and society*. Englewood Cliffs, N.J.: Prentice Hall.

Schenker, Hillel (1985). Every word of the most penetrating criticisms can only help save us. *Israel Horizons*, March–April, 7–9 and 28.

Schiff, Z., and Yaari, E. (1984). *Israel's Lebanon war* (I. Friedman, Trans. and Ed.). New York: Simon and Schuster.

Segev, Tom (1988). *Hanefesh ha'tova mi-Nahariya* (The good soul from Nahariya). *Ha'aretz*, March 3.

Shalit, E. (1987). Within borders and without: The interaction between geopolitical and personal boundaries in Israel. *Political Psychology 8*, 3, 365–79.

Staub, E. (1978). *Positive social behavior and morality: Social and personal influence* (Vol. 1). New York: Academic Press.

———. (1984). Steps toward a comprehensive theory of moral conduct: Goal orientation, social behavior, kindness, and cruelty. In W.M. Kurtines and J.L. Gewirtz, *Morality, moral judgment, and moral behavior: Basic issues in theory and research*. New York: Wiley.

Talmon-Garber, Y. (1970). *The kibbutz: Sociological studies*. Jerusalem: Magnes Press, Hebrew University.

Wundheiler, L.N. (1985/86). Oskar Schindler's moral development during the Holocaust. *Humboldt Journal of Social Relations 13*, 1–2, 333–56.

Von Cranach, M., and Harré, R. (eds.) (1982). *The analysis of action: Recent theoretical and empirical advances*. Cambridge,: Cambridge University Press.

Yirmiya, Dov (1983). *My War Diary: Lebanon, June 5–July 1, 1982*. Boston: South End Press.

# PART SIX

# PROMOTING ALTRUISTIC BONDS

*Edited by Samuel P. Oliner*

# INTRODUCTION

## Samuel P. Oliner

This section of the book addresses the factors and processes that help promote a more altruistic and caring society. In these introductory remarks, we shall describe the connectedness and the central message contained in the five chapters.

It is clear that each of the chapters deals with the promotion of prosocial behavior and concern for the other. The Oliners address the theoretical concept called extensivity, which was introduced in their book *The Altruistic Personality: Rescuers of Jews in Nazi Europe* (New York: Free Press, 1988). Extensivity implies attachment and commitment to one's family as well as including diverse others and feeling responsible for them. The questions that this chapter raises are, What kind of human beings are more likely to be altruistic? What are some of the major processes that could explain their concern for others and putting the interest of others before their own?

In their study on rescuers of Jews in Nazi-occupied Europe, the Oliners found that rescuers have a propensity to be more attached and committed to people in their relationships, and that they have a propensity to assume obligations and social responsibility for all other human beings, perceiving them as worthy and deserving of help, as well as empathy.

The Oliners offer eight processes that they deem to be helpful in promoting a more altruistic individual. Four processes are related to forming attachment to people in the immediate environment, which include bonding, empathizing, learning caring norms, and participating in caring behavior. And four processes are related to inclusiveness, which involves diversifying, networking, reasoning, and forming global connections. By "bonding," the Oliners mean forming enduring emotional attachment to people and places. These are objects—human and nonhuman—with which individuals feel intensely interconnected, related, affiliated, and identified. "Empathizing" implies understanding others' thoughts and feelings, and in some cases even feeling what others feel. Like bonding, empathy encourages caring behavior, particularly in situations where others are in difficulty or in pain. A more caring society can come about as a result of individuals learning caring norms. Included among these norms are ethical rules and guidelines by which to live. Parents, for example, model caring norms when they treat their children with dignity. In order to effect a more caring society, one should also strongly encourage participation in caring behavior. This means that one should be involved in the processes of helping and develop competencies in order to be able to help. Among these skills, or competencies, should be listening, advocating, caring, and intervening directly on behalf of other people who are in pain. The Oliners suggest that these processes can be inculcated not only by parents and peers, but by schools and various other institutions as well.

The other four processes involve creating linkages, diversifying, networking, reasoning, and making global connections. By "diversifying," the Oliners mean enlarging the group of people and objects with which one ordinarily interacts, eliminating the tendency to divide the world into "us" and "them." "Networking" denotes another way of making linkages to other, broader societies. Unlike diversifying, which is getting to know someone or something different, networking implies joining with others for the purpose of achieving some common goal or objective. By "reasoning," the Oliners mean forming rational solutions to problems based upon logic and empirical evidence, because such solutions have an important role to play in bringing about a more caring society. Making global connections connotes realizing the commonality of all humanity, and becoming aware of the shared problems and issues that concern us. Institutions of higher education have a major part to play in expanding global horizons for people.

Staub's chapter addresses the issues of what makes for a more caring, helping, and nonaggressive society. He suggests that child socialization, cultural values and ideals, moral rules, empathy, and attachment are processes that help develop a better understanding of others, and thereby lead to nonaggression while helping to connect people with each other.

Positive socialization and the experience of parental role models and how they cope with moral issues will affect the prosocial orientation of a child. Staub stresses the importance of warmth, affection, and interaction. Interaction with a child, even if it only lasts for ten minutes at a time, is a vitally important aspect of the development of a prosocial and empathic person. Staub stresses the importance of natural socialization, which consists of a child actually experiencing helping and caring for others. He puts heavy emphasis on child-rearing practices, which are strongly associated with prosocial or antisocial behavior. Connected with this is the development of positive self-identity, and the importance of emotional independence and the capacity for independent judgment. Staub emphasizes the role of the family in raising caring children. The family has to model justice and stress the connectedness with the rest of humanity.

Teachers and schools, however, also have an important role in the moral development of children; they should teach caring skills and give the student the opportunity to help others. Role playing is important in shaping morality. The type of personality that schools will turn out will depend upon its philosophy and its makeup. Schools can turn out authoritarian-type individuals or democratic-type individuals. Children in a democratic school can engage in moral discourse, be able to have a broader view of the world, and be able to take perspective of others more easily, while students who are educated in authoritarian schools will become more rigid, authoritarian-type individuals who may blindly obey malevolent authority.

Staub also addresses the important role that universities have to play. Teaching the subjects of history, sociology, anthropology, art, and literature are important because the student will gain information about diversity and other people's perspectives, views, and ideologies. This would help create a more nonviolent society.

Boland's chapter focuses on two points. He discusses the connection between altruism and benevolence. Then he uses the example of Alcoholics Anonymous as an institution actively engaged in altruistic behavior.

For Boland, altruism is a kind of benevolence that involves moral intuitions and a kind of spirituality. Altruism must be taught because one cannot innately acquire it. Teaching love and sensitivity to children involves risk. One has to stick one's neck out, because sometimes the norms of society are not prepared for such teaching. Some people believe that altruism might even be self-destructive. Caring for someone else may jeopardize one's own survival. Benevolence, for Boland, is a principle of love on a higher order, which may go unrecognized by the other person. A benevolent person seeks the very best for others, regardless of their personal merit or appeal.

Love, caring, understanding the troubles of alcoholics, helping them restore sobriety, creating an interdependent healing power, helping alcoholics to confront the destructiveness of alcoholism, providing the opportunity for self-revelation, and helping alcoholics to stay sober by providing them with a "sponsor," an experienced recovering alcoholic, are some of the methods employed in the teachings of Alcoholics Anonymous.

The Heller and Mahmoudi chapter addresses the issue of the existence of altruism and extensivity in the Bahá'í religion. They call the Bahá'í religion a social movement whose aims are to develop an altruistically oriented, global society. Its members' aim is to transform civilization, but to transform themselves as well as their own social institutions. This is, in essence, the teaching of the Bahá'í faith, which is found in 205 different countries around the world.

The Bahá'í faith, as a matter of course, teaches peace. It is other oriented, and includes all people within its universe of social responsibility. It teaches spirituality, and the recognition that all people of both sexes are equal, as well as that all faiths are of great and equal value. Love, justice, and equality are crucial elements within the Bahá'í faith, and vital to its prosocial orientation is that it is a democratic kind of social movement. Caring and equity are powerful elements of the Bahá'í faith: "Let them at all times concern themselves with doing a kind thing for one of their fellows, offering to someone love, consideration, thoughtful help. Let them see no one as their enemy or as wishing them ill, but think of all human kind as their friend; regarding the alien as an intimate, the stranger as a companion, staying free of prejudices, drawing no lines."

Osiatynski, in his chapter, asks some timely questions dealing with whether a collectivist society such as the USSR is more altruistic than an individualistic society, and whether the current transformation of Soviet society from collectivism to individualism will reduce prosocial orientation in the USSR. He assures us that, in his opinion, we shouldn't be concerned because collectivism was never strongly associated with altruism in the USSR. Rather, he feels that altruism is associated with individualism. In Russia, and later in the Soviet Union, individualism was never encouraged, and it was difficult to transform people so that they act and behave as individuals with free will, personal freedom, and choices. In the balance of the chapter Osiatynski looks at individualism and collectivism and the kind of help rendered to the needy in Russian society. The Russian Orthodox Church is noted for the lack of affirmation of individualism. The church encourages the notion that a person who is in pain, poor, disabled, blind, and even mentally ill must suffer just like Jesus Christ did, and therefore it constitutes a moral obligation for the individual to help those people. This help was regarded as a moral self-improvement for the helper. The duty to help, to take pity, to give charity, was deeply embedded in Russian religious teachings. The Russian concept of altruism was propagated by the philosopher Vladimir Solovyev, who believed that all morality was based on three emotions: shame, pity, and pious adoration. For him, love of God, not of one's fellow man, is the principle of charity. The principle of charity was hence well developed in Russian culture. For Marxism or Leninism, however, there was no place for charity, because for them, charity/altruism was merely a mask for capitalist selfishness and paternalism. The Soviet system was a substitute for charity, pity, philanthropy, and altruism. The new Soviet man or woman, by becoming a member of the Soviet system, no longer had need of charity and altruism, because the Marxist/Leninist system will provide all of their needs—the state will help, care, be concerned, and become responsible for all people. There is no need for paternalism of one group of people towards the other through the degrading action of giving somebody a handout.

More recently, there is a resurgence of charity in the Soviet system, because the population has come to realize that there is a need to help the unfortunate people at the bottom. The author Granin calls for the old-fashioned tradition of pity and "love for the fallen," which was strongly advocated by Pushkin and Sholokhov. The state can no longer be a substitute for individual and private altruism. Since the state could not effect help for "the fallen," Osiatynski feels that only through a successful transformation from collectivism to individualism will there be a foundation laid for individualistic altruism.

In sum, the Oliners and Staub offer empirically derived processes that are correlated with helping. Boland sees the AA as an institution actively engaged in helping victims of alcoholism, Heller and Mahmoudi inform us that the Bahá'í faith encourages the ethic of care and responsibility for all, and Osiatynski claims that only when the USSR can instill individualism in the Soviet person, with free will and the possibility of choices, will altruism take shape in the USSR.

# 16

# PROMOTING EXTENSIVE ALTRUISTIC BONDS: A CONCEPTUAL ELABORATION AND SOME PRAGMATIC IMPLICATIONS

*Pearl M. Oliner and Samuel P. Oliner*

Since the publication of our study of rescuers of Jews during the Holocaust (Oliner and Oliner 1988), we have had the opportunity to discuss our findings with many groups. Almost inevitably, we are confronted with questions regarding its practical implications. What people want to know is what they can do to promote a more caring society. This chapter is an attempt to suggest some parameters for promoting altruism in society at large.

The phenomenon of rescue provides a particularly rich source for inducing such parameters because of its nature and scope. Rescue was not only an altruistic behavior but also an example of heroic altruism. Whereas altruistic behaviors generally involve some costs, rescuers risked their lives, and frequently those of their families as well. Moreover, whereas altruistic behavior on behalf of one's own group is not uncommon, rescue behavior was directed toward *outsiders*, a religiously and ethnically different group. Non-Jewish rescuers of Jews were but a fraction of the total population under Nazi occupation; their behaviors thus suggest an uncommon commitment that transcended group loyalties. But a deep commitment to altruism and a broadly inclusive one among large numbers of the global population may well be necessary for planetary survival.

The parameters for our proposal are rooted in a basic concept, which we call extensivity. We begin by explaining this concept and its evolution as suggested by the theoretical and empirical work of others, and describe its empirical basis as it emerged from our study of rescuers. We then suggest its usefulness by applying it as the central focus for eight social processes that we deem essential for promoting extensive altruistic behaviors in diverse social institutions.

## EXTENSIVITY: A CONCEPTUAL ELABORATION

As we define it, *extensivity* means the tendency to assume commitments and responsibilities toward diverse groups of people. Extensivity includes two elements: the propensity to *attach* oneself to others in committed interpersonal relationships; and the propensity toward *inclusiveness* with respect to the diversity of individuals and groups to whom one will assume obligations.

The construct *attachment* is perhaps most familiar in the context that John Bowlby (1969) used and developed it. Based on his observations of infant-mother relationships, Bowlby concluded that the desire for proximity was a compelling drive among infants, and the ways mothers responded to this need became the prototype for all subsequent human relationships. Further research has amplified as well as modified some of Bowlby's conclusions. Ainsworth (1967), for example, distinguished between securely and nonsecurely attached children, while yet others have concluded that Bowlby may have exaggerated the importance of the mother as an attachment figure, and that others, including fathers, other relatives, and even strangers could serve this purpose (Schaffer and Emerson 1964). What this research nonetheless shares in common is the assumption that attachment to some figure in infancy and early childhood is essential for healthy development. A sustained connectedness with an adult figure who provides security and stability in responding to children's needs presumably shapes fundamental conceptions about trust and nontrust, self and other, relationships and autonomy.

That the need for attachment may be a life-long issue has been proposed by developmentalists in particular, although the concept of attachment is variously labeled. *Communion* is the term that Bakan (1966) used to describe connectedness with others; he argues that it, along with *agency* or individuation, is fundamental to all human experience. Kegan (1982) terms it *subject* relations—embeddedness in the other or joining of the self with the other—which he views as one of the two ongoing processes of *making meaning* throughout life (the other, *object* relations, involves disembedded-ness and separation.) Chodorow (1974) as well as Carlson (1972) and Gilligan (1982) have emphasized that while interconnected-ness and social relationships are fundamental maturity needs in both males and females, interconnectedness is more commonly the modality of women.

Most commonly, the word *attachment* implies interpersonal con-nectedness—that is, a sense of relationship with known others. The term is also generally used to suggest an intense form of interper-sonal connectedness, reserved only for very special relationships. In this sense, it is conceived as a dichotomous state; one either has it or one does not. As we conceive it, however, attachment is a dimension—that is, a sense of interpersonal connectedness that ranges in intensities, from love at one pole to alienation (extreme detachment) at the other. In between is a broad continuum reflect-ing varying intensities of attachment and detachment.

No single extant social science concept captures the notion of inclusiveness—that is, broad-ranging interconnectedness—al-though it is sometimes implied by the word *extensive*. For example, Sorokin (1954) used *extensity* to describe one of the five dimensions of love. Love, he noted, can be confined to self or one other person, or range as far as the love of the whole universe, including all living creatures. Between these polarities, said Sorokin, "lies a vast scale of extensities: love of one's family, or a few friends, or love of all the groups one belongs to—one's clan, tribe, nationality, nation, religious, occupational, political, and other group and associa-tions" (16). Epstein (1980) uses the term *extensive* to describe per-sonal theories of reality that are broad and wide ranging. While all people construct personal theories to structure their experiences and to direct their lives, says Epstein, individuals with *extensive* personal theories can accommodate and integrate new and diverse experiences without threat; individuals with narrow self-theories are rigid, defensive, and intolerant of differences.

However, the term *extensive* is sometimes also used to imply attachment—that is, intense interpersonal connectedness—with-out regard to breadth. This meaning is implied by some self-concept theorists, among whom the concept of *self* and *other* are particular concerns.

Common notions of the self imply ego boundaries, so that self and others are distinct (Perloff 1987; Waterman 1981). Individu-alism is commonly associated with firm ego boundaries, so that the sense of self in effect "stops at one's skin and clearly demarks self from nonself" (Spence 1985, 1288). Self-concept theorists have not been entirely persuaded by this notion of ego boundedness. Rather than bounded, some perceive the ego as mutable and fluid, expanding and contracting in the course of experience. This fluid, mutable self incorporates new external elements into it, while extruding others. *Ego extensions* is the term Rosenberg and Kaplan (1982) say is most commonly assigned to those external elements that are experienced as part of the self. As Rosenberg and Kaplan imply, extension in this sense implies an intense attachment, for as they explain it, external elements of this type are experienced as part of the self and defended with as much vigor as the self itself. Although they refrain from using the term, *love* seems an apt description of such an intense relationship.

Others, however, allow for varying intensities of ego extensions in which care for others may not be congruent with the total self proper. Reykowski (1984), for example, expresses the latter idea in the term *psychological proximity*, which includes a range of closeness to the self. The more psychologically proximate others are perceived to be, says Reykowski, the greater the likelihood that they will be treated similarly to the self. In this sense, the self appears to remain intact and bounded. Although capable of extending the self to assign varying degrees of value to others whom one recognizes as like the self, one does not quite experience the other as an actual part of the self.

As we define it, *inclusiveness* refers to the *breadth* of interpersonal connectedness feelings. Like attachment, it, too, is a dimension. As we conceptualize it, it is a dimension ranging from feelings of connection to the universe at one pole, to the exclusion of all others except the self at the other. In between is a broad continuum reflecting varying individuals and groups.

In view of the fact that no existing construct appears to characterize the propensity for both interpersonal attachments and inclusive connectedness, we propose the term *extensive* not only as a way of addressing this omission, but also because attachment and inclusiveness appear to be conceptually related.

Both attachment and inclusiveness imply ego extension: a propensity toward assuming committed responsibilities that differ only in the degree and breadth or range of persons to whom one accepts obligations. Proponents of the bounded self concept perceive such relationships emerging from autonomous and independent selves who may rationally conclude that self-interest is best served by recognizing the mutual interests of other selves. Proponents of the fluid self concept contend that the self emerges and is defined in relationships, so that the self includes the interests of others. Implicit in both these orientations is the notion of extending onself—reaching out, including and integrating others—although the underlying theoretical mechanisms that explain them differ.

As *extensivity* implies reaching out and integrating, *constrictedness* implies contracting and separating. As *extensivity* implies attachment and inclusiveness, *constrictedness* implies detachment and exclusiveness. *Detachment* implies a propensity to avoid committed and responsible interpersonal relationships, to remain apart and distant from others. This does not necessarily imply dehumanization of the other; it need not be based on ethnocentric views. Rather, detachment reflects a sense of boundedness in which the self is not only distinct from others but is also not bound to others in relationships of obligation. Avoidance of commitments is one of the hallmarks of detachment; at its extreme it becomes alienation, so that external objects generally—perhaps including even the self itself—are experienced as meaningless and without value.

Whereas *detachment* implies a general tendency to remain apart and separate from others, *exclusiveness* implies the deliberate expulsion of particular individuals or groups from consideration. Exclusive people may, however, feel strong attachments to particular people or groups. Exclusion may result from centration on self or selected others (such as one's family, religious or national group) so that *outsiders* are remote objects at best. Exclusion may also be the consequence of ethnocentrism and pseudospeciation, in which outsiders are viewed as inherently inferior. At its extreme, outsiders can be dehumanized.

*Extensivity* thus implies two dimensions: the attachment dimension, which ranges from alienation or extreme detachment at one pole to love at the other; and the inclusiveness dimension, which ranges from exclusion of all others except the self at one pole to the inclusion of the universe at the other. In between each pole is a broad continuum reflecting varying intensities of detachment and attachment, and varying degrees of inclusiveness. Yet another way to conceptualize extensivity is to say that it is a personality orientation that is rooted both in the particular and the general.

Conceptualizing extensivity as a two-dimensional continuum allows us to better understand the responses of nonrescuers as well as rescuers. Several nonrescuers were highly attached people, who were quite capable of altruistic behaviors on behalf of their families, church groups, or nation, but who nonetheless shut their doors in the face of supplicant Jews. Other nonrescuers were more detached generally; they felt little in the way of obligations to people of any kind and were unlikely to perform altruistic acts on behalf of any others. In the latter case, it was not so much a matter of excluding Jews as it was a general sense of remoteness from others.

Highlighting this distinction also helps explain why inclusive people, such as those who are intent on saving humankind, may nonetheless inflict great cruelties on individuals. Because of their disconnection from real people, who may cloud their vision or limit their options, they may become inured to the suffering of those around them. Billig's (1985) compelling account of terrorist Horst Mahler, cofounder of the Red Army Faction, suggests the evolution of an individual who, initially motivated to save the world, progressed to distinguishing between *them* (those outside the revolutionary circle) and *us*, finally becoming indifferent to the "us" as well. What this suggests is that unless tempered by the other, either propensity alone carries the seeds of its own social pathology: one denying obligations to others besides one's own, the other denying obligations to particular individuals or groups in the name of a transcendent ideal.

## THE EMPIRICAL BASIS OF THE CONCEPT "EXTENSIVITY"

The empirical basis for the concept *extensivity* was derived from a summary factor analysis of approximately 150 single variables or items we measured in our study of rescuers and nonrescuers.

Survey questions were grouped into topics and twenty-seven summary variables were constructed through selection, summation, and factor analysis of the items within the topic groupings. (See Oliner and Oliner 1988, 313–18, for the definition of each variable and how it was derived.) These twenty-seven summarizing variables were the basis for yet another factor analysis, which upon completion arranged the variables into four major orthogonal factors. Based upon the themes common to the variables that loaded highly on each factor, the factors were labeled Family Attachments, Jewish Friends, Broad Social Commitments, and Egalitarianism.

What do these factors signify? As we interpreted it, the first two major factors—Family Attachments and Jewish Friends—indicate strong attachments to people in the immediate environment: in one case to families of origin, in the other to friends. The third and fourth major factors—Broad Social Commitments and Egalitarianism—are more abstract and depersonalized. They suggest a linkage to a more generalized *other:* in one case, a sense of responsibility toward society at large, in the other a perception of a shared common humanity.

With respect to these four major factors, rescuers scored significantly higher on each than did the comparison sample of nonrescuers. Thus, rescuers scored significantly higher than nonrescuers on degree of family attachment, Jewish friendships, broad social commitments, and egalitarianism. More importantly, more rescuers scored highly on at least two factors: one that indicated *a strong attachment to the people in their immediate environment, as well as one that indicated a linkage to the broader world.* In short, these data appear to support the idea that rescuers, as compared with nonrescuers, were more likely to be extensive people.

## PROMOTING EXTENSIVE ALTRUISTIC BONDS IN SOCIETY

If an extensive orientation promotes altruistic behavior, what types of specific experiences might promote it? In the following, we propose a conceptual scheme that we believe synthesizes many of the experiences proposed by others as conducive to altruistic behavior specifically, as well as several others not yet so identified but that we believe are also likely to encourage it. The value of this schematic framework, we believe, lies in its potential applicability as a conceptual lens through which social institutions can be analyzed for the purpose of modifying or reinforcing current practices, or adding new ones.

Basing our framework on the concept of extensivity, we propose eight social processes that we believe can promote inclusive altruistic propensities. Four of these processes—bonding, empathizing, learning caring norms, and participating in caring behaviors—relate to forming attachments and a sense of obligation to others in the immediate environment. The remaining four—diversifying, networking, developing problem-solving strategies, and forming global connections—relate to making inclusive linkages to diverse groups in the broader society. Before we proceed to a description of these processes, and their potential applicability in varied social institutions, some underlying assumptions need to be addressed.

We presume that more consistent and stable expressions of extensive altruism depend on cumulative experiences interacting with evolving internal structures. Rather than being dependent on one type of social experience alone—such as bonding, empathy, or learning caring norms—we presume that extensive altruistic propensities are enhanced through various means and are reinforced to the extent that they are incrementally supported. While it is likely that some such experiences may be more important than others with respect to particular individuals or groups, our schematic framework is nonetheless an additive one.

While it is also probable that each process influences the other—bonding, for example, may encourage empathic feelings as well as receptivity to learning caring norms—their linkages are not certain. Since several of these processes have been directly and specifically associated with altruistic propensities, they warrant special attention. Since bonding, empathy, and caring norms can be restricted to particular groups only, we presume that they are more likely to be associated with an inclusive orientation if experiences directly address inclusiveness rather than rely on assumed extensions.

We further presume that an extensive altruistic orientation is primarily the product of nonrational processes, in which rationality plays but a secondary role. Whereas rationality implies logical reasoning and empirical justifications, nonrational behaviors are acquired in the context of cultural expectations interacting with personal proclivities, neither of which have necessarily been subjected to reasoning processes (Etzioni 1988). While rationality has a role to play in promoting an extensive altruistic orientation, it is most likely to resonate among people predisposed to use reason either because of personal preference or because of the nature of the culture with which they identify. Hence, the processes we emphasize do not exclude rationality, but include it as only one process among many others.

Our focus on multiple social institutions, rather than the family alone, stems from considerations regarding the age during which an extensive altruistic orientation is most likely to be acquired and the social contexts in which people spend most of their lives. While not denying the influence of later experiences, social psychologists have tended to emphasize early childhood as the shaping crucible for adult attitudes and behaviors. While early childhood experience strongly influences basic orientations toward life, its primacy is no longer universally accepted. Life-span researchers, such as Baltes and Reese (1984) suggest that each stage of life is accompanied by important developmental changes, and that no single period in the life cycle is more critical than another. Changes are associated with internal processes as well as external social role, task, and age expectations. We assume that the capacity for altruism is no exception. As Krebs and Van Hesteren propose (this volume), higher-stage altruism is dependent on the evolution of internal developmental capacities, themselves associated with age interacting with experiences. While some predisposition toward altruism is likely to be acquired in early childhood, we assume that experiences at all stages of the life cycle can either facilitate or inhibit it.

Related to the above is our assumption regarding the contexts in which encouraging experiences need to occur. Families— whether families of origin or acquired—continue to be one critical social institution for such encouragement. Families, however, are neither uniformly equipped nor uniformly inclined to promote an altruistic orientation toward others. Moreover, people spend large percentages of their time in social institutions other than families, and unmarried working people in particular frequently live alone and without access to families (Yankelovich 1982; Ludeman 1989). If peer groups, schools, religious or ethnic groups, and the workplace fail to provide experiences conducive to an extensive altruistic orientation, then even already-predisposed individuals may be threatened with losing it. When family beginnings are less than benevolent, the need for other institutions to provide such encouraging experiences increases. We thus assume that people are most likely to develop an extensive orientation toward others if the institutions in which they live most of their lives support it.

Finally, we assume that all social institutions—including the workplace—have the potential for encouraging the above processes without forfeiting other primary goals. In fact, examples of these social processes already exist in embryonic form in all types of social institutions, and many theorists argue that implementation of these processes may be essential not only for our mutual survival, but also to promote other primary institutional goals. Families are frequently presumed to contain the optimal opportunities for promoting experiences conducive to altruism, because such experiences do not necessarily conflict with other primary functions families are required to perform, such as maintenance and support of family members and the socialization of children into the larger society. Conversely, the economic sector in a capitalist society is presumed to be among those social institutions least conducive to altruism, because altruistic activity conflicts with its primary function, which is to maximize profits. Neither position, however, is necessarily the case. Impoverished and overburdened families, for example, may find maintenance and support functions overriding. Conversely, not all businesses, even in a capitalist society, are oriented exclusively toward maximum profits—some forego maximization in favor of social responsibility norms, for example. What this suggests is that social institutions, including the family, vary greatly with respect to their perceived constraints and opportunities for promoting experiences conducive to an extensive altruistic orientation.

Whether the processes we identify are sufficient to promote altruistic behavior under extreme circumstances—when the lives of self and others are jeopardized—is a matter not yet resolved. Evidence from our study of rescuers suggests that they increase the probability of altruistic behavior even under conditions of extreme terror. Whether they are sufficient to promote the development of the "ideal altruistic personality" type proposed by Krebs and Van Hesteren (this volume) is a matter of conjecture. As Smolenska and Reykowski propose (this volume), the motivation for rescue was essentially of three types, of which only one—the axiological—appears to approximate the highest level of altruistic development. According to that framework, most rescuers appeared to be motivated normocentrically or empathically, rather than axiologically (Oliner and Oliner 1988). While it may be the case that the highest level of altruistic development is more conducive to stable and more qualitative forms of altruism, such evidence suggests that the voluntary readiness to jeopardize life and limb for others does not depend on it.

**THE SOCIAL PROCESSES**

With the above assumptions in mind, we now proceed to a brief description of each of the above processes and its potential applicability in diverse social institutions, with particular emphasis on the family, education, and the workplace. (A more elaborate description of these processes and their application to varied settings in book length is in preparation.)

*Bonding* means forming enduring emotional attachments to people and places: those objects, human and nonhuman, with which individuals feel so intensely interconnected, related, affiliated, and identified that should they become transformed or even disappear, they remain ever real and present in their internal world. While the impact of bonding to place in relation to interpersonal relationships has not been studied, interpersonal bonding is often associated with a number of psychological characteristics presumably more conducive to altruism, including trust, optimism, and competence (Lieberman 1977; Ainsworth 1979; Sroufe 1979; Main and Weston 1981). Infancy is generally regarded as the critical period for bonding to occur. Egocentrism and excessive feelings of neediness are associated with those who fail to form satisfactory bonds during this period (Bowlby 1969; Rutter 1979; Shengold 1989).

But bonding can also occur in other contexts. Teachers, parents, and students can develop deep and sustaining relationships with their schools and colleagues, for example (Lightfoot 1983). The same is true for the workplace. Before divestiture, AT & T, for example, was almost uniformly described as a strongly bonded cultural institution (Tunstall 1985). The attitudes and behaviors of people in such environments are distinctly different from those in which bonding has not occurred.

Bonding environments, we propose, share some generic qualities. They stimulate, provide comfort and play opportunities, and, while also providing a net of safety and security, affirm individuality and autonomy as well. Without the latter, such environments risk engulfment and smothering—and as argued by many (see Osiatynski; Krebs and Van Hesteren, this volume), autonomy is essential for altruism. Bonding environments thus provide a sense of a "connected identity," a concept proposed by Staub (this volume), implying an independent self that is nonetheless connected with others.

The second process, *empathizing,* means understanding others' thoughts and feelings and feeling with them. (For varied definitions of *empathy,* see Eisenberg and Mussen 1989; Feshbach 1982; Batson 1987; Wispé 1986.) Empathy has been highlighted by several researchers as significantly associated with altruism (Eisenberg and Mussen 1989; Kohn 1990). Batson in particular regards empathy as the critical component for promoting altruistic behavior (Batson 1987). Empathic feelings, particularly for others' pain, were significantly associated with rescuers as compared with nonrescuers.

While several philosophers as well as contemporary psychologists believe that people may be born with some inherent potential for empathy, most of the latter agree that empathy is a product of development and experience. A number of studies suggest some generic experiences that encourage empathy. Among these, clarifying one's own values and feelings and having opportunities for taking the perspective of others (including interpreting others' feelings and thoughts as well as role playing) are frequently highlighted. The importance of the first process is emphasized in particular by Jarymowicz (this volume), who found that individuals who were more aware of their self-distinctiveness were more likely to respond to others on others' own terms (exocentric responsiveness). Although perspective taking is generally perceived as a cognitive endeavor that can be used for self-serving purposes as well as prosocial ones, studies suggest that its enhancement is frequently associated with the enhancement of prosocial behaviors (Feshbach 1979; Chandler 1973).

Environments that promote empathy encourage both clarification of one's own feelings and perspective taking. The initial motivation to engage in such processes may be self-enhancement, effectiveness, or mutual survival. In families as well as other social institutions, participants can be encouraged to develop empathic skills for the purpose of more effective communication and collegiality. As E. Wight Bakke (1946) observed more than forty years ago, until both labor and management recognized their mutual survival needs and understood each others' tasks and responsibilities, conflict was inevitable. But once a cognitive perspective-taking mode is adopted, the opportunity for affective arousal increases. Teachers, clerics, or managers, for example, who first are persuaded to develop perspective-taking skills for instrumental purposes—to achieve better ratings from supervisors or to be better liked—may eventually become concerned with their clients as ends unto themselves.

*Caring norms*—including rules, values, and principles—express expectations regarding appropriate helping behaviors. (Although scholars frequently distinguish among these terms, for our purposes, it is sufficient to note that values and principles are generally considered to be more abstract and less prescriptive than norms, with rules being the most concrete and specific of all.) Some theorists propose that norms serve as self-monitoring devices with regard to selected behaviors (Von Cranach et al. 1982), particularly when such norms are internalized (Schwartz and Howard 1984). Several psychologists view norms as values that people internalize sometime during the process of socialization and development (Staub 1978; Eisenberg 1986; Hoffman 1977).

Norms are communicated implicitly and explicitly through oral and written language, goals, myths, stories, codes of conduct, and models. Words like *love* and *care*, sometimes used in the educational context, and *social responsibility*, increasingly used in the business sector, suggest altruistic normative expectations. Myths and stories—about individuals or groups—as well as codes of conduct communicate cultural ideals. In the religious context, norms are commonly communicated through "sacred" texts: the sacred texts of the Bahá'ís, for example, encompass many extensive altruistic norms (see Heller and Mahmoudi, this volume.) In some schools and businesses, written codes of conduct prescribe caring norms (D. Solomon et al. 1990; Johnson and Johnson's Credo in Smith and Tedlow 1989; Norton Company in Weber 1990). In some schools as well as businesses, principals and chief executives are heralded as exemplars of caring models. They not only advocate policies with due consideration for their positive impact on others, and not only behave concordantly themselves, but also reward others for similar behaviors.

While some evidence suggests that learned values and norms—particularly when internalized—influence behavior, other evidence suggests that values and norms may follow rather than precede behavior. Regardless of its origin, the importance of actually *participating in altruistic behaviors* has been demonstrated by "foot in the door" research. People who do a small favor first are more likely to do a larger one subsequently and are more likely to continue doing them in varied circumstances (Freeman and Fraser 1966; Beaman et al. 1983; Staub, this volume)

Participation can range from reasonably low-cost behaviors, such as listening and supportive interchanges (Goffman 1971), to more costly behaviors, such as advocacy, protest, whistle blowing, and resistance. Low-cost prosocial behaviors are perceived as beneficial in many social institutions—teachers as well as business employees are frequently exhorted to become good listeners as well as engage in supportive social interactions. Some schools and businesses provide internal mechanisms to deal with conditions leading to protest and whistle blowing (Ewing 1981).

Participation encourages the assumption of personal responsibility for the welfare of others. While external expectations—of superordinates as well as peers—encourage the assumption of personal responsibility, the latter appears more likely to occur when individuals help contribute to the shaping of expectations and are encouraged to reflect on them. Such practices are evident in some schools—where students and teachers, as well as parents, are invited to create rules—as well as in a few businesses where employees have been charged with making policy with respect to such matters as product quality, confidentiality, and responsibility toward the homeless and the environment (e.g., Norwest Banking under CEO John W. Morrison and Vice President for Social and Policy Program Doug Wallace, interviewed by Freudberg 1986).

However much the above processes help integrate groups, they are not sufficient. While they help create caring communities among individuals who interact on face-to-face levels, they do not necessarily link such groups to the larger society. The larger society is no longer merely the local, state, or even the national community, but rather the globe and the ecosphere. Hence we propose the following as a means toward forming inclusive attachments.

*Diversifying,* as we define it, means enlarging the groups of people and objects with whom people normally interact for the primary purpose of promoting positive social relationships. Evidence suggests that people are more likely to engage in altruistic behaviors on behalf of known rather than unknown others, particularly if such known others are perceived as more similar to than different from the self. They are more likely to perceive others as similar under conditions that support the reduction of negative stereotypes and the promotion of positive interactions.

Learning *about* other groups is one means of diversifying one's orientation. Such learning is likely to be most beneficial if it encompasses both those characteristics that indicate a shared humanity as well as those conditions or characteristics that render the group distinct. As Blum and Seidler propose (this volume), it is not sufficient that people view others as part of a universal humankind; they must learn to prize others in their distinctiveness. Learning about other groups also implies viewing them not only from the perspective of one's own group, but from that group's perspective as well. Hence, learning about other ethnic groups provides opportunities to see commonalities and distinctions viewed from the perspective of one's own ethnicity as well as others'. The same principle can be applied in relation to businesses and consumer groups, for example, as well as to teachers and parents.

Diversifying also means having actual experiences with others different from the self, under conditions suggested by Allport's contact hypothesis—intensive *equal status* interactions (Allport 1954). While such contacts do not necessarily lead to diminution of group stereotyping (Brewer and Miller 1988), evidence suggests that it can succeed in promoting respect among individuals, even when the latter may have been highly prejudiced at the outset (Cook 1984, 1985). In the context of families, schools, the neighborhood, or the workplace, contacts may include such activities as sharing holidays and festivities with diverse others, as well as equal opportunities for listening to them and learning from them.

Equally important for diversifying are opportunities to learn about and have experiences with the nonhuman world—animals and plants, as well as rocks, streams, and lakes. As with diverse other humans, such learning and experiences need to emphasize relationships *with* rather than exploitation of our natural environment, living and nonliving.

Like diversifying, *networking* is another way for making linkages to the broader society. However, whereas the purpose of diversifying is merely to promote positive social relationships, the purpose of networking is to cooperate with diverse others in pursuit of some shared goal. Rather than maintaining boundaries, networking widens points of cooperation and builds coalitions among diverse groups.

Pursuit of a shared goal is an essential feature of Allport's contact hypothesis, and several experimental studies demonstrate that when it occurs, respect and empathy across groups increases. The jigsaw method, for example, devised by Aronson et al. (1978), as a teaching technique, has been demonstrated to cause such effects in diverse classrooms, including those marked by high racial tension (Aronson and Yates 1983; Blaney et al. 1977; Geffner 1978).

Networkers address a shared goal or problem in which all have a stake. Self-help groups, such as Alcoholics Anonymous (Dan Boland, this volume), are one type of networking group created to focus on a shared problem and provide mutual support. Rather than confront each other as adversaries, businesses can cooperate with consumers and environmental groups, for example, for the purpose of creating beneficial and nonpolluting products. Businesses, parents, teachers, and students sometimes cooperate for the purpose of improving teaching and learning relating to work skills. The opportunities for coalition building are as diverse as the visions of varied groups.

Cooperating requires perceiving others as part of the solution rather than the problem; hence the need for *developing shared problem-solving strategies.* Among other things, this requires concentrating on common positive goals and outcomes, and using skills relating to negotiation and conflict resolution.

One such skill is reasoning: finding rational solutions to problems on the basis of logic and empirical evidence. Prosocial reasoning uses such processes in the service of prosocial goals. As Van Hesteren (this volume) observes, an individual with an altruistic personality is a *knower:* one who is able to compare and organize information and construct concepts. Such abilities are particularly helpful in public arenas when diverse groups plan together and consider their mutual obligations to remedy some shared problem. Facts, inductive and deductive reasoning, and probability calculations can help resolve diverse points of view and conflicts. Planned procedures and policies can be evaluated with respect to such matters as justice and care.

Through modeling, listening, and reflecting, parents and teachers can help children to develop their reasoning skills and to apply them to social issues. Schools can invite students to examine public issues with respect to considerations of justice and care. Many colleges and universities now include courses in ethics in fields as diverse as marketing, forestry, and biology. Among some religious groups, ecumenical dialogue has resulted in reconceptions of prevailing religious caring and justice norms (Rubenstein and Roth 1987).

Other skills relate to resolutions of conflict through negotiation and arbitration in which peace and harmony, rather than justice or care, are the prevailing objectives. In such cases, both parties need to be persuaded that they have something palpable to gain from the resolution.

*Making global connections* implies learning to link the "here-and-now" with the global-ecospheric nature of life. It is the most encompassing process of the inclusive dimension, for it implies extending altruistic considerations to all elements of the cosmos—human and nonhuman, living and nonliving. While reasoning can help promote universal principles of fairness and care, making the global connection depends on many nonrational processes. The immediate objective in this process is to promote the recognition that the cosmos is an interrelated whole, and that small routine behaviors—whether acts of aggression or care, whether environmentally destructive or enhancing—have wide-ranging effects and are inextricably and mutually linked.

The affective dimension—the willingness to attend to global matters—is frequently born of pragmatic self-interest based on the recognition of global interdependence. Two issues appear to dominate in such mutual recognition: the avoidance of war and the avoidance of environmental disaster; of them, the latter may be more compelling as a collective interest.

While the relationship between interest in global affairs and altruism is not clear, it appears likely that those who are altruistically predisposed on the local level will incline to extend this orientation globally to the extent that their experiences are global in nature. In the family, children can be introduced early to cultures around the world through stories, songs, and personal acquaintances. The concentration on Western European cultures, common to many world history courses, needs to be modified so as to include a balanced perspective of other cultural regions. More emphasis needs to be given to understanding such cultures on their own terms. Student exchange programs, as well as letter and telecommunication exchanges, need to be vigorously encouraged. The multinational and transnational context of many businesses is forcing some to reconsider old assumptions about efficacy and long-term survival and to expand the notion of social responsibility. Discussion of the international context needs to increase in business training textbooks and seminars.

Globalization, however, cannot remain the province of specialized individuals with enlightened views. The linkages between small local behaviors in the contexts of habitual living in families, schools, the workplace, and the world need to be made routinely relevant, whether in respect to energy consumption or in respect to the promotion of peace.

It is in the global context that Americans, as well as affluent other nations, will be called upon to act altruistically—giving up and sharing some of their resources and consumption patterns in favor of the less privileged and in consideration of future generations. However, this view of altruism is a limited one. As Osiatynski argues (this volume), caring for others in the sense of sharing resources alone perpetuates dependency and resentment, often accompanied by higher expectations. As we conceive it, altruism also implies empowerment—helping others to care for themselves as well as for others. It is only through empowering others that they can be helped to overcome their sense of helplessness and preserve their sense of dignity. It is also the means toward overcoming hierarchical relationships based on dominance in favor of partnerships and collegiality.

While the above is meant to be but a sketch of the social processes we propose as conducive toward development of an extensive altruistic orientation, it nonetheless suggests an analytic framework for examining a variety of social institutions. As a pragmatic tool, it can serve as a means for proposing modifications as necessary. Thus, for example, while many schools require students to learn about diverse cultures and world history, they do far less with respect to forming intragroup attachments at the school site, particularly at the high school and university level. Conversely, some businesses manage to create coherent communities in which participants become strongly attached, but fail to address constituencies outside it.

As Durkheim proposed years ago, altruism is no mere ornament to social life, but its fundamental basis (Durkheim in Bellah 1973). If Durkheim was correct, then global social life will need to be predicated on altruistic values. If the concept of a *global community* is to have meaning for people at large, then it behooves all our social institutions to provide the experiential base upon which altruism rests. We believe the above processes can help move us in that direction and that all social institutions have the potential to include more of them in their routine activities.

## REFERENCES

Ainsworth, M. D. S. (1979). Infant-mother attachment, *American Psychologist* 34, 932–37.

—— (1967). *Infancy in Uganda: Infant care and the growth of attachment.* Baltimore, MD: Johns Hopkins University Press.

Allport, G. (1954). *The nature of prejudice.* Reading, MA: Addison-Wesley.

Aronson, E., Blaney, N., Sikes, J., Blaney, N., and Snapp, M. (1978). *The jigsaw classroom.* Beverly Hills, CA: Sage.

Aronson E., and Yates, S. (1983). Cooperation in the classroom: The impact of the jigsaw method on inter-ethnic relations, classroom performance, and self-esteem. In H. Blumberg and P. Hare (Eds.), *Small groups.* London: Wiley.

Bakan, D. (1966). *The duality of human existence: Isolation and communion in Western man.* Boston: Beacon.

Bakke, E. W. (1946). *Mutual survival: The goal of unions and management.* New York: Harper and Row.

Baltes, P. B., and Reese, H. W. (1984). "The life-span perspective in developmental psychology." In Marc H. Bornstein and Michael E. Lamb (Ed.), *Developmental psychology: An advanced textbook.* Hillsdale, NJ: Erlbaum, 493–532.

Batson, C. D. (1987). Prosocial motivation: Is it ever truly altruistic? In L. Berkowitz (Ed.), *Advances in experimental social psychology.* New York: Academic Press, 65–122.

Beaman, A. L., Cole, C. M., Preston, M., Klentz, B., and Steblay, N. M. (1983). Fifteen years of foot-in-the door research: A meta-analysis, *Personality and Social Psychology Bulletin* 9, 181–96.

Bellah, R. N. (Ed.) (1973). *Emile Durkheim: On morality and society.* Chicago: University of Chicago Press.

Billig, O. (1985). The lawyer terrorist and his comrades, *Political Psychology* 6, 29–46.

Blaney, N. T., Stephan, C., Rosenfeld, D., Aronson, E., and Sikes, J. (1977). Interdependence in the classroom: A field study, *Journal of Educational Psychology* 69, 139–46.

Bowlby, J. (1969). *Attachment and loss* (Vol. 1). New York: Basic.

Brewer, M. B., and Miller, N. (1988). Contact and cooperation: When do they work? In P. A. Katz and D. A. Taylor (Eds.), *Eliminating racism: Profiles in controversy.* New York: Plenum, 315–26.

Carlson, R. (1972). Understanding women: Implications for personality theory and research, *Journal of Social Issues* 28, 17–32.

Chandler, M. J. (1973). Egocentrism and antisocial behavior: The assessment and training of social perspective-taking skills, *Developmental Psychology* 9, 321–32.

Chodorow, N. (1974). Family structure and feminine personality. In M. Z. Rosaldo and L. Lamphere (Eds.), *Women, culture, and society.* Stanford, CA: Stanford University Press, 43–66.

Cook, S. W. (1985). Experimenting on social issues: The case of school desegregation, *American Psychologist* 40, 452–60.

—— (1984). Cooperative interaction in multiethnic contexts. In N. Miller and M. Brewer (Eds.), *Groups in contact: The psychology of desegregation.* New York: Academic Press.

Eisenberg, N. (1986). *Altruistic emotion, cognition, and behavior.* Hillsdale, NJ: Erlbaum.

Eisenberg, N., and Mussen, P. (1989). *The roots of prosocial behavior in children.* New York: Cambridge University Press.

Epstein, I. (1980). The self-concept: A review and the proposal of an integrated theory of personality. In E. Staub (Ed.), *Personality: Basic aspects and current research.* Englewood Cliffs, NJ: Prentice Hall.

Etzioni, A. (1988). *The moral dimension: Toward a new economics.* New York: Free Press.

Ewing, D. (1981). Constitutionalizing the corporation. In T. Bradshaw and D. Vogel (Eds.), *Corporations and their critics.* New York: McGraw Hill, 235–68.

Feshbach, N. D. (1982). Sex differences in empathy and social behavior in children. In N. Eisenberg (Ed.), *The development of prosocial behavior.* New York: Academic Press.

————— (1979). Empathy training: A field study in affective education. In S. Feshbach and A. Fraczek (Eds.), *Aggression and behavior change: Biological and social processes.* New York: Praeger.

Freeman, J. L., and Fraser, S. C. (1966). Compliance without pressure: The foot-in-the-door technique, *Journal of Personality and Social Psychology* 4, 195–202.

Freudberg, D. (1986). *The corporate conscience: Money, power, and responsible business.* New York: AMACOM (American Management Association).

Geffner, R. A. (1978). The effects of interdependent learning on self-esteem, inter-ethnic relations, and intra-ethnic attitudes of elementary school children: A field experiment. Doctoral dissertation, University of California, Santa Cruz.

Gilligan, C. (1982). *In a different voice: Psychological theory and women's development.* Cambridge, MA: Harvard University Press.

Goffman, E. (1971). *Relations in public: Microstudies of the public order.* New York: Harper and Row.

Hoffman, M. L. (1977). Moral internalization: Current theory and research. In L. Berkowitz (Ed.), *Advances in experimental social psychology* (Vol. 10). New York: Academic Press.

Kegan, R. (1982). *The evolving self: Problem and process in human development.* Cambridge, MA: Harvard University Press.

Kohn, A. (1990). *The brighter side of human nature.* New York: Basic.

Lieberman, A. F. (1977). Preschoolers' competence with a peer: Relations with attachment and peer experience, *Child Development* 48, 1277–87.

Lightfoot, S. L. (1983). *The good high school: Portraits of character and culture.* New York: Basic.

Ludeman, K. (1989). *The worth ethic: How to profit from the changing values of the new work force.* New York: Dutton.

Main, M., and Weston, D. R. (1981). The quality of the toddler's relationship to mother and to father: Related to conflict behavior and the readiness to establish new relationships, *Child Development* 52, 932–40.

Oliner, S. P., and Oliner, P. M. (1988). *The altruistic personality: Rescuers of Jews in Nazi Europe.* New York: Free Press.

Perloff, R. (1987). Self-interest and personal responsibility redux, *American Psychologist* 42, 3–11.

Reykowski, J. (1984). Spatial organization of a cognitive system and intrinsic prosocial motivation. In E. Staub, D. Bar-Tal, J. Karylowski, and J. Reykowski (Eds.), *Development and maintenance of prosocial behavior: International perspectives on positive morality.* New York: Plenum.

Rosenberg, M., and H. B. Kaplan (Eds.) (1982). *Social psychology of the self-concept.* Arlington Hts., IL: Harland Davidson.

Rubenstein, R. L., and Roth, J. K. (1987). *Approaches to Auschwitz.* Atlanta, GA: John Knox, ch. 2.

Rutter, M. (1979). Maternal deprivation, 1972–1978: New findings, new concepts, new approaches, *Child Development* 50, 283–305.

Schaffer, H. R., and Emerson, P. E. (1964). *The development of social attachments in infancy.* Monographs of the Society for Research in Child Development, 29, no. 3, 1–77. Chicago: University of Chicago Press.

Schwartz, S. H., and Howard, J. A. (1984). Internalized values as motivators of altruism. In E. Staub, D. Bar-Tal, J. Karylowski, and J. Reykowski (Eds.), *The development and maintenance of prosocial behavior: international perspectives on positive development.* New York: Plenum, ch. 11.

Shengold, L. (1989). *The effects of childhood abuse and deprivation.* New Haven, CT: Yale University Press.

Smith, W. K., and Tedlow, R. S. (1989). James Burke: A career in American business. President and fellows of Harvard College, 1989. In D. E. Goodpaster and T. R. Piper (Eds.), *Managerial decision making and ethical values: Course module.* Boston, MA: Harvard Business School, section 8.

Solomon, D., Watson, M., Schaps, E., Battistich, V., and Solomon, J. (1990). Cooperative learning as part of a comprehensive classroom program designed to promote prosocial development. In S. Sharan (Ed.), *Cooperative learning: Theory and research.* New York: Praeger, ch. 10.

Sorokin, P. A. (1954). *The ways and power of love: Types, factors, and techniques of moral transformation.* Boston: Beacon.

Spence, J. T. (1985). Achievement American style: The rewards and costs of individualism, *American Psychologist* 40, 1285–95.

Sroufe, L. A. (1979). The coherence of individual development: Early care, attachment, and subsequent developmental issues, *American Psychologist*, 34, 834–41.

Staub, E. (1978). *Positive social behavior and morality: Social and personal influences* (Vol. 1). New York: Academic Press.

Tunstall, W. B. (1985). Breakup of the Bell system: A case study in cultural transformation. In R. H. Kilmann, M. J. Saxton, R. Serpa, and associates (Eds.), *Gaining control of the corporate culture.* San Francisco: Jossey-Bass.

Von Cranach, M., Kalbermatten, U., Indermuhle, K., and Gugler, B. (1982). *Goal-directed action.* London: Academic Press.

Waterman, A. S. (1981). Individualism and interdependence, *American Psychologist* 36, 762–73.

Weber, J. A. (1990). Case: Corporate codes of conduct. In D. J. Wood, *Business and society.* Glenview, IL: Scott, Foresman/Little Brown Higher Education, 284–87.

Wispé, L. (1986). The distinction between sympathy and empathy: To call forth a concept, a word is needed. *Journal of Personality and Social Psychology* 50:2, 314–21.

Yankelovich, D. (1982). *New rules: Searching for self-fulfillment in a world turned upside-down.* Toronto: Bantam.

# 17

# THE ORIGINS OF CARING, HELPING, AND NONAGGRESSION: PARENTAL SOCIALIZATION, THE FAMILY SYSTEM, SCHOOLS, AND CULTURAL INFLUENCE

## Ervin Staub

What kind of socialization is required to raise caring, cooperative, helpful persons? What kinds of experiences are necessary for the development of characteristics that help people deal with crises by turning toward rather than against others, by inclusion rather than exclusion? What will help them resist movements, ideologies, and group influences that lead to confrontation and violence? How can they become self-assertive, able to stand up for their own rights and pursue their own goals, but also consider the rights, needs, and goals of others? What kind of socialization is required to develop people who are willing to make sacrifices to help others?

The way children are socialized is a basic manifestation of the culture and its institutions. Through socialization the culture recreates itself or creates itself anew. In order to socialize children in ways that lead to caring and nonaggression, a society (and its individual members) must value these characteristics. Currently, this is the case to a limited degree only in most countries; as compared with wealth, personal success, or patriotism, *the relative value* of caring about and helping others tends to be low. Therefore, changes in the socialization of children and in the values and institutions of society must progress simultaneously, supporting and reinforcing each other.

Sociobiologists (Trivers 1971; Wilson 1975) have proposed that altruism, the willingness to sacrifice in order to benefit others, is part of the human genetic makeup. However, our observations of each other clearly tell us that human beings vary greatly in their caring and help giving. While it is reasonable to believe that we possess a genetic potential for altruism (as well as aggression), the evolution of this potential depends on experience. Experience greatly affects even animals' response to the needs of other animals (see Staub 1978). Beyond a genetic potential, we possess "genetic building blocks" out of which altruism as well as aggression can evolve (Staub 1989). The fate of these potentials depends, however, on experience.

Socialization, the process whereby a culture transmits its values, rules, and roles to the child, is one type of important experience. What the culture teaches—by reward and punishment, through stories, and by example—is one source of the values and personal characteristics of individuals.

While the purpose of cultural transmission is to socialize children into prevailing values, norms, conceptions, and modes of behaving, none of these are static. Cultures evolve, as individuals do. For a group of people to survive, for group life to be possible, the culture must evolve values and rules that limit aggression and promote consideration for others' welfare and interest. However, the exact nature of standards and values that societies evolve will greatly differ as a result of different environmental conditions that groups have faced, different solutions they have created to resolve problems, their different routes of evolution. The rules and values they transmit represent their accumulated wisdom. Religions often elevate the accumulated wisdom of a culture to universalistic strivings.

In some cultures, the child is also exposed to human ideals that go beyond the existing culture. Philosophers as well as other thinkers have often gone beyond the peculiarities of the evolution of their own group and offered universal values and rules that would maximize human welfare. These ideals usually derive from conceptions of enlightened self-interest, the view that we can maximize our own welfare by considering the welfare of others, so that they will consider ours. Principles such as Kant's categorical imperative, according to which we are to act only in ways that we are willing to have others act, expand moral consideration beyond the group to all humanity. A less absolute principle is offered by utilitarianism, which regards the best conduct as the one that maximizes the ratio of benefit to harm (the greatest good for the greatest number). The combination of an absolute principle like the categorical imperative and the principle of utility may offer the best guide to moral conduct (Frankena 1973).

Yet another source of caring and nonaggression is the experience of a child in his or her relationships with both other human beings and the social system. How others behave towards the child, how as a result of the influences affecting him the child behaves towards others, as well as the limitations and opportunities within the social system itself determine whether the child feels valued or disregarded, comes to value rather than devalue other human beings, and sees others as benevolent or malevolent, as trustworthy or untrustworthy. Valuing people is essential for wanting to reach out to them and to respond to their needs. When socializing experiences are positive, the developing persons will come to value both themselves and others, and evolve generative capacities so that they can create values and ways of being that go beyond what is learned from transmission and direct experience.

Another likely source of values of mutual caring, connectedness, and love is the experience of connectedness. Having experienced such states (as a result of conditions that I will describe below) we transform them into values. Such experiences can be highly gratifying, which is reason for optimism; they make it possible to develop and/or adopt connectedness to others and caring for them as central values.

A constellation of characteristics, rather than a single one, is optimal both for individual positive functioning and positive human relationships. They include a *prosocial value orientation*—a positive view of others, concern for their welfare, and a feeling of personal responsibility for others' welfare (Staub 1974, 1978, 1980, 1989)—as well as *moral rule orientations*, which can be as general as holding a basic moral principle like justice, or specific such as adopting norms that prescribe helping. *Empathy* is a third important characteristic; it probably arises from a positive view of human beings, feelings of connection to them, and concern about their welfare (but without a feeling of personal responsibility, which would turn it into prosocial orientation).

A prosocial value orientation was related to people helping others in either physical (Staub 1974, 1978) or psychological (Feinberg 1978; Grodman 1979; Staub 1978) distress. It was found to be more strongly related to self-reports of helping than either moral rule orientation or empathy (Staub 1990b). Nonetheless, a combination of these characteristics, especially an integration in which rule orientation is not predominant, provides a strong basis for helpfulness while making it unlikely that the welfare of individuals will be sacrificed for abstract ideals.

*Personal goal theory* suggests that in order to be frequently activated, to be dominant over other motives and thus lead to helping, these value orientations should be high in people's hierarchy of values and goals (Staub 1978, 1980, 1989). This is to be one of the central outcomes of the positive socialization in the home and in schools that I will describe in this chapter. Supporting characteristics such as competencies and the capacity to infer or perceive others' internal states and take their roles are also essential for caring, empathy, and their expression in behavior (Staub 1978, 1980, 1989).

## CHILD REARING THAT PROMOTES CARING, HELPING, AND NONAGGRESSION

The education of the child in values and rules is less basic than the child's direct experience. Interpersonal relations and experiences with caretakers, with people in authority, and with peers are the sources of feelings, values, and beliefs about self, about other people, and about connections to others.

### Attachment and Differentiation

An important *genetic building block* is the capacity for attachment. Except under the most extreme conditions of deprivation in caretaking and stimulation, found in some institutions (Thompson and Grusec 1970), and probably also present in some of the fractured and disorganized families increasingly common in our society, the child will develop an attachment—an affectional tie—to a caretaker. The quality of attachment will vary. Researchers have identified three primary kinds: secure, anxious, and conflictual or avoidant. Secure attachment is the result of the caretaker touching and holding the infant, mutual gazing, the responsiveness of the caretaker to the infant's needs. The latter is an essential component. Infants who develop secure attachment to caretakers are less upset when this person leaves them with a stranger, more loving and responsive when he or she returns. They show less anxiety in strange situations and appear secure and loving with the person who is the object of their attachment.

Recent research findings confirm the long-held belief that the earliest relationships influence later ones. When they later interact with peers, securely attached infants are able to initiate interaction effectively, and are the recipients of positive behavior from peers (Sroufe 1979). Secure attachment is probably a rudiment of trust both in others and in the self, of positive valuing of other people and a positive identity.

The connection to some people that is inherent in attachment is also a starting point for fear of other humans. As attachment manifests itself, evolving gradually but becoming evident after infants develop object constancy, stranger anxiety also appears. This is a powerful rudimentary manifestation of the fear and distress by which both humans and animals respond to the strange, the unfamiliar, what is discrepant from the known. Experience, however, shapes the degree and extensiveness of fear of strangers. For example, infants who develop a secure attachment or are exposed to more people show less stranger anxiety (Shaffer 1979). Attachment and stranger anxiety are manifestations, both as metaphors and in reality, of the separation of us and them, the known and liked from the unknown that is feared. Continuing experience shapes the evolution of positive ties to some people and the inclination to separate from others.

Children learn to differentiate between their primary group, the family, and the rest of the world, and are frequently taught not to trust those outside the family. Moreover, there is often specific indoctrination against out-groups, be they religious, ethnic, national, or political. At a very early age children evaluate their nation, for example, in a positive way, while expressing stereotypic and negative views of other nations (Piaget and Weil 1951). Having learned to make differentiations between in-groups and out-groups, people will naturally create them under novel circumstances. Even if they develop prosocial and moral rule orientations and empathy, unless they become inclusive, that is, come to include a broad range or all people in the human and moral domain, their helping and caring may remain restricted to a narrow in-group (Oliner and Oliner 1988; Staub 1989; 1990a).

## Positive Socialization and the Child's Experience

Research findings from the last two or three decades, obtained both from examination of parental socialization practices and from laboratory settings, indicate that a *pattern of parental practices* contributes to prosocial behavior and values (for reviews, see Grusec 1981; Eisenberg 1986; Radke-Yarrow, Zahn-Waxler, and Chapman 1983; Staub, 1979, 1981, 1986; Zahn-Waxler et al. 1986). These include parental warmth, affection, or nurturance; the tendency to reason with the child, to explain why the parents expect certain behaviors while they disapprove of others, and especially "induction," pointing out to children the consequences of their behavior on others, both negative and positive; firm but not forceful control, the parents leading the child to actually act according to values they regard as important, to follow important rules; and natural socialization, the parents guiding the child to engage in behavior that benefits others, to cooperate with others, so that learning by doing can follow (Staub 1975, 1979). Modeling by parents, the example of the parents' own behavior, is also an important source of what children learn.

Parental warmth and affection, especially when combined with sensitivity in perceiving and responding to the child's needs, have important consequences. The child experiences the parents as loving and kind, as trustworthy and benevolent. Since interaction with parents is usually the young child's primary experience of people, these feelings will generalize to others. The parents' caring and kindness lead the child to experience himself or herself positively, to the evolution of positive self-esteem. Warmth and nurturance make the child feel safe, so that he or she can initiate new behaviors and experiment in the world without fear of punishment. Even a limited ten-minute-long interaction with a nurturant rather than an indifferent adult leads kindergarten-age children to initiate more action upon hearing sounds of another child's distress from another room (Staub 1970a). Finally, warmth and nurturance by parents lead to identification, to the child wanting to be like the parents. This increases cooperation with parents, and makes the relationship of parents and children more mutually satisfying and the socialization of the child easier.

The quality of interaction with adults results in selective attention to the world, a striking finding. Nursery school children who were cared for, over a two-week period, by either a warm or an indifferent adult remembered the same number of actions of small dolls that were manipulated by the adult. However, *what* they remembered differed; the former children remembered more positive, helpful acts, the latter more negative, aggressive acts (Yarrow and Scott 1972). In general, children's orientation to other people probably affects how they experience events and what they learn from experience.

Reasoning with children is a mild form of influencing and controlling them. As a mode of relating to them, it is consistent with affection and nurturance. Induction, the parents (or anyone else) pointing out to the child the consequences of his or her behavior for other people, communicates to the child his or her power to affect others' well-being, as well as his or her responsibility towards others. In addition, induction focuses attention on others' internal states, on how they feel and what they think, on their inner world. This is crucial for learning to consider others' needs, hopes, and desires.

Children have their own desires, intentions, their own agenda. If parents are to guide the child to a consideration of other people, or if they are to lead the child to respect values and rules, they must at times exert additional influence. Firm enforcement of at least a limited set of rules that the parents regard as highly important is necessary. It is essential, however, that this does not take forceful and violent forms (see below). Firm enforcement of rules that express important values can coexist with allowing the child substantial autonomy, choice, and self-guidance, to an increasing degree as the child's capacity for responsible choice and competence develops.

Parents can also guide children to act in helpful, generous, cooperative ways, an example of what I have called *natural socialization* (Staub 1975, 1979). Natural socialization is a pervasive but hidden aspect of socialization. In order to develop interest in and motivation to engage with activities, objects, and people, the child has to experience them. He or she has to engage with mathematical games and problems to evolve an interest in math, a desire to work with math, and to experience such activity as satisfying. Engagement can result in learning by participation: under supporting conditions, participation will enhance motivation. Such learning is of great importance for helping and harmdoing.

In a series of studies my associates and I found that children who teach younger children, or make toys for poor hospitalized children, or write letters to hospitalized children are later more likely to be helpful or generous (Staub 1975, 1979). These findings were stronger for girls, in that participation in a broader range of prosocial acts enhanced their later prosocial behaviors. With girls the combination of participation and pointing out the beneficial consequences of their behaviors to them had the strongest effect in increasing subsequent helpfulness or generosity.

Boys were more likely to later act to benefit others if they participated in helpful acts that responded to lesser and/or less personal need. Direct helping of needy others seemed to evoke their resistance. For example, when boys participated by making toys for poor hospitalized children, their helping behavior immediately afterwards declined. Still, this experience had a positive impact with the passage of time, in that these boys' helping was somewhat elevated on a "delayed posttest" several weeks later. In contrast, helping behavior that was not directed to alleviate distress or personal need, making toys to help an art teacher develop materials for teaching art, enhanced boys' subsequent helping of poor, hospitalized children. For girls, the initial experience of making toys for poor hospitalized children enhanced later helping most.

In our society, boys may see some acts of kindness as "goody goody," especially when adults induce them or guide them to engage in those acts. The caring these acts express may be inconsistent with the masculine image boys try to adopt. Being put in a situation where they were to engage in such acts may have resulted in resistance and evoked an oppositional tendency.

Finally, the parents' example, their kindness not only towards their own children but in interaction with people in general, is essential. Values, rules, and modes of behaving will not be acquired by children if they are verbally propagated by adult socializers but not manifested in their conduct.

The consequences of these experiences on children's personality appear manifold. First, they lead to a positive evaluation of other people, a respect for and concern about other people's welfare, and a feeling of responsibility to help others—that is, a prosocial value orientation. Second, out of their connection to other people and their capacity to understand others' internal states, feelings of empathy can arise. The experiences that I described, especially if they are combined with parents setting relatively high standards for their children that they can successfully fulfill at least some of the time, will also lead to the evolution of a positive self-esteem (Coopersmith 1967).

A pattern of child-rearing practices that is in essence the opposite of the one I just discussed will lead to the opposite consequences: to hostility and aggression. They include indifference and rejection by parents; hostility, especially between boys and their fathers, and the use of control over the child that relies on the parents' power, or power-assertive control, such as depriving the child of privileges and especially the frequent use of physical punishment. Such practices are related to aggressive behaviors in boys (Aronfreed 1968; Bandura and Walters 1959; Eron 1982; Huesmann et al. 1984; Huesmann, Lagerspetz, and Eron 1984; Staub 1986, 1989). One likely effect of their use is that children come to view people as hostile and aggressive; another is that they learn that aggression is normal, acceptable, even inevitable in human relations. Their own mistreatment may generate anger and hostility in them towards other people. In extreme cases, they may develop an *antisocial orientation*, a negative evaluation of people and the desire to harm them.

Experiences that are afforded by the culture and life in a society both affect parental socialization and combine with it to shape individual characteristics. For example, children who habitually watch aggressive television are more aggressive. But these tend to be children who are rejected, criticized, or are in other ways the objects of parental hostility (Eron 1982; Huesmann et al. 1984; Huesmann, Lagerspetz, and Eron 1984). Personal experiences affect the elements of culture to which children voluntarily expose themselves. But even children who experience positive socialization will usually be exposed to elements of culture that stress competition and focus on self-interest. And they usually lack guidance as to how to integrate conflicting values and goals.

### Self-awareness and Positive Identity

An essential aspect of *positive socialization* is to develop self-awareness and self-acceptance in children. Too much anxiety and threat make it necessary for children to defend themselves from feelings, to deny them and repress them. Even when socialization practices and the family environment are optimal, however, children require help to correctly read and code their own feelings and those of others. They require support to experience and be aware of their own sadness, disappointment, hurt, and anger. Parents can help children learn to perceive, accept, and deal with the whole range of feelings. Alternatively, they can guide children not to attend to and thereby not to perceive, or to negatively evaluate, deny, and repress some feelings.

The consequences can be profound. One of them is the projection of unacceptable feelings onto others, which generates moral indignation, anger, and hostile behavior. Another is diminished well-being and happiness and diminished capacity for informed choice which affect all relationships.

Life can never be painless. Even feelings of love often result in pain: the person we love returns less caring and love, or turns to another for love, or dies. It is essential for people to be able to experience feelings of sadness, grief, sorrow, anxiety, anger, and other painful and conflictful emotions. Only by experiencing them can people move through them, be done with them. The inability to perceive, accept, or experience such feelings in ourselves makes it unlikely that we will perceive them in others or, if we do, that we will respond with empathy, support, and help. It diminishes our capacity to accurately see and experience others; combined with our diminished well-being, it makes us less open to others' needs, pain, or suffering; and it decreases our willingness to subordinate our own needs and goals to helping others in distress.

Another essential consequence of positive child rearing is self-reliance, emotional independence, and the capacity for independent judgment. Such qualities will result from providing children with love and nurturance, from helping them become aware of their feelings, from allowing them increasing degrees of autonomy, from involving them in family decision making, and from exposing and guiding them to a wide range of activities. Such child rearing enables children to differentiate themselves from members of their family, to evolve separate identities. It provides the emotional strength to endure the vicissitudes and turmoils of life. All this reduces the likelihood that people will seek guidance from leaders and solace from ideologies that tell them how to live, or that they will accept definitions of reality by experts and those in authority that would lead them to harm other people (Staub 1989).

Being part of and committed to a valued group, like a nation, or to a faith or an ideology, gives people great courage, physical and moral. Frequently such courage serves destruction, as evi-

denced by kamikaze pilots, Shiite terrorists, or men in battle. However, great courage is evident as well in service to others that is
nonviolent and at time requires deviation from a larger social
group. When lives are in danger, due to accidents or persecution,
some people respond in heroic ways, endangering and at times
losing their own lives in saving others. The challenge of raising
children is to help them evolve strong, well-developed but at the
same time connected identities that embody caring about others'
welfare and the experience of deep feelings of satisfaction from
connection to other people. The term *connected identities* implies
both such connection and the capacity to stand apart and, at times,
in opposition.[1]

The preceding discussion shows the importance for children's
development of feeling safe, secure, and protected, especially when
young. A great problem today, at least in the U.S., is the large
numbers of children who grow up without either a family or an
alternative child-care arrangement that provides this.

## THE INFLUENCE OF THE FAMILY AS A SYSTEM

It is increasingly recognized that the family is a system with explicit and implicit, hidden rules. For children, these rules tend to
become blueprints of the world and of how to function in it. In
coercive family environments, members rely on aggression to exert
control over each other and to defend themselves from attack (Patterson 1982). Children come to learn that human beings are aggressive, and that only by aggression can they defend themselves
or exert influence.

In many families parents set rules in an authoritarian fashion.
They often prohibit not only aggression by children within the
family but also the expressions of anger or other feelings they
regard as antisocial or contrary to their ideals. The consequences
can include denial and repression of hostile feelings, lack of self-
awareness and self-acceptance, and a liking of or preference for
hierarchical relationships. Children who grow up in a democratic family, where values and rules are negotiated and children
participate in making decisions, will obviously learn greater
independence.

Family systems also have other characteristics. One parent may
be passive, with decisions made by the other. Once the system
evolves around this division of power, change will be resisted. The

greater power of one parent may arise from, or may be maintained by, a coalition with children. The child's personality will manifest both his or her own position or role in the system and what the system teaches about the roles, responsibilities, and relative power of males and females, adults and children.

Recent work by Boszormenyi-Nagy and Spark has focused on justice as a profoundly important aspect of family life (Boszormenyi-Nagy and Spark 1984). Injustice that the child suffers in the family will remain a legacy that the person will have to work out in his or her own life. The abuse of children, in this view, can be the balancing out of injustice that a person suffered as a child at the hands of parents.

One difficulty in raising children in ways that promote caring and nonaggression lies in the parents' own personalities. Even if parents value these characteristics in their children, they are limited by their own personalities in promoting them. Their ease or difficulty in allowing their growing children participation in family decisions, the extent to which they are aware of their own feelings and perceive those of their children, and the family rules they unknowingly establish are the result of their own past history and who they have become. People need mirrors to see themselves and to grow. To become capable of raising caring and nonaggressive children, many people need experiences that would bring to their awareness both their modes of relating to their children and the family systems they have unconsciously shaped.

To overcome the limitations imposed by the negative impact of certain parental characteristics, we ought to expand the range of adults with whom the child has significant contact. More cooperative child rearing would facilitate intimate contact with more people. My observations suggest to me that children whose early experience was potentially highly damaging, as a result of abandonment or bad treatment at the hands of adults, were sometimes "saved" by people who had reached out to them and become significant positive figures in their lives.

Methods of disciplining children and modes of relating to them are also affected by the parents' own life conditions. For loving, affectionate relationships with children, the use of reasoning, and the use of nonforceful modes of control, it is necessary that parents have relatively ordered and secure life circumstances. If their basic needs for food, shelter, health care, and emotional support are unfulfilled, and if they lack a feeling of reasonable control over

their lives, positive socialization becomes less likely. When unemployment increases, reports of child abuse increase, and periods
of economic problems are associated with increased incidence of
societal violence (Hovland and Sears 1940; Landau 1982).

If we are to raise children who feel connected to other human
beings, who are willing to help others, and who can resist pressures
towards individual or group aggression, society will have to provide parents with at least a modicum of security and the fulfillment
of basic needs. Thus, for the evolution of a pattern of personal
characteristics that significantly increase the potential for kindness
versus cruelty, in a large enough group of children to represent a
noticeable cultural change, at least minimally supportive societal
conditions are required.

We can instruct parents, train them in specific skills of child
rearing. This is not enough, however. Methods of raising children
partly derive from parents' values. Up to the twentieth century,
parents in many places—in Germany, but also in England and
elsewhere (DeMauss 1974; Stone 1977)—regarded children as innately willful. The child's will had to be broken, which usually
required forceful means, if the child was to be capable of goodness
and obedience. Obedience to parents was regarded as perhaps the
highest of all values. Belief in the use of physical punishment with
children (Straus, Gelles, and Steinmetz 1980) and other destructive
beliefs, values, and practices still abound.

How do such societal views change? Partly through the education of parents. They must be convinced that beneficial consequences follow from children acquiring characteristics that
promote positive behavior and diminish harmdoing: on the life of
the family, on the future success and happiness of the child, and
on the harmony and well-being of society. Some of these characteristics, like positive self-esteem and a feeling of efficacy, are also
important for people pursuing self-related goals. A positive orientation to other people contributes to harmonious, satisfying interpersonal relationships and, thereby, to personal satisfaction and
happiness. Reciprocity is perhaps the most basic law of human
relationships (Gouldner 1960): people return kindness and are unlikely to harm someone who has benefited them. However, reciprocity depends not only on actions but also on the motives
attributed to actors. We will best gain others' kindness, cooperation, trust, and affection if we impress them with our caring and
unselfish actions *and* intentions. The best way to accomplish this

is to be caring and unselfish. Self-assertion is also important, standing up for one's rights, so that those who might exploit a person's kindness will not be able to do so.

## Creating Change

Information, advocacy, and the availability of services with specifiable benefits may lead parents to accept and even seek education in parenting. Training parents in specific skills of child rearing can be highly effective. The state of Missouri, for example, initiated a demonstration project, starting with prospective parents and continuing until the children reached age three. Participants were taught simple skills such as setting clear limits for their children beginning in the first year of life, and creating stimulating environments and experiences (Meyerhoff and White 1986). Formal evidence showed that children whose parents received this training functioned at a more intellectually advanced level than children whose parents had not. Less formal evidence suggested that they also functioned better socially.

If such programs were widely available, and their benefits known, many prospective parents might turn to them to reduce the uncertainties of parenting and acquire the skills of "positive parenting." In the context of training in parenting skills, parents could examine and discuss their beliefs about the nature of children and evolve an attitude of benevolence, care, and consideration. As parents realize that positive modes of relating to children are effective in gaining their cooperation, they will acquire both a sense of power and an increased feeling of benevolence. They are likely then to be receptive to new views and positive practices. Social scientists and psychologists have an essential role in communicating information to the public that has accumulated in research, which provides the bases for new assumptions about and techniques for raising children.

It would also be of great value to create and make available *family systems diagnoses* to the general public. The purpose of this would be to make family members aware—by the use of vivid procedures like viewing and discussing videos of family interaction—the rules and procedures by which the family operates. The discussion of what is happening in the family could entail education in alternative ways of functioning, and their possible results. Such services may someday be practical tools to increase happiness and well-being in families, decrease the frequency of divorce, and contribute to the positive socialization of children.

## THE ROLE OF SCHOOLS

Many of the practices that I described need to be employed by other socializers as well, especially school teachers. Teachers can be warm, indifferent, or hostile. They can explain and discuss rules or set rules in an authoritarian fashion. And the schools have many opportunities for natural socialization, for teaching children by participation.

Through the use of cooperative learning techniques, children can teach each other and learn from each other (Aronson et al. 1978; Johnson et al. 1981; Hertz-Lazarowitz and Sharan 1984). Older children can teach younger ones. Or each child can become an expert on part of the material and teach it to others, each child's knowledge necessary for the whole. This is one of many cooperative learning techniques, the so-called jigsaw technique (Aronson et al. 1978). Such experiences enhance academic performance, especially of minority children, who in the framework of cooperative learning interact with other children as equals. Cooperative learning also contributes to the positive self-esteem and prosocial behavior of all children.

Teachers can also employ role playing, a form of "as if" participation that is highly effective in learning social interaction. Kindergarden children who role played helping later demonstrated more helping of a child in physical distress or more sharing with a poor child (Staub 1970b). Preadolescent delinquents who spent a substantial period of time role playing scenes they created, presumably enacting and in the course of it resolving life issues, showed increased capacity to take others' roles, and decreased delinquent behavior as evidenced by their police records (Chandler 1973).

Schools inevitably shape children's social and moral nature as a function of the experiences they provide and create, and secondarily as a function of what they teach. Teachers, like parents, can discipline and guide children by the methods of positive socialization that I have described, or by forceful and punitive practices. By the kind of rules that teachers set and enforce, they communicate to children what is acceptable and valued. The rules also influence how children interact with each other, aggressively or prosocially, cooperatively or competitively, and thereby influence what children learn in their interaction with peers. This is highly important, since increasingly the child's socialization becomes self-socialization: the child's behavior shapes others' behavior towards himself or herself and the child's responses to others shape the cycles of interaction, which in turn further shape and form the child's personality, self-concept, motives, and world view (Staub 1986, 1989).

The school can function as an authoritarian system, or as a democratic one in which children discuss and participate in resolving issues that affect their lives and relationships to each other. A democratic system will help children evolve both a capacity for responsible decision making, whether it is about classroom conflicts or authority relations, and positive modes of conflict resolution. Children can engage in moral discourse about matters both in the school and in the outside world. The school can offer the child participation in many roles and activities, from school plays to music groups to school councils and sports (Gump and Friesen 1964). As a consequence, the child comes to perceive himself or herself as an actor rather than an audience, as an agent rather than helpless in shaping events, as responsible for others' welfare as well as his or her own, and as a responsible member of the community (Staub 1978).

People are easily guided by leaders, experts, and other authorities. In *1984* George Orwell described how in his imaginary state today's enemy instantly becomes tomorrow's friend, and today's friend tomorrow's enemy. The minds and views of people can also be too easily molded in the real world. Upon Nixon's visit to China the former Chinese Communist hordes became ping-pong players. Negative views and feelings are perhaps even more easily created. Through education and experience we must strive to help every person evolve a *critical consciousness*. Although this makes for less ease in exerting authority and makes the life of leaders more difficult, it is an essential task (Staub 1989).

Both parents and schools have a further essential task, to teach children about the shared humanity of all people. This must happen in many interconnected ways. In the educational realm children can learn about the differences in customs, beliefs, and values of different groups of individuals while coming to appreciate commonalities in desires, yearnings, feelings of joy and sorrow, and physical and other needs. Orwell described his profound change of attitude during World War I when he saw, from his trench, an enemy soldier pull down his pants and relieve himself. By concretizing and particularizing human beings, rather than holding abstractions, we can enhance empathic responsiveess to a wide range of people. A shared humanity that is made concrete and manifest will diminish the tendency for "us-them" differentiation and devaluation.

An appreciation of both a shared humanity and differences in customs, beliefs, and values can be enlarged by attention to and respect for differences among children in the classroom, both personal and cultural. As just one of hundreds of possible issues, consider differences among children of varying cultural backgrounds in their relationship to time. Some children may have learned little concern about punctuality. While the child has to accept the need to be on time, the teacher must be aware of and show respect for the values and ways of life underlying the child's behavior. The child's values and the reasons for punctuality in the school setting can be discussed. Once such discussions become the normal operating procedure, without punitive connotations, they may make the children who are involved feel important rather than self-conscious, and enlighten all.

How can we convince schools to adopt practices that will contribute to prosocial goals and behaviors? Partly we must stress the inevitable consequences of the nature of the school environment and of school experience on children's personality, values, and social behaviors. Since the consequences are inevitable, the question is not whether but *what* values, characteristics, and behaviors are schools to promote. We must also advocate the values and goals of interconnectedness and cooperation and the harmful consequences of promoting extreme competitiveness. We must address the ways in which individualism and the affirmation of self on the one hand, and connectedness and a common spirit on the other hand, can be balanced and integrated.

We must also convince schools that practices that contribute to a positive orientation towards others also enhance the overall effectiveness of academic instruction. As I noted, cooperative learning procedures are at least as effective as more traditional procedures with academically advanced children, while much more effective with disadvantaged, underachieving, minority children. In addition, they help evolve positive self-esteem, positive interpersonal behaviors that extend across group lines, and the capacity to listen to and communicate with others.

On the basis of already existing and constantly evolving information, specific methods and procedures for school instruction need to be developed and disseminated, and their use advocated. For example, in an ongoing longitudinal study a set of practices and procedures have been employed by three schools that stress cooperative learning, opportunities for prosocial action as a basis for learning by doing, teachers' use of positive discipline techniques and other related procedures developed on the basis of research findings. The parents of participating children are also involved, so that they join the schools in positive socialization. The findings show that the participating children show an enhanced capacity for role taking and more prosocial behaviors in interacting with peers, in comparison to those children in control schools (Battistich et al. 1991). The procedures developed for this study lend themselves for adaptation and use in regular school curricula.

## THE ROLE OF UNIVERSITIES

Both our capacity to materially improve and our capacity to destroy lives have greatly advanced, while our capacity to live together in peaceful cooperation has not. It is essential that our institutions of higher learning also attend to the evolution of the human potential for caring and cooperation (Staub 1987).

### Further Learning about Us and Them

Learning about different cultures and ways of life can reduce stereotyping, devaluation, fear of the unknown and the different. Ideally, such education would create the capacity to see different cultural groups from within their own framework, and to adopt their points of view. Students should also become aware of different basic assumptions that frame experience and provide meaning.

It is important to bring a developmental framework to the study of the history, anthropology, sociology, art, and literature of different cultures. How did the characteristics of cultures evolve as a function of the circumstances they faced and the choices they made in dealing with life problems? Can we see each culture as an integrated whole, as a mode of adaptation? As we become aware of processes of change, we see cultures less as static entities. We will come to see our own culture and society as one mode of adaptation, one form of group life. Students may come to see the "goodness" of quite different values, ways of life, and religions, become aware of their functions and usefulness for different groups of people. Such education offers multiple and cross-cultural perspectives. It would hopefully enable students to understand and accept others more. At the same time it may help them experience less upheaval in response to changes in their own society.

Universities also provide a laboratory for learning about others' values and ways of life, given the intermingling of people from different backgrounds. Can we provide students with opportunities to learn about each other, to tell each other their "stories," their hopes, desires, and disappointments, their failures and successes? Universities guide students to relate to the institution and to each other in terms of their abilities and achievements, usually competitively. Coming to relate to each other out of shared experience can help students appreciate their shared humanness, can generate acceptance of self and others.

### Learning to See the Self, Others, and Society

We go about the world making us-them differentiations, and all too often devalue and scapegoat others, justify the suffering of victims by further devaluing them, and exclude them from the moral universe (Staub 1989, 1990a). We engage in these and many other psychological and social processes without awareness of them. Can we evolve the capacity to see ourselves in interaction, to see how our actions affect others' reactions, and to be aware of our psychological processes that generate our actions?

Recently I talked with and spent time with an elderly couple. The wife complained bitterly about her husband's anger, how he threatens her, the difficulty in living with him. Spending just a few hours with them, it became clear to me that she was frequently angry at him and criticized him for little or no reason. Stumbling over the curled-up corner of a rug, for example, she blamed him. She was unaware of her own behavior, however, and its likely impact on him.

Individuals and groups tend to focus on others' behavior; rarely do they see the whole interaction, including their own role in it. Moreover, rarely are people aware of their basic tendencies in perception and thinking, which powerfully influence their actions and emotions. They often see their own behavior, especially aggression, as a justified and necessary response to others' actions.

Universities can educate students about psychological and social science principles, about the processes by which cruelty and kindness arise in themselves and in the world around them. If education helps students evolve a deep awareness and the capacity to observe and see, an experiential knowledge, change in them is certain to follow. For example, their perception of the meaning of others' behavior can change and in turn their feelings evoked by it. They may also perceive earlier and more accurately drifts in their social group towards the mistreatment of subgroups or hostility towards other nations, and respond as active, caring bystanders.

### Learning about Ethical Views and Systems

The practice of thinking about right or wrong provides an important basis for ethical choice. The history of human thought is rich in ethical thought. Philosophers and social thinkers have long thought about the principles, the rules, the type of considerations for others' welfare that might best guide human relations. What are the consequences for oneself and others of living life by different moral principles and rules? Why should we be concerned about others' welfare? What is the nature of enlightened self-interest? The study and discussion of ethical thought should start early, and continue in a more systematic manner in the university.

### The Evolution of Critical Consciousness

I am advocating education that contributes to the capacity for independent judgment. If we are to create a caring and nonviolent world, it is essential that each person assume responsibility for both his or her own conduct, and for the conduct of his or her society. It is necessary to respect and cooperate with authority to an extent, if a society is to function. But this must be balanced with the responsibility of each individual to judge the effects of policies and practices by leaders and institutions on the welfare of members of the society, on relations with other countries, on human beings elsewhere. Each individual is responsible for participating in shaping those policies and practices.

In sum, developing caring and the tendency to help others, as well as promoting the capacity to resist influences that would lead to harming others, depend on varied socialization and cultural elements. Creating positive influences on children's lives requires concerted effort: by social scientists who can disseminate relevant information; by parents, teachers, and school administrators; and by any person who commits himself or herself to an ongoing effort to work for a caring society and a caring world.

## NOTES

1. I have proposed a classification of types of selves according to degree and nature of connection to others: disconnected; autonomous or independent; selves-in-relation (Surrey 1985); and embedded (Staub, in press). The connection of embedded selves to others includes dependency and need, which make deviation and independent action difficult. The term "connected selves" or "identities" has a similar meaning to, but for my purposes is preferable to "self-in-relation."

## REFERENCES

Aronfreed, J. (1968). *Conduct and conscience.* New York: Academic Press.

Aronson, E., Stephan, C., Sikes, J., Blaney, N., and Snapp, M. (1978). *The jigsaw classroom.* Beverly Hills, CA: Sage.

Bandura, A., and Walters, R. H. (1959). *Adolescent aggression: A study of the influence of child training practices and family inter-relationship.* New York: Ronald.

Battistich, V., Watson, M., Solomon, D., Schaps, E., and Solomon, J. (1991). The child development project: A comprehensive program for the development of prosocial character. In W. M. Kurtines and J. L. Gewirtz (Eds.), *Handbook of moral behavior and development. Vol. 3. Applications.* Hillsdale, NJ: Erlbaum.

Boszormenyi-Nagy, I., and Spark, G. M. (1984). *Invisible loyalties: Reciprocity in intergenerational family therapy.* New York: Bruner-Mazel.

Chandler, M. J. (1973). Egocentrism and antisocial behavior. *Developmental Psychology, 9,* 326–32.

Coopersmith, S. (1967). *Antecedents of self-esteem.* San Francisco: Fremont.

DeMauss, L. (Ed). (1974). *History of childhood.* New York: Psycho-history Press.

Eisenberg, N. (1986). *Altruistic emotion, cognition, and behavior.* Hillsdale, NJ: Erlbaum.

Eron, L. D. (1982). Parent-child interaction, television violence, and aggression of children. *American Psychologist, 37,* 197–211.

Feinberg, H. K. (1978). Anatomy of a helping situation: Some personality and situational determinants of helping in a conflict situation involving another's psychological distress. Doctoral dissertation, University of Massachusetts, Amherst.

Frankena, W. (1973). *Ethics* (2nd ed.). London: Prentice-Hall.

Gouldner, A. W. (1960). The norm of reciprocity: A preliminary statement. *American Sociological Review, 25,* 161–79.

Grodman, S. M. (1979). The role of personality and situational variables in responding to and helping an individual in psychological distress. Unpublished doctoral dissertation, University of Massachusetts, Amherst.

Grusec, J. (1981). Socialization processes and the development of altruism. In J. P. Rushton and R. M. Sorrentino (Eds.), *Altruism and helping behavior*. Hillsdale, NJ: Erlbaum.

Gump, P. V., and Friesen, W. V. (1964). Participation in nonclass settings. In R. G. Barker and P. V. Gump (Eds.), *Big school, small school: High school size and student behavior*. Stanford, CA: Stanford University Press.

Hertz-Lazarowitz, R., and Sharan, S. (1984). Enhancing prosocial behavior through cooperative learning in the classroom. In E. Staub, D. Bar-Tal, J. Karylowski, and J. Reykowski (Eds.), *Development and maintenance of prosocial behavior* (pp. 423–43). New York: Plenum.

Hovland, C. I., and Sears, R. R. (1940). Minor studies of aggression: Correlation of lynchings with economic indices. *Journal of Psychology, 9*, 301–10.

Huesmann, L. R., Eron, L. D., Lefkowitz, M. M., and Walder, L. O. (1984). Stability of aggression over time and generations. *Developmental Psychology, 20*, 6, 1120–34.

Huesmann, L. R., Lagerspetz, K., and Eron, L. D. (1984). Intervening variables in the television violence-aggression relation: Evidence from two countries. *Developmental Psychology, 20*, 746–75.

Johnson, D. W., Maruyama, G., Johnson, R., Nelson, D., and Skon, L. (1981). The effects of cooperative, competitive, and individualistic goal structures on achievement: A meta analysis. *Psychological Bulletin, 89*, 47–62.

Landau, S. F. (1982). Trends in violence and aggression: A cross-cultural analysis. Paper presented at the Tenth International Congress of Sociology, Mexico City.

Meyerhoff, M. K., and White, B. L. (1986). Making the grade as parents. *Psychology Today, 20*, September, 38–45.

Oliner, S. P., and Oliner, P. M. (1988). *The altruistic personality: Rescuers of Jews in Nazi Europe*. New York: Free Press.

Patterson, G. R. (1982). *Coercive family processes*. Eugene, OR: Castilia.

Piaget, J., and Weil, A. (1951). The development in children of the idea of the homeland and of relations with other countries. *International Social Science Bulletin, 3*, 570.

Radke-Yarrow, M. R., Zahn-Waxler, C., and Chapman, M. (1983). Children's prosocial dispositions and behavior. In P. H. Mussen (Ed.), *Carmichael's manual of child psychology*, Vol. 4 (4th ed.). New York: Wiley.

Shaffer, D. R. (1979). *Social and personality development*. Monterey, CA: Brooks-Cole.

Sroufe, L. A. (1979). The coherence of individual development: Early care, attachment, and subsequent developmental issues. *American Psychologist, 34*, 834–42.

Staub, E. (1970a). A child in distress: The influence of modeling and nurturance on children's attempts to help. *Developmental Psychology, 5*, 124–33.

——— (1970b). The use of role playing and induction in children's learning of helping and sharing behavior. *Child Development, 42*, 805–17.

——— (1974). Helping a distressed person: Social, personality, and stimulus determinants. In L. Berkowitz (Ed.), *Advances in experimental social psychology*, Vol. 7. New York: Academic Press.

——— (1975). To rear a prosocial child: Reasoning, learning by doing, and learning by teaching others. In D. DePalma and J. Folley (Eds.), *Moral development: Current theory and research.* Hillsdale, NJ: Erlbaum.

—— (1978). *Positive social behavior and morality: Social and personal influences,* Vol. 1. New York: Academic Press.

—— (1979). *Positive social behavior and morality: Socialization and development,* Vol. 2. New York: Academic Press.

—— (1980). Social and prosocial behavior: Personal and situational influences and their interactions. In E. Staub (Ed.), *Personality: Basic aspects and current research.* Englewood Cliffs, NJ: Prentice-Hall.

—— (1981). Promoting positive behavior in schools, in other educational settings, and in the home. In J. P. Rushton and R. M. Sorrentino (Eds.), *Altruism and helping behavior.* Hillsdale, NJ: Erlbaum.

—— (1986). A conception of the determinants and development of altruism and aggression: Motives, the self, the environment. In C. Zahn-Waxler, E. M. Cummings, and R. Iannotti (Eds.), *Altruism and aggression: Biological and social origins.* New York: Cambridge University Press.

—— (1987). The ideal university in the real world. *Occasional Papers,* Institute for Advanced Studies in the Humanities. University of Massachusetts, Amherst.

—— (1989). *The roots of evil: The origins of genocide and other group violence.* New York: Cambridge University Press.

—— (1990a). Moral exclusion, personal goal theory, and extreme destructiveness. In S. Opawa (Ed.), Moral exclusion and injustice. *Journal of Social Issues, 46,* 47–65.

—— (1990b). The power to help others. Unpublished manuscript, University of Massachusetts, Amherst.

—— (in press). Individual and group selves, motivation and morality. In W. Edelstein and T. Wren (Eds.), *Morality and the self.* Cambridge: MIT Press.

Stone, L. (1977). *The family, sex and marriage in England, 1500–1800.* New York: Harper & Row.

Straus, M. A., Gelles, R. J., and Steinmetz, S. (1980). *Behind closed doors: Violence in the American family.* Garden City, NY: Anchor/Doubleday.

Surrey, J. (1985). Self-in-relation: A theory of women's development. Wellesley, MA: Stone Center, Wellesley College.

Thompson, W. R., and Grusec, J. (1970). Studies of early experience. In P. H. Mussen (Ed.), *Carmichael's Manual of Child Psychology,* Vol. 2 (3rd ed.). New York: Wiley.

Trivers, R. L. (1971). The evolution of reciprocal altruism. *Quarterly Review of Biology, 46,* 35–37.

Wilson, E. O. (1975). *Sociobiology: The new synthesis.* Cambridge, MA: Belknap Press of Harvard University Press.

Yarrow, M. R., and Scott, P. M. (1972). Imitation of nurturant and nonnurturant models. *Journal of Personality and Social Psychology, 23,* 259–70.

Zahn-Waxler, C., Cummings, E. M., and Iannotti (Eds.). (1986). *Altruism and aggression: Biological and social origins.* New York: Cambridge University Press.

# 18

# ALTRUISM AMONG ALCOHOLICS

## Daniel M. Boland

In practice altruism means giving more to others than we are expected to give while taking less for ourselves than we're allowed to take. Expressions of this kind of practical altruism vary from everyday gestures of courtesy to selfless, heroic action. Altruism can mean accepting simple inconveniences for the benefit of loved ones or giving one's life for one's friends. Altruism motivates kindness to strangers and aid to weary colleagues, food and shelter for the needy and care for the friendless. Altruism inspires our concern for troubled others whose wisdom is less tested, whose temperament is less stable, and whose resilience is less tenacious than our own.

True altruism involves giving something personal: one's time or trust, one's loyalty or support. True altruism has no hooks; we act unreservedly, even anonymously, for others' well-being. We ask nothing in return, neither friendship nor loyalty, neither religious conversion nor ideological assent, neither appreciation nor thanks. The realization of this ideal may seem rare indeed; one might think only of Mother Teresa or the Dalai Lama as true altruists. Yet in everyday affairs, altruism is surely incarnated in the sacrifices of loving parents and in the tireless tutelage of diligent teachers. And there is another arena of life filled with examples of altruism: Alcoholics Anonymous (AA), in which altruism is daily demonstrated by the extraordinary emotional support and unheralded generosity recovering alcoholics extend to one another. This movement crosses every racial, religious, geographical, age, and language barrier and is still growing. AA's success exemplifies altruism's role in physical healing, psychological recovery, and spiritual transformation.

Alcoholism is both a physical disease and a spiritual malaise. It is also life-threatening: unchecked, it kills. If alcoholics do not quit drinking, their condition eventually becomes severe enough to require hospitalization; in time, they will die.

Sooner or later all alcoholics reach a point at which their drinking is completely unmanageable, their lives utterly out of their control. They each experience a moment in which they face a choice between further self-degradation, illness and eventual death or drastic action and dramatic change. They can no longer conceal or rationalize their condition.

When the alcoholic comes to that moment of crisis and decision, what can he or she do? For many alcoholics AA is the only effective channel to survival, sanity, and sobriety. AA provides the company of other successfully recovering alcoholics, which is critical at this point. True, alcoholics were once thought of as self-centered, irresponsible, aggressive, narcissistic, and hostile people. But the research of Tamerin and Neumann (1974) challenged that stereotype. Their studies concluded that alcoholics, who are often overcontrolled and inhibited, also seem to be unusually altruistic and selfless, hard working and highly idealistic. Together, recovering alcoholics have the one irreplaceable ingredient that seems to catalyze the healing process: personal experience.

Clinical and anecdotal evidence consistently indicates that almost all alcoholics are unable to initiate recovery and maintain sobriety by themselves. Good intentions are utterly insufficient for sobriety. Despite his or her remorse and subsequent sincerity, almost every alcoholic soon realizes that going it alone, especially in the early stages, is foolhardy and self-defeating; it almost universally results in relapse. The support, experience, and wisdom of other alcoholics is crucial.

The healing power in AA rests on a number of psychological elements: the nonintrusive listening of other alcoholics; the knowledge and experience of despair, which all alcoholics have undergone; supportive reassurances and unfeigned, nonthreatening intimacy with other alcoholics whose confrontations may be blunt and brutally frank but are clearly informed by personal suffering; the availability of successfully recovering alcoholics who tirelessly share their concern and time with no reservations or expectations of personal reward. These are the beneficial traits that newly arrived alcoholics routinely encounter, the psychological sparks that ignite AA's effectiveness.

AA is a surprisingly loose and informal confederation. To join AA the alcoholic merely locates an AA meeting, walks in (no invitation is necessary), sits down, and listens. The only requirement for AA is a sincere desire to stop drinking and the willingness to attend meetings. While joining AA is a very simple matter, doing so may require all the courage and humility an alcoholic can muster.

AA meetings are held many times each day in thousands of large cities and small towns around the world. AA has no admission fees, no dues, no formal registration procedures, no membership rolls, no age restrictions (some AA members are in their early teens), no uniforms or secret handshakes, no political or religious affiliations. The only quasi-structure in AA occurs at the beginning of each meeting when a list of twelve truths about the alcoholic's life—the so-called Twelve Steps—are read aloud.

AA members create an interdependent healing environment. Members understand one another; acceptance is tangible. A sense of kinship and inclusion are indispensable ingredients in the first steps toward sobriety. AA members need not know one another to help and be helped. Their particular brand of shared suffering binds them. In fact, the intensity and openness of their concern and support for one another often surprises and confounds new members and sober outsiders. Alcoholics' deepest failings are their common bond. Admitting their failures and unashamedly discussing shameful events usually elicit knowing nods and smiles of recognition from fellow alcoholics who know exactly what is being said; they've been there.

As alcoholics confront the destructive force of their drinking, they learn that they can redirect their addictive energy toward a healthy pathway that, for most alcoholics, also involves moral change and spiritual recovery. They recognize that sobriety is but one step along a lifeline of choices. Alcohol is a major symptom (but not the only problem) in alcoholics' addictive and avoidant lifestyles. They may, for example, find periods in which their craving erupts in indirect ways; alcoholics are often heavy smokers who also consume oceans of coffee and mounds of chocolate.

The indispensable core of AA's healing power—the sine qua non of its existence—is the group meeting. As each speaker addresses the group, the meeting becomes an arena of intense listening. No one speaks very long, a few minutes at most. No one interrupts. Group members (all of whom have "hit bottom" in their own way) listen with intensity and patience. Their noninterruptive listening has a rare empathic quality, and the atmosphere is clearly supportive.

Confidentiality and anonymity are taken for granted. A person may even speak, unseen, from the back of the room. In those few minutes, a speaker may reveal (perhaps for the first time) the self-defeating facades and self-destructive delusions that have constituted his or her alcoholic lifestyle. During these AA meetings each person introduces himself or herself to the group by first name only, adding that he or she is an alcoholic ("I'm Bill and I'm an alcoholic"). New members then make any brief, candid statements or comments they wish about their lives, particularly about alcohol's role in it, and what they are learning by being sober. Group members simply listen; no one is challenged or questioned; there is usually no dialogue or discussion, no rules about what to say.

Because of the alcoholic's history of denial, AA encourages frankness. Alcoholics tell harrowing, sometimes brutal tales about their excesses, often with little delicacy or reserve. In the group the recovering alcoholic finds honesty and support all around; lies and further denial are transparent and useless. Evasion and equivocation hinder recovery. This blunt, unadorned self-descriptive communication seems to possess extraordinary, life-saving properties. In the psychological complexities of hearing and accepting others, of unchallenged self-revelation and undefended self-disclosure, a powerful therapeutic milieu develops. Without the need for lies and facile dodges, the truth surfaces; alcoholics see the extent of their past rationalizations, excesses, and excuses. They see how completely alcohol has sullied their thinking, stultified their emotional lives, and twisted their reason and judgment. They realize how their thoughts have been profoundly convoluted. They see that self-delusion and lies are useless. They learn to face their self-indulgence, to accept responsibility for their past and present behavior. They also learn to avoid the destructive excesses of unproductive guilt, depression, and remorse. And, most critically, they learn how to live without alcohol. They see how others do it. They realize that they drink not because they have problems; they have problems because they drink. And at last they grasp the basic message that it's taken them their lifetimes to appreciate: if they don't drink alcohol, they won't get drunk! Thus, self-revelation is the first step to sobriety and self-discovery in AA.

Newcomers to AA are urged to attend meetings as often as possible, usually at least once a day for a minimum of thirty to ninety days; the more meetings the better. As one AA member put it, "We have all known the newcomers' terror and humiliation. In the group we all share the same kind of pain in personal ways. That's all we need to know about one another: the pain. There's no arguing or debating in group meetings, no right or wrong way of being sober, as long as you don't drink. There's just the reality of being an alcoholic with other alcoholics, admitting the worst to them and to yourself, knowing that just being with them, even briefly, is the way back to decency and sobriety and survival. Everyone understands the other person's search because everyone is still searching, no matter how long they've been sober, because sobriety never ends."

In the transformation from addiction to sobriety, from self-destruction to emotional and spiritual redemption, alcoholics have a healing benefit: knowledge of their self-defeating potential. They have learned the worst about themselves the hard way. The worst mistakes they might make have, in all likelihood, already been made long ago. They have little else to lose.

There are pitfalls to sobriety, however. Alcoholics always leave a wake of shattered relationships, broken promises, and disillusioned allies behind them. In the waning days of their drinking, the people closest to them are usually drinkers themselves or are well-meaning but ill-advised loyalists (the enablers) who actually abet, however, unwittingly, their addiction. When healing begins, alcoholics have to establish their priorities, often for the first time. They learn that it is now essential to honestly take inventory of their whole way of relating to other people (Johnson 1973). They soon realize that their entire lives have—without exception—been connected to or dominated by alcohol. Consequently, they may have to withdraw from certain relationships and social routines connected to alcohol. They may have to end long-term friendships and switch jobs. And, as much as they may have prayed for the alcoholic's recovery, the alcoholic's family (if they are still around) may find his or her sobriety a taxing and stressful experience.

At some point in their recovery, the newcomers may select a

"sponsor"—a more experienced recovering alcoholic whose sobriety and wisdom have been tested, someone more mature in the healing process, a mentor and counselor who will act as the alcoholic's immediate source of advice and support. But above all else, the crucial requirement for alcoholics' recovery and for those who still love them (or are trying to) is that they remain sober, no matter what the cost!

The religious overtones, the spiritual rhetoric and redemptive imagery in AA are difficult to accept for some critics who say the AA approach is naive or unscientific. There are also a few newly formed atheist AA groups who reject the mention of God or a higher power as a factor in their recovery. Some critics also feel that AA (and many of the self-help organizations based on the AA/Twelve Step recovery model) panders to uncritical, self-deceiving losers who are really kidding one another and who use meetings simply to blow off emotional steam, to achieve an inexpensive catharsis. These critics overlook the countless recovered alcoholics whose lives are sober evidence of something immensely powerful at work. In its brief history, AA has provided a path to sanity, sobriety, and serenity and restored life and hope to millions of alcoholics around the world.

The social scientist may ask, Is AA a valid example of altruism in the strict sense? Do recovering alcoholics give support and acceptance to one another altruistically or for their mutual benefit? Are they on a power binge or an ego trip or just trying to ease their own personal discomfort? Are AA members selflessly altruistic or are they really using one another, out for their own sakes, concerned only for their own sobriety (Batson 1990)?

From a clinical or research perspective, these are challenging questions. In the day-to-day world of the recovering alcoholic, however, they are utterly meaningless. Why and how AA works is less important than that it does work. In fact each AA meeting ends with the powerful admonition, "Keep coming back; it works!"

Viktor Frankl (1984, 113) once wrote, "Man is able to live and die for the sake of ideals and values which give meaning to life." AA helps people see sobriety as a life-saving ideal and each sober moment as a valued step in the life-long journey toward serenity. Success in AA terms is measured "one day at a time"; each day's success means life itself.

## REFERENCES

Al-Anon (1982), *Living with an Alcoholic,* Eleventh Printing. New York: Al-Anon Family Group Headquarters.

―――― (1985), *Al-Anon's Twelve Steps and Twelve Traditions,* Fifth Printing. New York: Al-Anon Family Group Headquarters.

Batson, C. Daniel (1990), "How Social an Animal? The Human Capacity for Caring," *American Psychologist,* 45, 336–46.

Conrad, Barnaby (1986), *Time Is All We Have.* New York: Arbor House.

Frankl, Victor (1984), *Man's Search for Meaning,* 3d ed. New York: Simon and Schuster.

Johnson, Vernon E. (1973), *I'll Quit Tomorrow.* New York: Harper & Row.

Monti, Peter M., Abrams, David B., Kadden, Ronald M., and Cooney, Ned L. (1989), *Treating Alcohol Dependence.* New York: Guilford.

Myers, Judy (1987), *Staying Sober: A Nutrition and Exercise Program for the Recovering Alcoholic.* New York: Congdon & Weed.

Tamerin, John, and Neumann, Charles P. (1974), "The Alcoholic Stereotype: Clinical Reappraisal and Implications for Treatment," *American Journal of Psychoanalysis,* 34 (4), 315–23.

U.S. Congress, Office of Technology Assessment (1983), *The effects and costs of alcoholism treatment.* Washington, D.C.: U.S. Government Printing Office.

# 19

# ALTRUISM AND EXTENSIVITY IN THE BAHÁ'Í RELIGION

*Wendy M. Heller and Hoda Mahmoudi*

Throughout history, religion has often been the cause of bitter, violent, and seemingly insolvable conflicts between groups of people. Yet religion also has the potential to transcend other group affiliations in uniting people into a community. Although religion has often been cited to justify prejudice and hostility against other groups, religious scriptures have furnished inspiring appeals to altruism and enduring exhortations to embrace the "other." This chapter will examine some of the ways in which one religious system, the Bahá'í faith, combines the unifying function of religion with altruism in its aspiration to develop an altruistically oriented global society.

Located in over two hundred countries, the Bahá'í faith has recently been identified as the second most widely distributed religion (geographically) after Christianity (Barrett 1988). Although the Bahá'í faith originated in nineteenth-century Iran, the vast majority of its multiracial and multicultural membership is now located in other countries, especially in the Third World, with the largest national community being in India. The Bahá'í faith has no clergy; its community administration is conducted by elected councils of nine members (at the local, municipal level by Local Spiritual Assemblies; at the national level by National Spiritual Assemblies; and at the international level by the Universal House of Justice). The Bahá'í teachings are contained in the writings of the religion's prophet-founder, Bahá'u'lláh (1817–1892); his son and successor, 'Abdu'l-Bahá (1844–1921); and 'Abdu'l-Bahá's grandson and successor, Shoghi Effendi (1897–1957). Bahá'ís accept these works as authoritative texts and the definitive model for belief and behavior, as well as the blueprint for social transformation and for the global social order that is the religion's ultimate goal (see Universal House of Justice 1985).

Bahá'ís aim to transform civilization by transforming themselves and their own social institutions on the basis of principles contained in the Bahá'í scriptures. Both altruism and extensivity—a pattern of personal commitment and responsibility that embraces diverse groups of people (see Oliner and Oliner, this volume)—are fundamental components of Bahá'í belief and practice, a factor that has important implications for the community Bahá'ís are attempting to construct.

The social change envisioned by Bahá'ís involves processes of individual and structural transformation that are interrelated and interactive. Individual transformation embodies more than a profession of belief; it is viewed as a process of acquiring distinctive personal characteristics and demonstrating them in social interactions as well as in working, together with other Bahá'ís, to develop the emerging Bahá'í social institutions.

In the Bahá'í view, spiritual life is not separated from the realm of social relations but integrated with it. The Bahá'í teachings shift the focus of religious practice from individual salvation or enlightenment to the collective progress of humanity as a whole (Arbab 1987, 10). They address social conditions and global problems as directly related to the individual's spiritual life; issues of world peace, the equality of men and women, harmony between science and religion, the equitable distribution of wealth and resources, and the elimination of prejudice are, for Bahá'ís, inseparable from religious belief and practice.

Such an emphasis on collective progress has important implications for the relationship of individual entities—whether individual persons, nations, or other groups—to the larger society of which they form a part. As Shoghi Effendi wrote in 1938, essentially, that relationship is based on the principle of the subordination of "every particularistic interest, be it personal, regional, or national, to the paramount interests of humanity." This, in turn, is based on the idea that

in a world of inter-dependent peoples and nations the advantage of the part is best to be reached by the advantage of the whole, and . . . no abiding benefit can be conferred upon the component parts if the general interests of the entity itself are ignored or neglected. (1955, 198)

Yet the "interests of humanity as a whole" are not conceived in terms of a vague abstraction that could be appropriated by a particular dominant group and interpreted as identical with its own interests but, rather, as a complex dynamic relationship between the parts and the whole, in which the viability of the whole is served by ensuring the well-being of all its individual parts, an enterprise for which all share responsibility.

This conception is demonstrated at its most basic in the relationship of the individual person and society, in which a complex balance is sought between individual freedom and responsibility. Cooperation between society and the individual is stressed, as is the fostering of "a climate in which the untold potentialities of the individual members of society can develop." Such a relationship, as it is envisioned, "must allow 'free scope' for 'individuality to assert itself' through modes of spontaneity, initiative and diversity that ensure the viability of society." Thus, even while the will of the individual is subordinated to that of society, "the individual is not lost in the mass but becomes the focus of primary development" (Universal House of Justice 1989, 20–21).

The fulfillment of individual potential is to be sought not in pursuing self-centered desires but in contributing to the benefit and well-being of others, and "the honor and distinction of the individual consist in this, that he among all the world's multitudes should be a source of social good" ('Abdu'l-Bahá 1957, 2–3).

As Farzam Arbab (1987), a member of the International Teaching Centre, a Bahá'í advisory institution, has noted, such emphasis on the progress of humanity is also reflected in a shift of emphasis on the particular qualities that Bahá'ís are enjoined to acquire; for example, justice is stressed more than charity, and the acquisition of attitudes conducive to unity is valued over simple tolerance. Even the qualities of love and of detachment from the material world are conceived as active and social rather than passive and inward directed:

The social dimension is also enhanced through the expansion of the meaning of most qualities to include a social vision. Love includes the abolition of social prejudices and the realization of the beauty of diversity in the human race. Detachment from the world is not taught in a way that leads to idleness and to the acceptance of oppression; it is acquired to free us from our own material interests in order to dedicate ourselves to the well-being of others. To this ... is also added a constant endeavor to acquire social skills, to participate in meetings of consultation, to work in groups, ... to reach and carry out collective decisions. (Arbab 1987, 11)

Thus, he concludes, the Bahá'í path of spiritualization "should not be confused with one that defines goodness passively and produces a human being whose greatest virtue is not to harm anyone; it is a path to create social activists and agents of change" (11).

Altruism is a major component of that desired social change and figures prominently in the Bahá'í texts. Many scriptural exhortations delineate altruistic norms explicitly, holding in high regard those who "nurture altruistic aims and plans for the well-being of their fellow men" ('Abdu'l-Bahá 1978, 72). Other teachings reflect values and attitudes conducive to an altruistic orientation (see Oliner and Oliner 1988), including a sense of unity with and responsibility toward others beyond one's own social group; a strong family orientation; emphasis on relationship rather than status; generosity; trustworthiness; appreciation of diversity; as well as ethical values of justice and caring.

Unity and interdependence, and their link to helping behavior, are prominent themes in the Bahá'í texts, often expressed through organic metaphors, as in this passage from the writings of Bahá'u'lláh (1952):

The utterance of God is a lamp, whose light is these words: Ye are the fruits of one tree, and the leaves of one branch. Deal ye one with another with the utmost love and harmony.... So powerful is the light of unity that it can illuminate the whole earth. (288)

Explaining this metaphorical reference, 'Abdu'l-Bahá (1978) writes that because all humans are interconnected and mutually dependent, they must "powerfully sustain one another" by caring for each other:

Let them at all times concern themselves with doing a kindly thing for one of their fellows, offering to someone love, consideration, thoughtful help. Let them see no one as their enemy, or as wishing them ill, but think of all humankind as their friends; regarding the alien as an intimate, the stranger as a companion, staying free of prejudice, drawing no lines. (1–2)

The theme of inclusiveness is emphasized in every aspect of Bahá'í individual and community life, beginning with the fundamental teachings of the oneness of humanity and the unity of religion. The Bahá'í teachings view divine revelation not as a static, unique event, but as a continuing process that is the central feature of human history. The spirit that inspired all the founders of the great religions of the past, the Manifestations of God, is recognized as one and the same. Their original teachings contain the same basic ethical and moral precepts, prominent among which are the teachings that promote altruism. The tenets that change from one religious dispensation to another are the social laws and practices. Thus, religious truth is understood to be relative, progressive, and developmental.

Such a perspective implies more than tolerance for the equality of individual religions as separate entities to be respected in a pluralistic society. It redefines the nature of their relationship to one another and thus sets new terms for a definition of identity that is based on connection rather than separation. Unlike religious groups that define themselves by their distinction from other groups based on the claim that their founder was the sole or the final source of truth, or their practices the only correct form of worship, the Bahá'í religious tradition accepts all the great spiritual teachers as equals. Bahá'ís are expected to revere Buddha, Zoroaster, Moses, Jesus, and Muhammad, as well as their own founder, Bahá'u'lláh, recognizing in them the same spirit of the Mediator between God and humanity. Thus, although the body of teachings composing the Bahá'í religion itself cannot accurately be called eclectic, the Bahá'í religious *tradition* includes all of the previous dispensations, which are viewed as "different stages in the eternal history and constant evolution of one religion, Divine and indivisible, of which it [Bahá'í] itself forms but an integral part" (Shoghi Effendi 1955, 114).

From the Bahá'í perspective, the principle of the unity of religion and progressive revelation restores the unifying role of religion in society, providing a basis for resolving long-standing, apparently unbridgeable division among religious communities as well as a resolution of the dilemma posed by the existence of numerous religions, each claiming divine origin. For Bahá'ís, the principle removes any pretext for disunity deriving from religious affiliation; in fact, all religious conflict is forbidden. The Bahá'í writings direct Bahá'ís to "love . . . all religions and all races with a love that is true and sincere and show that love through deeds" ('Abdu'l-Bahá 1978, 69). "That the divers communions of the earth, and the manifold systems of religious belief," Bahá'u'lláh (1952) writes, "should never be allowed to foster the feelings of animosity among men, is, in this Day, of the essence of the Faith of God and His Religion" (287).

Affirming the preeminence of the principle of religious inclusiveness and unity, the Bahá'í writings go so far as to state that if religion becomes the cause of division and disunity, it is better to have no religion at all ('Abdu'l-Bahá 1945).

Closely linked to the principle of the unity of religion is the distinguishing feature of the Bahá'í dispensation: the principle of the oneness and wholeness of humanity. The full equality of all members of the human species and their close relationship to one another mandates that Bahá'ís regard people from all racial, religious, ethnic, class, and national backgrounds as members of one global human family. Rather than offering mere "symbols of internationalism" in the hope that these might, as Allport (1954) suggested, "provide mental anchorage points around which the idea of world-loyalty may develop" (44), the Bahá'í religion begins with the underlying principle of world loyalty and human unity, which is itself the anchorage point, "the pivot," according to Shoghi Effendi (1955), "round which all the teachings of Bahá'u'lláh revolve" (42). The extension of the individual's personal commitments and relationships to include the diverse groups that compose humanity is repeatedly urged in Bahá'í texts in the strongest terms possible—that is, as no less than a divine commandment:

In every dispensation, there hath been the commandment of fellowship and love, but it was a commandment limited to the community of those in mutual agreement, not to the dissident foe. In this wondrous age, however, praised be God, the commandments of God are not delimited, not restricted to any one group of people, rather have all the friends been commanded to show forth fellowship and love, consideration and generosity and loving-kindness to every community on earth. ('Abdu'l-Bahá 1978, 20–21)

Far from being an abstract principle removed from real social conditions, the unity of humankind must be lived in practice, as 'Abdu'l-Bahá (1969) told a gathering in Europe in 1912:

Do not be content with showing friendship in words alone.... When you meet a [stranger], speak to him as to a friend; if he seems to be lonely try to help him, give him of your willing service; if he be sad console him, if poor succour him, if oppressed rescue him....

What profit is there in agreeing that universal friendship is good, and talking of the solidarity of the human race as a grand ideal? Unless these thoughts are translated into the world of action, they are useless. (16)

Although the Bahá'í writings speak of the absolute equality of all, the intent is not sameness or conformity to a dominant culture, nation, race, class, or any other group. In theory and in practice, cultural and racial diversity are valued in the Bahá'í community. Along with the expression of the ideal, a conscious awareness exists that effort is necessary to break down age-old barriers of prejudice and separation. The cultivation of friendships with people of different backgrounds is repeatedly encouraged, but perhaps the most notable evidence of the Bahá'í commitment to interracial unity is the attitude toward interracial marriage, which is actively welcomed and encouraged in the Bahá'í writings.

In consonance with the prosocial orientation of the Bahá'í teachings, the ideal Bahá'í personality as implied in the Bahá'í scriptures is other centered, extensive, and altruistic. In one passage, 'Abdu'l-Bahá (1945) makes altruism itself the touchstone for a new definition of true human nature:

Man should be willing to accept hardships for himself in order that others may enjoy wealth; he should enjoy trouble for himself that others may enjoy happiness and well-being. This is the attribute of man.
...He who is so hard-hearted as to think only of his own comfort, such an one will not be called man.
Man is he who forgets his own interests for the sake of others. His own comfort he forfeits for the well-being of all. Nay, rather, his own life must he be willing to forfeit for the life of mankind. (42)

Although personal transformation is seen as a life-long process, according to the Bahá'í texts the foundations of altruistic behavior can be developed in childhood. Children are believed to be born with the capacity for good or bad behavior; during the course of their development they can be influenced by their social interactions, especially in the family. The Bahá'í writings urge parents to "teach [children] to dedicate their lives to matters of great import, and inspire them to undertake studies that will benefit mankind" ('Abdu'l-Bahá 1978, 129). So crucial is the teaching of prosocial behavior that "training in morals and good conduct is far more important than book learning" ('Abdu'l-Bahá 1978, 135).

However, teaching children lofty ideas is not considered sufficient on its own. Emphasis is repeatedly placed upon behavior, rather than professions of belief—on deeds, not words. Thus the most powerful method by which children can be taught a prosocial orientation is the model of parents whose actions reflect the ideal personality characteristics.

The impact of modeling on children has received significant support in the literature on altruism and prosocial behavior. According to Mussen and Eisenberg-Berg (1977), "a substantial proportion of the individual's helping and sharing responses is acquired through observation and imitation of a model's behavior without direct reinforcements" (31). Yarrow, Scott, and Waxler (1973) conclude that "generalized altruism would appear to be best learned from parents who do not only try to inculcate the principles of altruism, but who also manifest altruism in everyday interactions" (256). The role of parental influence in fostering the development of the altruistic personality has been further underscored by Oliner and Oliner (1988).

Another area of related emphasis is parental discipline. The development of good character and behavior in children is to be encouraged through the love, understanding, and wise guidance of the parents, using reason rather than force. Bahá'í texts strongly discourage the use of physical punishment or verbal abuse of children, a view supported by contemporary social psychologists. Hoffman (1975), as well as others, suggests that the use of physical power or material resources to control the child's behavior (power assertion) is least effective in developing consideration for others. In contrast, the disciplinary technique of induction—reasoning and explanation based on the impact of the child's behavior on others— encourages prosocial behavior (Mussen and Eisenberg-Berg 1977).

Bahá'í child socialization aims to develop a prosocial orientation in children, who are encouraged to recognize themselves as members of a community that begins with the family and extends to include all of humanity. They are encouraged to develop a sense of personal spiritual responsibility to act toward others with empathy and compassion as well as justice and equity, and to sacrifice their own material self-interests for others in need. As adults, Bahá'ís are expected to make a commitment to continue internalizing such patterns until they become the foundation of the personality itself. Spiritual development is seen as an infinite process of self-transformation—that is, a continual, conscious refining of one's behavior in the crucible of social interaction. The cultivation of spiritual, altruistic qualities remains the aim and central focus of life for the adult Bahá'í.

In the light of recent research, it is noteworthy that both the ethical principles of justice and of caring, important motivators of altruistic behavior (Oliner and Oliner 1988), are emphasized in the Bahá'í writings, where they are not viewed as contradictory or exclusive but as inseparably connected. Even when the ethic of justice is enjoined, it is usually as a practice to be performed out of concern for others. Justice is presented as the practice of equity, often linked with "safeguard[ing] the rights of the downtrodden" (Bahá'u'lláh 1952, 247). The Bahá'í conception of justice means that all have a right to receive care.

Well over half a century before Carol Gilligan (1982) called attention to the complementarity of the "masculine" ethic of justice and the "feminine" ethic of caring, 'Abdu'l-Bahá (1978) had written, "The Kingdom of God is founded upon equity and justice, and also upon mercy, compassion, and kindness to every living soul. Strive ye then with all your heart to treat compassionately all humankind." Yet, he then qualified this statement, asserting that oppression must be opposed: "Kindness cannot be shown the tyrant, the deceiver, or the thief, because, far from awakening them to the error of their ways, it maketh them to continue in their perversity as before" (158).

The Bahá'í teachings recognize that the transformation of individuals into altruistic persons cannot take place outside the social context, which must provide a matrix for that transformation. Recent research has drawn attention to the importance of group norms in motivating moral behavior, whether directly, as a response to the social expectations as such, or indirectly, as internalized personal norms (Reykowski 1982). The findings of Oliner and Oliner (1988) further underscore the importance of the normocentric orientation in motivating the altruism of rescuers of Jews during World War II.

Such findings imply that not only must altruistic qualities be fostered in individuals, but a social framework must also be provided within which extensivity and altruism are valorized and represent the norms of the group itself. The creation of such a society is inseparable from the development of individual altruistic personalities, for so long as groups value egocentrism, unfettered individualism, status seeking, dominance, and a materialistic orientation, altruism will remain an exception to the rule, and the altruistic personality will appear as deviant in comparison to the rest of the group. In Bahá'í society, this situation is reversed: altruism is not an aberrant behavior contrary to convention, because the normative expectations (which individuals are ultimately expected to internalize) are altruistic.

It is beyond the scope of this discussion to describe in its entirety the social order Bahá'ís envision and to which they are committed. But they believe that

much of it will be the fruit of the process of integration of now isolated or even hostile races, groups, and nations who, as they come together and unite in the same cause, become transformed and help transform each other, and bring to the rising institutions of a new World Order the richness of different cultures and of different social thought and experience. (Arbab 1987, 11)

Thus, in the Bahá'í view, it is through the individual practice as well as the institutionalization of the principle of unity in diversity that human society can evolve to an unprecedented level of cohesion and cooperation, and transcend the limitations implicit in the current state of separation and competitiveness. While the Bahá'í conception of unity in diversity should not be construed as merely a version of liberal pluralism, the safeguarding and encouraging of diverse elements within the Bahá'í community is a major institutional principle. It is embedded within Bahá'í institutions through practices that, because they apply at all levels of administrative and community functioning—local, national, and international—require the participation and support of the entire Bahá'í community.

Most prominent of these practices is consultation, a group decision-making process whose goal is to reach solutions to problems by consensus. Bahá'í consultation encourages the open and frank expression of diverse views on the topic under discussion, in an atmosphere of love and respect that also allows the "clash of differing opinions" that can strike the "shining spark of truth" (Shoghi Effendi 1968, 21). Each member of the consultative group has an equal right of expression, and no blocs or factions—or any subdivisions of the group—are permitted. Inseparable from the Bahá'í consultative process is the development of sensitivity and respect for the different voices whose expressions of opinion may not fit into conventional or dominant cultural modes of communication. Since the group attempts to work toward consensus on an issue, voting only as a last resort, the process does not necessarily require reduction to duality: alternatives need not be narrowed down to the two poles "for" and "against." Instead, the consultative process itself, drawing on the interactive contributions of all its diverse members, is looked to as the creative source of new solutions.

Consultation is regarded both as a method for generative decision making and conflict resolution as well as an instrument for reinforcing the unity of a diverse group. It is the method by which the Bahá'í administrative institutions conduct the affairs of the Bahá'í community, but Bahá'ís are also encouraged to use consultation in all aspects of their lives, whether in the family, neighborhood, or workplace.

Another way in which Bahá'í administrative institutions are structured to implement unity in diversity involves practices intended to ensure the participation of minority ethnic populations (the definition of what constitutes a "minority" is left to the discretion of the National Spiritual Assembly in each country). "To discriminate against any race, on the ground of its being socially backward, politically immature, and numerically in a minority," is considered to be "a flagrant violation of the spirit" of the Bahá'í teachings (Shoghi Effendi 1963, 29). In principle, protecting the "just interests of any minority element within the Bahá'í community," and ensuring that all have the opportunity to contribute their perspectives to the collaborative efforts of the group, is considered so important that representatives of minority populations "are not only enabled to enjoy equal rights and privileges, but they are even favored and accorded priority" (Universal House of Justice 1976, 49). Bahá'í communities are instructed that it is their duty to ensure that "Bahá'í representative institutions, be they Assemblies, conventions, conferences, or committees, may have represented on them as many of these divers elements, racial or otherwise, as possible" (Shoghi Effendi 1963, 30).

One way in which this principle is practiced is the minority tie rule of Bahá'í elections. In the course of elections for Bahá'í administrative institutional membership—elections that are conducted without nominations or campaigning, and are decided by plurality vote—if voting results in a tie between persons, one of whom represents a minority, "priority should unhesitatingly be accorded the party representing the minority, and this for no other reason except to stimulate and encourage it, and afford it an opportunity to further the interests of the community" (Shoghi Effendi 1963, 30). In addition to its direct effect in increasing minority representation in Bahá'í administrative institutions, the practice of this rule heightens the sensitivity of the group to its minority membership and reaffirms the group commitment to valuing and encouraging minority participation. For the individual believer, conceding a tie vote to the minority representative becomes a concrete opportunity to practice sacrifice of self-interest for the other, within a context of social approval.

Whether applied in community administration, in the family, in education, or in the economy, the Bahá'í principles and practices are viewed as catalysts whose application will ultimately bring about social transformation leading to the development of an altruistic global society. Such a society, in the Bahá'í context, begins with the individual striving daily toward personal transformation—the deliberate internalization of spiritual teachings incorporating altruistic, extensive values as personal norms. The Bahá'í teachings strive to imbue individuals with an inclusive orientation transcending—though not suppressing—other group loyalties and valuing the well-being of the entire planet and all its inhabitants. Throughout the Bahá'í writings, the vision imparted to the individual is that of a peaceful, just, and caring civilization whose foundation rests on the cornerstone of the unity of all human beings, a unity that is to be consolidated and protected by institutions that reflect and promote the principles of unity, equity, and altruistic service as normative expectations.

## REFERENCES

'Abdu'l-Bahá (1945). *Foundations of world unity.* Wilmette, IL: Bahá'í Publishing Trust.

———. (1957 [1875]). *The secret of divine civilization.* Wilmette, IL: Bahá'í Publishing Trust.

———. (1969 [1912]). *Paris talks: Addresses given by 'Abdu'l-Bahá in Paris in 1911–1912* (11th ed.). London: Bahá'í Publishing Trust.

———. (1978). *Selections from the writings of 'Abdu'l-Bahá.* Haifa: Bahá'í World Centre.

Allport, G.W. (1954). *The nature of prejudice.* Reading, MA: Addison-Wesley.

Arbab, F. (1987). The process of social transformation. In *The Bahá'í Faith and Marxism: Proceedings of a conference held January 1986* (pp. 9–20). Ottawa: Association for Bahá'í Studies.

Bahá'u'lláh (1952 [1939]). *Gleanings from the writings of Bahá'u'lláh.* Trans. Shoghi Effendi (rev. ed.). Wilmette, IL: Bahá'í Publishing Trust.

Barrett, D. B. (1988). World religious statistics. *Encyclopedia Britannica book of the year* (1988, p. 303). Chicago: Encyclopedia Britannica.

Gilligan, C. (1982). *In a different voice: psychological theory and women's development.* Cambridge, MA: Harvard University Press.

Hoffman, M. (1975). Moral internalization, parental power, and the nature of parent-child interaction. *Developmental Psychology 11,* 228–39.

Mussen, P., and Eisenberg-Berg, N. (1977). *Roots of caring, sharing, and helping: The development of prosocial behavior in children.* San Francisco: Freeman.

Oliner, S. P., and Oliner, P. M. (1988). *The altruistic personality: Rescuers of Jews in Nazi Europe.* New York: Free Press.

Reykowski, J. (1982). Motivation of prosocial behavior. In V. J. Derlaga and J. Grizelak (Eds.), *Cooperation and helping behavior: Theories and research* (pp. 355–75). New York: Academic Press.

Shoghi Effendi (1955 [1938]). *The world order of Bahá'u'lláh* (rev. ed.). Wilmette, IL: Bahá'í Publishing Trust.

———. (1963 [1939]). *The advent of divine justice* (rev. ed.). Wilmette, IL: Bahá'í Publishing Trust.

———. (1968 [1928]). *Bahá'í administration* (5th rev. ed.). Wilmette, IL: Bahá'í Publishing Trust.

Universal House of Justice (1976). *Messages from the Universal House of Justice, 1968–1973.* Wilmette, IL: Bahá'í Publishing Trust.

———. (1985). *The promise of world peace.* Haifa: Bahá'í World Centre.

———. (1989). *Individual rights and freedoms in the world order of Bahá'u'lláh: A statement by the Universal House of Justice.* Wilmette, IL: Bahá'í Publishing Trust.

Yarrow, M. R., Scott, P., and Waxler, C. Z. (1973). Learning concern for others. *Developmental Psychology 8,* 240–60.

# 20

# ALTRUISM IN THE SOCIALIST WORLD

*Wiktor Osiatynski*

The subject of this discussion is "ordinary" altruism, that is, acts of disinterested help rendered to others. I interpret "altruism" as voluntary help rendered by an individual to another individual or group who does not arouse in that individual the biological instinct of help and care. Culture may encourage or discourage it, but the final choice whether to help or not rests with the individual. The actual motivation of that help is less important here. I leave it for the reader to appraise to what extent the opinions represented here may apply to the saving of people in extreme situations.

In the years 1987–1990, as a participant in the Altruistic Spirit Project of the Institute of Noetic Sciences in Sausalito, California, I had talks with many scholars of altruism and persons involved in practical altruistic activities in Poland, the USSR, and other Eastern European countries. I was particularly interested in the impact of the current political reforms in the USSR and Eastern Europe on altruism and other acts aimed at helping others. An important element of those reforms is to create mechanisms to reinforce individualism. Thus the question arises whether an increase in individualism will reduce the traditional altruism and prosocial orientation in those countries.

This study argues that this will not happen, because individualism and altruism do not clash with each other. On the contrary, altruism is based on individualism and together they are complementary to each other in a free society. There can be no altruism without individual freedom of choice; at the same time, altruism provides a moral balance for individualism and the related rise in egoism. Moreover, individualism and altruism oppose collectivism: thus a lessening of collectivism and reinforcement of individualism may pave the way for a rise in altruism in post-Communist societies.

This study will concern only the model of collectivism created in Russia under the tsars and developed in the Soviet Union. In the Soviet Union, Communist collectivism developed in favorable conditions because of the collectivist tradition particularly noticeable in the Orthodox religion, the village community, and even in the progressive social thought of the Russian intelligentsia.

## 1. INDIVIDUALISM, COLLECTIVISM, AND HELP TO THOSE IN NEED IN RUSSIAN CULTURE

Prerevolutionary Russian traditions largely shaped the thinking and aims of today's reformatory elites in the Soviet Union. It is therefore worthwhile to consider the role of individualism and collectivism and the model of help that prevails in Russian culture. I have assumed individualism to include 1) the separation of the individual from community; 2) the grant to that individual of certain elementary rights that may not be infringed by the state authority or by the community; 3) the conviction that the individual has the right independently to decide about his/her life, provided such decisions do not encroach on other persons' rights; 4) the conviction that the individual is responsible for his/her acts and fate; 5) the conviction that the individual voluntarily establishes or at least confirms social bonds with definite persons, and that the community is woven from such bonds; 6) the conviction that the individual may have duties in relation to the state and society, but those duties cannot be imposed arbitrarily and cannot encroach on that individual's rights. However, what is not an indispensable element of individualism is the conception of social contract—that is, the notion that the state arises from a contract between individuals who preserve a part of their inalienable rights, transferring some powers only to that state.

Here collectivism means a negation of the above elements of individualism, in particular 1) a poor separation of the individual from the community; 2) the primacy of the community over the individual and of the individual's duties over rights—lack of the right independently to decide about one's own life; 3) a minimal economic and social security provided by the community; 4) the conviction, related to the claim for the sense of security, that the individual is not responsible for his/her own fate; 5) weakness of the civil society composed of an economic sector independent of the state or community, and of voluntary associations and self-government; and 6) weakness of voluntary social bonds between the separate individuals acting as individuals and not members of the community.

## 1.1. The Orthodox Religion

One of the main traits of the Orthodox religion that differentiates it from Catholicism and the Protestant religions is a lack of affirmation of the individual. No conception of individual rights exists; rather, an explicit anti-individualism is expressed in the individual's subordination to community.

This subordination appears already on the cognitive plane. Eastern Christianity and its institutions claim to possess the one and only truth, which is collective in its substance. A logical consequence of such a conception and practice is the rule that the individual should submit to that truth and to the institutions that proclaim it, hence the duty of obedience to and imitation of the path shown by the church. With the church's complete subordination to the state, that duty was extended to include unconditional obedience to the state.

The unity of church and state additionally impaired the position of the individual: namely, extinguishing the conflict between church and state, it removed the force that had limited the absolutism of both of those authorities, secular and spiritual. As a result, there was in the entire Orthodox state system nowhere that the individual could find shelter from constraint and oppression; nor were there forces to demand respect for individual rights.

The only counterbalance to the unrestricted absolutism of the state was the principle of inner freedom that functioned in the Orthodox consciousness. In his/her inner substance, the individual was free and had an absolute value. That freedom, however, was not achieved in society but in religious feelings directed toward the other world. Rather than get involved in life on earth, it was thought better to concentrate on the improvement of inner freedom expressed in one's communion with God.

Even those individual actions that concerned others served the purpose of self-improvement. According to the Orthodox religion, the faithful are obliged to give alms and render help to orphans and the destitute and to protect widows. Yet those "charitable acts are to serve the giver's moral health, and do not have in view the possible beneficial effects for the recipient" (Wieczynsky, in press, 560). This tradition was expressed in the duty to give a penny to each of the beggars in the churchyard, irrespective of one's appraisal of the actual needs or conduct of the person asking for help.

Related to this is an equally old tradition of seeing Christ in every person in pain, in poverty, or in need, and even in those imprisoned. Hence the phenomenon we know from Russian literature: the kindness of ordinary people toward prisoners and convicts. Hence also the custom of following those sent into exile to Siberia: the exiles were nearly as sacred as Christ because they suffered like Christ.

### 1.2. The Village Commune

The religious dictate of rendering unconditional help to those in need was universally accepted in Russian rural life. However, such help was quite selective, involving persons—*yurodivi*, cripples, beggars—whom the commune considered "morally" authorized to receive help. In relations with other persons, however, who were equal to one in position, rights, and duties, the dictate to help lacked any particular impact.

The duty to render help was imposed first of all on the family and was only transferred to the community if the family was unable to perform it. In practice, mutual help was rendered in cases concerning the mutual interests of all inhabitants, such as fire, flood, or epidemic. According to custom, individual families received help in situations such as childbirth, weddings, funerals, and particular hardships. The village community usually recognized and duly performed its duties toward deserted and abandoned children and orphans; the dictates to help the elderly, the ailing, and the lonely were less strictly observed (Atkinson 1988).

At the same time, the commune consolidated all the anti-individualistic traits of Russian culture. The supreme value was equality, which was interpreted as equal living conditions—that is, within a single peasant class; the gulf separating peasants from landowners was universally accepted. From the seventeenth century on, that equality was served by the periodic redistribution of land within the commune, to give an equal portion to every man and boy. Those who had previously had more land lost, while those who had a greater number of children profited.

Another trait of the peasant commune was strong resentment both toward those who happened to be better off and more resourceful and toward those who simply chose to stay poor without the commune's approval—there was danger that such persons might abuse the commune's duty to help. It may be presumed that those very resentments were the source of measures, introduced later on, to fight the so-called social parasites. The predominating value of equality in the Russian village made the emergence of any trend towards individualism impossible.

### 1.3. The Individual and Help to Those in Need in Russian Social Thought

The village commune became the ideal model of the future for the strongest philosophical trend among the Russian intelligentsia in the latter half of the nineteenth century—populism. The anticapitalist populists gave priority to social over political change, considering the basic social value to be not freedom but equality. They considered political freedom and its protective constitutional mechanisms to be tools of capitalist oppression.

Two other trends in Russian thought were also antiindividualistic: Slavophilism and pan-Slavism, which combined messianic imperialism with glorification of the tsar's autocracy. Of all the trends in nineteenth-century Russian thought, those closest to individualism were the so-called occidentalists and Constitutional Democrats, such as Vissarion Belinsky and Alexander Hertzen, who understood the Western principle of individual freedom. But even these occidentalists despised the middle class and all its mechanisms of protecting individual freedom.

All these main trends of Russian social thought had one feature in common: a program of more or less radical social change introduced by the elite, in most cases the intelligentsia. None of the philosophical trends, however—not even Russian liberalism—recognized individual freedom as an essential value. This does not mean that the Russian intellectuals were indifferent to the individual and individual fate. On the contrary, all the criticism of the middle class and capitalism, particularly in the case of the populists, referred to the good of the individual. The populists (*narod-*

*niks*) intended to improve the village commune to create the best possible conditions for the development of the human being.

Freedom, interpreted positively as the full development of human abilities, naturally went along better with equality than with human liberties and rights. Here the *narodnik* philosophical conceptions approached Marxism, which also rejected political freedom, stressing the vision of the full realization of human potential. With the trend towards Marxism, the role of individualism in Russian thought was even further reduced. The intellectual conception of helping those in need also changed.

While in the village community help was rendered outside the family only in exceptional cases, in the higher classes the duty to help was interpreted more broadly. The entire upper-class Russian culture was permeated with a sense of guilt and duty towards those in need and a profound sympathy toward the suffering. This can be seen in particular in nineteenth-century Russian literature, which went beyond the appeal to be charitable and made heroes of the wronged and humiliated, the poor and lonely, the unfortunate and the fallen. For the Russian intelligentsia, those "wronged and humiliated" meant the entire Russian people, only just liberated from serfdom. The sense of being indebted to the poorer always characterized the Russian intelligentsia, regardless of ideological affiliation.

Concern about the fate of the people was accompanied by a sense of mission and a certain paternalism, expressed above all in the belief that the greatest possible gift for the people would be their mental and moral instruction and elevation to the level of the intelligentsia itself.

### 1.4. Altruism in Russian Thought: *Landmarks* and the Philosophy of Vladimir Solovyev

The authors of the 1909 volume *Landmarks* accused the socialist-minded populists of mental aristocratism toward the people, treated as the object and not the subject of change, as immature children in need of help from better-educated protectors. They argued that social radicalism was bound to lead to the rejection of absolute values and the explanation of all evil by external conditions, and to the blurring of individual responsibility for human acts and life, thus consolidating the people's immaturity.

Rejecting the intellectuals' concern for the abstract "cause" of the people, the authors of *Landmarks* opposed the conception of an altruism that increases the responsibility of both the helper and the recipient of help. For altruism to become possible, the belief had to be renounced that man's only worthy aim was to serve the common good, and some egoism had to be permitted (Gershenzon 1977 [1909], 86–87). Only if the individual's right to satisfy one's own needs and to choose one's own happiness were accepted could truly altruistic and responsible bonds be formed between the individual and the community.

The conception of altruism postulated by the authors of *Landmarks* drew on the works of the greatest Russian idealist of the late nineteenth century, Vladimir Solovyev, who believed all morals to be based on three emotions: shame, pity, and pious adoration. Shame expresses the individual's attitude toward all that is inferior; its development is conscience, aimed at restoring integrity in the individual's inner life. Pious adoration expresses the attitude toward all that is superior, while pity is a social emotion that, according to Solovyev, expresses humanity's attitude towards all that is equal and similar to it—that is, toward its fellow human beings (Walicki 1979, 388).

Pity originates from maternal love, which is then extended to others, then to humanity at large, and eventually to all the universe. Pity (compassion) is best expressed in the principle of altruism, which should reign in human relations. Altruism based on pity prevents the individual from doing to others what he/she would not like to suffer from them, and makes the individual do what he/she would like them to do. Pity and altruism are aimed at "transforming the society into an integral organism, to bring to pass the 'truth of coessentiality,' the real solidarity of all beings" (Walicki 1979, 388).

Solovyev combined the love of God and the love of one's fellow human being in the principle of charity—that is, of alms—which he formulated and developed in his treatise *The Spiritual Foundations of Life*, written in the years 1882–1884. He believed that a "kingdom of alms" where "the strong and rich would offer themselves up as a sacrifice to the weak and poor" would be the supreme stage of social development. The duty of charity imposed on the "strong and rich" was to be the essence of a nonrevolutionary and basically religious social transformation. In turn, the implementation of the dictate of charity should be the chief aim of the state. The state should renounce the traditional order and serve the moral one.

It is worth stressing here that despite his different grounds, for Solovyev the duty to give alms was, as in Orthodox tradition, a duty of unconditional help where the helper had no right whatever to appraise the requests and needs of the recipient of help. "True alms consist in giving what is necessary and requested," Solovyev stressed (1988, 48–64).

In formulating this perspective Solovyev attempted to square the Russian tradition with the Western conception of individualism and human rights. Recognizing the primacy of morality and moral rigorism over statutory law, Solovyev nevertheless considered subjective rights to be the necessary guarantee of a minimum of morality in society. Admittedly, morality is much closer to perfection than law, yet there is no mechanism to enforce respect for moral principles. Law, however, has such coercive measures at its disposal. "Thus law is not to change the world into the Kingdom of Heaven but rather to prevent it from changing into hell." While morality tends to be maximalistic, law "lets one be immoral" within specific limits, "defining the conditions of balance between individual freedom and common good" (Stremoukhoff 1980, 280).

Human rights and dignity, freedom of conscience, and the principle of individualism itself were for Solovyev the Western values Russia had to adopt if the restoration of human integrity was ever to be possible. The Kingdom of Heaven in this world could be composed of free human beings only, and a separate individual living in society was the chief aim of moral progress, Solovyev argued. He was probably the only Russian philosopher who tried to combine the common good with individual interests not through subordination of the individual to the community but through recognition of human dignity and individualism as the basis of free altruistic activities aimed at implementation of the principle, traditional in the East, of the universal unity of all people and beings.

### 1.5. The Tradition of Philanthropy

The principle of help was realized in practice in Russia through philanthropic activities that developed rapidly late in the nineteenth century. Philanthropy originated in charity, but unlike alms and charity, which rendered help directly to those in need, philanthropy involved the establishment of permanent institutions of social welfare: schools, almshouses, hospitals, publishing houses, etc. But ever since Nikolai Novikov's charity schools in Petersburg were found to be a threat to the empress's autocratic power, philanthropy, as well as all other civic initiatives, was regularly persecuted.

It is therefore not surprising that in the days of great reforms after 1861, philanthropy was prominent among the rights for which progressive reformers struggled. The liberalization of the period resulted in an exceptionally rapid development of philanthropic activities, led by Russian factory owners trying to win public approval and a position equal to that of the nobility. Philanthropic activity was also among the most frequently used methods of establishing social institutions other than the state-controlled ones in Russia.

In tsarist Russia, charity and philanthropy had provided a counterbalance for autocracy, a complete lack of freedom, and the system's everyday cruelty. After the 1917 revolution, even that counterbalance ceased to exist.

## 2. COLLECTIVISM AND ALTRUISM IN THE SOVIET UNION

### 2.1. Altruism in Marxism and Leninism

For Marx, altruism is merely a mask for class egoism and the selfishness of the capitalists. It has nothing to do with love of one's neighbor; at best, philanthropy serves the "fulfillment of the money aristocracy's self-love, it serves well their pride and their desire for amusement" (Fritzhand 1961, 145; translation mine).

Marx's critique of altruism went hand in hand with his rejection of individualism. Three important tenets describe his attitude toward both concepts:

1. Individual freedoms are barriers that separate people from one another. To overcome those barriers it is necessary to a) reject the notion of individual rights and b) subordinate the selfishness of the individual to the interests of the public sphere.

2. Marx's public sphere is not the same as the social sphere. The public sphere is identical with the state, which is to take over the private sphere and civil society alike. Since all bonds between individuals, including altruism, belong to civil society, there is no room for such bonds or for interpersonal relations in the public

sphere—that is, in the state-controlled society. In Marx's ideal society, all activities are to be planned rationally by the state and the needs served by altruism will be taken care of by the state. Individual interests should be subordinated to the interests of the state and, at the same time, all bonds between individuals within civil society (not organized and controlled by that state) should disappear.

3. In the ideal Communist society, the natural kindness of people will triumph over their selfishness, which is induced merely by defective social relations. With those relations mended by revolutionary means, there will be no room for selfishness or for altruism, as the purpose of the latter is to countervail individual selfishness.

Similarly, there was no room for altruism, compassion, or help in Marx's theory of social development, in which capitalism, with its harsh primitive accumulation, was accepted as a necessary sacrifice on the road to communism.

For Marx, private capitalist exploitation was a tool efficient enough to drive energy out of individuals and to increase the nation's wealth on the road to communism. Thus, when communism was reached in a relatively affluent society, everybody could afford, so to say, to be "naturally good" and the contradiction between the individual and society could be transcended: everyone would do what he or she liked, with no need for sacrifice, and all the others would benefit.

But after communism took over in Russia, where primitive accumulation had not yet taken place, the Communists, who had taken power on behalf of the people, now faced the necessity to exploit that same people as a precondition of the future material progress they promised. The need for a drastic change in ideology emerged. Thus, Lenin introduced the concept of a "prosocial man," and the notion of "social interest" became the most venerated idea of Soviet communism. While Marx's "new man" was a superman who—by virtue of the revolutionary change in social relations— was able to develop all his individual potential, Lenin's "new man" was a being who gave up his willingness to develop his potential and sacrificed his personal interests and needs for the good of a society represented by the state. Thus, Lenin introduced the original blend of Marxism with traditional tenets of Russian Orthodoxy, populism, and collectivism.

## 2.2. Rejection of Altruism and Charity in Communist Russia

In the early years of communism, a number of additional factors repressing the altruistic or simply charitable behavior of Soviet citizens emerged.

During the campaign against *kulaks* in the twenties as well as the ruthless crushing of all political opposition in the thirties, feelings of charity, pity, and mercy were the only remaining obstacles to the imprisonment and execution of innocent people and to the cruelty and lawlessness of the entire system. Therefore, they were ridiculed in the official propaganda as proof of weakness and of lack of revolutionary principles. Mercy was synonymous with betrayal, according to the revolutionary "ethics of struggle," which required merciless annihilation of all "enemies of the people."

Although charity and mercy reemerged in extreme situations during World War II, with the return of Stalinism in relatively safer and more normal times, other factors began to undermine, with more durable effects, the traditional ethics of mercy and pity. Many of them had to do with Communist ideology.

The most visible ideological influence was the atheism imposed on Soviet society, particularly during the party-controlled education of the young generations. With mass rejection of religion, all absolute values became weaker and were challenged ever more effectively. A related development was the outright rejection of the entire Russian philosophical tradition after the revolution.

At the same time the monopoly of an omnipotent Communist state weakened the individual's sense of social responsibility; the state was there to take care of the needy. A new ethics emerged based on the principle of the "pride of the Soviet citizen," which forbade citizens to accept help from private persons, including the family.

With these developments there was less and less room for charity in the Soviet state. Charity Street in Leningrad was renamed Textile Street, and in the dictionary the very word *miloserdie* (charity) was annotated as "obsolete." The notion of "altruism," never really accepted by the Russian intelligentsia before the revolution, was repudiated outright after the revolution. The educational system neglected the development of charity or help to others and of such feelings as compassion or pity. As Danil Granin puts it, the natural sensitivity to others' pain ceases to exist when it is not upheld by education or exercised daily. Thus, the word "charity," purged from Soviet art, literature, and education, actually went out of use.

These developments were not accidental by-products of the Communist system. They were the logical consequences of the Marxist-Leninist interpretation of the relationship between individuals and society.

### 2.3. The Individual and Society in Soviet Collectivism

The most important idea of Soviet social thought and ethics is the concept that an individual has to give priority to social interests, as defined by the state, over personal needs and desires. The worst moral offense for a Soviet citizen is to be selfish or "nonsocial." While this may sound like it paves the way for philanthropy and altruism, actually it does not. Social interests are never defined in Soviet science as the needs of a definite individual or a group of individuals within the civil society. Nor is another individual supposed to be a recipient of a good Soviet citizen's unselfish deeds. In the entire body of Soviet Marxist-Leninist social and philosophical writings, one can hardly find a single mention of this particular type of prosocial behavior. Moreover, one cannot find any attention given to the direct relationship among individuals and/or between an individual and a group of individuals within the civil society.

On the contrary, rejection of such relations is the main target of the Leninist critique of altruism and bourgeois ethics in general. "Scientific ethics of Marxism-Leninism has proven that what lies at the very foundation of morals are not the relationships between separate individuals in general but relations between social classes," claimed the authors of the *Great Soviet Encyclopaedia* (1960, 2: 187; translation mine).

In general, Leninist social thought is limited to collectivism— that is, to relations between people as members of groups organized and controlled by the state. In fact, the essence of Marxism-Leninism can be interpreted as the identification of society with the state and the elimination of the non-state usage of the term "society."

In Leninism, the very definition of the individual is put in collective terms—that is, the boundaries between an individual and various collectives he/she is part of are blurred and imprecise. One has a feeling that a greater part of the individual's identity rests in the collective. Such nonindividualized individuals are not fully grown up: they have obligations to the collective but no rights to protect their autonomy from that collective.

A good example of this collectivist philosophy is a work by a noted Soviet scholar, director of the Institute of Marxism and Leninism in Moscow, Georgi Smirnov (1977), on the formation of the so-called Socialist personality. Writing about "the combination of the common and personal interests in the individual of a new type," Smirnov quotes a standing authority of Soviet pedagogy, Antoni Makarenko, who wrote, "A man inside whom the interests of the collective prevail over personal interests is already a Soviet type of man" (292; translation mine).

Describing the highest social ideals of the Soviet man, Smirnov writes, "One does not need much to live for oneself; to live for others one needs many good characteristics, powers, and talents. There is truth in saying that an individual is rich not in what he owns but in what he gives to others" (294; translation mine). However, in his entire book Smirnov does not point to a single mechanism by means of which an individual could give anything to other definite individuals. Society and social interest are defined in abstract terms and are represented solely by the state.

This seems to be the essential difference between Leninism and traditional Russian collectivism. While in prerevolutionary Russia the cruelty of the system was balanced by pity, charity, and mercy, which linked individuals, under communism all efforts were made to break the bonds between individuals, including those within the family. Altruism, help, charity, and pity were remnants of the old social network and had to be wiped out to pave the way for one monolithic and hierarchial system of oppression and exploitation. An ever more isolated and atomized individual was totally controlled by the state, which represented society. "Prosocial" ideology was to persuade victims to accept willingly their exploitation and dependence.

### 2.4 Return to Charity in Recent Years

Despite all efforts to banish it, the old Russian tradition of pity, charity, and mercy remained alive in people's hearts and in some forms of art, particularly war literature and movies, where expressions of humane feelings and charitable acts were permitted.

Another literary arena in which moral issues were present was the wave of rustic literature in the 1960s, by folk writers called *derevenshchiki*, (village-dwellers), among whom the most influential were Vladimir Soloukhin and Victor Likhonosov (Jarco 1988; Drawicz 1988). A great majority of them tried to revive the Russian tradition of human interconnectedness, combining a warm attitude toward the church with the affirmation of faith, perceived as the foundation of all other values.

The issues raised by the *derevenshchiki* began to reemerge in the mainstream of Soviet cultural life with the beginning of the current changes in the USSR. Today, a great number of writers claim that "conscience, compassion, and pity are the foundations of ethics," and join forces with the moral and religious revival in Soviet society (Bykau, in Drawicz 1988, 7).

This revival was particularly visible in 1988, during the celebrations of the millennium of the Orthodox church in Russia. But since early in 1986, a growing number of churches have been reopened after many decades as museums, civic centers, or grain stores. There has been an upsurge in the number of baptisms of both children and adults. The most important part of the teachings given to the newly baptized adults concerns morals in general and the development of virtues of charity, compassion, and pity in particular.

The Orthodox church has also asked the Soviet government to restore the traditional social services of the church, especially the training for nuns to serve as nurses in hospitals, and the provision of help to the needy. While awaiting the decisions, Orthodox priests exercise charity by giving alms to people who ask them for help. An important aspect of this help is a clearly expressed sense of the obligation to help unconditionally.

An increase in charitable and helping activities outside the church became especially visible after the 1986 nuclear plant explosion in Chernobyl. Ordinary men and women volunteered to help the victims, took strangers to their houses, and helped them resettle in new places. Throughout the USSR people collected over five hundred million dollars to help the victims. Similar reactions were also becoming common in less dramatic situations.

In February 1987, Danil Granin published a long essay, "On Charity," in the leading Soviet cultural magazine *Literaturnaya Gazeta*. Granin, who defended his city during the siege of Leningrad, was a coauthor of the *Book of the Siege*. Based on his personal experience during the war and the research done for the book, Granin came to believe that every individual is endowed by nature with an innate feeling of compassion and an instinct to help. In recent years, however, Granin had noticed that people stopped acting on those positive feelings in their relationships with others. He realized that if those feelings are not exercised in daily life, they tend to abate slowly and eventually vanish completely.

In his article, Granin described in detail the disappearance of charity and compassion in Soviet society and analyzed the reasons why charity was going "out of usage" in the USSR. He recalled the old Russian traditions of pity and "love of the fallen" praised by great Russian writers from Pushkin to Sholokhov. Finally, Granin not only called the readers to charity and philanthropy but asked for the creation of various institutional mechanisms that would help people to exercise those virtues in everyday life.

Granin's article resulted in thousands of letters to the editor of *Literaturnaya Gazeta:* a great number of readers supported Granin and gave practical advice as to how charity could be introduced into Soviet life; some claimed charity "is against the very principles of Marxism, for it hampers attempts to give to everyone according to his work and breeds social parasites," while the last group supported Granin in principle but claimed that taking care of the needy should remain the obligation of the Communist state.

Granin himself kept out of the debate. From a number of letters he learned that many people, including a great portion of the youth, had already been doing what he called for. They helped the needy and elderly. They cooked dinners for sick people and kept them company. All those activities were illegal or at least extralegal. In order to help, the helpers had to overcome bureaucratic obstacles and risked persecution or penalties. Granin decided to use his position and influence to give protection and help to the helpers. In the fall of 1988 he created the Charitable Association "Leningrad."

The primary purpose of the association is not to render direct help to the needy but to help volunteers fulfill their commitments. The majority of helpers are young people. According to Granin, some of them are motivated by their religious beliefs. Some have themselves experienced difficulties and were helped out by others. A majority, however, are people who more or less accidentally helped others and liked it. This is the source of Granin's ultimate optimism, and proof that the only requirement for the spread of charitable acts is simply to create for young people an opportunity to exercise charity.

The example of the "Leningrad" association was followed by a number of similar charitable organizations throughout the Soviet Union. At the same time, other helping organizations were created. In Moscow, the "Children's Fund" and the "Cultural Fund" were established. Press articles and radio and television features repeatedly call for charitable activities, and the most popular TV program, "Vzgliad" (Outlook), includes a lengthy section on needy or neglected Soviet citizens and asks for help for them. Subsequent programs reported about thousands of people who responded to the previous week's call for help.

All these activities have a similar purpose: to propagate help to the needy. They share a similar set of underlying assumptions, two of which are especially important: first, the admission that the Soviet system has failed to solve social problems and alleviate individual misery, and second, a call for the restoration of the best prerevolutionary traditions of pity, charity, and philanthropy that were banned from Soviet culture and life for over seventy years. Therefore, the analysis of those traditions seems crucial for an understanding of the meaning of charity today and for the future of altruism in the Soviet Union, especially in view of the marked continuity of many Russian and Soviet ideas, practices, and values.

## 3. CONCLUSIONS: INDIVIDUALISM, ALTRUISM, AND COLLECTIVISM IN RUSSIA AND THE USSR

As a trait of Russian and Soviet culture, the duty to help those in need, usually rendered in the form of alms, philanthropy, or radical social activity for the people, has a number of characteristics the consequences of which can be seen in the culture and social life of the Soviet Union.

First, that help is unconditional, independent of the helper's appraisal of the actual needs and attitude of the recipient. This is a natural consequence of the attitude towards helping in which salvation, alleviation of the sense of guilt, or the helper's frame of mind mattered more than the interest of the person receiving help. This motive seems to have been particularly strong in the case of radical revolutionary activities pursued "in the name of the people." Definite individuals disappeared entirely from view in

Marxist-Leninist philosophy and in Communist social practice, where the state was the only recipient of "prosocial" activities.

Related to this is a highly controversial problem of interdependence between helping activities and interhuman bonds. The faithful would give alms never looking the beggar straight in the eye. The populists acted for the benefit of the masses, not definite individuals. In the collectivist model of help formulated by Lenin, an attempt was made to remove all interpersonal relations, including those within the family, replacing them with an anonymous system of help distributed by the state. In time, all helping activities were depersonalized, and the notion of "prosocial attitudes" served as a mask of exploitation carried out by the state, and as a tool to obtain consent to oppression from those exploited.

Thus both philosophical and religious Russian tradition and Soviet practice seem to leave little room for direct bonds between the helpers and the helped. Observations and memories of those who received help from Russians (or other nations of the USSR), however, clash with that conclusion. Those once transported to Siberia and to labor camps, as well as refugees from Siberia and escaped prisoners, are practically of one mind in contrasting the cruelty and soullessness of official representatives of the system with the self-sacrificial help they received from "ordinary" people, sometimes perfect strangers. Moreover, they all stress the spontaneous and profound bond established nearly at once in contacts with Russians, particularly with those rendering help. This was pointed out by Krzyzstof Pomian.

I was similarly impressed during many journeys in the Soviet Union. I believe we deal here with an element of the former Russian system of natural bond, which has resisted time and Communist propaganda. That bond consists of participation in the unity of the universe, in a basic union in which people participate through a "metaphysical submersion" rather than the establishment of direct bonds between one another. This community spirit, derived possibly from the poor personal individualization of self characteristic of the Orthodox religion, is evident throughout Russian culture, both in the intellectual populists and their critics, in the authors of *Landmarks*, in Solovyev, and in the *derevenshchik* writers of the 1960s.

A basic difference between traditional Russian collectivism and its Communist counterpart is precisely that attempt to remove such primitive bonds or at least to subordinate them to the state

and party control. The fact that this attempt proved not fully effective might indicate that the only way to loosen such bonds is
by replacing them with cultural and economic individualism, as
occurred in the developed countries. Only following such loosening
of natural unity can the establishment of new, this time more
voluntary, bonds between the individualized individuals take
place.

Another important trait of the Russian model of helping is its
rigorism. Help, particularly that which was to secure salvation for
the helper, not only had to be disinterested but also had to involve
a sacrifice of the helper's interest. Any grain of profit, or even
satisfaction, deprived help of its moral value. This attitude seems
to persist to the present day: Danil Granin considers a religious
motivation of helping to be "inferior," as it follows from a wish
for reward in the shape of future salvation. One leading Soviet
psychologist discontinued his research on altruism, saying, "If I
were to carry on then, and to remain honest and faithful to my
research, I would have to give all I had away to the needy. I was
not prepared for such a gesture, so I changed the topic of my
research."

Such rigorism deprived help of its everyday nature, making it
assume heroic dimensions and discouraging those incapable of
great achievements and sacrifices from any helping activities whatever. At the same time, with a strong cultural stress on helping, it
was difficult to say to what extent help was actually rendered
spontaneously.

Still another trait of the Russian cultural model of help is its
paternalism. Recipients of help were treated as children unable to
choose a life path unaided and who therefore must be guided by
the educated helpers. Exclusivity and paternalism were also characteristic of the Russian model of philanthropy in which factory
owners and merchants took the lead. Among the weak Russian
middle class, philanthropy was an attempt to gain at least a minimum of control over social life through philanthropic institutions,
financed and controlled by capitalists. In any case, philanthropy
consolidated the helper's exclusive and paternalistic attitude towards those helped and did not contribute to establishing bonds
between individuals in civil society.

The paternalistic model of helping left the greatest impression
on the consciousness of those helped, encouraging helplessness and
a lack of responsibility for one's own fate. Unconditional helping

did not allow for the "tough love" where, as a result of refusal to help, the fallen person must make an effort to rise.

The "cult of the fallen," exceptionally strong in Russian literature, often added heroic value to failure, thus providing the grounds for the negative leveling characteristic of Russian social consciousness. Combined with the duty to help, intraclass egalitarianism favored a sense of entitlement and expectation of sacrifice by others. This in turn often gave rise to selfish requests for help, for things and services that were not necessary or that the supplicant could have obtained unaided.

Also worthy of note are the interpretation of land and other property as a burden rather than a chance for individual development; the notion of economic activity as a no-score game where all profit must involve another person's loss; intolerance of those who willfully situate themselves outside the social division of labor ("social parasites"); prejudice against competition; lack of a sense of relationship between effort expended and reward received; and the expectation of socioeconomic security and equality.

It is not by chance that all the abovementioned traits are connected with the Russian anti-individualism that they consolidate: they are elements of a broader and consistent system of collectivism where the valid model of charitable help at the same time fanned and balanced anti-individualism.

Subordinating the individual to the community, collectivism negated individualism. At the same time, forcing out charity, collectivism also negated altruism with its essentially voluntary character. Altruism, however, seems not to negate individualism: they counterbalance each other. It is not by chance, for that matter, that the notion of altruism was used for the first time by Auguste Comte already after the emergence and establishment of the notion of individualism. Nor was it by chance that in the rare cases where Russian thought approached individualism, it departed from the simple duty of charity toward a kind of help that establishes bonds between people.

The problem acquires a special importance in the face of the reforms now being undertaken in the Soviet Union, reforms aimed not only at de-Stalinization and transformation of the petrified political and economic structures but also at stimulating the Soviet people to activity, to take risks, and to assume responsibility for their own fate. This change of attitude cannot be accomplished if the traditional anti-individualism is preserved. Such change will also be impossible if the traditional conception of charity is revived, as a large part of the modern Russian intelligentsia would do, for like Russian and Soviet collectivism, that conception of charity includes many factors that reduce the individual motivation to assume responsibility for one's own life.

It seems, therefore, that the success of reforms in the Soviet Union depends largely on a renunciation of collectivism and a trend toward both individualism and altruism. The instruments of change towards individualism may be primarily economic and political. However, only moral consciousness can transform collectivistic into altruistic attitudes. While the changes towards individualism may indeed be forced with growing effectiveness by the current economic and political situation, there are reasons to fear that Soviet culture is still poorly prepared for the task it now faces—transforming traditional collectivistic charity into individualistic altruism—a foundation on which a noncollectivist community composed of autonomous human beings might be based in the future.

## REFERENCES

Atkinson, D. (1988). "Egalitarianism and the commune." *Slavic Review*.

Billington, J. H. (1966). *The icon and the axe: An interpretative history of Russian culture*. New York: Vintage.

Drawicz, A. (1988). "Ku wiecznosci wyciagam dlonie" (I point my hands toward eternity). *Wiez* (Warsaw) 5 (May) 3.

Fritzhand, M. (1961). *Mysl etyczna mlodego Marksa* (Ethical thought of the young Marx). Warszawa: Ksiazka i Wiedza.

Gershenzon, M. O. (1977 [1909]). "Creative self-cognition." In B. Schragin and A. Todd (Eds), *Landmarks: A collection of essays on the Russian intelligentsia, 1909* (64–87). New York: Karz Howard.

Granin, D. (1987). "O milosierdii" (On charity). *Literaturnaya Gazeta* 12 (March 18) 13.

*Great Soviet Encyclopaedia*, vol. 2. (1960). Moscow.

Jarco, J. (1988). "Nurt religijno-moralny w rosyjskiej prozie radzieckiej lat szescdziesiatych i siedemdziesiatych" (The moral and religious trend in Russian Soviet novels of the 1960s and 1970s"). *Odra* (Wroclaw, Poland) 2 (February).

Smirnov, G. L. (1977). *Oblicze czlowieka socjalizmu* (The face of Soviet man). Warsaw: Ksiazka i Wiedza.

Solovyev, V. S. (1988). *The spiritual foundations of life*. Warsaw.

Stremoukhoff, D. (1980). *Vladimir Soloviev and his messianic work* (Translated by Elizabeth Meyendorff). Belmont, Mass.: Norland.

Walicki, A. (1979). *A history of Russian thought: From the enlightenment to Marxism.* Stanford, Cal.: Stanford University Press.

Wieczynski, J. L. (in press). "Philanthropy and charity in Russia from early times to 1861." In *Modern Encyclopedia of Russian History.* Vol. 50. Edited by Joseph L. Wieczynski. Gulf Breeze, Fl.: Academic International Press.

# INDEX

# DATE DUE

| SE 16 07 | | | |
|---|---|---|---|
| | | | |
| | | | |
| | | | |
| | | | |
| | | | |
| | | | |
| | | | |
| | | | |
| | | | |
| | | | |
| | | | |
| | | | |
| | | | |
| | | | |
| | | | |
| | | | |
| | | | |
| | | | |

WITHDRAWN

DEMCO 38-296